PASS the CCNA

The Implementing and Administering Cisco Solutions

v1.0 200-301

EXAM

Hazim Gaber, B.Sc. (ENG), CSSBB, PMP

Published By

HSM Press
HSMG Services & Consulting Inc.
34th Floor
10180 101 ST NW
Edmonton, AB T5J 3S4
Canada
Phone: 1-800-716-8955

www.hsmglobal.ca
books@hsmglobal.ca

ISBN: 978-1-64921-378-5

Foreword

I am delighted to have the opportunity to help you pass the Cisco Certified Network Associate Exam..

This book has been organized to make it easier to absorb and understand the information. I have included practical examples where appropriate.

This is a work in progress. If you have any suggestions to improve this book, or if you see any errors, or if you need help, I would be grateful if you contacted me. My e-mail address is hazim@hsmservices.ca

Visit the CCNA Page at hsmpress.ca/ccna

Regards,
Hazim

May 2020

Table of Contents

Part A: Introduction

Who is Cisco?

Cisco is arguably the most well-recognized manufacturer of network hardware in the world. Some of their products include

- Routers, Switches, Wireless Access Points
- VoIP Telephones and Controllers
- SD-WANs
- Firewalls
- Cloud devices

Cisco equipment is used everywhere, from small businesses to ISPs that run the backbone of the internet.

Some acquisitions that Cisco has made include

- Viptela
- Meraki
- Acacia Communications
- Broadsoft

Cisco offers certifications on all their network hardware.

What is the CCNA?

The CCNA is an entry level credential for IT Professionals to design, configure, identify issues and solve problems with computer networks on Cisco hardware.

The CCNA allows you to do the following

- Install and configure Cisco network equipment such as switches, routers, and wireless access points
- Understand network concepts like NAT, ARP, DNS, and DHCP
- Understand physical cabling principles and wireless principles
- Understand virtualization
- Configure switching and routing protocols, ACLs, VLANs, EtherChannel
- Understand cloud-based networks
- Understand automation in network configuration

You should have

- At least two years experience in IT administration and security
- Day-to-day knowledge of technical network information
- Broad knowledge of security threats
- Experience with computer networks

CCNA overlaps with

- Vendor neutral networking certifications (CompTIA Network+ for example)
- Virtualization Certifications (VMWare)
- Security Certifications

What can you do with a CCNA Certification?

- System Engineer
- Systems Administrator
- Network Administrator
- Network Field Technician
- Network Analyst

What's new?

The exam has been completely changed for February 2020. The structure of the CCNA has changed.

In the past, there were nine separate CCNA tracks:

- Collaboration
- Data Center
- Routing & Switching
- Wireless
- Security
- Service Provider
- Cloud
- Cyber Ops
- Industrial

Routing & Switching was the most popular. When people say "CCNA", they usually mean CCNA Routing & Switching. There was too much overlap between the different CCNA tracks. It is important to have some knowledge about each area to properly configure a network.

Now there is only one CCNA.

When you obtain your CCNA, you can advance to the CCNP (Cisco Certified Network Professional) credential. There are five CCNP tracks:

- Collaboration
- Data Center
- Enterprise
- Security
- Service Provider

You can go further in each track to get your CCIE (Cisco Certified Internetwork Expert), or you can challenge the exam.

How do I obtain the CCNA Certification?

You must pass the exam, 200-301. The passing score is 825 (out of a possible score of 1000). The exam is 120 minutes long and contains a maximum of 90 questions. The actual number of questions will depend on the difficulty. If you receive an exam with more difficult questions, there may be fewer questions.

The score of 825 is not a percentage (such as 82.5%). It is not clear how much weight each question is given or whether questions have equal weiht.

About the Exam

- You can register online to take the exam. The online system will show you the dates and times that are available.
- You may be able to write the exam on a Saturday or Sunday, depending on the Prometric Test Center.
- You may reschedule the exam for free, if you do so at least 30 calendar days before the exam.
- You may reschedule the exam for USD$325, if you do so at least 2 calendar days before the exam.
- You may not reschedule the exam if there are less than 2 calendar days before the exam.
- If you do not show up to the exam or are more than 15 minutes late to the exam, you will not be allowed to write the exam, and will forfeit the entire fee.

- At the exam center, you are required to show a piece of government-issued photo ID.
- You will be required to empty your pockets and place the contents in a locker.
- If you are wearing eyeglasses, they will be inspected.
- You may be checked with a metal detector.
- You can only bring your photo ID and locker key into the exam room.
- The test center will provide you with scratch paper, a pencil, and a basic calculator.

- While you write the exam, you will be monitored via audio and video surveillance.
- Each exam is up to 90 multiple-choice questions, and you have 90 minutes to complete the exam.
- You can't go back to a question after
- You can take a break at any time, but the time on the exam will continue to elapse.
- It goes without saying that cheating will not be tolerated!

- The questions are
  - Multiple-choice (single, and multiple responses)
  - Drag & Drop
  - Simulated Lab – you are given several virtual (simulated) Cisco devices and must fix the configuration
  - Simlet – like the Lab, but you are given several questions about the state of the simulated network

About this Book

- The Exam has 6 Main Topics
- We're going to cover each topic in order
- This is the best way because some readers have advanced knowledge and just need to brush up on specific topics, while other people are starting from the very beginning
- Sometimes that won't make sense because we are explaining an advanced concept before explaining a basic concept, but I will explain concepts as necessary
- Keep everything in the back of your mind; you might choose to go back and re-read a section
- You can think of the topics as three parts
  - Part 1 covers Sections 1 to 4, and is related to configuration of routers, switches. It also covers physical network infrastructure (cabling).
  - Part 2 covers Section 5 and is related to security.
  - Part 3 covers Section 6 and covers automation.

Breakdown of 200-301

Coverage Amount	Coverage Details
20%	**1.0 Network Fundamentals** 1.1 Explain the role and function of network components 1.1.a Routers 1.1.b L2 and L3 switches 1.1.c Next-generation firewalls and IPS 1.1.d Access points 1.1.e Controllers (Cisco DNA Center and WLC) 1.1.f Endpoints 1.1.g Servers 1.2 Describe characteristics of network topology architectures 1.2.a 2 tier 1.2.b 3 tier 1.2.c Spine-leaf 1.2.d WAN 1.2.e Small office/home office (SOHO) 1.2.f On-premises and cloud 1.3 Compare physical interface and cabling types 1.3.a Single-mode fiber, multimode fiber, copper 1.3.b Connections (Ethernet shared media and point-to-point) 1.3.c Concepts of PoE 1.4 Identify interface and cable issues (collisions, errors, mismatch duplex, and/or speed) 1.5 Compare TCP to UDP 1.6 Configure and verify IPv4 addressing and subnetting 1.7 Describe the need for private IPv4 addressing 1.8 Configure and verify IPv6 addressing and prefix 1.9 Compare IPv6 address types

- 1.9.a Global unicast
- 1.9.b Unique local
- 1.9.c Link local
- 1.9.d Anycast
- 1.9.e Multicast
- 1.9.f Modified EUI 64

1.10 Verify IP parameters for Client OS (Windows, Mac OS, Linux)

1.11 Describe wireless principles

- 1.11.a Nonoverlapping Wi-Fi channels
- 1.11.b SSID
- 1.11.c RF
- 1.11.d Encryption

1.12 Explain virtualization fundamentals (virtual machines)

1.13 Describe switching concepts

- 1.13.a MAC learning and aging
- 1.13.b Frame switching
- 1.13.c Frame flooding
- 1.13.d MAC address table

20% **2.0 Network Access**

2.1 Configure and verify VLANs (normal range) spanning multiple switches

- 2.1.a Access ports (data and voice)
- 2.1.b Default VLAN
- 2.1.c Connectivity

2.2 Configure and verify interswitch connectivity

- 2.2.a Trunk ports
- 2.2.b 802.1Q
- 2.2.c Native VLAN

2.3 Configure and verify Layer 2 discovery protocols (Cisco Discovery Protocol and LLDP)

2.4 Configure and verify (Layer 2/Layer 3) EtherChannel (LACP)

2.5 Describe the need for and basic operations of Rapid PVST+ Spanning Tree Protocol and identify basic operations

2.5.a Root port, root bridge (primary/secondary), and other port names
2.5.b Port states (forwarding/blocking)
2.5.c PortFast benefits

2.6 Compare Cisco Wireless Architectures and AP modes
2.7 Describe physical infrastructure connections of WLAN components (AP, WLC, access/trunk ports, and LAG)
2.8 Describe AP and WLC management access connections (Telnet, SSH, HTTP, HTTPS, console, and TACACS+/RADIUS)
2.9 Configure the components of a wireless LAN access for client connectivity using GUI only such as WLAN creation, security settings, QoS profiles, and advanced WLAN settings

25% **3.0 IP Connectivity**

3.1 Interpret the components of routing table
3.1.a Routing protocol code
3.1.b Prefix
3.1.c Network mask
3.1.d Next hop
3.1.e Administrative distance
3.1.f Metric
3.1.g Gateway of last resort

3.2 Determine how a router makes a forwarding decision by default
3.2.a Longest match
3.2.b Administrative distance
3.2.c Routing protocol metric

3.3 Configure and verify IPv4 and IPv6 static routing
3.3.a Default route
3.3.b Network route
3.3.c Host route
3.3.d Floating static

3.4 Configure and verify single area OSPFv2
3.4.a Neighbor adjacencies
3.4.b Point-to-point

	3.4.c Broadcast (DR/BDR selection) 3.4.d Router ID 3.5 Describe the purpose of first hop redundancy protocol
10%	**4.0 IP Services** 4.1 Configure and verify inside source NAT using static and pools 4.2 Configure and verify NTP operating in a client and server mode 4.3 Explain the role of DHCP and DNS within the network 4.4 Explain the function of SNMP in network operations 4.5 Describe the use of syslog features including facilities and levels 4.6 Configure and verify DHCP client and relay 4.7 Explain the forwarding per-hop behavior (PHB) for QoS such as classification, marking, queuing, congestion, policing, shaping 4.8 Configure network devices for remote access using SSH 4.9 Describe the capabilities and function of TFTP/FTP in the network
15%	**5.0 Security Fundamentals** 5.1 Define key security concepts (threats, vulnerabilities, exploits, and mitigation techniques) 5.2 Describe security program elements (user awareness, training, and physical access control) 5.3 Configure device access control using local passwords 5.4 Describe security password policies elements, such as management, complexity, and password alternatives (multifactor authentication, certificates, and biometrics) 5.5 Describe remote access and site-to-site VPNs 5.6 Configure and verify access control lists

	5.7 Configure Layer 2 security features (DHCP snooping, dynamic ARP inspection, and port security) 5.8 Differentiate authentication, authorization, and accounting concepts 5.9 Describe wireless security protocols (WPA, WPA2, and WPA3) 5.10 Configure WLAN using WPA2 PSK using the GUI

10%	**6.0 Automation and Programmability**
	6.1 Explain how automation impacts network management
	6.2 Compare traditional networks with controller-based networking
	6.3 Describe controller-based and software defined architectures (overlay, underlay, and fabric)
	    6.3.a Separation of control plane and data plane
	    6.3.b North-bound and south-bound APIs
	6.4 Compare traditional campus device management with Cisco DNA Center enabled device management
	6.5 Describe characteristics of REST-based APIs (CRUD, HTTP verbs, and data encoding)
	6.6 Recognize the capabilities of configuration management mechanisms Puppet, Chef, and Ansible
	6.7 Interpret JSON encoded data

How to Practice

There are three ways to study for the CCNA.

- Just read the book. If you're smart, you can read the book and pass the exam. But probably not. The new CCNA has a lot of concepts that need reading, but you need experience configuring real Cisco equipment.

- Build a simulator. You should read the book and then practice on your simulator. Ideally, you should have
    - A couple of Cisco routers
    - A couple of Cisco switches
    - Some ethernet patch cables (copper)
    - Some fiber patch cables
    - Some SFPs
    - A console cable
    - A laptop with a terminal emulator

  You can buy used Cisco equipment online for a few hundred dollars.

  If you're planning to advance to the CCNP or CCIE, you might need additional equipment.

- Use an online simulator. There are several online simulators that let you practice different scenarios. They may charge a monthly fee. The advantage is that you can scale up to build and simulate large networks, which won't be possible if you build a real simulator. Also, the simulator can introduce problems that you can troubleshoot, whereas your own simulator can just be configured.

  The best simulator is the Cisco Packet Tracer, available for free from Cisco.

  You will also need a Cisco Wireless Controller and some wireless access points.

Notice that each topic starts with a verb. When you study, you should think about the meaning of the verb because it will tell you how much understanding is required.

The more difficult tasks that require practice

- **Configure** – set up a feature in a Cisco device using commands or a graphical user interface, as applicable. Configure requires us to remember the necessary commands and their parameters.
- **Verify** – check that a device is functioning in a specific way or that specific settings have been configured. Verify tasks can be used to troubleshoot issues.
- **Interpret** – view an output from a router or switch and understand what it means

Moderately difficult tasks that require understanding

- **Explain** – describe how a process or technology functions or how it works
- **Compare** – list the similarities between two or more protocols, devices or methods.
- **Differentiate** – list the differences between two or more protocols, devices or methods

Tasks that require memorizing

- **Describe** – list the characteristics of an item or protocol
- **Identify** – choose the correct choice from a list of options
- **Define** – state the meaning of something

On a final note, the Cisco website is a great resource. There is a ton of information on the Cisco website and on the internet about the CCNA, router/switch/WLC configurations, and many other topics.

Recommended Tools, Hardware & Software

Every job requires tools, and the CCNA is no different. You won't need the tools for your exam, but you will need them for your job.

I recommend

- Buy high quality tools that will last a long time. Cheap tools are more expensive in the long term. They break down and cause frustration.
- Ask for advice, read reddit reviews, read reviews on Amazon, watch YouTube videos, until you find the tools that are best for you. Ask me!

The Cisco curriculum doesn't require a lot of tools. What you need to think about is whether you are going to be a Cisco technician who solely works on connecting and troubleshooting Cisco equipment configurations, or whether you will be troubleshooting other things.

Will you need to troubleshoot or install physical wiring, access points, etc.? Probably. It's better to have the tools and not need them then to need them and not have them.

What you really need

- Laptop
- Cisco console cable
- Patch cables
- Cable tester
- A few screwdrivers or a drill with some screwdriver bits

It would be nice if you had the following

Laptops & Smartphones

Apple Tablet/Smartphone
Android Tablet/Smartphone
Windows Tablet/Smartphone

Software

Some of the software may also be incorporated into hardware

Packet Sniffer

Protocol Analyzer
Terminal Emulation Software such as PuTTy
Linux/Windows OS
Software Firewall
Software IDS/IPS
Network Mapper
Hypervisor Software
Virtual Network Environment
Wi-Fi Analyzer
Spectrum Analyzer
Network Monitoring Tools
DHCP Service
DNS Service
Knowledgebase / Ticket Management Software such as AutoTask or Service Now

Equipment

Layer 2/3 Switch
Router
Firewall
VPN Concentrator
Wireless Access Point
Laptop that supports virtualization
Media Converter
Configuration Terminal (with Telnet and SSH)
VoIP System (including a phone)
SOHO Router/Switch
Surge Suppressor
Power Distribution Unit (PDU)
Uninterruptable Power Supply (UPS)
Managed Switch
Hub

Tools

RJ-11/RJ-45 Crimper
Cable tester

Punchdown Tools with Cutting and Non-Cutting 110, 66, BIX, and Krone Blades
Cable Stripper
Coaxial Crimper
Wire Cutter
Tone Generator and Probe
Fiber Termination Kit
Optical Power Meter
Butt Set
Multimeter
Power Supply Tester
Screwdriver, Drill, or Screw Gun and Assorted Bits

Spare Parts

Optical and Copper Patch Panels
Punchdown Blocks – 66, 110, and BIX
NICs
Power Supplies
GBICs
SFPs
Patch Cables – cat5e, cat6, fiber
RJ-45 Connectors
RJ-45 Jacks
RJ-11 Connectors
Unshielded Twisted Pair Cable Spool or Box
Coaxial Cable Spool or Box
F-Connectors / BNC Connectors
Fiber Connectors
Antennas
Bluetooth Wireless Adapters
Console Cables and RS-232 to USB Serial Adapter
Rack Screws
Assorted Sheet Metal, Wood, & Drywall Screws
Velcro
Zip Ties
Grounding Cable and Lugs

1.0 Network Fundamentals

1.1 Explain the role and function of network components

1.1.a Routers

1.1.b L2 and L3 switches

1.1.c Next-generation firewalls and IPS

1.1.d Access points

1.1.e Controllers (Cisco DNA Center and WLC)

1.1.f Endpoints

1.1.g Servers

What is a router? What is a L2 switch? What is an L3 switch? What is all this stuff and what does it do? We are already too deep into the material. Let's take a step back and figure something out here.

A network is a bunch of connected devices. Think about your home or office. I have an office downtown, which has a network. All my office devices – laptops, servers, printers, etc. can connect. I also have a home. All my home devices – laptops, phones, printers, cameras can connect. If I'm working from home, I can still connect to my office network.

Google has a big network. I can connect to Google's network from my home or office.

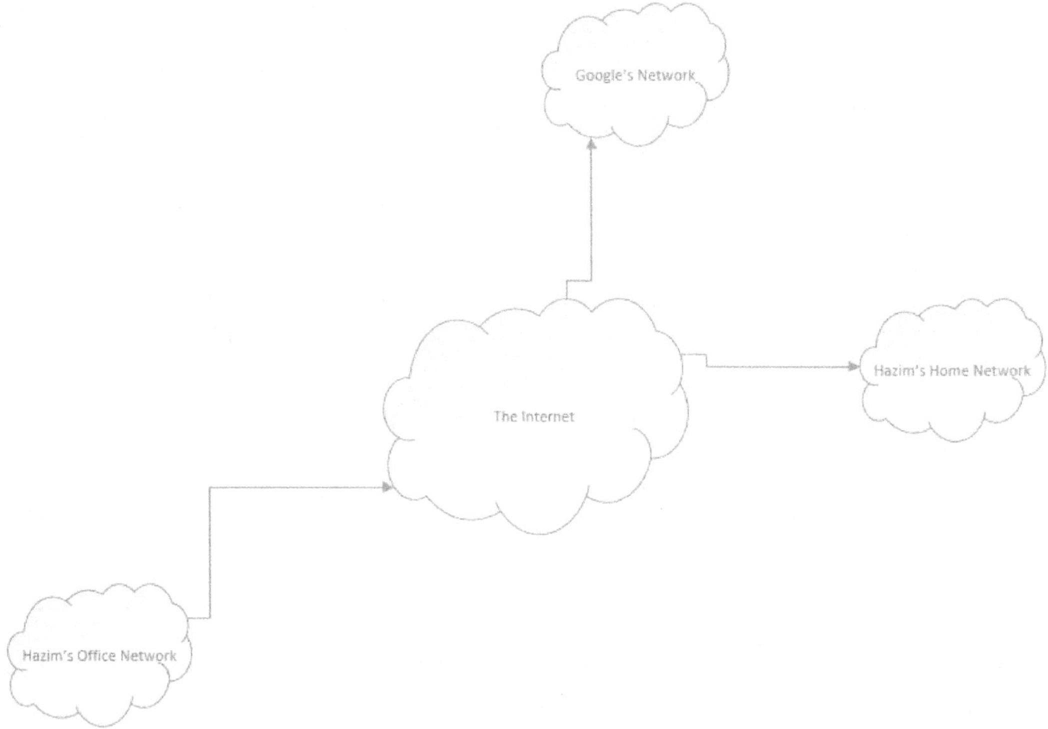

In the world, there are millions, or hundreds of millions of networks, all connected somehow. How does it all work?

Well, at the edge of each network is a **router**. We're going to learn more about these routers later. But for now, we should understand that a router moves traffic between one network and another. It might move traffic between your home network and the internet. Or it might move traffic between your work network and your home network.

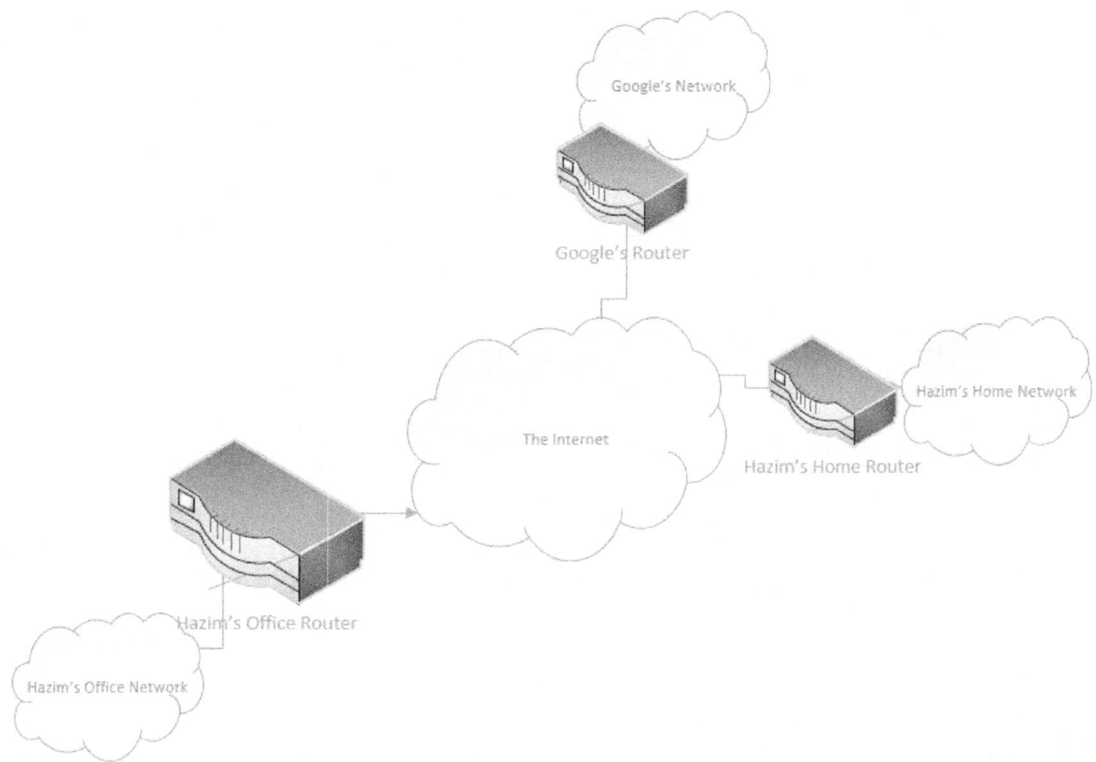

In each office, I also have a **switch**, or maybe I have several switches. Let's take a closer look at my home network. I connected all my devices to a switch, like my TV, my desktop computer, and my printer. The switch forwards traffic between the devices on my network. If I want to print something, the traffic goes from my computer, to the switch, and then to the printer. We might call the network in my home a **Local Area Network**. That is, any equipment behind the router is a Local Area Network, or **LAN**.

If I want to access something on the internet (on another network – outside my LAN), the traffic must pass through the router.

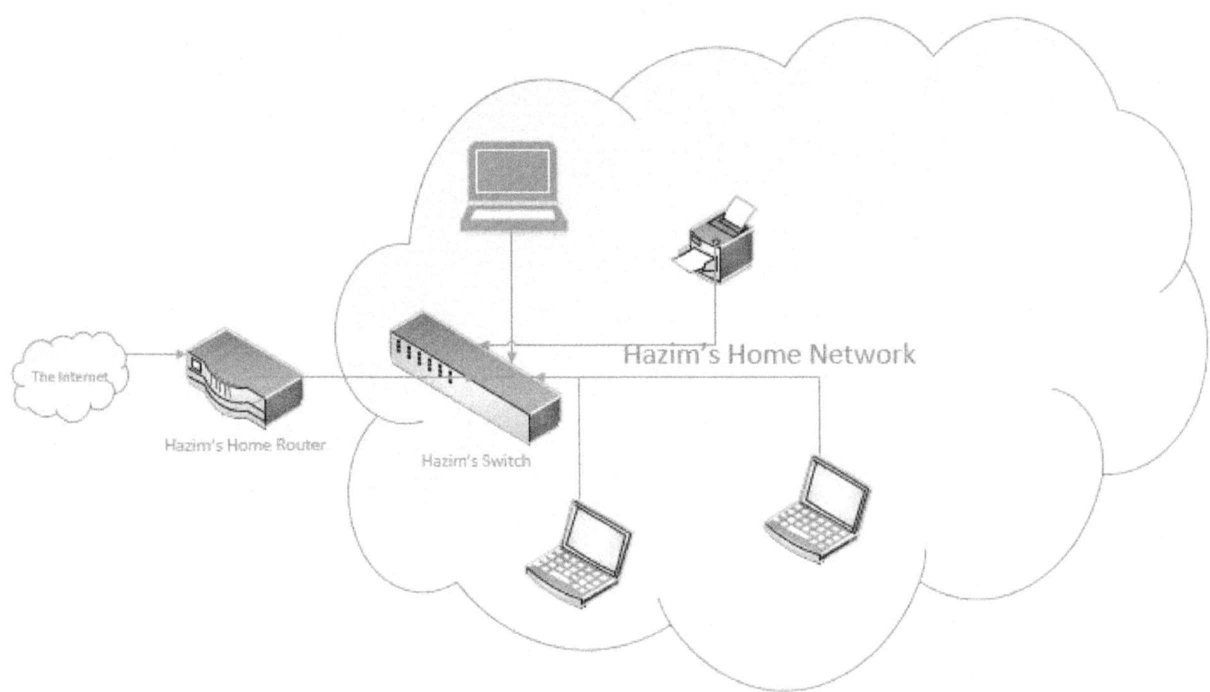

Going back to my switch – we call this type of Switch a **Layer 2 Switch**. More advanced switches are known as **Layer 3 Switches** (or **multi-layer Switches**). We'll come back to the difference later, when it makes more sense.

I also need to keep bad people out of my network. So, I add a **firewall** between the router and the rest of my network.

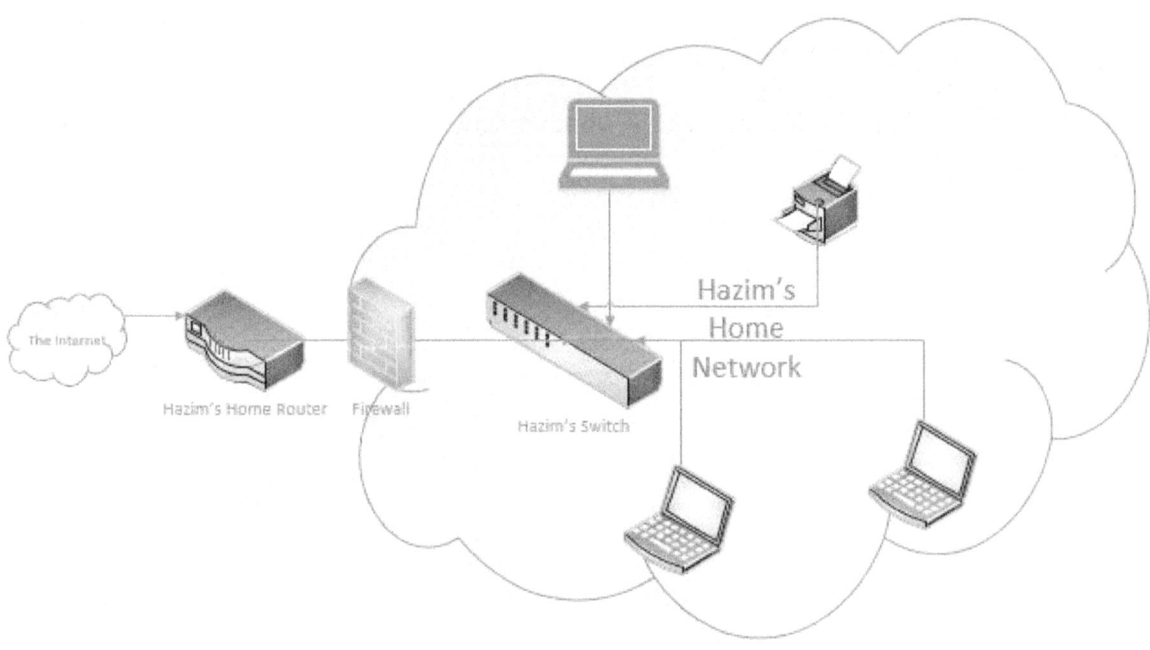

There are many types of firewalls. The most basic ones ask only a few questions

- Where is the traffic coming from? What is the source IP address of the traffic?
- Where is the traffic going? What is the destination IP address of the traffic?

The firewall has some rules. It compares the source and destination of the traffic to the rules and decides whether to let it through. It's like looking at the to and from fields on an envelope before deciding whether to mail it.

Newer firewalls – known as **Next Generation Firewalls** – take a deeper look. They look at the contents of the traffic to decide if it's good or bad. A Next Generation Firewall can ask some more questions

- What type of traffic is it? What is the port number? Is it HTTP traffic, VoIP traffic, FTP traffic, etc?
- If it's HTTP or HTTPs traffic, what is the URL of the website? Is this a safe website?
- What is the state of the traffic? Did the connection originate from inside the network or from outside the network? This is known as **stateful inspection**.

  For example, if you're visiting a website, we would expect the connection to originate from inside the network. If a website originates the traffic, it's probably from an imposter.
- How many packets did this host send? A sudden surge of traffic from a specific source could be a symptom of an attack. If the firewall notices that we're receiving a lot of traffic from a specific source, it could throttle it or slow it down.

A firewall can also use **security zones**. A security zone is a set of hosts (which could be internal or external). We might call each device on our network a "host". Each zone can have different rules for what its hosts can access. For example, we could have trusted internal servers in one zone, trusted external webservers in a second zone, and untrusted sites in a third zone.

The most important zone in our network is the **DMZ** or **Demilitarized Zone**. We put servers that must access both the internal network and the internet in the DMZ. These could include web servers and e-mail servers. We need to access our e-mail from inside the network, and people on the internet need to access our e-mail server to send us e-mails.

Cisco next generation firewalls were called **Cisco Adaptive Security Appliances** or **ASAs**. The newer firewalls are called **Cisco Firepower**. The Firepower firewalls take a deeper look at each packet. It's like opening each envelope and reading the contents before deciding whether to send it.

Why do we need to take a deeper look? A hacker can hide malicious information inside a legitimate-looking piece of data. For example, legitimate web traffic might come in disguised as legitimate web traffic. If a legitimate web server is compromised (through a virus or trojan), the hacker could use it to send malicious traffic.

This deep packet inspection is performed with a tool called **Cisco Application Visibility and Control** (**AVC**). The firewall can predict the application that is running inside the data.

We also use **Intrusion Prevention Systems**, or **IPSs**. The IPS is like a firewall, but more advanced. It checks every packet against a signature database to determine what to do with it. The IPS can detect viruses, worms, and DDoS attacks. Usually, the IPS comes preloaded with a signature database, and no configuration is required. The IPS might connect to the cloud and download new threat signatures to its database in real time. It might also share threats that it detects with other IPSs; if one IPS detects an early threat, it can share it with other IPSs, so that they all benefit.

In addition to its database, the IPS uses heuristics, or artificial intelligence to detect threats. If it detects a packet that might be a threat, but it's not sure, it sends it to the cloud for further analysis. Researchers take a closer look at the packet and decide whether to include it in the database.

Cisco has created **Next Generation IPSs**, which can look deeper inside the hosts on the internal network. The Next Generation IPS will identify the types of operating systems, applications, and protocols running on the internal network. They also identify the ports in use on the internal network. This is known as **Contextual Awareness**.

With this information, the NGIPS can do two things

- Detect abnormalities in the network, such as devices with unrecognized or non-typical operating systems and applications
- Avoid spending time looking for threats against devices that do not exist in the network

Like the firewall, the Cisco NGIPS provides Application Visibility and Control. It also provides **Reputation-Based Filtering**. Cisco tracks bad people on the internet based on their domain names, IP addresses, and names. Cisco assigns each network resource (web server, website, etc.) a reputation score. With this information, your NGIPS can block traffic that has a bad reputation.

Each time the IPS matches a packet, it creates a security alert. Over time, an IPS can create millions of security alerts; it's not possible for a human to read all of them. The NGIPS also uses **Event Impact Levels** to help rank each alert, so that an administrator can focus on the issues that could cause the most harm.

In summary, a Cisco Next Generation Firewall/IPS can do the following

- All the functions of a traditional firewall
- Application Visibility and Control
- Blocking specific URLs (websites) based on the reputation of the website. This is called **Reputation-Based Filtering**.

- Detection of malware
- All the functions of a standard Intrusion Protection System

Going back to my network, I have many laptops. Some of these laptops don't want to sit in one spot. I want to sit on the patio and do some work. So, I install a **Wireless Access Point**, or **WAP**. The WAP connects to the switch and broadcasts a Wi-Fi signal, which all my (wireless-capable) devices can connect to.

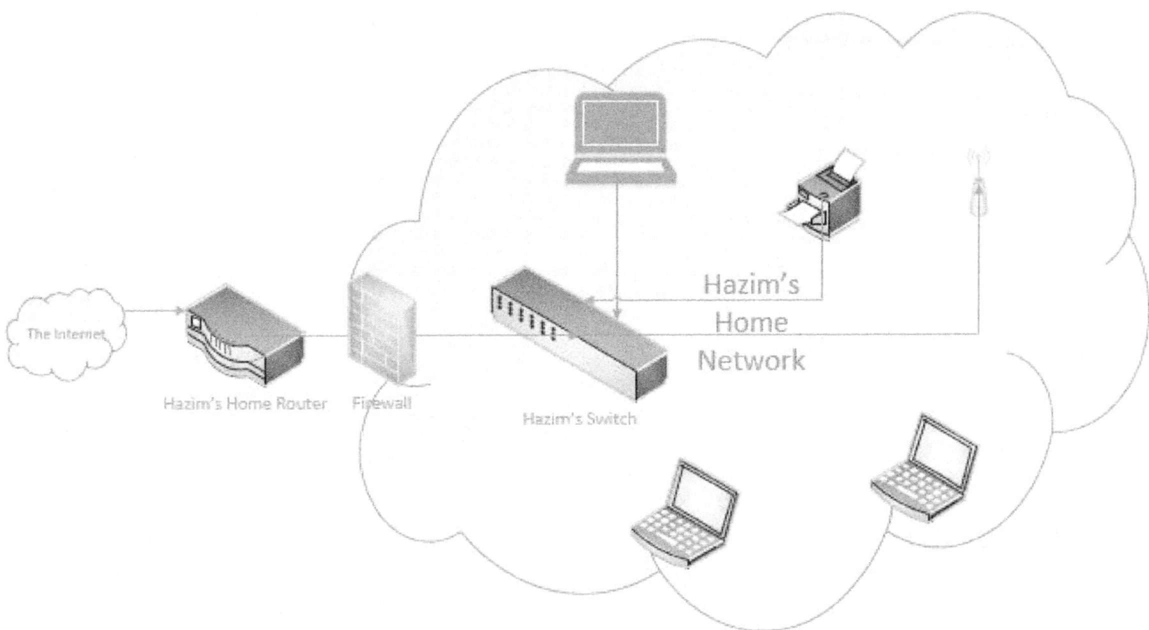

If I have lots of WAPs, then I need to add a controller. If I had an office with 20 or 30 or 100 access points, I wouldn't want to manually configure each one. The controller configures and monitors the WAPs automatically. The controller is known as a **WLC** or **Wireless Controller**. A more advanced Cisco controller is called the **Cisco DNA Center**. We will learn more about it later.

My network might also have a **server**. Servers are computers that serve multiple users. For example, I might have a server for sharing important files with multiple users. Or I might have a server that handles my e-mail.

Each of the end user devices (printers, laptops, desktops, phones, etc.) is known as an **endpoint** or an end-user device.

In a home network, we might have one physical device that performs all the functions: router, firewall, switch, and wireless access point all in one. It doesn't have a wireless controller, but the access point functions independently.

The home network device also functions as a modem and connects to a cable, DSL, fiber optic, or 4G connection.

We will learn more about the different devices and how to configure them later in this book.

1.3 Compare physical interface and cabling types

1.3.a Single-mode fiber, multimode fiber, copper

1.3.b Connections (Ethernet shared media and point-to-point)

1.3.c Concepts of PoE

I've been drawing switches and connecting them with lines, but how do we physically connect all this stuff together?

There are two types of network cable: Copper and Fiber. When do we use copper and when do we use fiber?

Most of the copper wiring in use is **Unshielded Twisted Pair (UTP)**. This is a standard ethernet cable that contains eight wires, twisted into four pairs. The twists are designed to cancel out most forms of **electromagnetic interference** (from radio waves and nearby power lines), or noise. A single UTP cable can be up to 100 meters in length.

For more advanced applications, we can use a **Shielded Twisted Pair (STP)** cable. This is also known as F/UTP cable. The difference is that the STP cable contains a foil around the wires. The foil blocks out even more electromagnetic interference than the twists. The foil connects to the termination point on each end of the cable and acts as an electrical ground. STP cable is used in applications such as video transmission and in areas where there is a large amount of interference. If we peel back a cable, we can see the difference between a shielded cable and an unshielded cable.

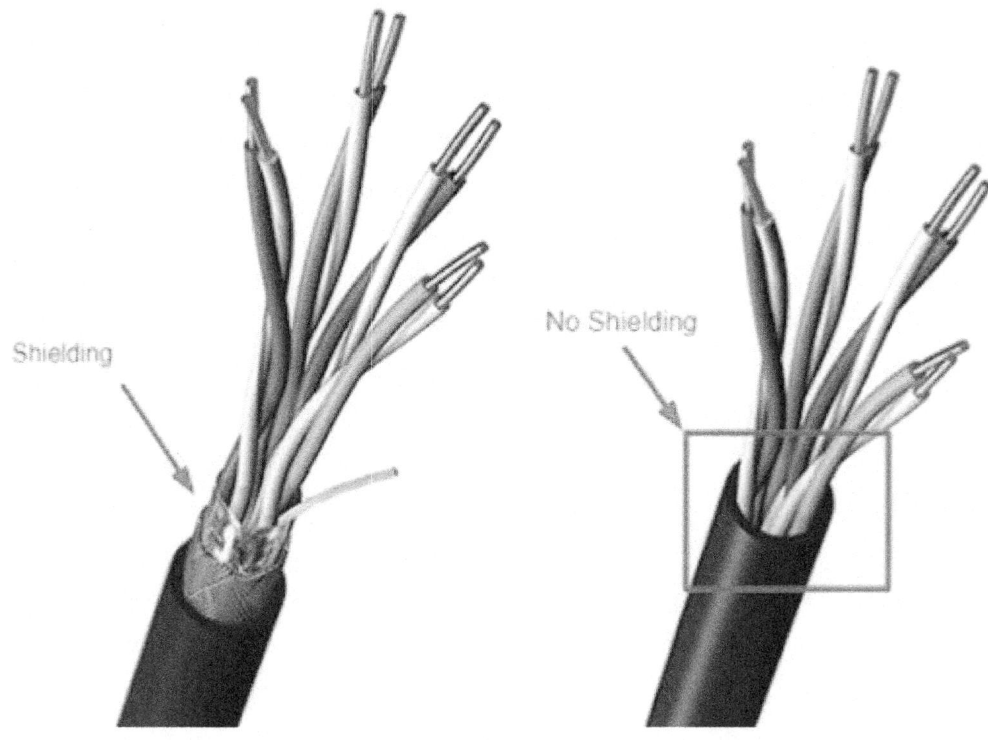

If we went crazy, we could buy a cable that had a separate shield around every pair. The shield protects the wires from electromagnetic interference. It also protects individual wire pairs from cross-talk (interference from a neighboring wire pair).

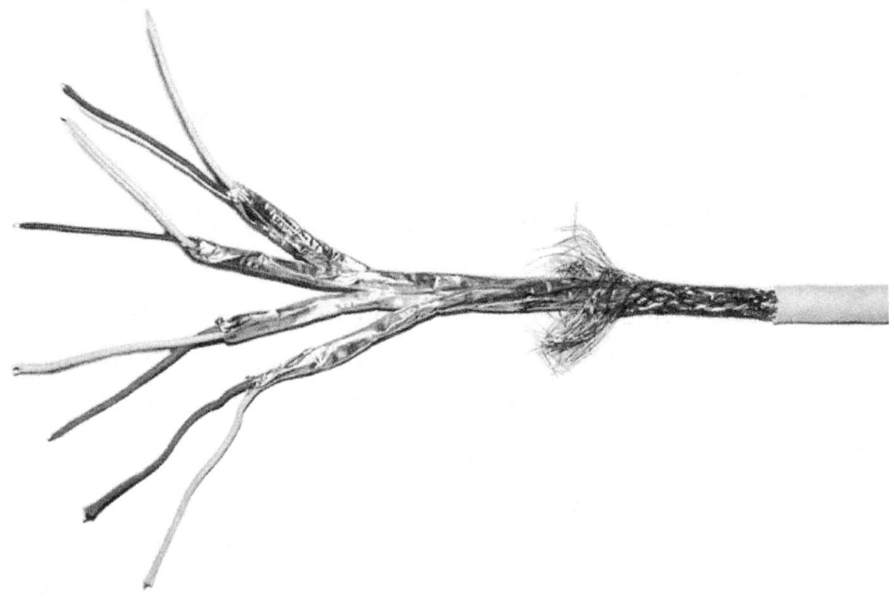

Most network devices are designed to accept a copper (UTP or STP) connection. That includes switches, IP cameras, computers, and VoIP phones.

Fiber optic cable can be run longer distances than copper. It also has a larger bandwidth (a fiber optic cable can carry more data than a copper cable). But fiber is more difficult to install than copper. It requires specialized equipment to test and terminate. A fiber optic cable uses light to transmit data, not electricity.

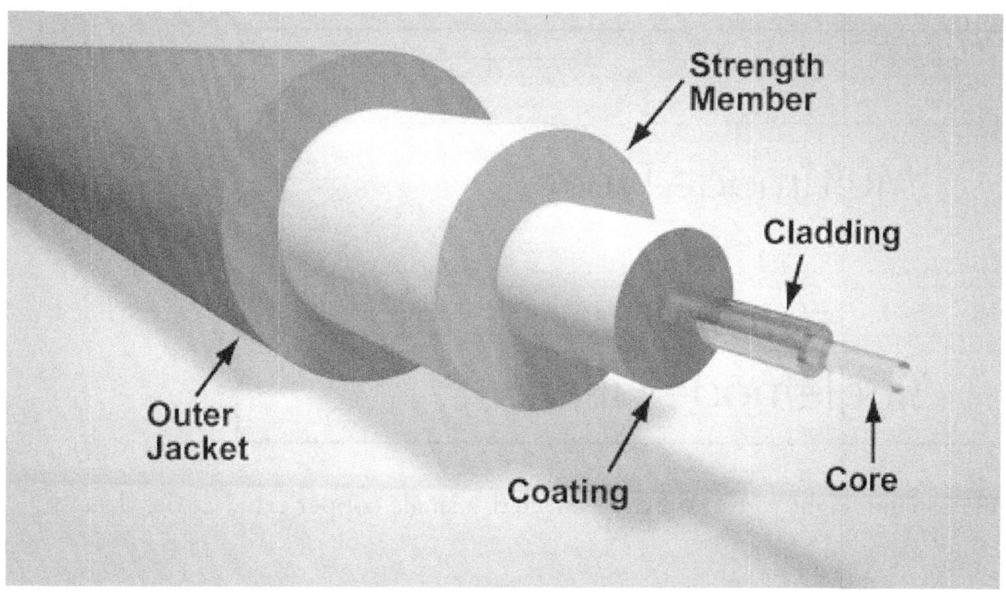

At the center of the cable is a glass core. Light travels through the core. Surrounding the core is a cladding, which prevents the light from escaping. The strength member is present in some cables and keeps it from breaking. Finally, the outer jacket protects the cable from rats that might chew on it.

We can't connect a fiber optic cable to standard endpoint devices. For example, a VoIP phone or computer will not have a fiber optic cable connector. If we ran a fiber optic cable to a far away computer, we would need a device called a media converter to convert the fiber light signal to a copper electrical signal.

Fiber comes in two forms: **single-mode**, and **multimode**. Single mode cable can be run upwards of 200 km. A powerful laser generates a light signal, which travels down the center of the core as a single signal.

Multimode cable can be run up to 1 km. A weaker LED generates a signal, which bounces up and down inside the core. We can send multiple multimode signals at the same time. The cladding keeps it inside.

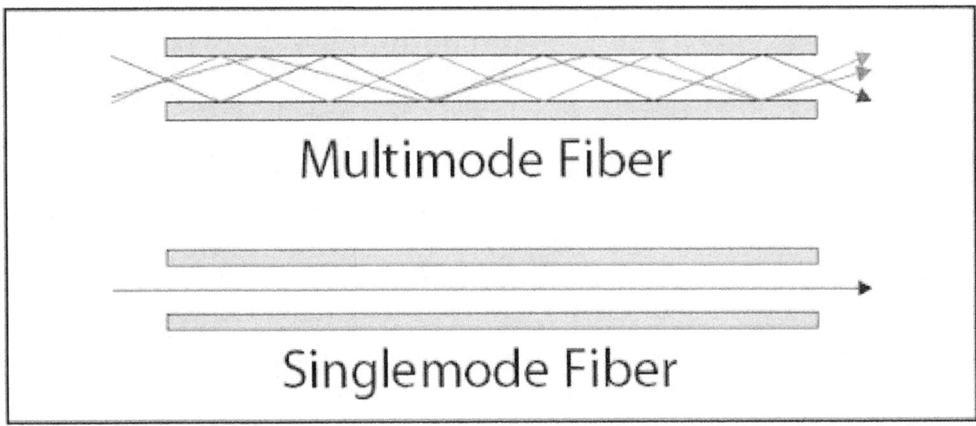

A single copper cable contains eight wires. When connected, a single copper cable carries data in both directions.

But a single fiber optic cable can contain multiple strands. A single strand carries data in only one direction. When we peel back the cable, we find multiple strands, which can be color-coded. We need at least two strands to make a circuit and carry data. Fiber optic cable typically comes with six or twelve strands.

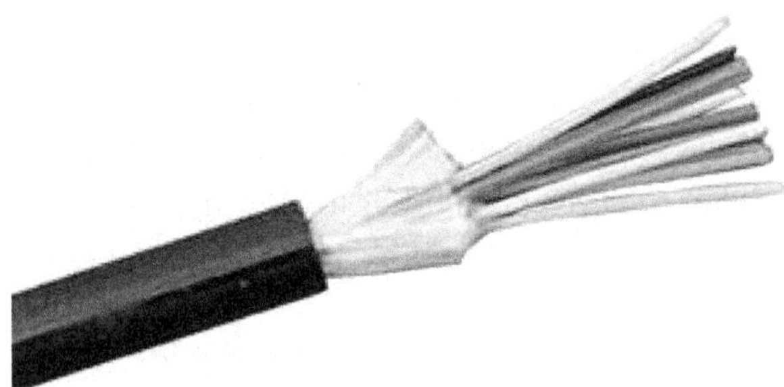

There are three benefits to fiber (vs copper)

- It can be run longer distances
- It is not affected by electromagnetic interference. Powerful electrical signals or radio waves can distort the signal carried by copper wiring.
- Copper wiring gives off a signal. We could possibly try to spy on the signal carried by a copper cable.

Let's say we wanted to connect a VoIP phone, an access point, or a surveillance camera to a network switch. These devices require power. But it's a hassle to connect the device to an ethernet cable and to a power outlet.

What if we're installing some surveillance cameras and don't have nearby power outlets. We would need to hire an electrician to install some power outlets. A better solution is called **PoE (Power Over Ethernet)** comes in. PoE lets a switch power a network device.

PoE sends power down the Ethernet cable (it only works on copper, not fiber) to power a network device. That means a device can get power and data on the same cable.

There are several types of PoE.

- PoE is governed by the 802.3af standard and delivers up to 15.40 W.
- PoE+ delivers up to 30W.
- UPoE delivers up to 60W and UPoE+ delivers up to 100W.
- Cisco also offers a proprietary PoE standard called Cisco Inline Power, which delivers up to 7 Watts.

PoE and PoE+ use two pairs of wires to deliver power, while UPoE and UPoE+ use all four pairs.

When designing a network, you might consider the following

- A switch capable of delivering PoE is called a **PoE switch** and is typically more expensive than a non-PoE switch.

- You must choose a switch that has enough overall capacity to power all the devices connected to it. Just because UPoE+ can deliver up to 100W per port doesn't mean that a 48-port switch will be able to deliver 4800W.

- Just because a device operates on UPoE+ and can accept up to 100W doesn't mean that it will draw all 100W. It might draw much less. That means that overall, you don't need as much power.

- A switch might be able to supply PoE on all its ports or only on some of its ports.

- In general, only the switches connected to endpoints need to support PoE. Switches that connect to other switches don't need PoE.

- Some switches have hot-swappable power supplies. It is important to choose a power supply that supplies the switch with enough power to pass on to its connected devices and to operate the switch.

A switch that supplies power is called **a Power Sourcing Equipment**, or **PSE**. A device that receives power is called a **Powered Device**, or **PD**.

If you only had one or two devices that required PoE, you might connect a **power injector** instead. A power injector sits between the switch and the device requiring power. It takes data from the switch, adds power, and sends it to the device.

We don't want to fry a device that doesn't require power by sending it power. For example, we don't want to send power into the Ethernet port on a desktop or laptop computer. How do we know that a device doesn't need power if it hasn't powered on yet?

The switch sends it a low power signal via Ethernet autonegotiation and wait for a reply. If the device doesn't require any power (like a laptop or desktop), and its powered on, it will reply, and the switch will know that it doesn't need to supply any power. Otherwise, if the switch can identify that the device requires power, it sends it enough power to boot up. The switch sends it the correct amount of power based on its power class.

The switch continues to monitor the device to determine whether its power class has changed. The device might tell us how many Watts of power it requires.

At the most basic level, all network devices need to be able to communicate with each other. Manufacturers gather together and develop common languages called **protocols**. As we will find out, some protocols are proprietary to Cisco devices – only Cisco devices understand them. But many are common to all network devices.

Why? Well, nobody has a monopoly on network and computing hardware. That means that devices from thousands of different manufacturers must work together. If you buy a laptop, it connects to the internet, and it doesn't matter whose network you're on. It just works, and that isn't an accident. It's because your laptop understands the same protocols as the network that you're on.

One of these protocols is called **Ethernet**. Ethernet works at different speeds.

The most common is **100BaseT**. It can transmit at a speed of up to 100 Mbit/s. 100BaseT is also called **100BaseTX** or **Fast Ethernet** and uses two wire pairs – orange and green. One device listens on the orange pair and talks on the green pair, while the other device does the opposite. On a router, you might see ports labelled as FE for Fast Ethernet.

Pin	Pair	Wire	Color
1	2	+/tip	white/orange
2	2	−/ring	orange
3	3	+/tip	white/green
4	1	−/ring	blue
5	1	+/tip	white/blue
6	3	−/ring	green
7	4	+/tip	white/brown
8	4	−/ring	brown

1000BaseT is also known as **Gigabit Ethernet**. It uses all four pairs of an ethernet cable. 1000BaseT is the current standard, and you should not install a new network with components that operate at a lower speed than 1000BaseT.

1000Base-X is the standard for communication over fiber at 1Gbit/s. There are two main standards: **1000BaseLX** uses single-mode fiber and can achieve distances of up to 10km, while **1000BaseSX** uses multi-mode fiber and can achieve distances of up to 220 meters.

A 1000BaseLX SFP costs around $10 while a 10GBase-L SFP may cost up to $2000. Therefore, organizations prefer to use 1000Base-X when they can. 10 Gbit/s ethernet ports are only found on high-end equipment.

10GBaseT or **10 Gigabit Ethernet** is a newer standard that allows devices to communicate at a speed of 10 Gbit/s. It can function over copper wiring or fiber. There are several fiber standards, including **10GBase-S** (multi-mode fiber) and **10GBase-L** (single-mode fiber).

Gigabit Ethernet over fiber sends a different type of signal than gigabit Ethernet over copper, but all the different 10 Gigabit Ethernet standards use the same signal regardless of the type of cable.

Look at this Cisco switch. On the left are 48 copper ports. Each one can accept a single RJ-45-terminated cable (a copper cable). On the right are four additional ports – the bottom two are copper and the top two are "**SFP**", or **small form-factor pluggable transceiver**.

You can't plug a cable into an SFP port.

So, what's the point? Well, there are many types of cables and available speeds – copper, single-mode fiber, multi-mode fiber, 10Gbit speeds, Gbit speeds, etc. Cisco can't sell a different type of switch for every possible connector. And what if we had a network with several different types of cable? There could be millions of possible switch port combinations.

Cisco can't manufacture millions of different switch models. Instead, the Cisco adds some "SFP" ports. Some switches have a few SFP ports and some have many.

Look at this switch. Almost all its ports are SFP ports.

You figure out what kind of connections you require – copper or fiber (single-mode or multi-mode). And you decide the speed that you require – 1GB, 10GB, or 40GB. And if you're using fiber, you decide what kind of connector you're using LC, SC, etc.. Then you buy the right SFPs and insert them into the switch. An SFP could cost between $10 and $2000 depending on the speed. You can mix and match SFPs on a single switch.

An example of a copper SFP is below. You insert the SFP into an SFP port and then you insert the cable into the SFP. SFPs are hot-swappable. That means we can change them while the switch is powered on.

The maximum speed of an SFP is 1 Gbit/s, but the maximum speed of an SFP+ is 10Gbit/s. An SFP+ is also known as an **enhanced small form-factor pluggable transceiver**. An SFP+ works with fiber and copper connectors.

For even faster speeds, such as those required in the networks of major Internet Service Providers, the **QSFP** or **Quad Small Form-factor Pluggable transceiver** can be used. The QSFP can provide speeds between 4 Gbit/s and 200 Gbit/s.

Below is an example of a fiber SFP. You will notice that it has space for two fibers. That is because a single stand of fiber typically operates in one direction at a time, whereas an ethernet cable operates in both directions at the same time. Thus, we would need two fiber strands to complete a "circuit".

Now that we've connected our devices, let's see what they actually say.

Ethernet works only on the **LAN** (**Local Area Network**) – that is the stuff behind your router. Ethernet only works between host devices (endpoints) and switches. When a device on a LAN wants to talk to another device on the same LAN, it breaks the message up into chunks. These chunks are called frames.

We sandwich our chunks between a header and a trailer. The headers contain important information like the sender and the destination. When we sandwich data between two headers, we say that it is **encapsulated**. This is very important, and we will come back to it later!

Ethernet Header	**Data**	**Ethernet Trailer**

What is inside the header and trailer?

Ethernet Header					**Data**	**Ethernet Trailer**
Preamble	SFD	Destination	Source	Type		FCS

- **Preamble** (7 bytes long) – this is a warning that lets the recipient device know that important data is coming so that it can get ready to listen. It gives the recipient some time to get ready. Think of a switch or computer just sitting there. Frames are electrical signals travelling down the Ethernet wire, bit by bit. The switch can't predict when the next frame will show up, and a new frame might catch it off guard. So, the preamble kind of makes it pay attention.
- **SFD** (1 byte long) – this is a warning that important data will start on the next byte. The switch knows that the preamble is over, and it must record any data after the SFD.
- **Destination** (6 bytes long) – the destination MAC address. Every network device has a unique address called a MAC address. The MAC address is burned into the device from the factory. It's kind of like a serial number.
- **Source** (6 bytes long) – the source MAC address.
- **Type** (1 byte long) – the type of data we are using.
- **Data** (between 46 and 1500 bytes) – the actual data (the chunk). If our data is less than 46 bytes, we add some "padding" to make it at least 46 bytes.
- **FCS** (4 bytes long) – the **Frame Check Sequence** - kind of a signature. The sending computer calculates an FCS from the data that he sends. The receiving computer performs the same calculation on the data that is received. If the recipient obtains the same result, then he knows that the data was received without any errors.

If the FCSs don't match, the recipient assumes that the data has been corrupted and throws it out. We call this **error detection**. We'll worry about how we recover from errors later.

This isn't a big deal, because we broke our data up into frames. We don't need to resend all the data – only the bad frames.

1.4 Identify interface and cable issues (collisions, errors, mismatch duplex, and/or speed)

I was talking about cables earlier. When two devices are connected via an Ethernet cable, they will evaluate the wiring between themselves and agree on a speed and duplex setting, in a process known as **autonegotiation**. In a **half-duplex** setting, only one device can transmit at a time; the other device must listen when the first one transmits. In a **full-duplex** setting, both devices can transmit and listen at the same time.

A 100BaseT connection could be either full duplex or half duplex. A 1000BaseT connection must always be full duplex.

An administrator can manually set an ethernet port on a switch or router to a specific speed and duplex setting but must then be careful to ensure that both the sending and receiving device have the same settings, or they will not be able to communicate.

There are two methods for terminating a cat5e/cat6/cat6A cable. The methods are known as **568A** and **568B**. Remember that an Ethernet cable contains four pairs of wires (colored as blue, orange, green, brown). The difference between 568A and 568B is that the position of the orange and green wires is swapped.

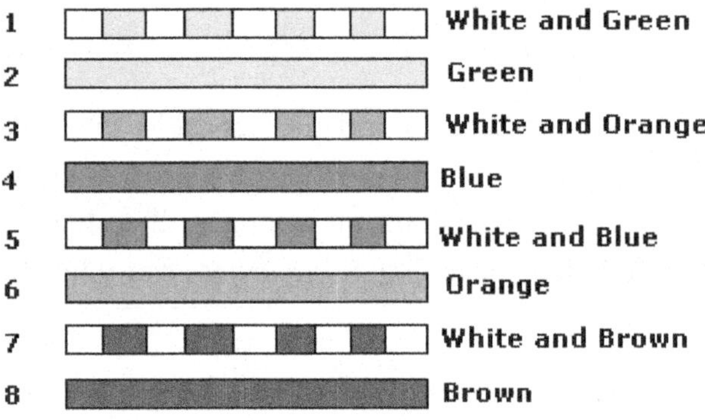

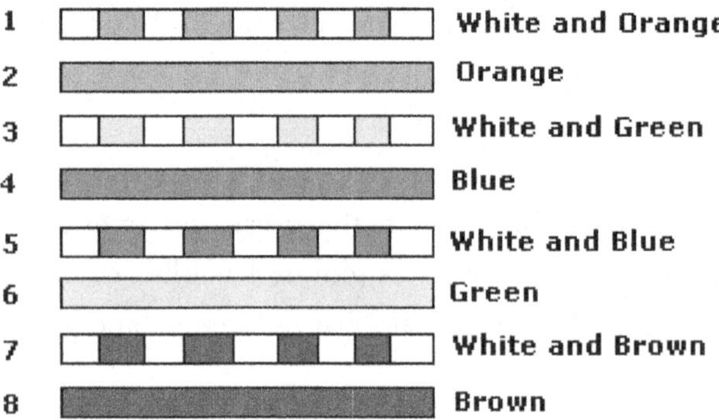

If we look at the side of a cat5e jack, we can see that the manufacturer has marked a color code for "A" style terminations and "B" style terminations. On the other side of the jack, we would see similar markings.

We should insert the wire into the correct colored slot on the jack or patch panel and then terminate it with a punch-down tool of the appropriate size.

We could also terminate the cable to a male connector. The male connectors follow the same color code as the female connectors. We use a tool called a crimper to secure the wires inside the connector.

Both 568A and 568B are acceptable termination methods. A cable should be terminated with the same method on both sides. An organization may require the cable to be terminated using a specific method. Most organizations prefer 568B, and most governments prefer 568A.

If we terminate the cable in the same order on both ends, we call it **a straight through cable**. If we terminate the cable as 568A on one end and 568B on the other end, the orange and green pairs become crossed. This is called a **crossover cable**.

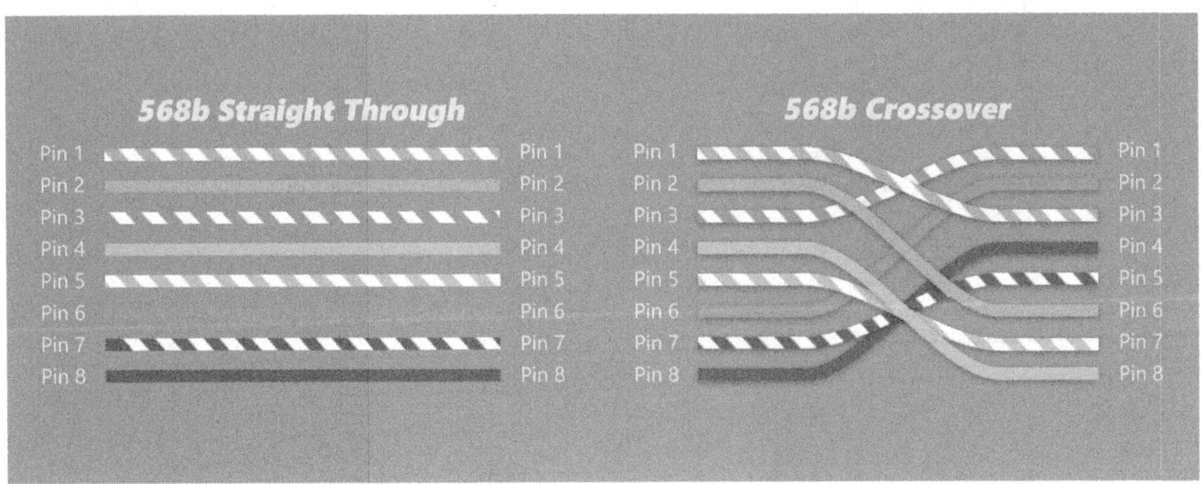

Why would we make a cross-over cable? Network devices usually use the orange and green pairs to communicate. A device like a switch transmits over the orange pair and listens on the green pair. A device like a computer transmits on the green pair and listens on the orange pair. If we connect a computer to a switch, collisions do not take place.

The device doesn't know the color of the wire; it only knows the position of the wire. If you punched the blue wire in the orange wire's spot, the device would communicate over the blue wire. Technically, a computer uses wires one and two to transmit data and three and six to receive data. A switch uses wires three and six to transmit data and wires one and two to receive data. Routers and wireless access points also use wires one and two to transmit data, which is why they can connect to a switch.

If we connect a computer to a switch, the switch will send data on wires three and six, which the computer will receive. The computer will send data on wires one and two, which the computer will receive.

If we want to connect two computers together or two switches together, they will try to talk on the same pair and listen on the same pair. No data will get through.

But if we use a cross-over cable, then one switch will transmit over the orange pair (wires one and two) and listen over the green pair (wires three and six). The other switch will transmit over the green pair (wires three and six) and listen over the orange pair (wires one and two). The wires "cross over" so that the traffic goes from position three and six to position on and two.

Technically, we don't need crossover cables to connect switches together anymore. If two modern switches are connected via a straight through cable, they will immediately detect the collision and agree on which switch will use which wire pairs. This is called **auto-mdix**.

1.13 Describe switching concepts

1.13.a MAC learning and aging

1.13.b Frame switching

1.13.c Frame flooding

1.13.d MAC address table

I wanted to explain each section in order, but it just doesn't make sense. I tried, but when I got to Section 1.2 I realized that I couldn't explain some concepts without background information. The entire model of the internet is built on layers and we shouldn't jump to another layer until we understand the one below it. I'm also going to start using the Cisco icons in my diagrams because we need to get serious.

Every network device – from the factory – receives a **MAC address**. It's like a serial number. It's unique to that device. The MAC address is twelve characters long, and it's also known as the **physical address** or a **global MAC address**.

How big is the MAC address again? It's 12 characters – 12 Hex digits to be exact (Hex digits are the numbers 0 through 9 and the letters A through F – no other characters are allowed). That makes it 24 bytes long. When we write a MAC address, it's common to separate every two digits with colons. AA:AA:BB:BB:CC:CC could be a MAC address. The MAC address isn't case sensitive. We might also separate every four digits with a period. aaaa.bbbb.cccc is also a MAC address.

How do we ensure that every device receives a unique MAC address? An international organization (IEEE) assigns a unique 6-digit prefix to each device manufacturer. If I'm a manufacturer and my prefix is AA:BB:CC, then all my MAC addresses must start with AA:BB:CC. Then it's up to me to make sure that the remaining six digits are unique for every device that I manufacture.

My network is below, and I have several devices connected to my switch. On the right is a printer. How does data get from my computer to my printer? For the sake of simplicity, we're going to pretend that the MAC address is four characters long. And we're going to ignore the switch's MAC address because it isn't important. And we're going to ignore other devices like routers. We just want to focus on the local network.

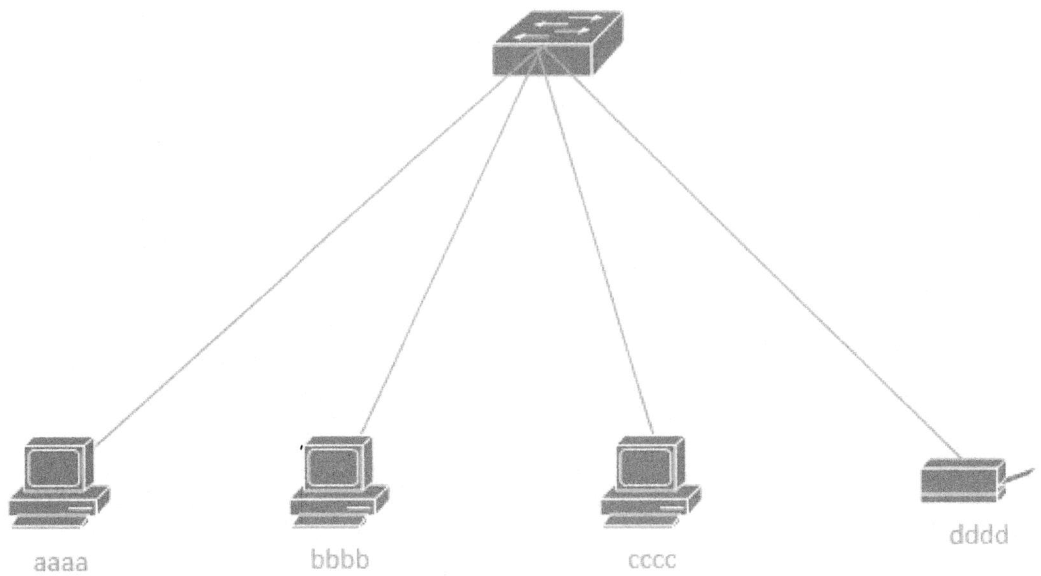

My computer's MAC address is "aaaa", and my printer's MAC address is "dddd". My computer already knows that "dddd" is on the LAN (Local Area Network). We're not going to worry about how it knew that just yet. Just know that my computer thought about where the printer was and concluded that it is on the local network. Thus, my computer sends an Ethernet frame to the address "dddd".

The frame looks like this

Ethernet Header	Data, IP Address, etc.	Ethernet Trailer

The frame travels to the switch. Let's pretend that this is a brand-new switch, and that each of my devices is connected to the switch via an Ethernet cable. My computer is in port #1, and the printer is in port #4.

The switch receives the frame on port #1. It learns two things from this frame

- The device connected to port #1 has a MAC address of "aaaa" (from the "from" address of the frame)
- I need to send this frame to a device with the MAC address "dddd", wherever that is

I'm going to backtrack here and talk about **MAC Address Tables**. A switch remembers the MAC address of every device that is connected to it. Well, the switch has a huge table called the MAC Address Table. When the switch first powers on, this table is completely blank. Each time the switch receives a frame, it checks the source MAC address on the frame, and it updates the table.

When the switch powers on, its MAC Address Table looks like this:

PORT #	MAC ADDRESS(ES)

It's blank.

When the first frame enters, its MAC Address Table looks like below. The switch learns that "aaaa" is connected to port #1 because the source MAC address of the frame that arrived on port #1 was sent from "aaaa".

PORT #	MAC ADDRESS(ES)
1	aaaa

The switch checks the table to see which port it should send the frame out of. It should send it out of port #4, but it doesn't know that the printer is in port #4, because "dddd" is not in the MAC Address Table. There is no "dddd' entry in the table yet.

What does the switch do? It sends the frame out of all the ports (except the one that sent it). If it's a 48-port switch, then it sends the frame out of 47 ports. If it's a 24-port switch, then it sends the frame out of 23 ports. All the ports except port #1. It doesn't send the frame out of the port that it entered through because that would be pointless. This action is known as **frame flooding**.

If the printer (dddd) replies to the computer (aaaa), the switch learns what port the printer is plugged into. Now the table looks like this:

PORT #	MAC ADDRESS(ES)
1	aaaa
4	dddd

The switch doesn't have to flood the frame received from the printer. It knows that the destination is "aaaa" and according to the table, "aaaa" is in por #1. Thus, the switch sends the frame out of port #1 only.

The entries in the table only last about five minutes. If the switch doesn't see traffic from a specific MAC address after five minutes, it deletes the corresponding entry in the table. This lets the switch keep track of changes and delete incorrect entries. We can adjust this time up or down when we configure the switch.

These addresses such as "aaaa" and "bbbb" are known as **unicast addresses** because each one has a single destination. When we send a frame addressed to "aaaa", it goes to only one device.

There is a special MAC address (FF:FF:FF:FF:FF:FF). This is the **broadcast** MAC address. If a device wants to send a frame to everybody on the LAN, it addresses it to the broadcast address. Every network switch knows to forward this address, and every device knows to accept traffic on this address.

The switch will flood a frame addressed to FF:FF:FF:FF:FF:FF on all of its interfaces regardless of what's in the table.

Before we had switches, we had **hubs**. Some networks still use hubs. A hub is like a switch without a MAC address table. It floods every frame that it receives, no matter what.

In my network here, every device can talk at the same time. If this network was connected via a hub, only one device could talk at the same time. Think about it. If 'aaaa' sends a message, the hub receives it and repeats it to 'bbbb', 'cccc', and 'dddd'. While those devices are receiving the message, they won't be able to talk.

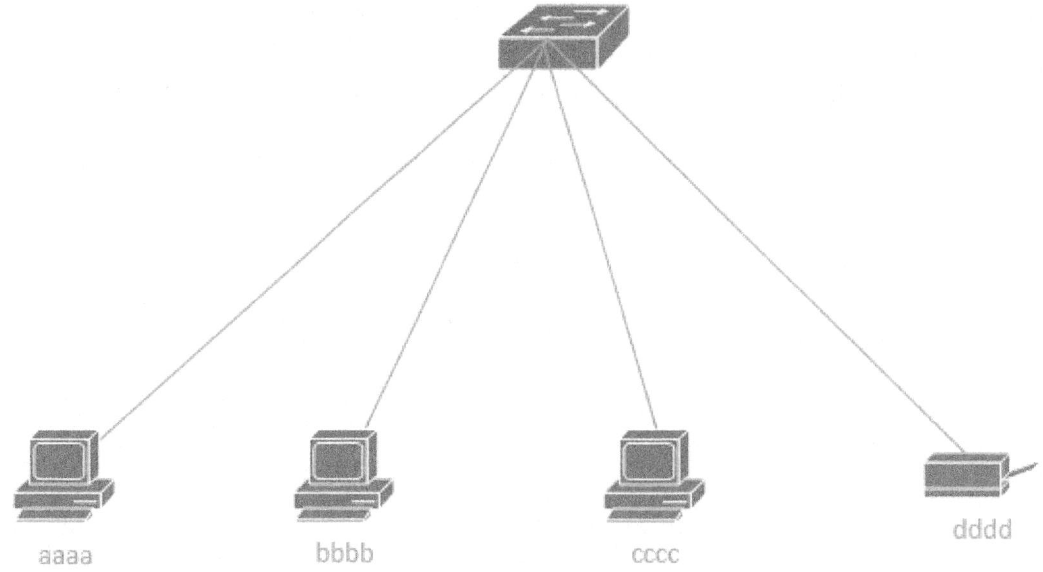

What happens if two devices try to talk at the same time? It results in a collision.

We can stop collisions through **CSMA/CD**, or **Carrier Sense Multiple Access with Collision Detection**. What happens if two devices try to talk at the same time on the same cable? Each device transmits a frame at the same time and a collision takes place.

A collision is bad, but with CSMA/CD, at least we know that it happened. Both devices stop talking immediately. Each device sends a "jam signal" – a message to the other devices that tells them to be quiet. Each device picks a random amount of time to wait and then resends its frame. Hopefully, the next time, the line is free, because each device waited a different length of time.

The collision detection method depends on the type of ethernet wiring in use.

In modern networks, CSMA/CD is not required. Collisions only took place on the old form of ethernet wiring, where many devices were connected to the same cable. Today, you won't see multiple devices connected to the same cable, but you might find hubs.

Cisco calls networks that use hubs **ethernet shared media** and networks that use switches **ethernet point to point**.

1.5 Compare TCP to UDP

But how do devices talk to each other, really? What do they say? How do messages get from one LAN to another? Remember I said that devices on a LAN talk to a switch and the switch forwards the frame based on the MAC address. What if they are on different LANs? Their traffic must pass through the router.

Devices speak a language called **TCP** or **Transmission Control Protocol**.

TCP involves a connection between two devices, with a three-way handshake. When using TCP, each time a device receives data, it verifies that the data has been received correctly. If not, the recipient requests that the sender retransmit the data.

TCP works with another protocol called **IP**, or **Internet Protocol**, and together they are called **TCP/IP**.

We think of TCP as being a **connection-oriented** protocol. It's like two people approaching each other at a park and agreeing to have a conversation:

- Person One: "Hey can I talk to you?"
- Person Two: "Sure"
- Person One: "Okay, I acknowledge that you agree to let me talk to you. Here is what I need to say: blah, blah, blah"
- Person Two: "I acknowledge what you said"
- Person One: "Thanks, blah, blah, blah some more"

What are these messages called?

- The first message is called the SYN (hey can I talk to you?). It is actually requesting that the parties synchronize their communication method.
- The second message is called the SYN-ACK (sure). The second party is requesting synchronization and acknowledging receipt of the first message.
- The third message is called the ACK (Okay, I acknowledge…). The first party is acknowledging receipt of the second party's message.

When we want to terminate the connection, we send a message called FIN.

TCP is a **connection-oriented protocol** because it requires us to create a connection before we can transfer data.

Under TCP/IP, every device has a unique address called an **IP address**. The IP address is 12 digits, and every three digits are separated by a period. We call each set of three digits an **octet**, and the value of each octet ranges from 0 to 255. For example, 111.111.111.111 is an IP address. So, every device has unique IP address and a unique MAC address.

In my example, I have two LANs connected over the internet. On the left is a LAN where the router IP address is 1.1.1.1, and on the right is a LAN where the router IP address is 2.2.2.2.

Right now, it's not important how they got these addresses. The devices inside the LAN also have IP addresses, but it's also not important.

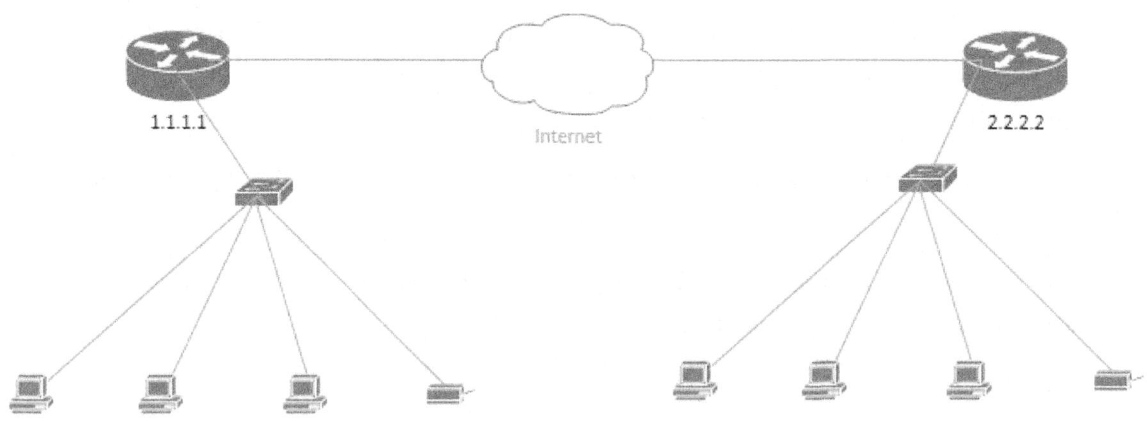

Remember how Ethernet breaks long messages up into frames? Well, in TCP/IP, these chunks of data are called **packets**.

What happens when a computer in the LAN on the left wants to send data a computer in the LAN on the right?

- The computer on the left determines that the destination computer isn't on the same LAN. Based on that, it creates a packet with the destination IP address. The destination IP address is the IP address of the router on the right. It's the IP address of the router, not the computer.

  As we will see learn later, we might never know the IP address of the computer on the right, and the LAN on the right is responsible for forwarding the packet to from the router to computer. The LAN on the left only has to worry about getting the packet to the LAN on the right.

  Our IP header might look like this

IP Header	TCP Header	Data

- We still need to take this packet from the computer on the left to the router on the left. Thus, our computer encapsulates this packet into an Ethernet frame. The frame is addressed to the MAC address of the local router.

Ethernet Header	IP Header	TCP Header	Data	Ethernet Trailer

- The switch receives the frame and, based on its MAC address, forwards it to the router. It checks the table to see what port the router is connected on.
- The router receives the frame, and strips the Ethernet header and trailer, revealing the IP Header inside.

IP Header	TCP Header	Data

- Based on whatever magic is inside the router, it sends this packet to the router on the right.
- The router on the right receives the packet and realizes that it is addressed to a computer inside its LAN. It adds new Ethernet headers, which include the MAC address of the destination computer. Now this is a frame again.

Ethernet Header	IP Header	TCP Header	Data	Ethernet Trailer

- The switch in the network on the right receives the frame from the router and forwards it to the correct computer.

How all this works deep inside each device is something we will learn more about in the coming chapters.

By the way, a UDP Header only has four components and is a total of eight bytes.

Source Port	Destination Port	Length	Checksum

The **OSI Model** was invented to explain the internet. It has seven layers and even though it doesn't make a whole lot of sense anymore, we still teach it to people. A better model is the **TCP Model**, which has five layers that follow the OSI Model.

Data is created at the top layer and works its way down until it gets to the bottom layer where it is transmitted. You can think of it as an assembly line. Each layer adds something to the data –

specifically, each layer adds a header and possibly a trailer to help the data get to its destination. What are the layers of the TCP Model, and how do they correspond to the OSI Model?

- **Application Layer** (Equivalent to the Session, Presentation, and Application Layers of OSI). The application layer allows programs to talk to the network. It contains the raw data generated by each computer program.

- **Transport Layer** (Equivalent to the Transport Layer of OSI). The transport layer moves the packets. Data from the application layer enters the transport layer and is encapsulated into **segments**.

- **Network (Internet) Layer** (Equivalent to the Network Layer of OSI). **IP Packets** are created on the Internet Layer. Segments from the transport layer receive IP Headers with their source and destination IP addresses.

- **Link Layer** (Equivalent to the Data Link Layer of OSI). TCP isn't concerned with the link layer, because the TCP/IP protocol doesn't define the physical link. Packets from the Internet layer receive Ethernet Headers and Trailers, resulting in frames.

- **Physical Layer** (Physical layer of OSI). The physical layer is the actual wiring with 0's and 1's traveling along it. The data is transmitted in this layer via an electrical signal (or light if we're using fiber optic cables).

We can summarize the information in the following table

TCP LAYER NAME	**CONTENTS**					**WHAT'S IT CALLED**	**OSI MODEL LAYER NAME**
APPLICATION				Raw Data			Application Presentation Session
TRANSPORT			TCP Header	Raw Data		Segment	Transport
NETWORK		IP Header	TCP Header	Raw Data		Packet	Network
DATA LINK	Ethernet Header	IP Header	TCP Header	Raw Data	Ethernet Trailer	Frame	Data Link
PHYSICAL							Physical

If we don't want to use TCP, we can use UDP. **UDP** is a **connectionless protocol** because it does not require a connection. UDP is like if I went to the top of a hill and started yelling. Nobody agreed to hear my message and it's possible that nobody will hear me. VoIP and other services use UDP.

When we communicate within a TCP layer (from computer to computer), we call it **same-layer communication**. When we communicate on a single computer between layers, we call it **adjacent-layer communication**.

Let's take a closer look at our routers. Behind each router is a LAN. Your home network is a LAN. Your work network is a LAN. Each device on a LAN knows that it is on a LAN and it can tell whether other devices are on the same LAN.

What if I had two offices, or five offices, or hundreds of offices, all over the country, and I wanted to make them into one big LAN? Let's say I have a server in Baltimore and I need to access it from my office in Los Angeles.

The solution is a **WAN**, or **Wide Area Network**. A phone company or an internet service provider lets some magic happen between our routers so that they can pass traffic over the internet but pretend to be part of the same physical network. We call this connection a **leased line**, **WAN**, **Point-to-Point**, etc..

The ISP provides you with an internet connection that works on the most basic layer. It's up to you to find a protocol to transmit the data between your routers. The two most popular protocols are **HDLC** or **High-Level Data Link Control**, and **PPP**, or **Point-to-Point Protocol**.

Since we're pretending that our LANs are part of the same physical network, it would be logical for our routers to transfer frames and not packets.

The HDLC frame is slightly different from an Ethernet frame. HDLC is an international standard, but Cisco routers use a proprietary version. Let's take a look.

HDLC Header	Data	HDLC Trailer

Preamble	Address	Control	Type		FCS

- **Preamble** (1 byte) – this lets the receiving router know that some data is coming
- **Address** (1 byte) – the destination MAC address
- **Control** (1 byte) – this field is no longer in use
- **Type** (2 bytes) – **proprietary to Cisco**; tells us the type of data in the HDLC frame
- **Data** – the data that we're transmitting
- **FCS** (2 bytes) – Frame Check Sequence

What happens in our network when the computer on the left wants to send some data to the computer on the right? Now these computers are on separate LANs connected via a WAN. We need to understand that every computer has an IP address – now it's relevant.

- The computer on the left determines that the destination computer on the right isn't on the same LAN. Based on that, it creates a packet with the destination IP address. The destination IP address is the IP address of the computer on the right.

  In this example, we have a WAN, so the computer in the left knows the IP address of the computer on the right (4.4.4.4) but can't reach it through the LAN.

IP Header	**TCP Header**	**Data**
Dest: 4.4.4.4		

- The computer encapsulates this packet into an Ethernet frame. The frame is addressed to the MAC address of the local router.

Ethernet Header	**IP Header**	**TCP Header**	**Data**	**Ethernet Trailer**

- The switch receives the frame and, based on its MAC address, forwards it to the router.

- The router receives the frame, and strips the ethernet header and trailer, revealing the IP Header.

IP Header	TCP Header	Data

- The router encapsulates the frame into an HDLC header and sends it to the router on the right.

HDLC Header	IP Header	TCP Header	Data	HDLC Trailer

- The router on the right strips the HDLC headers to reveal the original IP packet created by the computer on the left

IP Header	TCP Header	Data
Dest: 4.4.4.4		

- The router on the right adds new Ethernet headers, which include the MAC address of the destination computer

Ethernet Header	IP Header	TCP Header	Data	Ethernet Trailer
Dest: dddd				

- The switch in the network on the right receives the frame and forwards it to the correct computer

As I said earlier, every router only must worry about its own LAN, and nothing else. Now we can see that every router needs to get traffic to the next router (the neighboring router). If it can get traffic to the other network, it isn't concerned with how the other LANs operate internally.

Increasingly, ISPs are providing customers with ethernet connections known as **ethernet WANs**. An ethernet WAN acts like if we connected two routers together with a cross-over ethernet cable, no matter how far apart those routers are. Some other names for this service are **Ethernet Line Service**, or **Ethernet over MPLS (EoMPLS)**.

When we use an Ethernet WAN, we don't need to worry about the HDLC protocol anymore. Routers forward normal ethernet packets between themselves.

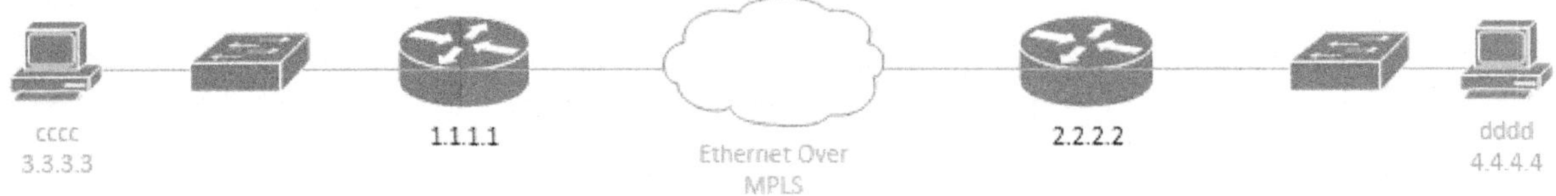

How?

- The computer determines that the destination computer isn't on the same LAN. Based on that, it creates a packet with the destination IP address. The destination IP address is the IP address of the computer on the right.

IP Header	TCP Header	Data
Dest: 4.4.4.4		

- The computer encapsulates this packet into an ethernet frame. The frame is addressed to the MAC address of the local router.

Ethernet Header	IP Header	TCP Header	Data	Ethernet Trailer

- The switch receives the frame and, based on its MAC address, forwards it to the router.
- The router receives the frame, and strips the ethernet header and trailer, revealing the IP Header.

IP Header	TCP Header	Data
Dest: 4.4.4.4		

- The router encapsulates the frame into a new Ethernet header and sends it to the router on the right. This new header has the MAC address of the router on the right as the destination.

Ethernet Header	IP Header	TCP Header	Data	Ethernet Trailer

- The router on the right strips the Ethernet headers to reveal the original IP packet created by the computer on the left

IP Header Dest: 4.4.4.4	TCP Header	Data

- The router on the right adds new Ethernet headers, which include the MAC address of the destination computer

Ethernet Header Dest: dddd	IP Header	TCP Header	Data	Ethernet Trailer

- The switch in the network on the right receives the frame and forwards it to the correct computer

What if my network is more complicated? In the previous scenario, each router only had one destination. What if there are more than two routers? A large corporate network has hundreds of routers.

Let's look at a more complicated network. I have four LANs now

- LAN 1, where IP addresses start with 1
- LAN 2, where IP addresses start with 2
- LAN 3, where IP addresses start with 3
- LAN 4, where IP addresses start with 4

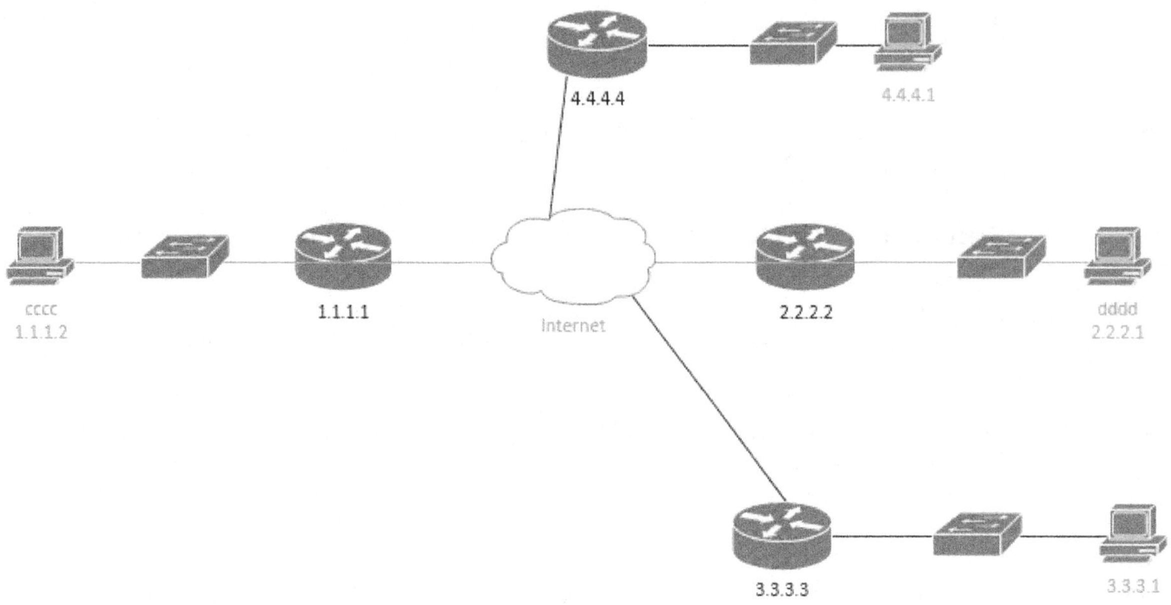

First, think about the computer on the left. It's preprogrammed to understand that if a packet's destination is outside its own LAN, then it should send it to the LAN router. This router is known as the **default gateway**. The computer has no other choice – a LAN could have multiple routers, but this is a rare setup. The router is responsible for sending the packet to the next network (the next router).

But how does the router (1.1.1.1) know where to send the packet to? It has a routing table. Router 1.1.1.1's table might look like this

INTERFACE #	DESTINATION
FE0/0/0	2.2.2.2
GE0/0/0	3.3.3.3
GE0/0/1	4.4.4.4

By the way, a router can have multiple **interfaces**, or ports to connect to. You will see interfaces labelled as "FE" for Fast Ethernet (100 Mbps) or "GE" for Gigabit Ethernet (1 Gbps), and then a number such as FE0/0/0.

- Let's say that computer 1.1.1.2 wants to send a packet to computer 3.3.3.1. It knows that computer 3.3.3.1 is on network 3.
- It knows that network 3 is different from its own network (network 1), so it encapsulates the packet in a frame and sends the frame to its default router. The frame contains the MAC

address of the default router. The switch sends the frame to the router.

Ethernet Header	IP Header Dest: 3.3.3.1	TCP Header	Data	Ethernet Trailer

- The router receives the frame and checks the FCS to ensure that there are no errors
- It strips the ethernet header and trailer, leaving just the IP header

IP Header Dest: 3.3.3.1	TCP Header	Data

- The destination is 3.3.3.1, which is part of the 3.3.3.3 network
- From the table, the router knows that network 3.3.3.3 is connected to GE0/0/0
- The router creates a new frame addressed to the router running the 3.3.3.3 network. The frame's sender field contains the MAC address of the 1.1.1.1 router, and destination field contains the MAC address of the 3.3.3.3 router.

Ethernet Header	IP Header Dest: 3.3.3.1	TCP Header	Data	Ethernet Trailer

- It sends this frame out of interface GE0/0/0
- The router on network 3.3.3.3 receives the frame. It strips the ethernet header revealing the IP address 3.3.3.1
- It creates a new frame and sends it to computer 3.3.3.1 (addressed to the computer's MAC address). The switch is responsible for forwarding the frame.

We call each of these networks (1.1.1.1, 2.2.2.2, 3.3.3.3, 4.4.4.4) **subnets**. If a group of computers is connected over a switch, then they should be part of the same subnet. If they are separated by a router (or multiple routers), then they are part of different subnets.

Remember our routing table? How did the router fill this table out?

INTERFACE #	DESTINATION
FE0/0/0	2.2.2.2
GE0/0/0	3.3.3.3

GE0/0/1	4.4.4.4

I made the network a little bit more complicated. Now there are multiple pathways. If router 1.1.1.1 needs to send data to 6.6.6.6, it has a couple of options. It must go through 2.2.2.2, and then it can either go through 3.3.3.3 or 4.4.4.4. How does it decide which route to take? How does it even know what routes there are?

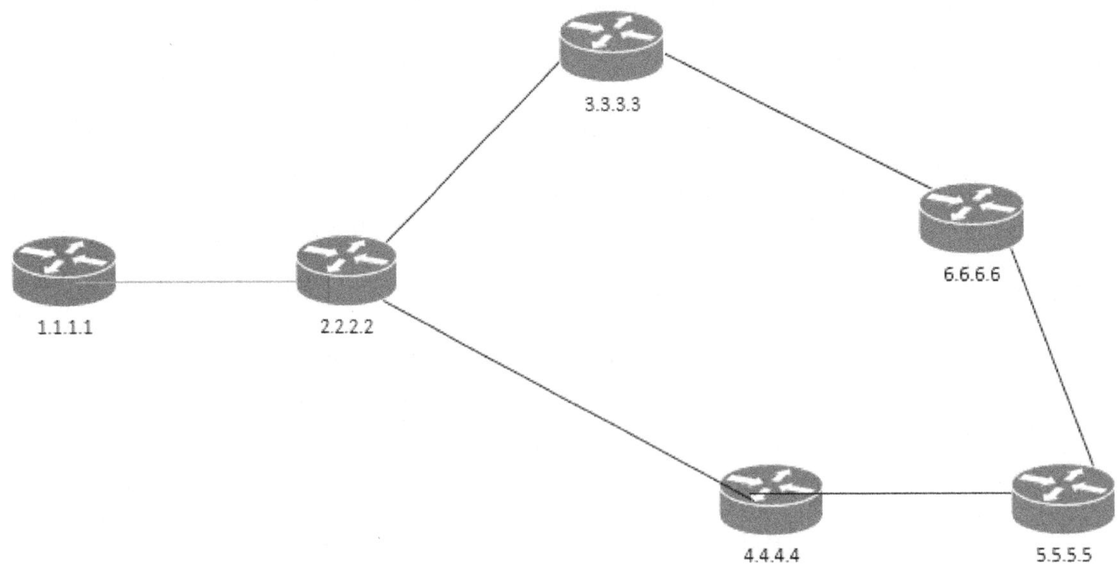

When we first connect a router, it automatically learns about the subnets that it's directly connected to. It adds those subnets to the table

- Router 1.1.1.1
    - Router 1.1.1.1 knows about subnet 1.1.1.1 (its own local network)
    - It also knows that it's connected to subnet 2.2.2.2 (the neighbor)
- Router 2.2.2.2
    - Router 2.2.2.2 knows about subnet 2.2.2.2 (its own network)
    - It also knows that it's connected to subnets 1.1.1.1, 3.3.3.3, and 4.4.4.4 (its neighbors)
- By the same logic
    - Router 3.3.3.3 knows about subnet 3.3.3.3, 6.6.6.6, and 2.2.2.2
    - Router 4.4.4.4 knows about 2.2.2.2, 4.4.4.4, and 5.5.5.5

- Router 5.5.5.5 knows about 4.4.4.4, 5.5.5.5, and 6.6.6.6
- Router 6.6.6.6 knows about 3.3.3.3, 6.6.6.6, and 5.5.5.5

That means router 2.2.2.2 might have a routing table that looks like this

INTERFACE #	DESTINATION
FE0/0/0	2.2.2.2
GE0/0/0	1.1.1.1
GE0/0/1	3.3.3.3
GE0/0/2	4.4.4.4

And router 1.1.1.1 might have a table that looks like this

INTERFACE #	DESTINATION
FE0/0/0	1.1.1.1
GE0/0/0	2.2.2.2

Once each router fills out its own table, it shares the table with its neighbors

- Router 1.1.1.1 tells 2.2.2.2 about 1.1.1.1
- Router 2.2.2.2 tells 1.1.1.1 about 3.3.3.3 and 4.4.4.4
- Router 2.2.2.2 tells 3.3.3.3 about 1.1.1.1 and 2.2.2.2
- Router 2.2.2.2 tells 4.4.4.4 about 1.1.1.1 and 2.2.2.2

Each router updates its table

- Router 2.2.2.2 doesn't need to update its table with the info it learned from 1.1.1.1, because it's directly connected to 1.1.1.1 and 1.1.1.1 is only connected to 2.2.2.2. Thus, 1.1.1.1 has no new information to share with 2.2.2.2.
- Router 1.1.1.1 updates its table to include routes to 3.3.3.3 and 4.4.4.4. Now it knows that it can reach networks 3.3.3.3 and 4.4.4.4 through router 2.2.2.2.
- Now router 1.1.1.1's table looks like this

INTERFACE #	DESTINATION
FE0/0/0	1.1.1.1
GE0/0/0	2.2.2.2, 3.3.3.3, 4.4.4.4

- Although it's not directly connected to 3.3.3.3 or 4.4.4.4, router 1.1.1.1 knows that it can reach those networks through 2.2.2.2. Thus, any traffic with a destination of 3.3.3.3 or 4.4.4.4 can travel through the GE0/0/0 interface.

  Router 1.1.1.1 doesn't have to worry about how Router 2.2.2.2 gets traffic to 3.3.3.3 or 4.4.4.4. It just needs to know that it can do so.

How do the routers actually talk? How do different brands of routers talk to each other? We will find out later.

We're going to stop and learn some background information.

I've been talking about MAC addresses for a while. A router or computer needs to address Ethernet frames to another router or computer's MAC address. How do devices learn the MAC address of the destination?

That's where **ARP** or **Address Resolution Protocol** comes in. Let's say my computer has a MAC address of AA:AA:AA:AA:AA:AA and an IP address of 192.168.1.2, and my printer has a MAC address of BB:BB:BB:BB:BB:BB and an IP address of 192.168.1.3. I want to print a document. My computer knows my printer's IP address, but it needs to find out its MAC address.

My computer sends out a message known as an **ARP request message**. It addresses the message to the broadcast MAC address FF:FF:FF:FF:FF:FF. Remember that messages to this address go everywhere.

My computer's message in effect says, "if your IP address is 192.168.1.3, then tell me your MAC address". This message is flooded over the entire network, but only the printer responds (because only the printer has that IP address). The printer sends an **ARP response message** back to my computer, indicating that its MAC address is BB:BB:BB:BB:BB:BB. By the way, the switch on my network sees these messages and uses them to learn MAC addresses of the connected devices.

My computer maintains a table called the **ARP table**. It adds the information learned from the printer's ARP response to the table. The ARP table contains a list of device MAC addresses and their corresponding IP addresses. The next time my computer wants to talk to the printer, it doesn't need to follow the ARP process and send out an ARP request message. It just checks the table. In fact, every time a computer needs to send an ARP message, it checks the ARP table first to make sure that there isn't already a valid entry.

Routers also keep records of ARP addresses. They need to know the MAC addresses of computers on their subnets and of neighboring routers. A router lets the entries in its ARP table expire after a period, because addresses can change.

We can look up the ARP entries on our computer by typing **`arp -a`**

The second item I want to mention is DNS. Humans are good at remembering names but bad at remembering numbers. A human can remember hostnames and website URLs like google.com and amazon.com. Unfortunately, for a computer to access a website, it must know the IP address of that website's server. How does a computer convert a URL like google.com into an IP address like 8.8.8.8?

The **DNS** or **Domain Name Server** converts human-readable domain names into machine-readable IP addresses.

It's easy for me to remember a name like "fileserver01", but my router/computer needs to know it as 192.168.5.5. When I type in "fileserver01", my computer calls the DNS and says "hey, what's the IP address for fileserver01" and the DNS replies with "192.168.5.5". Now I can send my traffic to 192.168.5.5 (or use ARP to learn 192.168.5.5's MAC address).

ICMP is a special protocol. It does not carry user traffic, but machine-to-machine communications. Network equipment use ICMP messages to communicate errors and status updates with each other. ICMP messages are used by **ping** and **tracert** commands. These commands are important for network troubleshooting.

For example, if I want to check whether a device with the IP address 192.168.5.5 is online, I can send it a "ping", also known as an **ICMP Echo Request**. If the computer is online, it sends a reply, known as an **ICMP Echo Reply**.

We will look at the benefits of TCP/IP in greater detail

- Multiplexing. We can use virtual ports to send different streams of traffic to the same computer.
- Segmentation. Data is segmented into packets before being transmitted instead of being sent as a continuous stream. It's like if I ripped pages out of a book and sent them to you one at a time.
- Error Recovery. The system numbers each packet so that the recipient is forced to acknowledge receipt. Any packet not received is sent again.
- Flow Control. We can use buffers to prevent high traffic flows from overloading network devices. If a computer receives a ton of traffic all at once, it can hold some of it in a buffer until it has the resources to process it.
- Connections. Devices must agree to communicate before they can communicate. We talked about this at the beginning of this chapter.

What is a **port**? For the purposes of this section, a port isn't something physical. If you look at the back of your computer, you'll see USB ports, HDMI ports, VGA ports, and probably a single network (Ethernet) port. We're not talking about those ports. A port is simply a virtual channel that an application can use to communicate with a specific protocol. All the data entering your computer travels through that single physical Ethernet port (or through a Wi-Fi connection), but it must be separated somehow so that every application receives the information it needs.

Say your computer's IP address is 192.168.1.5, and you're receiving the following traffic

- Email
- A file transfer through FTP
- Some web pages through Google Chrome
- A Zoom meeting or a Skype meeting

This traffic is all addressed to your computer's IP address – 192.168.1.5 and is divided into packets. How does each application know which packets belong to it? For example, how does Google Chrome know which packets contain web pages?

That is where these "virtual" ports come in. There are 65,535 different ports. Some of the smaller numbered ports are reserved for specific protocols. For example, HTTP is port 80. Unencrypted website (HTTP) traffic travels on port 80.

Each application only sends data out of, and listens for data on, the specific ports that it requires. For example, Google Chrome sends and receives web traffic over HTTP (port 80) and HTTPS (port 443). Therefore, Google Chrome only listens for traffic on ports 80 and 443 and sends traffic only on ports 80 and 443. It cannot see data on other ports.

When we send a packet with a webpage, we address it to 192.168.1.5:80. Google sees this traffic and takes it.

In general, a port is reserved for only one protocol, and the applications that use a protocol will use the ports reserved for that protocol.

In more advanced cases, two devices could choose to use a different port. For example, an HTTP web server could choose to listen/transmit on a different port than port 80 or port 443, such as port 8343. Then a device attempting to access the web server would need to know to use the non-standard port 8343. When a user instructs Google Chrome to visit a website, it tries to communicate with the web server over port 80 or port 443. If the web server is configured for another port, Google Chrome will display an error. Google Chrome must be configured to look for the website data on the non-standard port.

The real-world equivalent of a port is a set of post office boxes. Each tenant has his own box. The mail comes in to the post office from many locations. The street address on each envelope is the same, but the post office box is different. The post office sorts the mail into each post office box.

When a recipient comes in to check his mail, he can only look inside his own box. He doesn't see any mail addressed to another person, even though they share the same street address.

Some of the most common protocols are summarized in the following table. Remember that an administrator can run a protocol over a non-standard port number. The port number has no effect on the contents of the traffic.

Port Number/Name	Use
20 and 21/FTP	**File Transfer Protocol** FTP is a protocol for transferring files between two devices FTPS adds a security layer to the file transfer. It requires that the server have an SSL certificate installed. The entire session can be encrypted or only specific portions of the session can be encrypted.
22/SSH	**Secure Shell** Secure Socket Shell (or Secure Shell) allows a user to connect to a remote computer. SSH authenticates the identity of the remote computer to the user and the user to the remote computer. SSH creates a tunnel between the user and the remote computer. The user will require an SSH client such as PuTTY, and the remote computer will require an SSH daemon. Each remote computer must be set up to accept SSH logins (typically over port 22). Network firewalls must be configured to allow traffic over port 22. The user's IP address should be whitelisted on the firewall (do not allow SSH connections from any IP address)

22/SFTP	**SSH File Transfer** SFTP is a file transfer protocol within the SSH protocol. Provided that the SSH session is secured and properly configured, then the SFTP session will be as well.
23/Telnet	**Telnet** Telnet provides a text-based terminal to communicate with a network device or server. Telnet is like SSH but does not contain any security. It is no longer popular due to lack of security.
25/SMTP	**Simple Mail Transfer Protocol** Used to communicate with an e-mail server (for sending e-mail only). Can be secure or insecure, depending on whether the client and server agree to encrypt data between them.
53/DNS	**Domain Name Server** Translates Domain Names/Hostnames to IP addresses (necessary to locate network resource) Consider that a human can remember text names (such as google.ca or amazon.com), but for a web browser to access a website, it must figure out the corresponding server IP address. The DNS converts human-readable domain names into machine-readable IP addresses.
67/68/DHCP	**Dynamic Host Configuration Protocol**

	Allows a device to request a dynamic IP from a DHCP server. Allows a DHCP server to dynamically assign IP addresses to other devices. When a device first joins a network, it may not need an IP address and must request one.
69/TFTP	**Trivial File Transfer Protocol** TFTP is like FTP in that it allows a user to transfer files over a network. TFTP has a simple design. An important use of TFTP is to allow a device to boot over a network. A device with no operating system can load one over the network into memory.
80/HTTP	**Hyper Text Transfer Protocol** Used to transmit web site data (insecure)
110/POP	**Post Office Protocol** Allows an e-mail client like Outlook to retrieve messages from a server. With POP, the e-mail server receives messages on behalf of the user. The e-mail client asks the server if there is any new messages. If so, the e-mail client downloads messages from the server. The server deletes the messages after they have been downloaded. POP is no longer common; it has been replaced with IMAP and Exchange, which allow an e-mail client to "sync" with a server.
123/NTP	**Network Time Protocol**

	NTP allows network-connected devices to sync their clocks, to within a few milliseconds of UTC. NTP can function accurately even when the network has high latency through the clock synchronization algorithm. NTP can obtain the time from a central server or from a peer.
137-139/NetBIOS/NetBT	**NetBIOS/NetBT** Developed by Microsoft in the 1980s. Allows computers to communicate with each other over a network and exchange basic information. When a computer booted up, it broadcast its information (MAC address and hostname) so that other computers on the network could find it. NetBIOS only worked for small networks of up to 40 devices, with no router. NetBIOS over TCP/IP (or NetBT) was an upgrade. Provides name services (provides each computer with a unique hostname), and communications.
143/IMAP	**Internet Message Access Protocol** Allows an e-mail client to communicate with an e-mail server. The client and server "sync" so that both have the same data (e-mails, calendar entries, contacts, etc.). If an e-mail is deleted in the e-mail client, then it is also deleted on the server.

	IMAP may be secure or insecure.
161/162/SNMP	**Simple Network Management Protocol** Allows a user to collect and manage data about managed network devices, including routers, switches, servers, and printers.
389/LDAP	**Lightweight Directory Access Protocol** Allows users to access different directories Directories include e-mail directories, users, phone numbers, printers, and services
427/SLP	**Service Location Protocol** Allows computers to find services on a local network A device will broadcast a URL containing the location of a service that it offers over SLP Other devices can connect to the URL over SLP to use the service
443/HTTPS	**Hyper Text Transfer Protocol-Secure** Used to transmit web site data (secure)
445/SMB/CIFS	**Server Message Block/Common Internet File System** Allows computers on a network to share files and printers
548/AFP	**Apple Filing Protocol** Allows Apple devices to share files
636/LDAPS	**Secure Lightweight Directory Access Protocol**

	Like LDAP but secure
1720/H.323	Allows devices to communicate audio-visual content over a network. Used in videoconferencing applications.
3389/RDP	**Remote Desktop Protocol** Allows a user to remotely connect to a Windows server or computer via a Graphical User Interface
5060/5061/SIP	**Session Initiation Protocols** Used for real-time communications involving VoIP and video conferencing. Also used by mobile devices for voice over LTE.

Ports 0 to 1023 are **well known ports** reserved for specific applications. Only those applications should be using those ports. Ports 1024 to 49151 are called **user ports** or **registered ports**. An application developer can apply to have his application use one of those ports. Ports 49152 to 65535 are called **private ports**, **dynamic ports** or **ephemeral ports**. An app can borrow one of those ports temporarily if it needs to communicate.

In TCP/IP, an IP address combined with a port and a transport protocol (TCP or UDP) is called a **socket**. For example, 192.168.5.5:80 over UDP is a socket. The use of ports is called **multiplexing**.

Reliability or **error recovery** allows the sender to ensure that its message is received. Each TCP packet is numbered with a **Sequence number**. It's kind of like pages in a book. How does it work?

Computer A sent Packet #1 and Packet #2 to Computer B. The packets are numbered sequentially. The next packet will be Packet #3.

Computer B replies with an acknowledgement telling Computer A that it received the two packets. It numbers its acknowledgement "3". Notice that it didn't number it "2", or "1". It doesn't have to acknowledge all the packets that it received. Instead, Computer B is saying that it received all the packets up to (but not including) Packet #3. This is known as a **forward acknowledgment**, because it is acknowledging that it expects to receive Packet #3 next.

By the way, remember I said that in a TCP handshake the computers send a message called "SYN"? "SYN" is short for synchronize. Basically, each computer is telling the other one to synchronize its sequence numbers. Computer A doesn't have to start with Packet #1. It could start the could at 23424 or something. It doesn't matter, if both computers agree on a starting value.

Anyways, Computer A knows that Computer B received Packet #1 and Packet #2 because it receives ACK #3. It can send more packets.

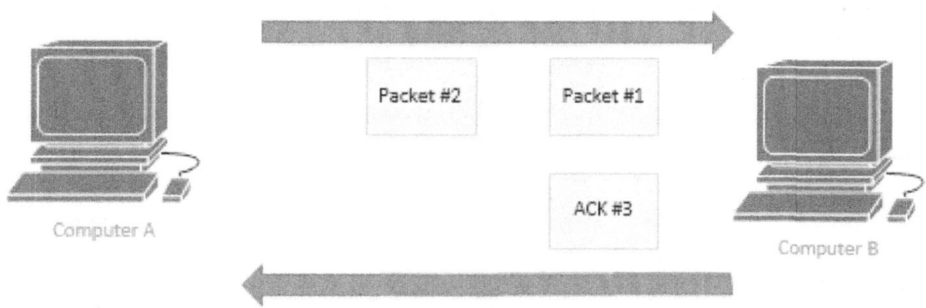

Now, let's look at a different example. Although they look alike, this is a different Computer A and Computer B than in the previous example, believe me.

Computer A sends four packets to Computer B. Packet #1 through Packet #4 are sent but Packet #3 fails to reach its destination. Computer B receives Packet #1, Packet #2, and Packet #4, and realizes that Packet #3 is missing. It sends Computer A an acknowledgement for Packet #3. Computer B is saying that it expects to receive Packet #3 next.

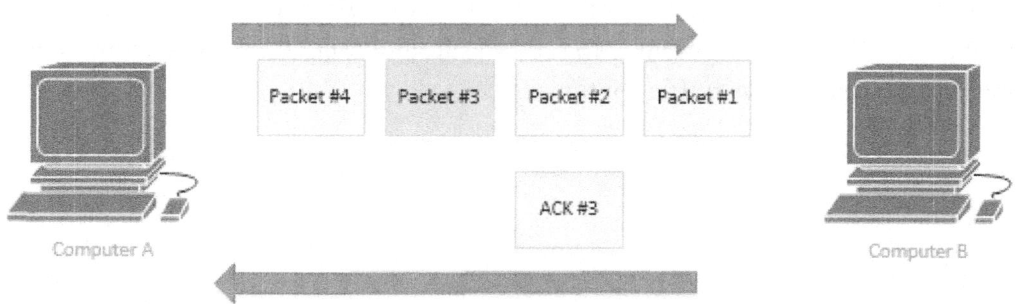

Computer A reads the ACK #3 and realizes that Computer B didn't receive Packet #3. It's not sure whether Computer B received Packet #4. Thus, Computer A resends Packet #3.

Upon receipt of Packet #3, Computer B responds with an acknowledgement expecting the next packet to be Packet #5. Computer B already received Packet #4 earlier, so it doesn't need to receive it again.

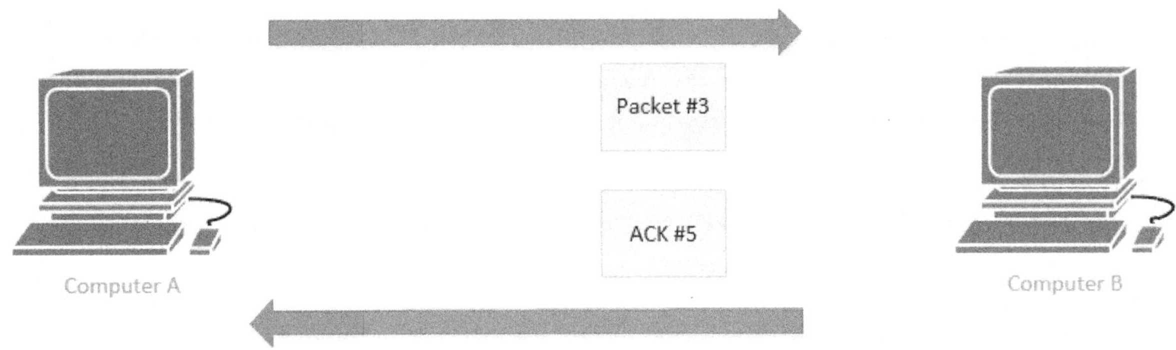

By not having to send an acknowledgement for every packet, we can reduce the amount of traffic that we send over the network.

The concept of **Flow Control** or **windowing** allows two computers to decide how many packets can be awaiting acknowledgement. For example, if the size of the window is five, then Computer A will send Computer B five packets. Once Computer B has acknowledged receipt of the five packets, Computer A can send more packets.

The two computers can adjust the size of the window during their connection. They can adjust the size of the window during each transmission. When they do, it is known as a **sliding window** or a **dynamic window**. The receiving computer uses the ACK message to tell the sender the size of the new window.

Each time a computer receives messages successfully, it increases the size of the window. Each time it receives messages unsuccessfully, it reduces the size of the window. A good network is like a well-oiled machine. Computers are not usually waiting to send traffic, and eventually, the window is so big that the computers send and receive traffic continually.

1.6 Configure and verify IPv4 addressing and subnetting

Remember that hosts on the same LAN have the same subnet. Anything behind the router has the same subnet.

If I have a large network, I should make one subnet for

- Each LAN or VLAN. We will learn about VLANs later – but for now, you can think of a VLAN like cutting your LAN into multiple segments. This is done through configuration on the switch (logically) and not physically.
- Each WAN
- Each point-to-point serial connection

Once I figure out how many subnets I need, I should figure out how big each subnet must be.

Remember that when a computer wants to access another computer it first must ask itself: is this device on my local network or is it somewhere else? If it is local, the computer users ARP to figure out the destination's MAC address. It sends the data to the destination MAC address; a switch (or multiple switches) on the network carries the data

What happens when the destination is not local? Then the device must send the data to a router. But how does it know which router to send it to? And how does it know whether a device is local?

Every device has network settings, which include at least three items

- **IP address** – this is the IP address of the device
- **Subnet mask** – this tells the device how big its local network is; the local network is known as a subnet
- **Default gateway** – this is another name for a router

The device uses its IP address and the subnet to figure out the range of IP addresses in its local network. If the destination IP address of a packet is not in the local network, then it is sent to the default gateway.

This is going to be the hardest part of the book. Learning the complicated math about subnets is difficult.

Networks are classified based on size. The entire IP address space is from 0.0.0.0 to 255.255.255.255. But you can't have all of it. A company can be assigned a portion of the space, called a network. Networks can be divided into classes.

- A **Class A** network contains 2^{24} addresses. Networks in the range of 1.0.0.0 to 126.0.0.0.0 are Class A networks. So, a network with a range of 2.0.0.0 to 2.255.255.255 is a Class A network.

  These are used for unicast in large networks.

- A **Class B** network contains 2^{16} addresses. Networks in the range of 128.0.0.0 to 191.0.0.0 are Class B networks. So, a network with a range of 130.0.0.0 to 130.0.255.255 is a Class B network.

  These are used for unicast in medium networks.

- A **Class C** network contains 2^{8} addresses. Networks in the range of 192.168.0.0 to 223.0.0.0 are Class C networks. So, a network with a range of 200.0.0.0 to 200.0.0.255 is a Class C network.

  These are used for unicast in small networks.

We have two more classes of networks

- Networks in the range of 224.0.0.0 to 239.0.0.0 are Class D networks. They are used for multicast.

- Networks in the range of 240.0.0.0 to 254.0.0.0 are Class E networks. These are reserved for future use.

These networks do not have subnet masks. They are strictly experimental, and most routers will not accept traffic from IP addresses in their ranges. The use of a Class A, B, or C network is called **Classful Subnetting**.

A subnet mask looks like an IP address. It is 32-bits long (each octet is 8-bits). If I must go deep down into how computers work, I will. Remember that computers are electrical. They only think in terms of "on or off", like an electrical switch. So, a 1 is on, and a 0 is off.

8-bits makes up one byte. A computer with 8-bits can only count to 255 in one operation. If I make a table that is base-two (every entry is double the previous entry), I can combine these eight numbers to make any number from 0 to 255. Look at the table below. You can add these numbers up to make any number you think of between 0 and 255.

128	64	32	16	8	4	2	1

If you look at the 8-bits in a byte, each bit is assigned to one of these numbers. If the bit is a one, or in "on' position, then the number is added, and if the bit is a zero, or in the "off" position, then the number is ignored.

For example, the computer might represent the following number

128	64	32	16	8	4	2	1
1	1	0	1	1	0	0	1

The value of this byte is 128 + 64 + 16 + 8 + 1 = 217

Thus, we have two ways to write out this number, either as 217 or as 11011001

So what? 255.255.255.252 is an example of a subnet mask. We could write it out as

11111111.11111111.11111111.11111100 if we wanted to. We call this a **binary number**. How did we get the binary number?

Well, the first three octets are "255". We get "255" from the table full of 1's (11111111).

128	64	32	16	8	4	2	1
1	1	1	1	1	1	1	1

128 + 64 + 32 + 16 + 8 + 4 + 2 + 1 = 255

The fourth octet is 252. We get "252" from the table with six 1's (11111100).

128	64	32	16	8	4	2	1
1	1	1	1	1	1	0	0

128 + 64 + 32 + 16 + 8 + 4 = 252

We could also call 255.255.255.252 a /30 subnet mask, because it has 30 "1's" in it. Note that you'll never see a subnet mask like 255.255.255.217. Why not?

If you wrote 217 in binary, it would look like 128 + 64 + 16 + 8 + 1 = 217, or 11011001. The whole subnet mask would be 11111111.11111111.11111111.11011001.

The 1's in a subnet mask always appear on the left and the 0's always appear on the right. Thus, the only numbers that can fit into a subnet mask are 0, 128, 192, 224, 240, 248, 252, 254, and 255.

Many network engineers like to refer to a subnet mask as a "/30" or "/28" or "slash whatever number it is", instead of saying the entire name.

But how do I use a subnet mask? If my IP address is 192.168.0.29 and my subnet mask is /28, how big is my network? What IP address does it start on and where does it end? We can figure it out

- /28 is my subnet. We can write it out as 255.255.255.240. We can also write it out as 11111111.11111111.11111111.11110000
- 192.168.0.29 is my IP address. We can write it out as 11000000.10101000.00000000.00011101
- We use the subnet mask to "mask" the IP address.

  Masking is a special kind of addition.

  For each place, if there is a zero in either the subnet or the IP address, then the result is zero. For each place, if there is a one in both the subnet and the IP address, the result is one.

  11111111.11111111.11111111.11110000 (subnet)

  11000000.10101000.00000000.00011101 (IP address)

  11000000.10101000.00000000.00010000 (result)
- We convert the result back to the decimal: 192.168.0.16
  This gives us our network name.
- So, my network starts at 192.168.0.16
- Where does it end? How big is my network? I know that my subnet is a /28, and since there are 32 total bits in an IP address, I can subtract to get 4 bits.

  32 bits total – 28 bits in the subnet = 4 bits in the network.

Remember that, **32 – subnet bits = network size**

There are 4 bits left for my network.

If I count the 4 bits from the end of the table, I get 8 + 4 + 2 + 1 = 15. So, my network has 15 more IP addresses.

It starts at 192.168.0.16 and it ends at 192.168.0.31

- In any network, the starting IP address is known as the subnet. It can't be assigned to a device. Although my network is called 192.168.0.16, 192.168.0.16 is not a usable IP.
- The first usable IP address is 192.168.0.17
- The last IP address in a network is the broadcast address for the network. Remember broadcast IP addressees? If a device wants to send a message to all the devices within its network, it sends it to the broadcast address. In this case, it is 192.168.0.31. I can't assign this IP address to a device either.
- Thus, the last usable IP address is 192.168.0.30
- Notice that this is a Class C network. The whole range is 192.168.0.0 to 192.168.0.255. That is a range of 256 addresses. Our subnet is 16 IP addresses wide. Therefore 256 / 16 = 16.

  If our company was assigned this entire Class C network, we could create up to 16 subnets that each contain 16 IP addresses.

- If this was a Class B network, it would have a range of 65,536 addresses. Therefore 65536 / 16 = 4096. We can create up to 4096 subnets that are 16 IP addresses wide, in a Class B network.

  Of course, we can create subnets that are smaller or larger than 16 IP addresses, but that would change the number of subnets we could create.

- In summary
  - My IP address is 192.168.0.29
  - My subnet mask is 255.255.255.240
  - The subnet name is 192.168.0.16
  - The first useable IP address is 192.168.0.17

- The last useable IP address is 192.168.0.30
- The broadcast IP address is 192.168.0.31

The default gateway can be any IP address in the range of 192.168.0.17 to 192.168.0.30. Typically, an administrator will give the gateway either the first usable IP address or the last usable IP address, but he doesn't have to.

The gateway is the IP address the router has facing the internal network. It's the IP address a device will contact when it wants to send traffic out the local network.

By the way, I can write the IP address as 192.168.0.17 or as 192.168.000.017. The extra zeroes at the beginning of each octet don't matter.

The opposite of Classful Subnetting is **Classless Subnetting**. How does it work?

If my network is 192.168.0.0 to 192.168.0.255, I have 256 IP addresses. I can break it down into one network of 256 addresses, or I can break it down into 2 networks of 128 addresses each, or 4 networks of 64 addresses each, or 8 networks of 32 addresses each, etc.. If my network was a Class A or Class B network, I could break it down into even more subnets and/or have even more IP addresses per subnet.

Look at the following table. We have a choice of seven subnet masks

SUBNET MASK	NUMBER OF IPS PER SUBNET	NUMBER OF SUBNETS
/24	254	1
/25	126	2
/26	62	4
/27	30	8
/28	14	16
/29	6	32
/30	2	64

There is no /31 or /32 subnet because we need at least three IP addresses in a subnet – the network name, the useable IP, and the broadcast address. A /31 subnet would be two IP addresses wide (meaning there would be a network and a broadcast address and no useable IP addresses), and a /32 subnet would be one IP address wide.

We could choose to break down our network into subnets of any size based on our requirements. We ask ourselves what the largest required subnet is and go from there. This is known as **Fixed Length Subnetting**.

What if I need subnets of different lengths? What if my network range is 192.168.0.0 to 192.168.0.255 (Class C) and I need

- A subnet with 100 IP addresses for computers
- A subnet with 20 IP addresses for servers
- A subnet with 20 IP addresses for network equipment
- A subnet with 10 IP addresses for surveillance cameras

The smallest subnet that could accommodate 100 IP addresses is the /25, with 128 usable IP addresses per subnet. But I can only make two /25 subnets out of the network that I have, and I need four subnets.

Introducing the **Variable Length Subnet Mask**. If we don't follow the traditional rules, we can do the following

- Create a /25 subnet (192.168.0.0 to 192.168.0.127) for the subnet that requires 100 IP addresses. This subnet has 126 usable IP addresses.
- Create a /27 subnet (192.168.0.128 to 192.168.0.159) for the subnet that requires 20 IP addresses. This subnet has 30 usable IP addresses.
- Create a /27 subnet (192.168.0.160 to 192.168.0.191) for the second subnet that requires 20 IP addresses. This subnet has 30 usable IP addresses.
- Create a /28 subnet (192.168.0.192 to 192.168.0.207) for the subnet that requires 10 IP addresses. This subnet has 14 usable IP addresses.
- I still have the address space 192.168.0.208 to 192.168.0.255 left over, which is 48 IP addresses. I can create a /27 and /28 subnet out of it. Or I can create three /28 subnets out of it. Or some other combination depending on my needs.

We write the subnets I created as follows

- 192.168.0.0/25
- 192.168.0.128/27
- 192.168.0.160/27
- 192.168.0.192/28

This notation is called **Classless Inter-Domain Routing**, or **CIDR**. We are writing the name of the network followed by the subnet size (as the number of bits).

If you want to remember an easy formula for the number of usable IP addresses in a subnet, it is 2^n-2, where n is the size of the subnet.

For example, if the subnet is /27, then the subnet size is 32 – 27 = 5

2^n -2 = 2^5 -2 = 30 (I have 30 usable IP addresses in a /27 subnet)

In summary, for subnetting

- I should choose a class of network (A, B, or C) if I can (if it hasn't been assigned to me)
- I figure out how many subnets I need – one for each LAN, VLAN, and WAN
- For each subnet I calculate the size based on the number of devices inside it. How many usable IP addresses do I need in each subnet?
- I divide my network into subnets, taking care that I have enough subnets and that they each have an adequate number of IP addresses.
- If I don't have enough IP addresses, I can try variable length subnetting or choose a larger class of network.

Going back to my three classes of networks

- A **Class A** network contains 2^{24} addresses. Networks in the range of 1.0.0.0 to 126.0.0.0.0 are Class A networks. So, a network with a range of 2.0.0.0 to 2.255.255.255 is a Class A network.
- A **Class B** network contains 2^{16} addresses. Networks in the range of 128.0.0.0 to 191.0.0.0 are Class B networks. So, a network with a range of 130.0.0.0 to 130.0.255.255 is a Class B network.
- A **Class C** network contains 2^8 addresses. Networks in the range of 192.168.0.0 to 223.0.0.0 are Class C networks. So, a network with a range of 200.0.0.0 to 200.0.0.255 is a Class C network.

Think about the IP address in a Class A network. If my network has a range of 2.0.0.0 to 2.255.255.255, that means the first octet doesn't change. It's always "2" or "002". We call the first octet the "network" portion. The remaining portion can be changed (assigned to hosts) and is called the "host" portion. That means that a Class A network has 8 bits in the network portion and 24 bits in the host portion.

Now apply the same logic to a Class B network. If my network has a range of 130.0.0.0 to 130.0.255.255, that means the first two octets don't change. It's always "130.0" or "130.000". That means that a Class B network has 16 bits in the network portion and 16 bits in the host portion.

Now apply the same logic to a Class C network. If my network has a range of 200.0.0.0 to 200.0.0.255, that means the first three octets don't change. It's always "200.0.0" or "200.000.000". That means that a Class C network has 8 bits in the network portion and 24 bits in the host portion.

So an IP address has two portions

Network Portion	Host Portion

When we apply a subnet mask, our IP address has three portions

Network	Subnet	Host

For example, if our network is a Class B, 130.0.0.0 to 130.0.255.25, and our subnet is a /27, there are 27 bits in the subnet mask.

Now remember that the first two octets – or 16 bits – are fixed in a Class B network.
That leaves 27 – 16 = 11 bits for the subnet.
Subnet– Network Bits = Subnet Bits
That leaves 32 – 27 = 5 bits for the host.
32 Bits – Subnet = Host Bits

Network	Subnet	Host
11111111.11111111	11111111.111	00000

Or in other words, **2^h-2 = number of usable IP's in the subnet, where h is the number of host bits.** For example, $2^5 - 2 = 30$ usable IP addresses in my example.

And, **2^s = number of subnets, where s is the number of subnet bits.** For example, $2^{11} = 2048$ /27 subnets in my Class B example.

If our network is a Class C, 200.0.0.0 to 200.0.0.255, and our subnet is a /27, there are 27 bits in the subnet mask.

Now remember that the first two octets – or 24 bits – are fixed in a Class C network.
That leaves 27 – 24 = 3 bits for the subnet.
Subnet– Network Bits = Subnet Bits
That leaves 32 – 27 = 5 bits for the host.
32 Bits – Subnet = Host Bits

Network	Subnet	Host
11111111.11111111.11111111	111	00000

Or in other words, **2^H-2 = number of usable IP's in the subnet, where H is the number of host bits.** For example, $2^S - 2 = 30$ usable IP addresses in my example.

And, **2^s = number of subnets, where S is the number of subnet bits.** For example, $2^S = 8$ /27 subnets in my Class C example.

Notice that if the network changed, the number of IP's per subnet doesn't change, but the number of subnets per network does.

In summary, we can calculate the number of subnets and IP addresses by

- Finding the number of network bits from the network type (8 for a Class A, 16 for a Class B, and 24 for a Class C)
- Finding the number of subnet bits **(S)** from **32 – subnet size**
- **2^H-2** is the number of usable IP addresses, **where H is the number of host bits**
- **2^s = number of subnets, where S is the number of subnet bits**
- Network Bits + Subnet Bits = Network Prefix Length

1.7 Describe the need for private IPv4 addressing

I touched on IP addresses earlier but now it's time to go into more detail. Remember that an IPv4 address looks like this: 192.168.222.234? I mentioned that we have three classes of IP addresses (A, B, and C). I also mentioned that the range of IP addresses is from 0.0.0.0 to 255.255.255.255.

How many IP addresses are there in the whole range? 4,294,967,296. When we consider that many of those IP addresses are used as broadcast addresses or the network name, there are much less available to be assigned to end user device. Are there enough IP addresses to go around if you consider that each person probably has a work computer, a home computer, a cell phone, and that there are many other servers and internet of things devices running in the background? Of course not.

IPv4 addresses are scarce because there are more devices than IP addresses, and because in the early days of the internet, organizations were assigned large blocks of addresses. Nobody thought that the internet would grow to be as big as it is today. For example, the US Department of Defense owns about 5% of the IPv4 addresses (addresses that start in 6, 7, 11, 21, 22, 26, 28, 29, 30, 33, 55, 214, and 215).

How did we solve the IP address scarcity problem?

- We used Classless Interdomain Routing (CIRD) to let customers have a portion of an IP network instead of the whole thing.
- We started working on IPv6 (we will talk about IPv6 in the next chapter) – a new version of IP that offers more addresses.
- We invented NAT to allow us to use private IP addresses in the internal network

There are **public networks** and **private networks**. You can't use an IP address in a public network unless it is assigned to you. IP addresses are assigned by the American Registry for Internet Numbers or ARIN.

But ARIN left three sets of IP addresses – three networks – open for anybody to use on their internal network. These are known as **private IP networks.**

There are three sets of private IP networks.

- 10.0.0.0 to 10.255.255.255 is the largest private network, with a range of 16,581,375 possible addresses. This type of network is known as a class A network.
- 172.16.0.0 to 172.16.255.255 is the second largest private network, with a range of 65,025 possible addresses. This type of network is known as a class B network.

- 192.168.0.0 to 192.168.0.255, is the smallest private network, with a range of 256 addresses. This type of network is known as a class C network.

ARIN assigns blocks of IP addresses to each major ISP and to larger organizations. These larger ISPs sub assign blocks of their IP addresses to smaller ISPs, who assign even smaller blocks of their IP addresses to their customers.

Most of the IP address space is public. In theory, any device with a public IP can reach any other device with a public IP (unless a firewall blocks it).

Let's go back to my example office. Our ISP assigned us one public address: 44.3.2.1.

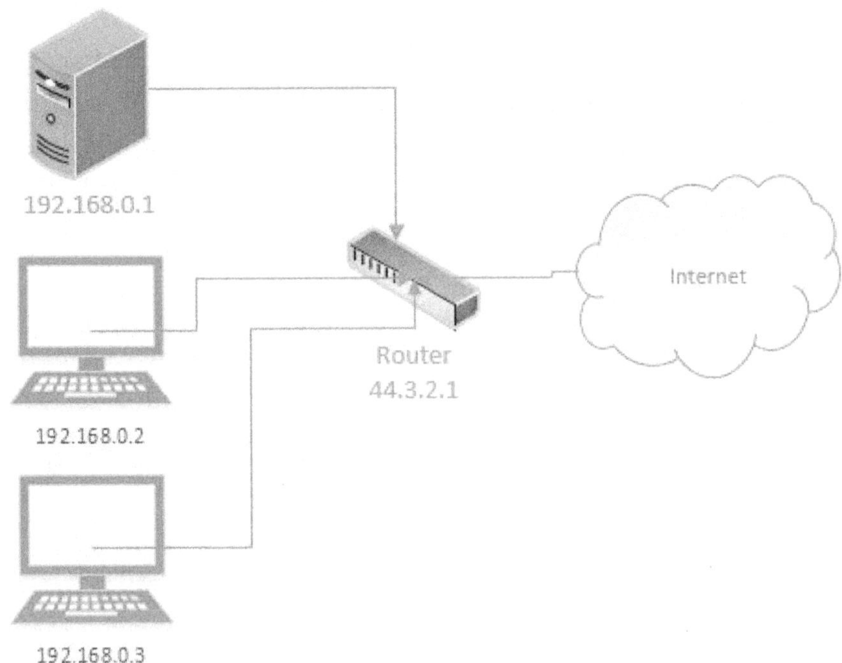

If you have an office or internal network, you can set up an internal addressing scheme by choosing one of the above three ranges. In my example office, I chose the range 192.168.0.0 to 192.168.0.255. What range should we choose?

If we have a small network, we should choose a small range. Smaller network equipment (such as in a home or small business) might not be able to handle a larger range of IP addresses.

If our business was so large as to require multiple locations, we could choose the range 10.0.0.0 to 10.255.255.255 and then subdivide it further so that each location receives a block (a subnet) from our range. For example, one location receives the range 10.0.0.0 to 10.0.255.255, and the second location receives the range 10.1.0.0 to 10.1.255.255, etc. It might look like the drawing below

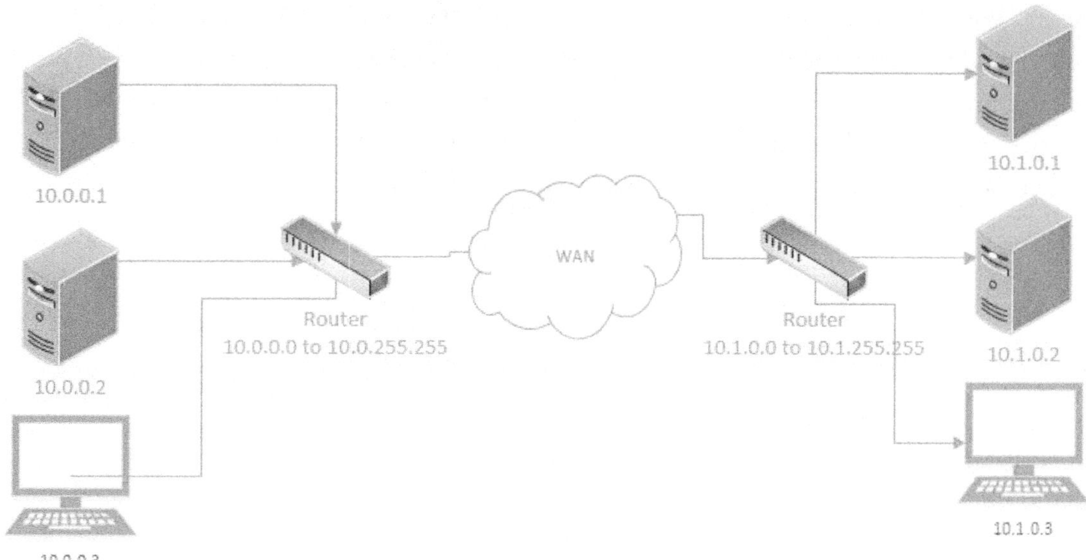

This would require us to implement a Wide Area Network or point-to-point VPN. The WAN allows us to configure the routers so that all the computers in all our offices think that they are on the same network.

In the IPv6 world, fc00::/7 is the only private range of IP addresses. It is better written as fc00:0000:0000:0000:0000:0000:0000:0000 to fdff:ffff:ffff:ffff:ffff:ffff:ffff:ffff.

How did I get from fc00::/7 to all of that gibberish? We'll find out later. But the point is, the IPv6 range is massive. There is no need for each private network to have the same address as any other private network.

If we connect two private IPv4 networks together, we will probably find some IP address conflicts. We might find that two devices have the same IP address, and one of them will have to change. But if we mash two private IPv6 networks together, we probably won't have any conflicts, because each private IPv6 address is randomly generated.

The private IP address space helped us in three ways

- Routers don't have to worry about the private IP addresses, so they won't keep track of routes involving private IP addresses. That means that each router has less routes to keep track of.

- The entire world doesn't need as many IP addresses because of NAT.

- We stop using other people's public IP addresses in our private networks. Before ARIN created the three private IP address ranges, people were using public IP addresses inside their private networks.

For example, I might create a private network using the IP address space 200.0.0.0 to 200.255.255.255. This would work in theory because devices don't attempt to verify that their IP addresses belong to a private network. But if my network ever connects to the internet, and another device on the internet uses the same IP address as me, I won't be able to access it. Why? My computer assumes that 200.0.0.0 to 200.255.255.255 is a local network and therefore won't pass any traffic addressed in that range to the router.

1.8 Configure and verify IPv6 addressing and prefix

We invented **IPv6 (Internet Protocol Version 6)** because we ran out of IPv4 addresses. There was never an IPv5 – it was invented but never made it past the design stage.

A few protocols were upgraded so that they could be compatible with IPv6. We will learn more about these protocols later on.

- OSPF was updated to OSPFv3
- ICMP was upgraded to ICMPv6
- ARP does not work on IPv6. IPv6 uses Neighbor Discovery Protocol instead.

IPv6 uses hexadecimal (not decimal) and an IPv6 address is 128 bits long.

I mentioned hexadecimal earlier when I talked about MAC addresses. Hexadecimal means "base 16". Imagine, from basic elementary school math that you can count from 0 to 9. When you reach "9", you get to add another digit to your number, and you get 10. Notice 10 has two digits and 9 has one digit? Now, if you get to "99" and you add one, you reach "100". Notice that "100" has an extra digit. So, we have ten different numbers (0, 1, 2, 3, 4, 5, 6, 7, 8, 9). We call this system "base 10".

What if we could count to 16 without adding another digit? We would need to invent six more numbers.

How do we do that? We didn't invent six more numbers, but we did use the first six letters of the alphabet. The hexadecimal digits are 0, 1, 2, 3, 4, 5, 6, 7, 8, 9, A, B, C, D, E, and F. So, if we add 9 + 1, then answer isn't 10, it's A. If we add A + 1, we get B. See what I'm saying? We can fit more numbers into a smaller space. It adds up quickly.

How many numbers can I fit in a two-digit number? Up to 100 (10 x 10 = 100). How many numbers can I fit into a two-digit hexadecimal number? Up to 256 (16 x 16 = 256).

The IPv6 header is larger than the IVv4 header

Version	Class	Flow Label	Payload Length	Next Header	Hop Limit	Source Address	Destination Address

For a device to be able to send IPv6 packets to another IPv6 device, it must have an IPv6 address. It must also know the IPv6 address of a router. The router must have an IPv6 address on its interface. That means along the entire route from sender to recipient, all devices must have an IPv6 address. The router encapsulates and deencapsulates IPv6 packets just like it would with an IPv4 packet.

The router will maintain an IPv6 routing table, which works in parallel with IPv4. A router can manage both IPv4 and IPv6 traffic at the same time. End user devices can send traffic through this router regardless of whether they support both IPv4 and IPv6 or only IPv4. IPv6 was designed to work in parallel with IPv4 devices because its inventors knew that the internet couldn't just switch over to IPv6 overnight. In fact, although it has been many years since IPv6 was made available, many networks still use IPv4. We call this a **dual stack configuration**.

We can write an IPv6 address as a1b2:c3d4:a1b2:c3d4:a1b2:c3d4:a1b2:c3d4. It is 32 characters long. A character can be a number from 0 to 9 or a letter from a to f (not case sensitive). We separate every four characters with a colon. There are ways to shorten the IPv6 address, which we will learn later.

In the IPv6 scheme, we can have subnets, sub-subnets, and sub-sub-subnets. How does it work? An IPv6 address has two parts. The first part is called the **prefix**. A /48 prefix is common.

For example, an organization would be assigned a 2001:0db8:1234:/48 prefix. That means that all of their IP addresses must start with 2001:0db8:1234:.

This prefix is 48 bits long (it's not 24 bits long because each character is 4 bits, not two). The organization has 80 bits left, since an IPv6 address is 128 bits long.

If we were to make subnets out of it, we could

- 2001:0db8:1234:1000: might be our first subnet. That means that all IP addresses in this subnet start with 2001:0db8:1234:1000
- 2001:0db8:1234:2000: might be our second subnet. That means that all IP addresses in this subnet start with 2001:0db8:1234:2000
- 2001:0db8:1234:f000: might be our sixteenth subnet. That means that all IP addresses in this subnet start with 2001:0db8:1234:f000

That makes for 16 subnets. Each subnet is 64 bits long (48 bit network size and 16 bit subnet), which contains 2^{64} IP addresses. Since each subnet is massive and since there is a massive number of subnets, there's no point in getting more complicated and picking subnets like 2001:0db8:1234:f001:, etc.

The number of available IPv6 addresses is massive. There are 340,282,366,920,938,463,463,374,607,431,768,211,456 IP addresses. Enough so that each person on earth could have trillions of them.

We can break each subnet down further. Let's say our organization operates worldwide. We can assign one subnet to each part of the world.

We could break down 2001:0db8:1234:1000: into 16 more sub-subnets, such as

- 2001:0db8:1234:1000:1000:
- 2001:0db8:1234:1000:2000:, etc.

Each of these sub-subnets contains 2^{48} IP addresses. We could break these down even further so that

- 2001:0db8:1234:1000:1000:1000: is a subnet
- 2001:0db8:1234:1000:1000:2000: is a subnet, etc.

Now each sub-sub-subnet contains 2^{32} IP addresses.

The point is that there is a lot of IP addresses. More than you'll ever use. You can pick the subnets however you want and not have to worry about selecting a too small subnet and running out of addresses.

There's no such thing as a subnet mask in IPv6. There is just a prefix.

If 2001:0db8:1234:1000:1000:1000: is my prefix, then my first IP address is 2001:0db8:1234:1000:1000:1000:0000:0000, and my last IP address is 2001:0db8:1234:1000:1000:1000:ffff:ffff.

I just fill in the blanks for the missing portion remembering that every IPv6 address is 128 bits long, and complicated math is not required.

If I have a bigger subnet then that means I have a shorter prefix. If I have a smaller subnet that that means I have a longer prefix.

We can shorten some IPv6 addresses. If our IP address looked like this: 2002:0de8:0000:0000:0300:8b2e:0360:7234, we could shorten it to 2002:0de8::300:8b2e:0360:7234. See what we did there? We hid the sections with "0000", and replaced them with '::', or two colons.

In any IPv6 address, we can hide the longest string of 0's, if they fill up an entire four-digit section, or more than one section in a row. We can only hide one string per IP address, otherwise it gets confusing.

If my address looked like this: 2002:0de8:0000:0000:0300:8b2e:0000:7234 and I shortened it to 2002:0de8::8b2e::7234, you now have two "::", but you don't know which one had four 0's and which one had eight.

Also, we can get hide any 0's that are before a ":". That means 2002:0de8:1824:2383:0300:002e:4e4e:7234 can be shortened to 2002:de8:1824:2383:300:2e:4e4e:7234

IPv6 addresses are written as a hexadecimal number, and then a /#. The /# is the prefix length which is between 0 and 128. There is no subnet, but there is a prefix. If we have an address and a prefix length, we can find the prefix.

How do we calculate the prefix? If the prefix length is a multiple of 4, divide the prefix length by 4 (since an IPv6 address has 4 bytes per digit). We keep the IP address up to the prefix length (P). We change the rest of the bits in the IP address to 0.

For example, if 2002:0de8:1824:2383:0300:002e:4e4e:7234 /48 is our IP address, we divide 48 by 4. That gives us 12. We count the first 12 digits (2002:0de8:1824) as our prefix length. If we set the remainder of the IP address to 0, then 2002:0de8:1824:0000:0000:0000:0000:0000 is our network. Therefore our prefix is 2002:0de8:1824:: (notice the two colons at the end).

Since the IPv6 protocol is still being adopted, not all networks understand it yet. What happens when a router communicating over IPv6 reaches a router that only understands IPv4? Let's say that you are trying to access google.com. You're in Florida and google.com is in California. Both of you understand IPv6, but the routers in between understand IPv4 only. Your computer and google.com's server create an **IPv4 tunnel** and send your IPv6 data through it. The most common tunneling protocol is called **6to4**.

A better approach is for each device to obtain both an IPv4 address and an IPv6 address. This is known as **dual stack**. Most modern ISP's assign both IPv4 and IPv6 addresses to their customers. A device will try to connect over IPv6, and if it can't then it will try to connect over IPv4.

Remember that we talked about ARP earlier? Well, IPv6 doesn't work with ARP. There is no broadcast IPv6 address, so a device can't send out a message saying, "hey if this is your IP address, reply you're your MAC address". What happens if you want to discover a MAC address that belongs to a specific IPv6 address? You must use the **Neighbor Discovery Protocol**.

How does it work? When a device connects to a new network, it generates a random IP address, known as a **link-local address**. Then it sends a multicast message to all the routers. All IPv6-enabled routers listen for messages addressed to FF02::2. The long version is FF02:0000:0000:0000:0000:0000:0000:0002.

The device tells the router "hey look at me, I'm at this random IPv6 address". If the device does not receive a reply, it assumes that there are no routers on the network and keeps the link-local address. If a router is on the network, it replies with some configuration information. The router tells the device what address it should have. The device starts using the address given to it by the router.

What do I mean when I say multicast? Multicast is like a mailing list with an IP address. A device can "subscribe" to a multicast and then it will receive messages addressed to that multicast's IP address. If we want to send a message to all the devices belonging to a specific multicast, we send a message to the multicast address.

As I said, FF02::2 is a multicast address that all routers subscribe to. If I want to send a message to all the routers on my network, I address it to FF02::2.

1.9 Compare IPv6 address types

1.9.a Global unicast

1.9.b Unique local

1.9.c Link local

1.9.d Anycast

1.9.e Multicast

1.9.f Modified EUI 64

Since there are so many IP addresses in the IPv6 space, it is possible for every device in the world to have a unique public IP address. The idea is that every device can be reached from every other device.

IANA (Internet Assigned Numbers Authority) gives out IP addresses to the different organizations. It assigns the largest blocks of IP addresses to the regional authorities. In North America, that is ARIN (American Registry for Internet Numbers). ARIN assigns smaller blocks to ISPs. ISPs assign smaller blocks to their customers.

IPv6 has a **global unicast** feature which is equivalent to the IPv4 public and private IP addresses. Each company is assigned a group of IP addresses, which they can subnet as they see fit. The block of IPv6 addresses that each company is assigned is called a **global routing prefix**.

A company could also use private IPv6 addresses for their network – these are known as the **unique local** IPv6 addresses.

The reserved addresses

- Global Unicast addresses start with 2 or 3. As of the end of 2019, IANA hasn't assigned any addresses that start with 3, but they are reserved for future use as Global Unicast addresses. A global unicast address is unique across the entire internet.

- Unique local IPv6 addresses start with FD. A local network can use addresses that start with FD, but they aren't guaranteed to be unique across the internet.

  We can assign a global unicast address to our router and unique local addresses to our internal devices, or we can assign global unicast addresses to all our devices.

- Multicast IPv6 addresses start with FF. A multicast address is an address we can send packets to so that they will reach multiple devices.

- Link Local IPv6 addresses start with FE80. The link local address is used by a device for internal testing. Packets addressed to a link local address stay on the local area network. The full range is fe80:0000:0000:0000:0000:0000:0000:0000 to febf:ffff:ffff:ffff:ffff:ffff:ffff:ffff.

- 2002:0000:0000:0000:0000:0000:0000:0000 to 2002:ffff:ffff:ffff:ffff:ffff:ffff:ffff was used by the **6to4** IP address conversion protocol

- ff00:0000:0000:0000:0000:0000:0000:0000 to ffff:ffff:ffff:ffff:ffff:ffff:ffff:ffff is the multicast address range

- The :: address, which is all zeros is called an **unknown address**. If a host has an issue with its IP address or if it has not been assigned an IP address, it uses the unknown address.

- The **::1** address is all zeros except for a one at the end. A host uses this address to test its own interface. It is equivalent to the IPv4 127.0.0.1 address (also known as the **loopback** address).

  A host uses the loopback addresses to test its internal applications. Traffic addressed to the loopback address must never leave the host. For example, if we're hosting a website on a server, we can type "127.0.0.1" in the server's web browser and should be able to view the website. If we can't then there is an internal error with the server.

How do we subnet an IPv6 network? We should have one subnet for each LAN or VLAN and one subnet for each WAN connection.

We have three parts again – the network, the subnet, and the host. In IPv6, the network is the global routing prefix. The host is called the interface ID. Between them is the subnet.

Global Routing Prefix	Subnet	Interface ID

The total length is 128 bits. There are no address classes (Class A, B, or C) like in IPv4, so we can build our network how we choose.

The global routing prefix is fixed by our ISP. The most common length is 64-bits (16 characters) or 48-bits (12 characters). It is convenient for ISPs to use a 64-bit or 48-bit length because it falls on the **nibble boundary** (the colons). But an ISP can use a prefix of 63 bits, 62, bits, etc.

The Interface ID is usually 64 bits long.

The subnet makes up the difference (but the total length of the address must be 128 bits. That means the Global Routing Prefix + Subnet + Interface ID = 128.

If our prefix is 64 bits and our interface is 64 bits, then our subnet is 0. If our prefix is 48 bits and our interface is 64 bits, then our subnet is 16 bits.

When we create our subnets, we should determine

- The prefix and prefix length
- The size of the interface ID (the host bits). 64 is a common length and we will learn why later.
- The subnet length (calculated from the prefix length and interface length)

We don't really need to worry about the size of each subnet or the number of subnets, because the address space is so large.

If our ISP assigned us 2002:0de8:1824:/48 and our interface length is 64 bits, then we have 16 bits for our subnet. We just need to think about all the unique numbers that fit inside the subnet area, and those are our subnets.

- Each subnet starts with our global routing prefix (2002:0de8:1824)
- The subnet portion is unique for all subnets
- The interface portion is all 0s

Then we assign the subnets. For example,

- 2002:0de8:1824:0001:0000:0000:0000:0000 or 2002:0de8:1824:1:: is our first subnet
- 2002:0de8:1824:0002:0000:0000:0000:0000 or 2002:0de8:1824:2:: is our second subnet
- 2002:0de8:1824:0003:0000:0000:0000:0000 or 2002:0de8:1824:3:: is our third subnet
- 2002:0de8:1824:ffff:0000:0000:0000:0000 or 2002:0de8:1824:ffff:: is our last subnet

We have 65,536 subnets (remember due to hexadecimal it is 16 x 16 x 16 x 16). Each subnet has 16^{16} possible IP addresses.

The subnet ID is called the **subnet router anycast address**. We should not assign it as an IP address. Devices can send a message to the subnet ID if they want to reach every router in the subnet. By having a subnet router anycast address, any device can reach the router without having to know the default gateway.

We can assign an IP address to a device statically, via DHCP, or via **SLAAC** (**Stateless Address Autoconfiguration**). We will learn more about this later.

An address that starts with FD only works on an internal network. It is called the **unique local address**. A device with no IP address can choose a unique local IP address that starts with FD. How?

- Use FD as for the first two digits
- Pick a 40-bit prefix (this prefix plus FD makes 48 bits) randomly
- The next 16 bits are the subnet
- This leaves us with 64 bits for the interface

If a device wants to use a static IP address (choose its own IP address), and wants to ensure that it is unique, it can calculate the modified **EUI-64** (**extended unique identifier**) address.

A link-local IPv4 address is only unique in its own local network, but an IPv6 link-local address is globally unique. Why? A MAC address is considered globally unique (no two devices have the same MAC address). Therefore, if an IPv6 address can be generated from a MAC address, it is also globally unique. The IP address is generated using a process called **EUI64**.

Remember that a MAC address is 48 bits (6 bytes) and follows the format 11:22:33:44:55:66. Like an IP address, a MAC address can be converted into 0's and 1's (binary).

We split the MAC address in half and add 16 bits (2 bytes) to the middle. This results in a 64-bit address, which is the standard sized interface portion of an IPv6 address.

If our IP prefix was aabb:ccdd:aabb:ccdd and our MAC address was 11:22:33:44:55:66, we split it in half, and add two bytes to the middle: 11:22:33:FFFE:44:55:66.

Now we add it to our prefix and the result is: aabb:ccdd:aabb:ccdd:1122:33FF:FE44:5566

Finally, we need to invert the seventh bit of the MAC address. This is a little tricky. I wrote the 11:22:33:44:55:66 MAC address in binary – every two digits makes up one byte.

00001011:00010110:00100001:00101100:00110111:01000010

The seventh bit is in bold

000010**1**1:00010110:00100001:00101100:00110111:01000010

If we invert it, we change it from a 1 to a 0.

Thus, the MAC address is

00001001:00010110:00100001:00101100:00110111:01000010

We can write it out as (only the first set of two digits changed).

09:22:33:44:55:66

That means our IP address is actually

aabb:ccdd:aabb:ccdd:0922:33FF:FE44:5566

Why do we bother inverting our MAC address? If our MAC address is unique than our inverted MAC address would also be unique.

Remember that a MAC address is assigned by the manufacturer. Some network devices allow us to manually change the MAC address. When the seventh bit is "1", we know that the MAC address was changed by the user. When the seventh bit is "0", we know that the MAC address was assigned by the manufacturer.

In summary, our IP address looks like this

Prefix	First half of MAC address	FFFE	Second half of MAC address

The FF30::/12 address is a multicast address. A **multicast address** lets you send a message to several hosts at the same time. It is different from a **broadcast address,** which lets you send a message to all the hosts on a subnet. The problem with a broadcast is that every host must read the packet and decide whether they needed it or not.

We don't use broadcasts in IPv6, because the multicast allows hosts that don't need the message to ignore it. For example, the FF02::5 address is intended for routers only. Routers will receive and process packets sent to this address, but other hosts will ignore it.

The most important multicast addresses

FF02::1	Everybody
FF02::2	All routers
FF02::5	All routers using
FF02::6	OSPF protocol
FF02::9	All routers using RIPng protocol
FF02::A	All routers using EIGRP
FF02::1:2	All routers using DHCPv6

The most important link local addresses prefixes are in the following table. These are also multicast addresses.

FF01	**Interface-Local** Local just to a specific device interface
FF02	**Link-Local** Local just to a specific subnet
FF05	**Site-Local** Local just to a site (office)
FF08	**Organization-Local** Local to an entire organization's network Used to pass router configurations
FF0E	**Global** Can go anywhere

For example, FF02:1111:2222:3333:4444:5555:6666:7777 is a link local address that can be used to address other devices on the same subnet.

A router knows whether it must keep a packet within its subnet or if it should forward it. With global addresses, a router must be configured to understand where the organization boundary is so that it does not forward a packet outside the organization.

Remember that the link-local unicast address prefix is FE80. For example, a device might use FE80:1111:2222:3333:4444:5555:6666:7777 as its link local address.

How can we use NDP to find the MAC address of another host on our subnet? Every device calculates a unique address called the **solicited-node multicast address** for every unicast address on its interface. If a device has a unicast address and a link-local address, then it will have to calculate two solicited-node multicast addresses.

We take the generic address FF02::1:FF00:0, which can be written as FF02:0000:0000:0000:0000:0001:FF00:0000 and add the last 24-bits (6 digits) of our IP address to it.

For example, if our IP address is FA01:ABCD:1111:2222:3333:4444:5555:6666, then the last six digits are 55:6666. When we add them to the generic address, we get FF02:0000:0000:0000:0000:0001:FF55:6666.

If the device address ends in 55:6666, then it will subscribe to the FF02:0000:0000:0000:0000:0001:FF55:6666 multicast address and receive messages addressed to it.

Now, if I want to send a message to a device with IP address FA01:ABCD:1111:2222:3333:4444:5555:6666, and it is on my local network, I still need to learn its MAC address. I calculate the device's solicited-node multicast address.

Then I send an NDP message to FF02:0000:0000:0000:0000:0001:FF55:6666. All the devices whose IP address end in 55:6666 will see the message and respond with their MAC addresses. Now I know the MAC address of the device with IP address FA01:ABCD:1111:2222:3333:4444:5555:6666.

The benefit of multicast as opposed to broadcast is that I didn't have to send my NDP message to all the devices on my network. Given how big an IPv6 subnet can be, there might be thousands of active devices, and I don't want to consume resources on all of them just so that I can learn one MAC address.

Some benefits of NDP

- **Neighbor MAC Discovery** – a host can learn the MAC addresses of the other hosts on the sane network
- **Router Discovery** – a host can learn the IPv6 addresses of the routers on its subnet
- **SLAAC** – a host can learn the subnet of its network
- **DAD** – a host needs to be able to verify that the address it chooses for itself is not duplicated somewhere else using **Duplicate Address Detection**

We learn the MAC address of other devices using two messages

- **Neighbor Solicitation** (**NS**) – NS is basically "hey if you are using this IPv6 address, reply with your MAC address". This address is sent to the **solicited-node multicast address** so that only hosts whose last six IPv6 address digits match will see the message.
- **Neighbor Advertisement** (**NA**) – NA is basically "look at me, this is my IPv6 address and my MAC address". The NA is sent as a reply to the NS. It can also be sent standalone (known as an **unsolicited NA**). When sent unsolicited, the other devices that see it will store it.

  An unsolicited message is sent to the FF02::1 address, which is a local-scope multicast address that all IPv6 hosts on a subnet listen to.

We learn the default gateways using two messages

- **Router Solicitation** (**RS**) – "hey if you're a router, identify yourself". This message is only sent to FF02::2 – a multicast address which local routers respond to.
- **Router Advertisement** (**RA**) – this is sent as a response to an RS. "hey, I'm this router, and this is my link-local IPv6 address". The router can send it to the host that created the RS or

it can send it to FF02::1, which is seen by all IPv6 hosts.

A router can periodically advertise itself by sending unsolicited RA messages to the FF02::1 address.

Remember that if a host needs to obtain an IP address, it can use DHCP. It calls the DHCP server and asks for an IP address. The DHCP server replies with an IP address that the host can use. We will learn more about DHCP later.

In IPv6 a device can generate an IP address using SLAAC, or **Stateless Address Autoconfiguration**. How?

- The device learns the IPv6 prefix that is on its link (local network). It learns this from an NDP Router Advertisement (RA) message.
- Then it generates an IP address that begins with that prefix. It can use the EUI-64 address, or it can choose a random value.
- It uses DAD (Duplicate Address Detection) to make sure that nobody else is using that address before assigning it to itself.

Each time a host joins a network (even if just powered off and already has a static IP address), it checks the DAD. Even if a host has a statically configured IP address, if it detects another host with the same address, it will not use its static address.

- The computer sends out a DAD message, which says "this is the address I chose, is anybody else using it"? It sends this message to the IP address that it selected. If another device is using the same IP address, it will receive the message.

- If the other address is in use, the host that is using it will reply with an NA (Neighbor Advertisement) message. The first host will realize that it must select a new IP address.

1.10 Verify IP parameters for Client OS (Windows, Mac OS, Linux)

On Windows, we can see the IP address details by opening a command prompt and typing **`ipconfig /all`**, or by going to the network adapter settings and viewing its properties.

For example, on my computer, the adapter shows the following properties

View your network properties

Properties

Name:	Wi-Fi
Description:	Intel(R) Dual Band Wireless-AC 8260
Physical address (MAC):	7c:2a:31:47:20:ed
Status:	Operational
Maximum transmission unit:	1500
Link speed (Receive/Transmit):	866/866 (Mbps)
DHCP enabled:	Yes
DHCP servers:	10.0.0.1
DHCP lease obtained:	May 1, 2020 9:18:54 PM
DHCP lease expires:	May 8, 2020 9:18:54 PM
IPv4 address:	10.0.0.168/24

From the command prompt, I see the following

```
Connection-specific DNS Suffix  . : ed.shawcable.net
Description . . . . . . . . . . . : Intel(R) Dual Band Wireless-AC 8260
Physical Address. . . . . . . . . : 7C-2A-31-47-20-ED
DHCP Enabled. . . . . . . . . . . : Yes
Autoconfiguration Enabled . . . . : Yes
IPv6 Address. . . . . . . . . . . : 2604:3d09:7a80:8700::acf8(Preferred)
Lease Obtained. . . . . . . . . . : May 1, 2020 3:23:12 PM
Lease Expires . . . . . . . . . . : May 4, 2020 10:51:00 AM
IPv6 Address. . . . . . . . . . . : 2604:3d09:7a80:8700:56a:1e74:90e5:7cec(Preferred)
Temporary IPv6 Address. . . . . . : 2604:3d09:7a80:8700:3ceb:c275:9c6b:ae2f(Preferred)
Link-local IPv6 Address . . . . . : fe80::56a:1e74:90e5:7cec%9(Preferred)
IPv4 Address. . . . . . . . . . . : 10.0.0.168(Preferred)
Subnet Mask . . . . . . . . . . . : 255.255.255.0
Lease Obtained. . . . . . . . . . : May 1, 2020 3:23:13 PM
Lease Expires . . . . . . . . . . : May 8, 2020 9:18:54 PM
Default Gateway . . . . . . . . . : fe80::be9b:68ff:feaa:9050%9
                                    10.0.0.1
DHCP Server . . . . . . . . . . . : 10.0.0.1
DHCPv6 IAID . . . . . . . . . . . : 192686641
DHCPv6 Client DUID. . . . . . . . : 00-01-00-01-24-0F-49-12-10-62-E5-EA-29-EE
DNS Servers . . . . . . . . . . . : 2001:4e8:0:4004::14
                                    2001:4e8:0:4019::14
                                    64.59.184.15
                                    64.59.190.245
                                    2001:4e8:0:4004::14
                                    2001:4e8:0:4019::14
NetBIOS over Tcpip. . . . . . . . : Enabled
```

It shows me

- My IPv4 address and my IPv6 address
- DNS Servers, Subnet Mask, and Default Gateway
- DHCP Lease expiry date and time
- MAC address

If we type **`netstat -rn`**, we can see a list of routes.

```
IPv4 Route Table
===========================================================================
Active Routes:
Network Destination        Netmask          Gateway       Interface  Metric
          0.0.0.0          0.0.0.0         10.0.0.1      10.0.0.168      35
         10.0.0.0    255.255.255.0         On-link       10.0.0.168     291
       10.0.0.168  255.255.255.255         On-link       10.0.0.168     291
       10.0.0.255  255.255.255.255         On-link       10.0.0.168     291
        127.0.0.0        255.0.0.0         On-link        127.0.0.1     331
        127.0.0.1  255.255.255.255         On-link        127.0.0.1     331
  127.255.255.255  255.255.255.255         On-link        127.0.0.1     331
  192.168.234.224  255.255.255.240         On-link  192.168.234.225    5256
  192.168.234.225  255.255.255.255         On-link  192.168.234.225    5256
  192.168.234.239  255.255.255.255         On-link  192.168.234.225    5256
        224.0.0.0        240.0.0.0         On-link        127.0.0.1     331
        224.0.0.0        240.0.0.0         On-link       10.0.0.168     291
        224.0.0.0        240.0.0.0         On-link  192.168.234.225    5256
  255.255.255.255  255.255.255.255         On-link        127.0.0.1     331
  255.255.255.255  255.255.255.255         On-link       10.0.0.168     291
  255.255.255.255  255.255.255.255         On-link  192.168.234.225    5256
===========================================================================
Persistent Routes:
  Network Address          Netmask  Gateway Address  Metric
          0.0.0.0          0.0.0.0   192.168.100.10  Default
===========================================================================
```

My computer remembers the gateway for several destinations. The computer knows that all of them are "on link", which means that they are on the local network. That is, all of them except for the destination "0.0.0.0", which it sends to my router located at 10.0.0.1.

If I was using a Mac or Linux, I could view the same information from the network settings or by typing **ifconfig** in the terminal.

```
Hazim's-iMac: ifconfig
en0:
        ether 0a:1b:2c:3d:4:5f
        inet 10.10.1.105 netask 0xffffff00 broadcast 10.10.1.255
```

If I type **netstat -rn**, I can also view the routing table.

1.11 Describe wireless principles

1.11.a Nonoverlapping Wi-Fi channels

1.11.b SSID

1.11.c RF

1.11.d Encryption

A radio signal (like the one used in Wi-Fi and cell towers) is like a wave. It goes up and down. It is actually in three dimensions, but I can't show 3D in a book. This wave is moving towards its target.

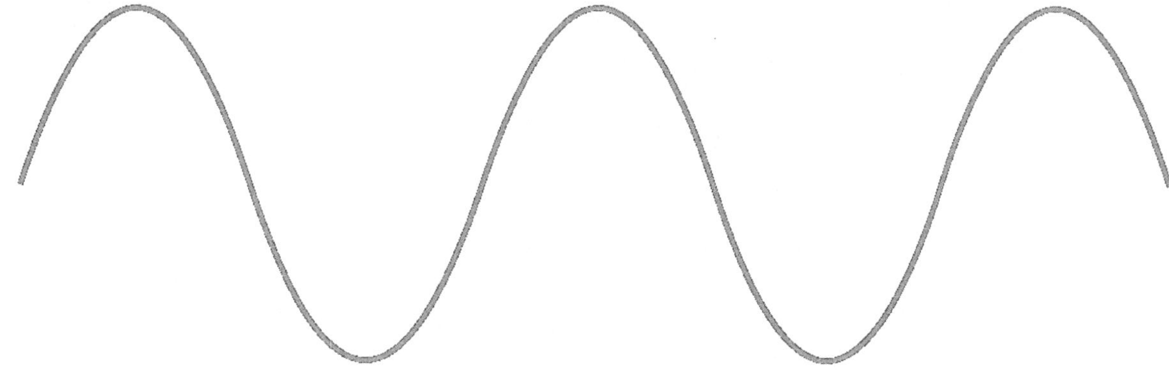

The height of the wave is called the **Amplitude**. The width of the wave is called the **wave length**. We can measure the wave from peak to peak.

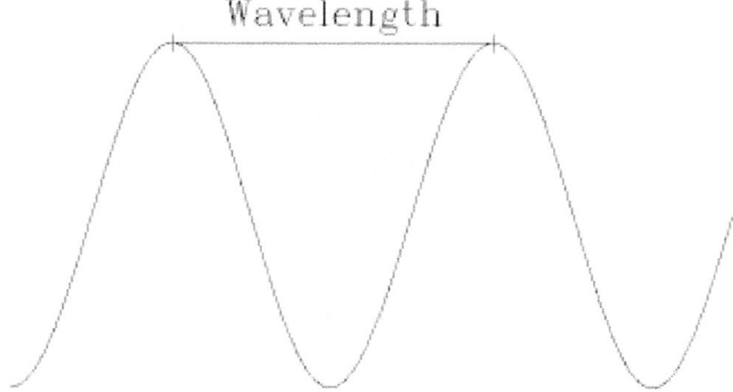

No matter the height or the width, the wave travels at the speed of light (300,000,000 m/s). You can think of a Wi-Fi signal like light that you can't see, because scientifically, that's exactly what it is. It's kind of like how we can't hear a dog whistle, but dogs can – our ears filter our many sounds. Well, our eyes filter out many types of light.

Since all waves travel at the same speed, the wider the wave (the larger the wavelength), the less waves will pass through a point each second. We call this the **frequency**, measured as the number of waves that pass through a point per second. We measure frequency in **Hertz (Hz)**.

If you had special glasses that would let you see radio waves in the air, it would look like a big mess of waves travelling everywhere. What we do is design each type of device to "look" for waves at a specific frequency and ignore the rest.

The government regulates the frequency that each type of technology can use. If everybody could broadcast signals at any frequency they wanted, the air would be a mess and no device would be able to keep track of their signals. Signals would interfere with each other.

Wi-Fi signals travel at a frequency of 2.4GHz and 5GHz.

If we change the Amplitude of the wave over time (up and down), but keep the wavelength the same, we can use it to convey information.

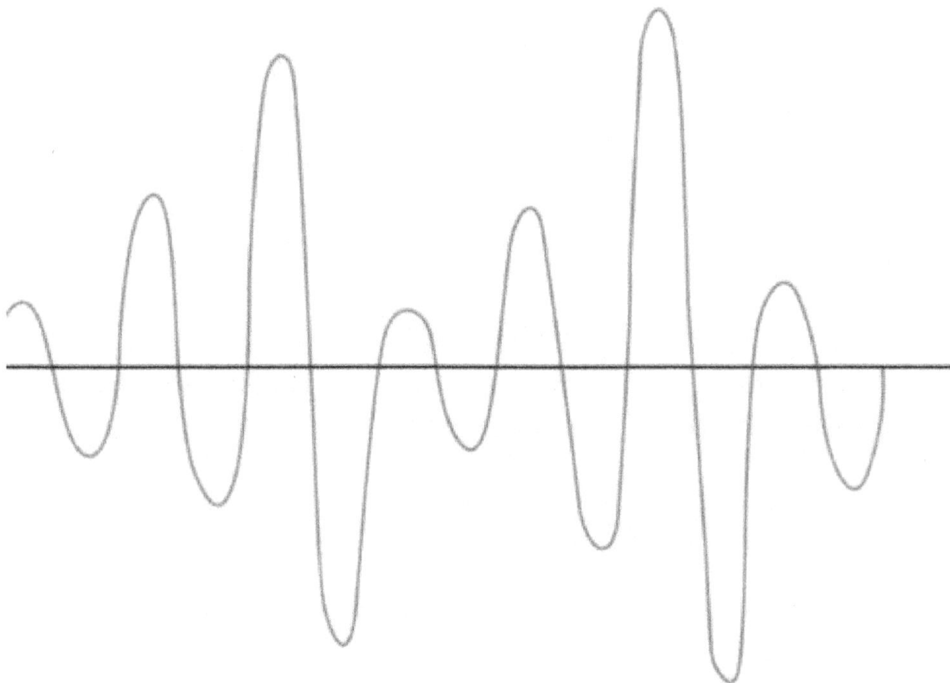

The range of a Wi-Fi signal is between 50 and 300 feet. It is affected by signal interference (noise) from neighboring networks. Different wall types can block or reduce the signal (glass, concrete, steel will block signals more than drywall).

The 2.4GHz range has eleven channels. It has a longer range and is less vulnerable to noise than the 5GHz range, which has twenty-three channels. Older devices use the 2.4GHz range. But what's a channel?

If I have a Wi-Fi network and my neighbor has a Wi-Fi network, the signals will interfere, and nobody will be able to understand anything. It's like if two cars crash into each other from opposite directions. What happens? Both cars stop.

To solve this problem, we divide the 2.4GHz spectrum into 11 channels: Each channel is 22MHz wide, spaced 5MHz apart. Therefore, a 2.4GHz network is technically broadcasting on 2.412GHz, 2.417GHz, 2.422GHz, etc.

If two neighboring networks choose different channels, they will each broadcast on a slightly different frequency – different enough that their signals won't interfere. We can manually select the channel that we want to broadcast our Wi-Fi on. We should survey the neighboring networks to see what channels they are broadcasting on and select a different channel from all of them. If we have multiple wireless access points in a building and their signals overlap, we should select a different channel for each of them.

The channel concept applies to 5GHz networks as well. A 5GHz spectrum is divided into 23 channels, each is 20MHz wide. A 5GHz spectrum can broadcast on 5.150GHz, 5.1570GHz, etc. There are more regulations for the 5GHz network and some countries do not allow some frequencies (they could interfere with weather radar and other systems).

Interference is when two Wi-Fi signals cancel each other out. Consider the following access points, both of which are broadcasting on Channel #1. The signal is good, except where it overlaps, where it cancels out. A device in the red area is bombarded with signals from both access points at the same frequency. It doesn't know which signal to listen to and won't be able to connect to anything. The solution is to change the channel on one of the access points.

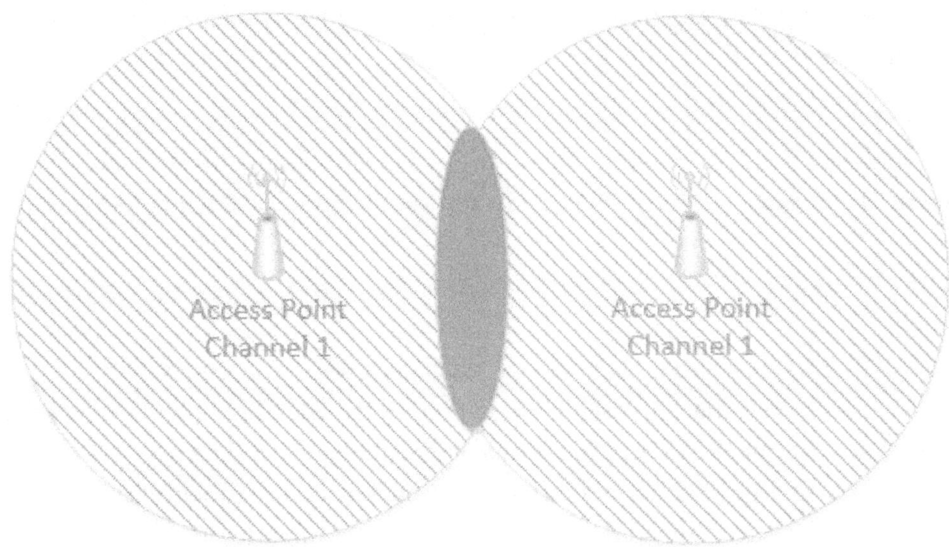

Remember how I said that a Wi-Fi channel is 22 MHz wide and that the channels are spaced 5 MHz apart? That means that on the 2.4 GHz range, the first channel is 2.412 GHz, but it actually ranges from 2.401 GHz to 2.423 GHz. The second channel is 2.417 GHz, but it actually ranges from 2.406 GHz to 2.428 GHz. That means that channels one and two overlap. If we look at the following diagram, we can see the overlap.

Channel #1 overlaps with Channels #2, #3, #4, and #5.

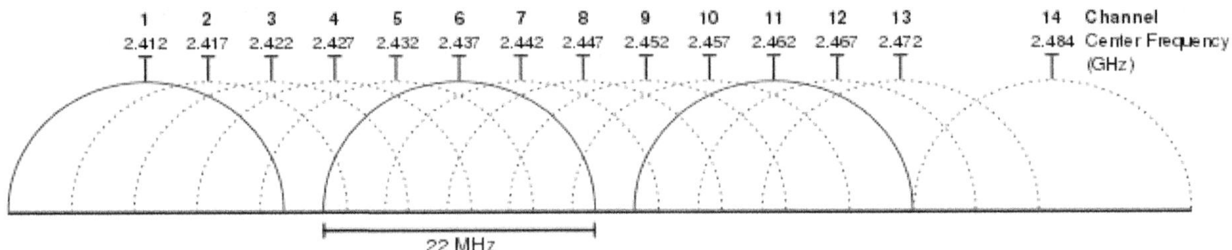

Thus, we should pick two channels that are far enough apart so that interference does not take place. The sixth channel ranges from 2.426 GHz to 2.448 GHz. In the above example, I should set one access point to broadcast on Channel 1 and the other access point on Channel 6.

5 GHz channels don't overlap, so we don't need to worry about selecting overlapping channels.

There are two other things we need to consider. An access point may only be able to handle fifty connections – this is an estimate for a high-quality access point; a poor-quality access point may only be able to handle twenty. If I have a conference room or theater with 200 or 400 occupants, even if the access point provides a good signal across the entire room, it may not have the capacity to connect to all the devices. Thus, we should install multiple access points to ensure that we have enough capacity.

In a larger area such as a warehouse with metal shelves, we may only have a few users, but the signal doesn't travel far enough. It might get blocked by the shelves. We should install access points to ensure that the signal is at least -70 dBm everywhere.

We should also verify that our **Signal to Noise Ratio** (**SNR**) is at least 24. Noise is caused by wireless signals that are outside of our network. Devices such as cell phones, cordless phones, and microwaves can cause noise. Other wireless networks can also cause noise. If our SNR ratio is too low, we might need to add additional access points, move the existing access points, install shielding in the building, or remove the sources of noise.

On the 2.4 GHz network, only four channels don't overlap – 1, 6, 11, and 14. Where possible, we should limit our Wi-Fi design to these four channels.

Consider this small rectangular room, which requires six access points due to many users.

If I space out the access points evenly and set them as best as I can so that there are no neighboring channels, they might look like this.

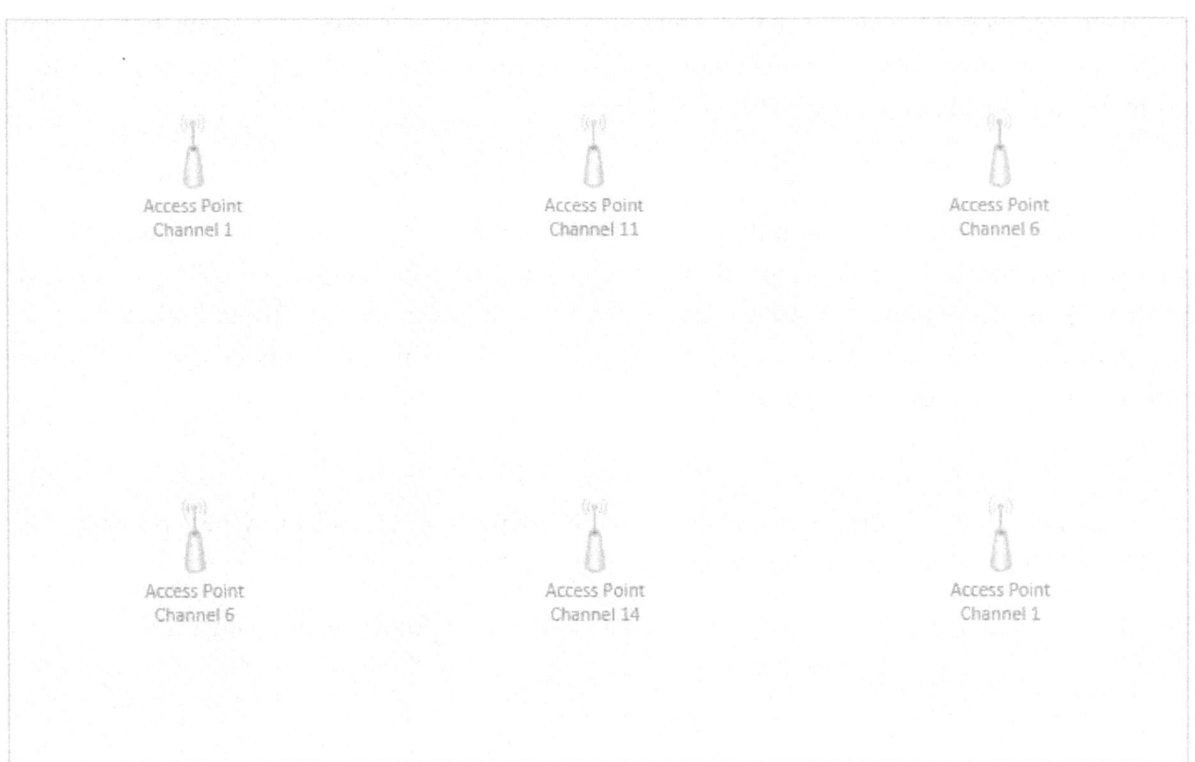

The access points that are on Channel #1 are in the top left corner and bottom right corner. If we highlight the coverage area of just those two access points, we can see that there is a significant overlap in the middle of the room (shown in red). The red area will have terrible coverage due to interference – there will be signals from two access points on Channel one. What can we do?

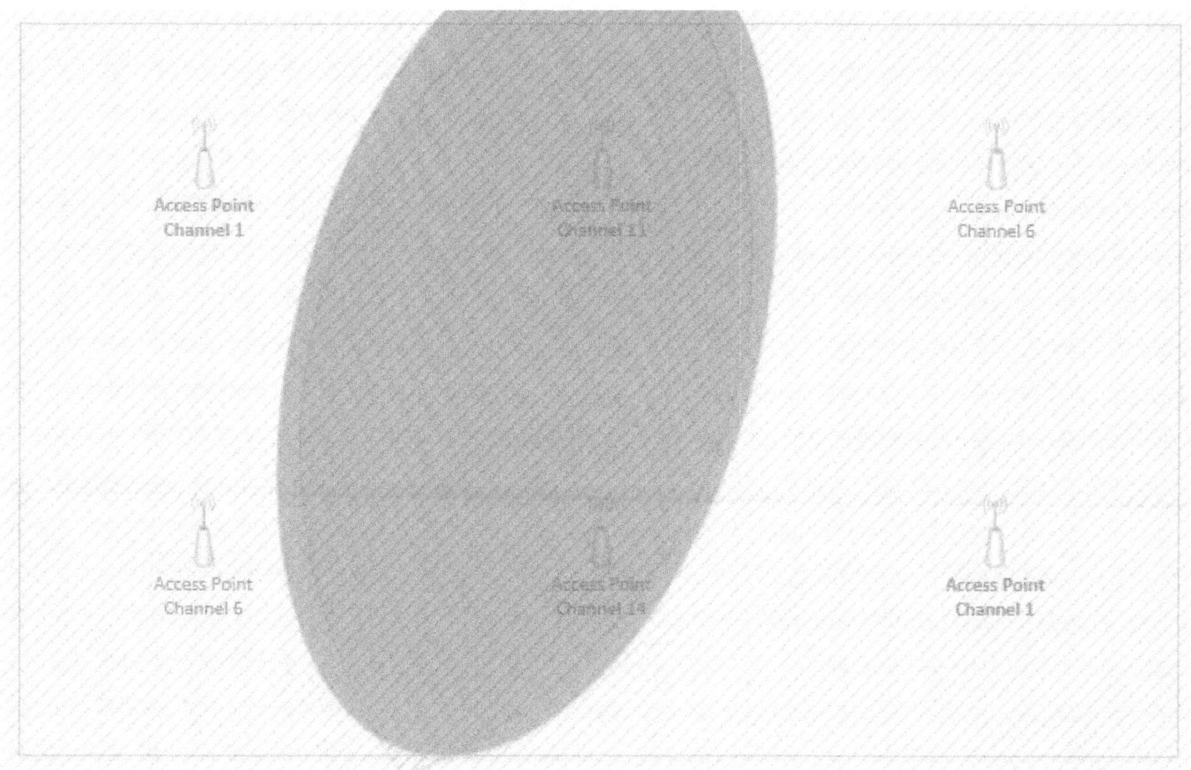

We can reduce the **transmit power** of each access point, so that the signal range is weaker. This way, the signals don't overlap, but we can still cover the entire room with an adequate Wi-Fi signal. I can adjust the signal strength of an access point so that it doesn't overlap with other access points or so that it does not leave the building.

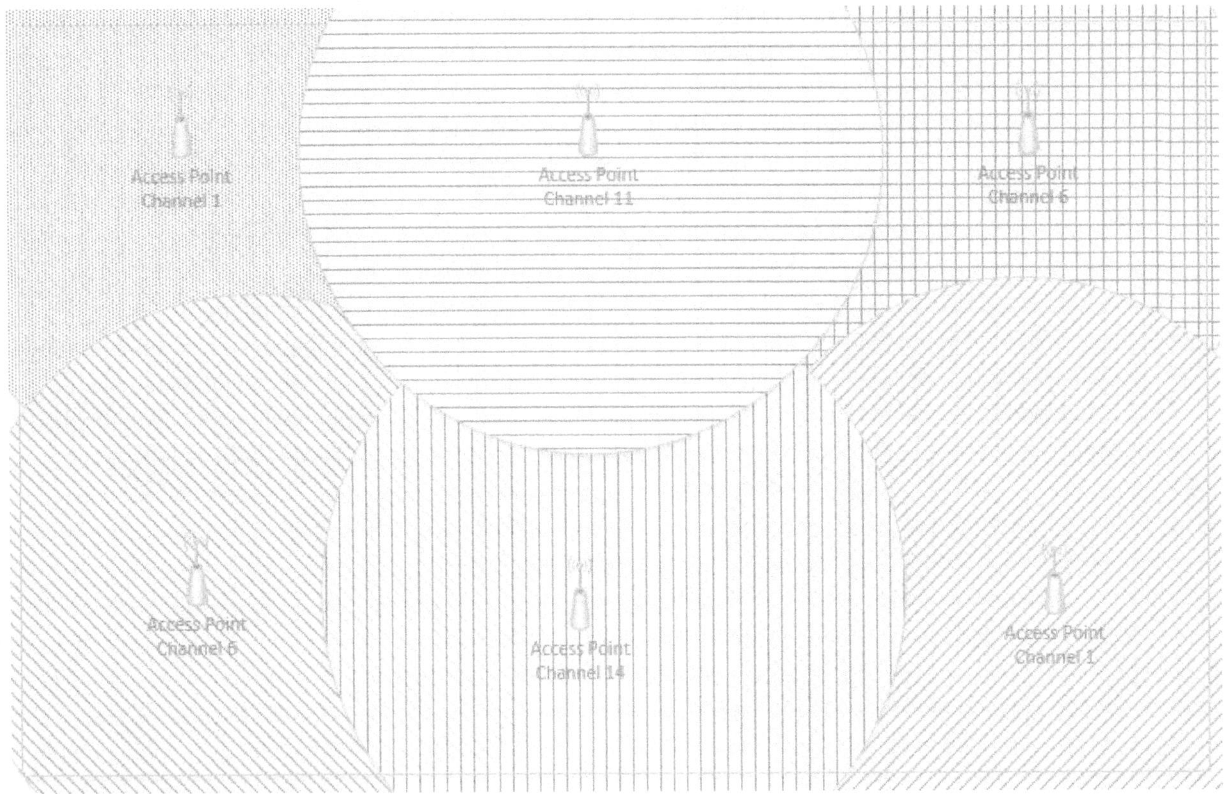

Now, I still have overlapping signals. But the overlap doesn't extend across the entire room. The access points that overlap are broadcasting on slightly different frequencies; therefore, their signals do not interfere.

The **BSSID** or **Basic Service Set Identifier** is the name of the network. A **Wireless Access Point**, or **WAP**, advertises its capabilities and allows devices to join. The area where a WAP operates is known as the **Basic Service Area**, or **BSA**. It is the area where the WAP's signal can reach host devices. In the example above, the BSA might be the room's perimeter.

On an **ad hoc network**, The BSSID it is typically the MAC address of the device we are connecting to. We might call this the **Independent Basic Service Set** or **IBSS**. The purpose of an ad hoc network is so that two wireless devices can connect to each other without using a WAP. For example, I can print directly to a printer from my laptop or smartphone. The printer broadcasts an ad hoc wireless network and we connect to it from a laptop.

On an infrastructure network, the BSSID is known as an **SSID** or **Service Set Identifier**. On a larger network, it's called an **Extended Service Set Identifier** or **ESSID**. When we have multiple access points, we force all of them to have the same ESSID so that users have the same experience regardless of where they are. Each access point has a unique BSSID, but all of them have the same

SSID. We don't want a user to change Wi-Fi networks when they move from room to room (or even within the same room).

We might call an end user device a **client**. When a client has connected to an access point, we call this an **association**. The purpose of a WAP is to allow wireless clients to reach the Ethernet network, and to allow clients on the Ethernet network to reach wireless clients.

A client will connect to the access point that is closest (technically, the access point that has the strongest signal). When a client moves from one WAP to another (on the same SSID), we call this **roaming**.

For example, say I have a large warehouse with hundreds of WAPs providing even coverage. If I turn on my laptop and walk around the warehouse, my laptop's Wi-Fi connection will jump from one WAP to another, but it will appear like I'm always connected.

A single WAP can broadcast multiple SSIDs (for example guest, and corporate).

A **wireless range extender** is also known as a **repeater**. When placed at the edge of a wireless network, the range can be increased. Essentially, it repeats the signal that it "hears" from the nearest access point. It acts as a relay between the nearest access point and a user who is further away.

Consider the following scenario. On the left, I have an access point connected to a switch. Its range is shown by the circle around it. On the right, I have a user who wishes to connect, but is out of range. I don't have the network infrastructure to install a second access point closer to the user.

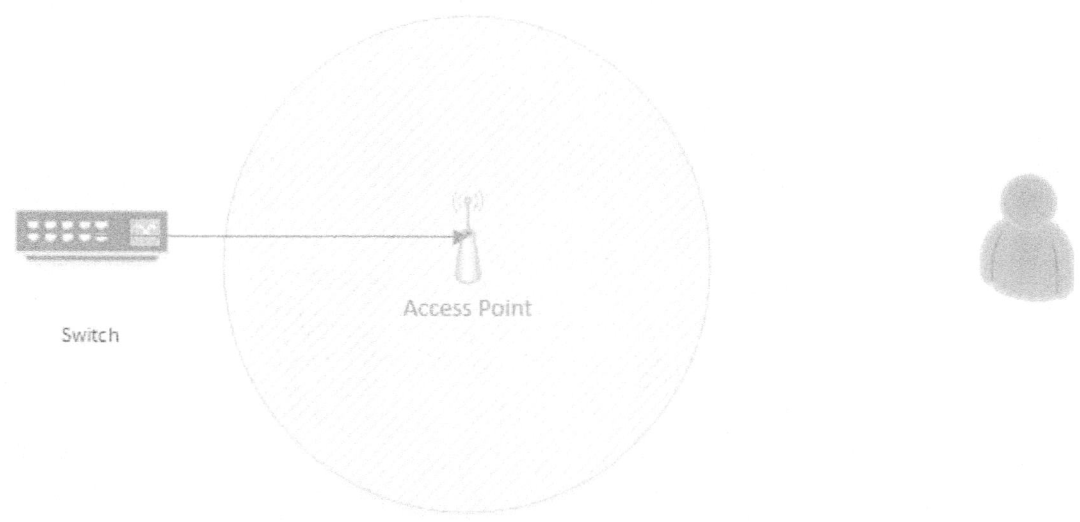

If I install a repeater, I now can extend the range of the access point to the user.

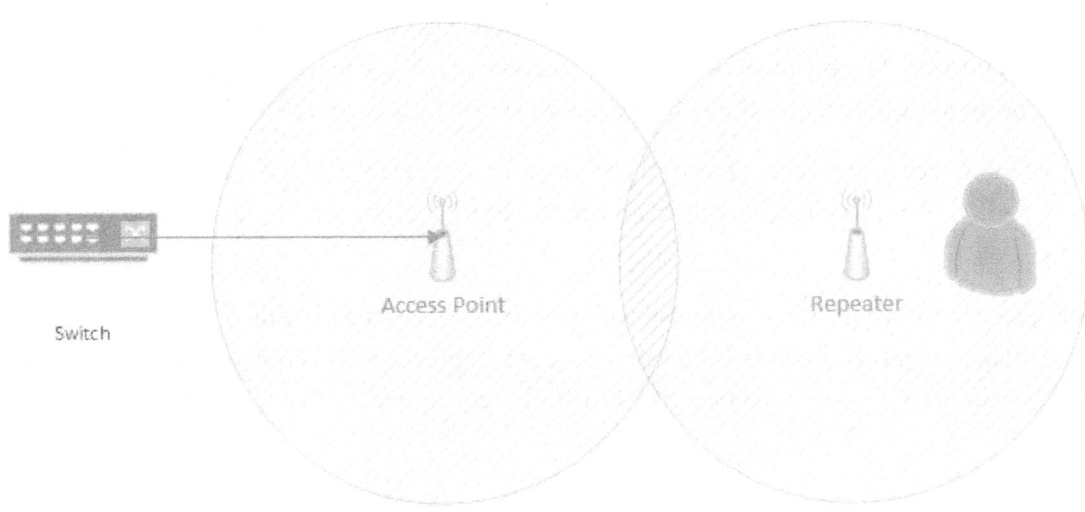

A repeater can be a normal AP that is set to "repeat" mode or it can be a special device. We usually change the repeater's channel so that it doesn't interfere with that of the original access point.

We can also use a **workgroup bridge**. A workgroup bridge is a device that connects to the Ethernet port of a host and allows it to connect to the wireless network. For example, if I have a portable X-ray machine or medical cart that moves around the hospital, but its only connection is to an ethernet port, I would connect it to ia bridge. The bridge can be a WAP that is set to **bridge mode**.

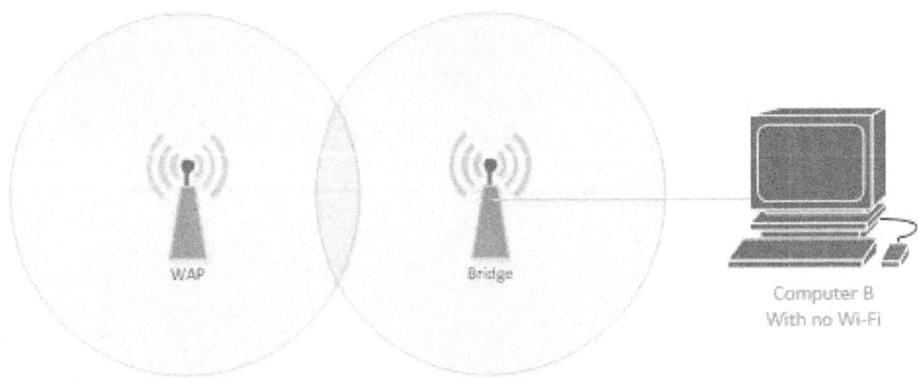

There are two types of bridges

- **Universal Workgroup Bridge (uWGB)**. In a uWGB, one wired device connects to a wireless network.
- **Workgroup Bridge (WGB)**. In a WGB, multiple wired devices connect to a wireless network.

What happens when we have multiple locations that must be connected via Ethernet, but can't, due to distance or cost? For example, if I have two office buildings that are 1000m apart, but I would like to connect their networks together, I have several options. I can install a fiber optic cable between the buildings, but this would be expensive, and I may not have the right to dig up the land between them. I could install a WAN connection, but this may be expensive. Another option is to install a **Point-to-Point** antenna.

Below are two buildings, each with an Ethernet network. I can install an antenna on the roof of each building and point them at each other. I connect the antenna in each building to its respective Ethernet network via an Ethernet cable. The two antennas serve to bridge the networks and make them act like one.

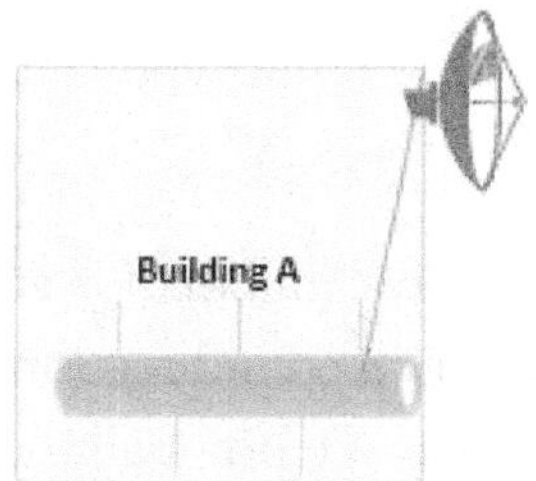

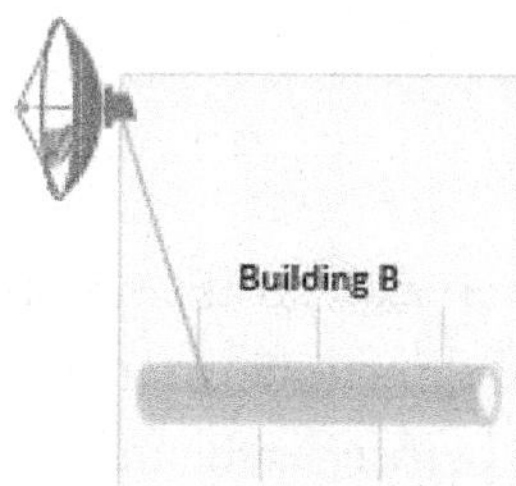

The antennas used in this case are highly specialized and must be pointed at each other. An example of a point-to-point antenna is the Ubiquiti AirFiber. This is not a Cisco product, but it is highly recommended by me.

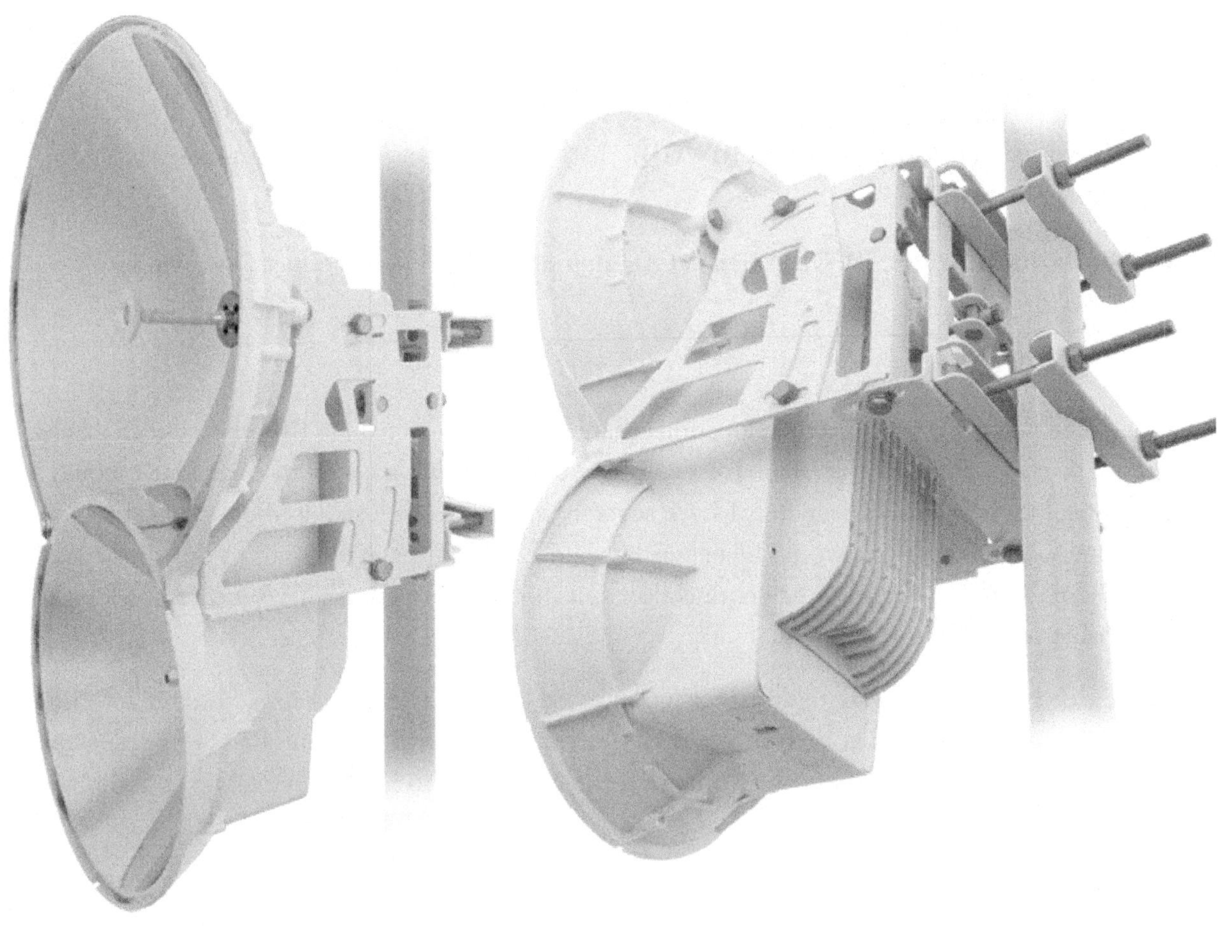

We can also create a **point to multi-point configuration**. One antenna (the central antenna) is an omni-directional antenna (it broadcasts its signal in all directions), while the others are unidirectional. Like before, each antenna connects to its Ethernet network via an Ethernet cable. We point all the unidirectional antennas at the central antenna.

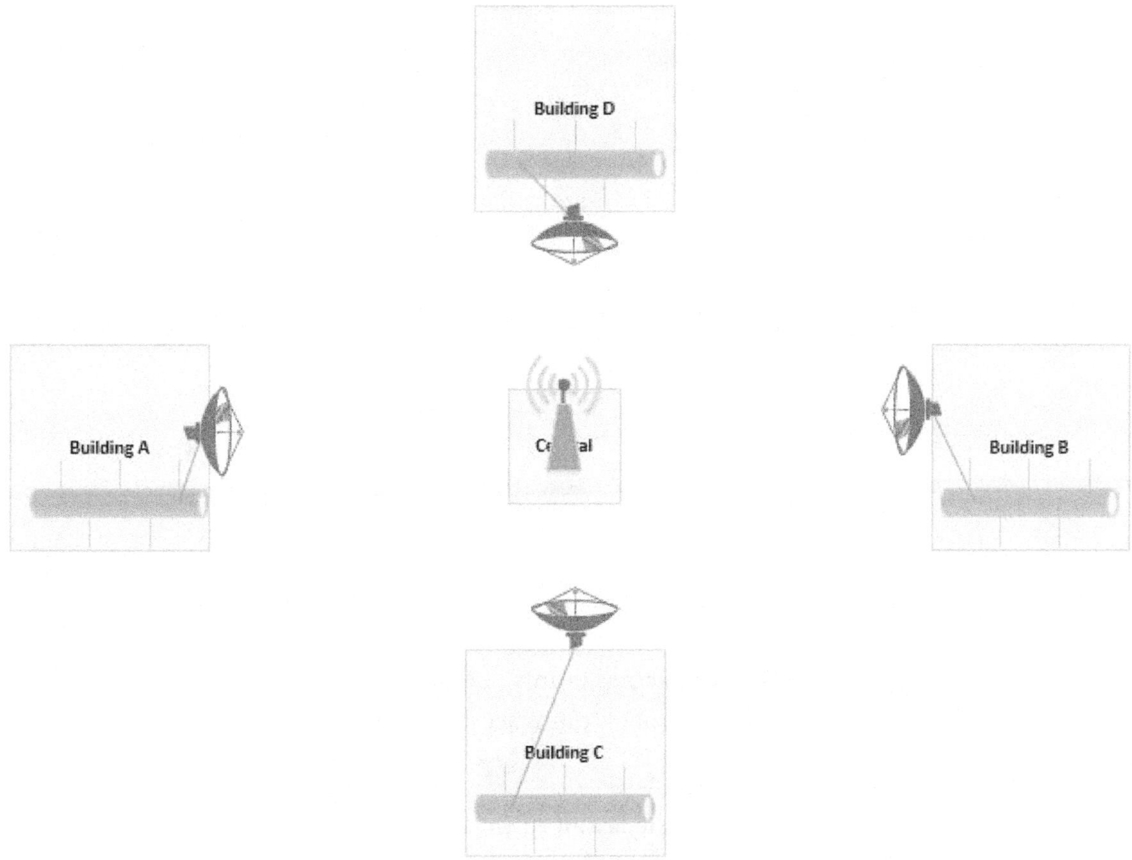

A **wireless mesh network** is where multiple network devices such as access points form connections with each other and with clients. The mesh network is necessary in areas where we require Wi-Fi, but an access point cannot physically reach a switch or router.

Consider my crude mesh wireless network below. The access point on the left has as direct physical connection to the router. It can allow clients to connect to the network. The access point on the right is too far from the router or any wiring to connect over a direct physical connection. It forms a mesh wireless connection with the first access point. Devices on the right cannot connect to the access point on the left because they are out of range. With the mesh network, devices connecting to the access point on the right can connect to the network because the traffic will travel to the access point on the left, and then to the router.

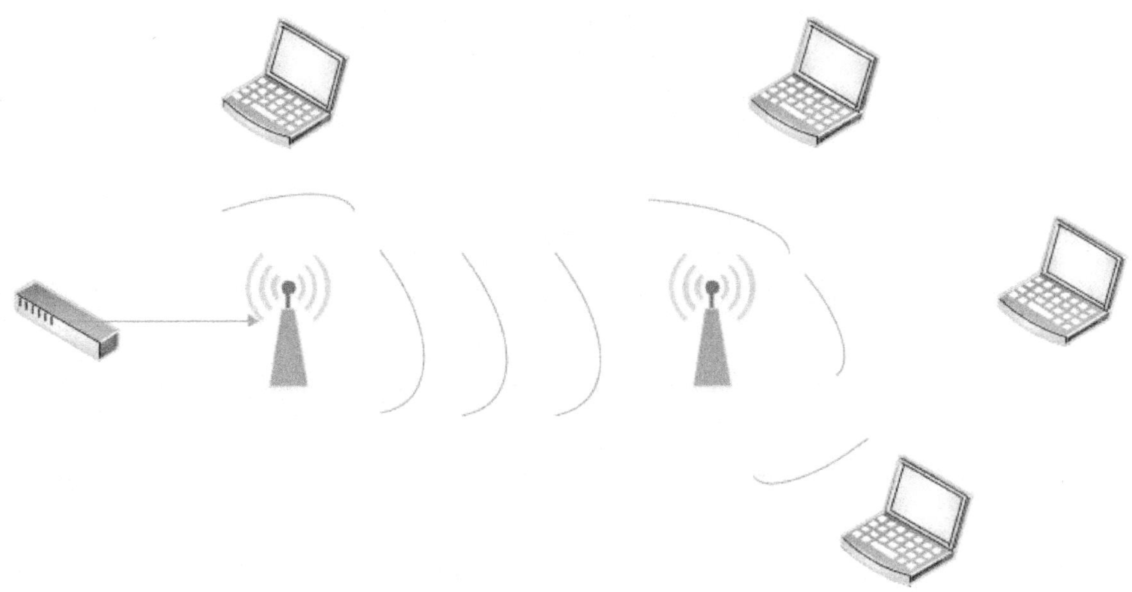

We can continue to add more wireless mesh access points in a row or wherever we choose. But as the mesh grows, the data will need to pass through more access points, and therefore latency will increase.

The members of the mesh must understand the layout of the entire network so that they can route traffic to the appropriate neighbor and get it to its destination. There are dozens of mesh routing protocols; some are better than others.

All Wi-Fi protocols are regulated by IEEE (Institute of Electrical and Electronics Engineers). Collectively, we call them 802.11. As the demand for technology increases, new standards are released. The current standard is 802.11ac.

An access point or client (computer, phone, Wi-Fi adapter) may support multiple standards. The standards are backwards compatible (for example, an 802.11ac device will work with an 802.11a device).

Five standards have emerged

802.11a	1999 Standard Supports up to 54 Mbps in the 5GHz range
802.11b	1999 Standard Supports up to 11 Mbps in the 2.4GHz range

802.11g	2003 Standard Up to 54 Mbps in the 2.4GHz range If all the devices on a network are at the 802.11g level, then the network operates at 54 Mbps. Otherwise, it operates at 11 Mbps to support the older devices.
802.11n	2009 Standard Supports **multiple-input, multiple-output** (MIMO) – an access point device with multiple antennas Up to 72.2 Mbps with one send and one receive antenna Up to 450 Mbps with three send and three receive antennas Also supports **transmit beamforming** which focuses the signal so that there are no dead zones It has a better way of supporting older devices. It can operate in one of three modes • **Legacy** means it sends separate packets for older devices, which is not efficient • **Mixed** means it sends out standard packets that support older devices and newer devices. We might also call this high-throughput or **802.11a-ht** or **802.11g-ht.** • **Greenfield** means that it sends out 802.11n packets that support newer devices, but not older devices
802.11ac	2014 Standard Supports multiuser multiple-input, multiple-output (MIMO)

Up to 433 Mbps per antenna, or 1.3Gbps with three antennas

The standard provides guidelines that manufacturers of wireless devices use when making devices. With a reliable standard, products from different manufacturers all work together. Just think about it – it doesn't really matter what brand laptop or phone you have, it generally works with the Wi-Fi at your office, your home, the airport, the mall, your friend's house, etc. That's because the Wi-Fi card in your device follows the same standard as the Wireless Access Points installed everywhere.

1.2 Describe characteristics of network topology architectures

1.2.a 2 tier

1.2.b 3 tier

1.2.c Spine-leaf

1.2.d WAN

1.2.e Small office/home office (SOHO)

1.2.f On-premises and cloud

I bumped this section to the end because it wouldn't make sense without some background information. Here is a switch. It has 48 ports. That means we can connect up to 48 ethernet devices to it (one might be a router). Actually, it has 52 ports, but we will worry about those ports on the end of the switch later.

What if I have a big office with hundreds or thousands of computers? What if I have a massive network like at a University campus? I need to buy a bunch of switches and connect them together because one won't be enough. But I need to think about it carefully. I can't randomly connect switches, or they will become overloaded. You know if you have one power outlet and you randomly daisy chain power strips, you will have a big mess, and maybe even a fire. Well, it is worse with switches.

Some switches are powerful, and some are weak. Thus, I need to create a hierarchy.

At the top, I can install a powerful switch, like a Cisco Catalyst 6500 switch. This is known as the **core switch**. On the second layer, I connect my less powerful switches to the core switch. We call these **access switches**, because the endpoints connect to them to access the network. This is a **two-tiered network**. A two-tier network is also called a **collapsed core** network.

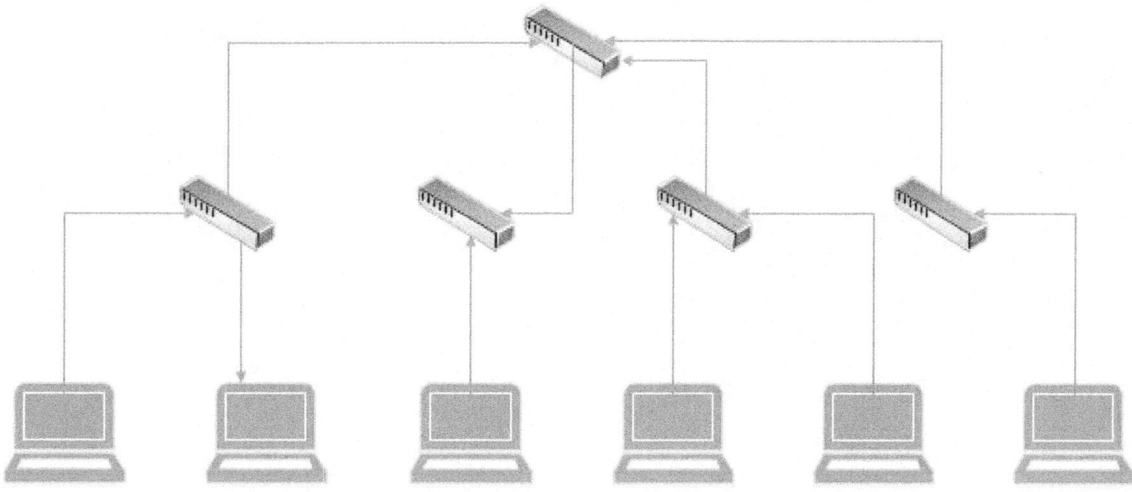

If I have a really, really big network, I can build it as three layers, or **three-tiered**. The switch at the top is called the **core switch**. The switches in the middle are called **distribution switches**. The switches at the bottom are called **access switches**. Ideally, each access switch should connect to two distribution switches in case one connection fails.

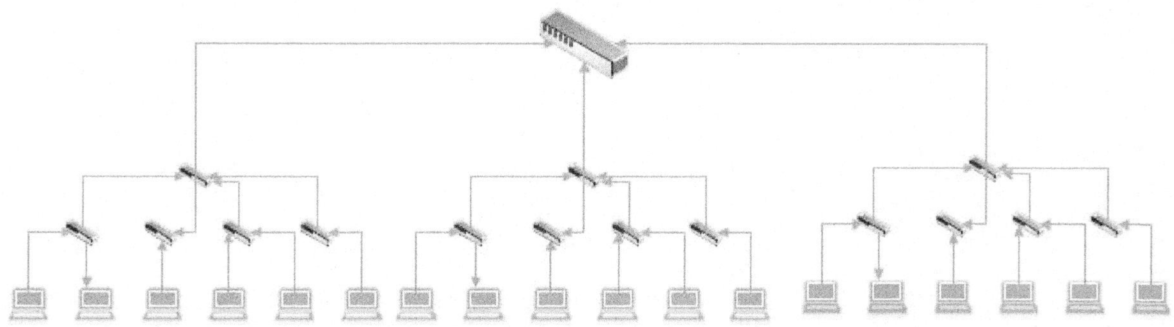

This kind of network is also called as a **star network**, because the points radiate from the switch.

An access switch connects to end user devices, but it does not connect to other access switches. A distribution switch aggregates data from access switches but does not connect to end user devices. A core switch forwards data between distribution switches, but it doesn't connect to any end user devices or access switches.

This is opposed to a **mesh network**, where all the switches connect to each other. There is no central switch. When there are only a few switches, a mesh network might be acceptable. The problem with this network is that every switch needs to connect to every other switch. If we have 40 switches, then 39 out of 48 ports on every switch are used for cross-connects. That means that 39 ports are used to connect to switches and 9 ports are used to connect to endpoints.

If I have a network with 49 switches, then each switch needs 48 ports to connect to the other 48 ports and none of them can connect to endpoints.

That is a lot of cables and not very efficient.

When all the switches connect to all the other switches, we call it a **Full Mesh**.

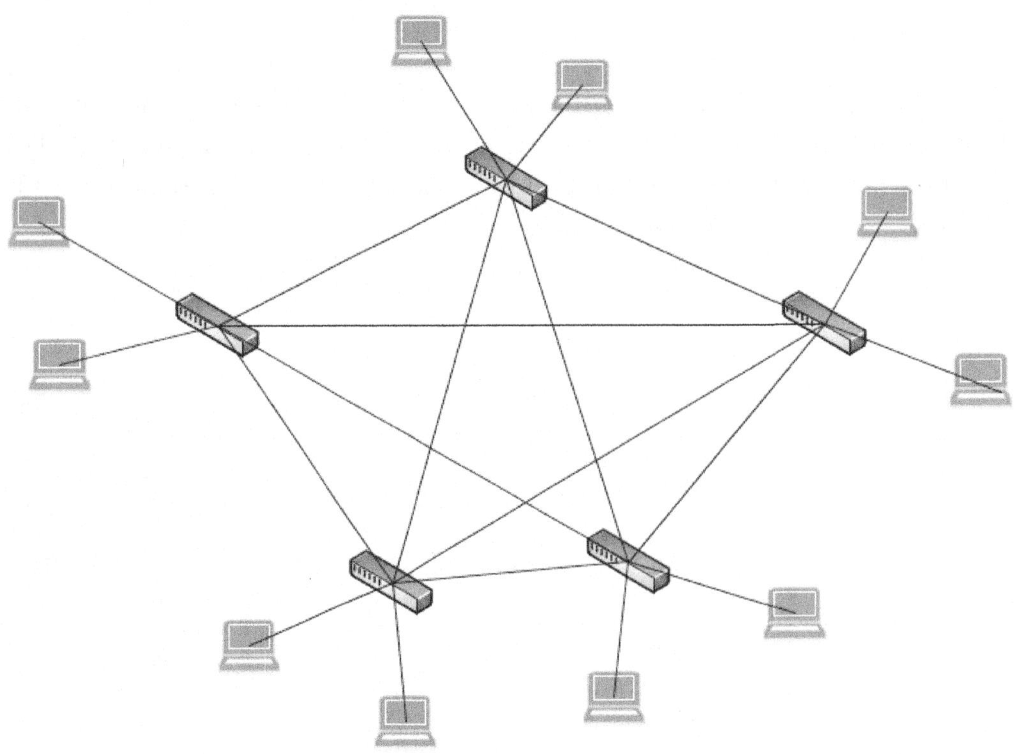

If only some of the switches connect to other switches, it is called a **Partial Mesh**.

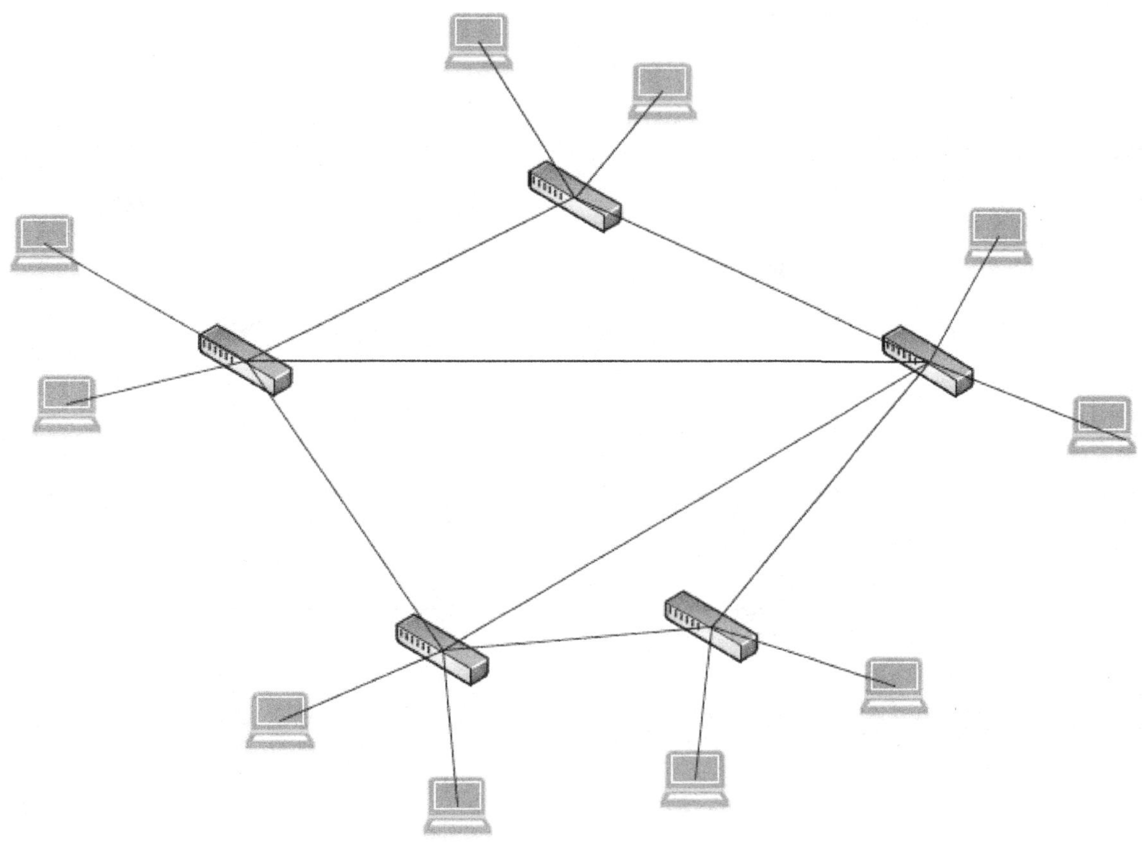

We can also combine a Mesh Network with a Star Network to make a **Hybrid Network**.

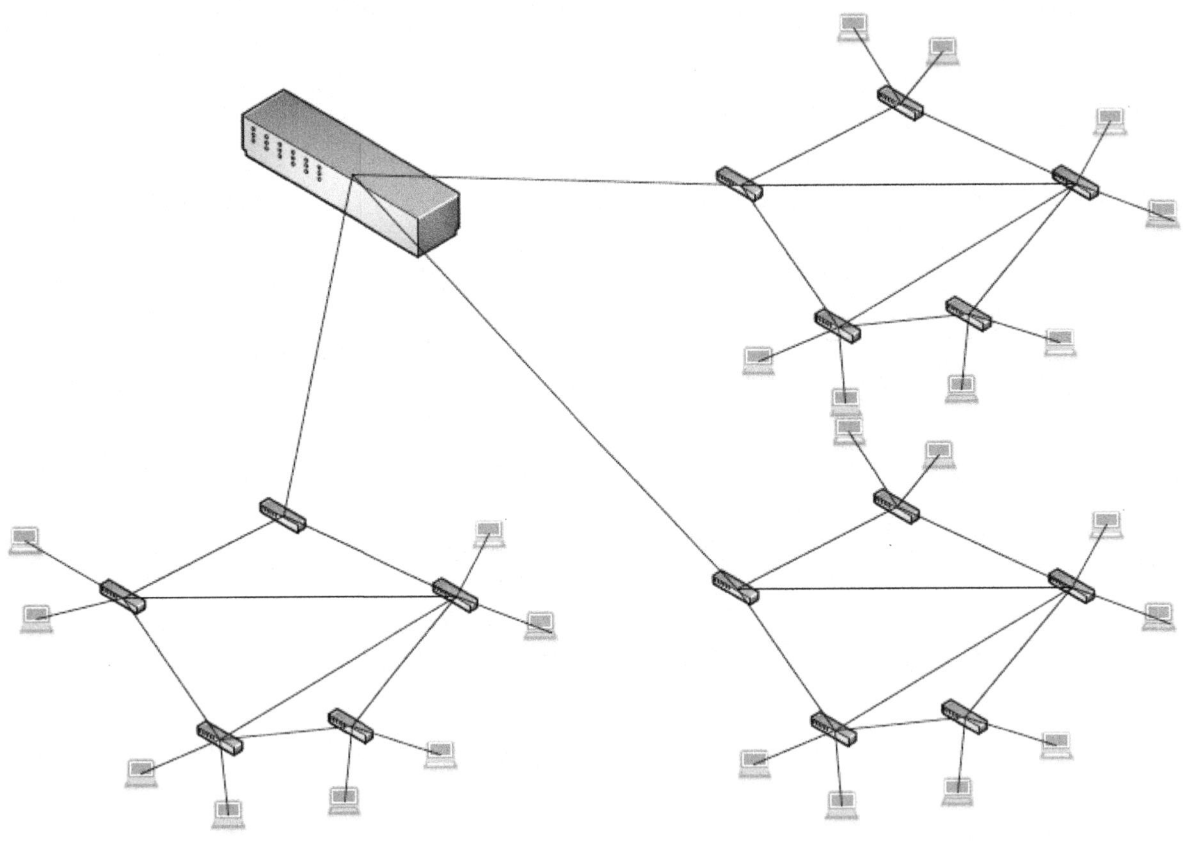

We also have a **Spine-Leaf Network**. At the top of the network is the spine (the spine switches). In the middle are the leafs (leaf switches). Each leaf switch connects to each spine switch, but a leaf switch never connects to another leaf switch. This kind of network is common in data centers and does not require core switches.

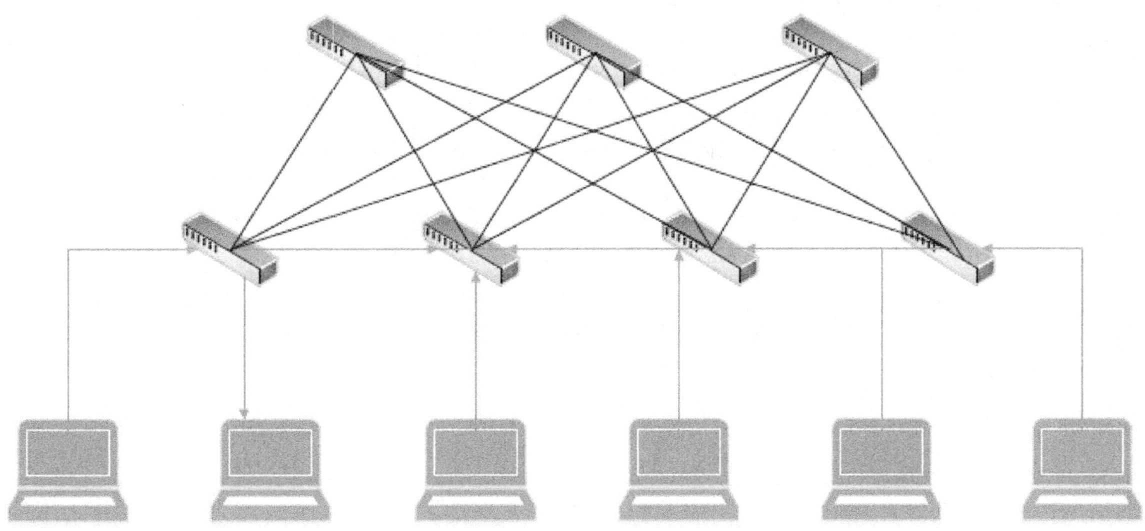

Okay, we are going to switch topics and look at how the internet gets into your home or office.

With a traditional internet connection, an Internet Service Provider (ISP) supplies you with a modem. The modem takes the signal from the ISP (a fiber, satellite, cellular, cable, or telephone connection) and converts it into an Ethernet connection that your network can use.

You connect the modem to your router or firewall and then you can access the internet. The problem with a traditional internet connection is that the ISP must install special equipment at its data center to transmit the signal to your modem (and to convert the signal to/from an Ethernet connection). The ISP must also supply and maintain modems at each customer location.

They had an idea. What if the ISP can build a massive Ethernet network across an entire city. Then you can just connect to their network without a modem.

A **Metro Ethernet**, or **MetroE**, is a WAN service that improves upon the traditional internet connections. An ISP creates a large Ethernet network in a city. A MetroE is commonly found downtown but can be extended to the suburbs. The ISP provides the customer with an Ethernet connection directly to their network.

Typically, the customer connects its router's outgoing port to the Ethernet connection provided by the ISP. The benefit is that the ISP doesn't need to install or maintain any specialized equipment and doesn't need to provide the customer with a modem. A customer could connect a switch to the ISP's connection, but most people choose to use routers.

One benefit of a MetroE is that we can connect multiple physical locations together via an ethernet connection instead of via a dedicated WAN link.

What's a WAN link? Well, let's say I have offices in Atlanta, New York City, and Baltimore. I want to connect all three offices together so that their networks pretend like they are one big network. I would need to run a big long cable from New York City to Baltimore and Atlanta, which would be impossible. What I can do is pay my internet service provider to give me a special type of internet connection called a **WAN**, or **Wide Area Network**. The ISP carries my traffic from one local network to another and my networks don't realize that they are physically separated. We will learn more about this later.

The connection to the ISP's network is called an **Ethernet Access Link**. The spot where the ISP's equipment ends, and the customer's equipment starts is called the **Point of Presence**. The customer's connection is called a **User Network Interface**.

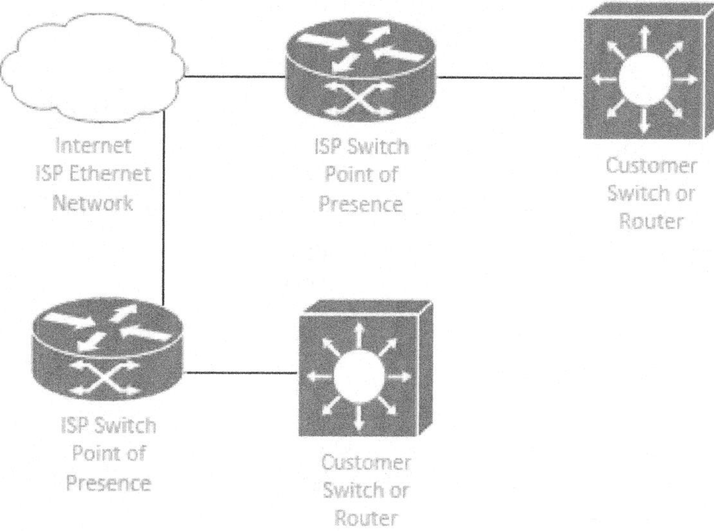

There are several types of MetroE

- **Ethernet Line Service** or **E-Line**. This is a Point-to-Point connection between two devices. It is like a leased line in that each device thinks that it is physically connected to the other device.
- **Ethernet LAN Service** or **E-LAN**. This is a connection between multiple devices that acts like a Full Mesh network. All the connected devices think that they are physically connected to the same LAN and can exchange Ethernet frames.
- **Ethernet Tree Service** or **E-Tree**. This is a Hub-and-Spoke between multiple devices. The central device can communicate with the remote devices, but the remote devices can only communicate with other remote devices through the central device.

The Ethernet Line Service

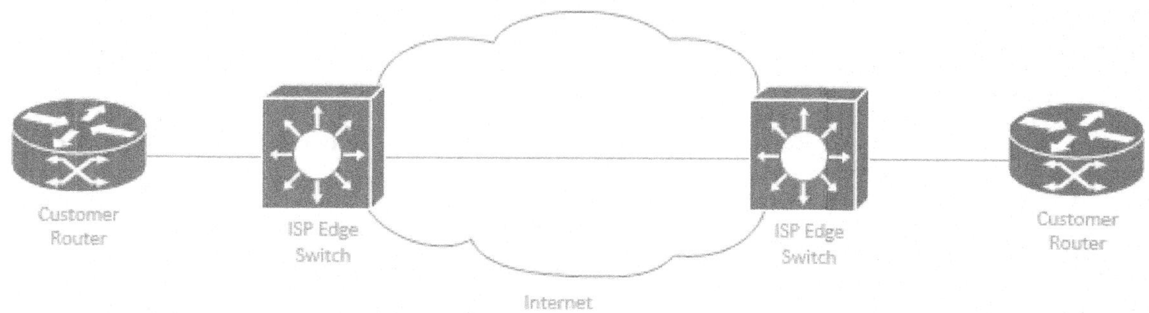

We configure each router to use a physical Ethernet interface. The IP addresses on the Ethernet interfaces are in the same subnet. The routers can exchange routes and become neighbors. Remember earlier I said that we need to allocate a subnet for each WAN interface.

On the edge of the ISP network is a switch (not a router or a modem). The switch helps carry Ethernet packets across the internet.

Every line needs its own subnet. That means that every router interface needs a unique IP address. The routers learn directly connected routes for any router connected by point-to-point.

In my example below, Customer Router "aaaa" connects directly to Customer Router "bbbb" and to Customer Router "cccc". Thus it learns a direct route to each of them.

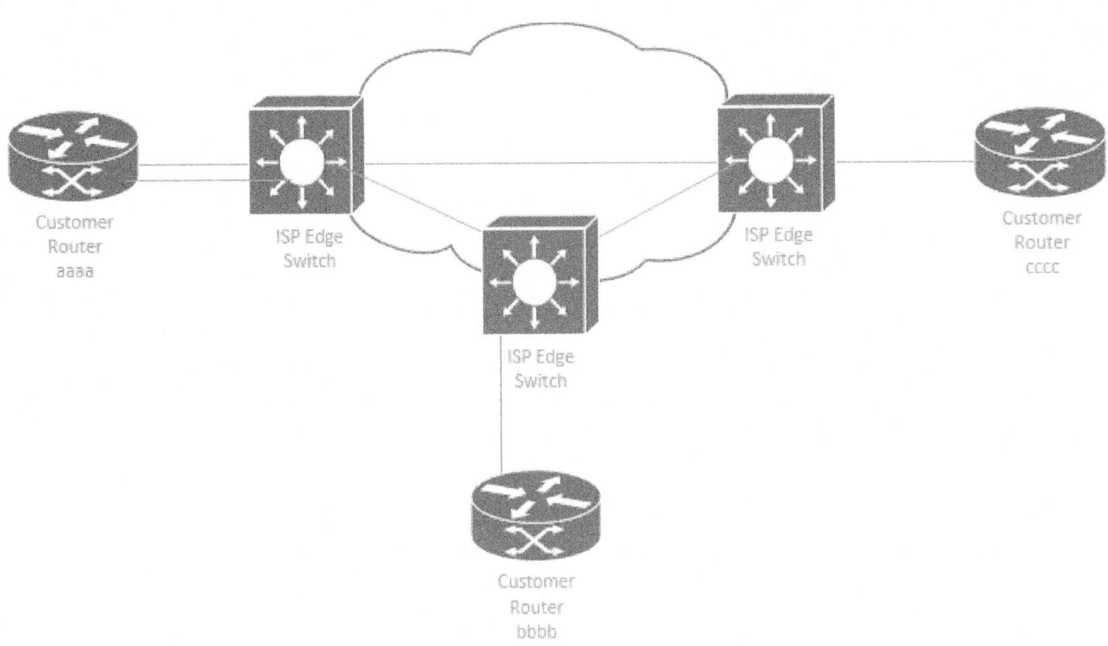

I created five subnets

Subnet Name	Description
10.10.10.0/24	The local subnet for Router aaaa
10.10.11.0/24	The local subnet for Router bbbb
10.10.12.0/24	The local subnet for Router cccc
10.10.13.0/24	The WAN subnet for the Router aaaa-Router cccc connection • 10.10.13.1 is Router aaaa's external IP address on this WAN • 10.10.13.2 is Router cccc's external IP address on this WAN
10.10.14.0/24	The WAN subnet for the Router aaaa-Router bbbb connection • 10.10.14.1 is Router aaaa's external IP address on this WAN

- 10.10.14.2 is Router bbbb's external IP address on this WAN

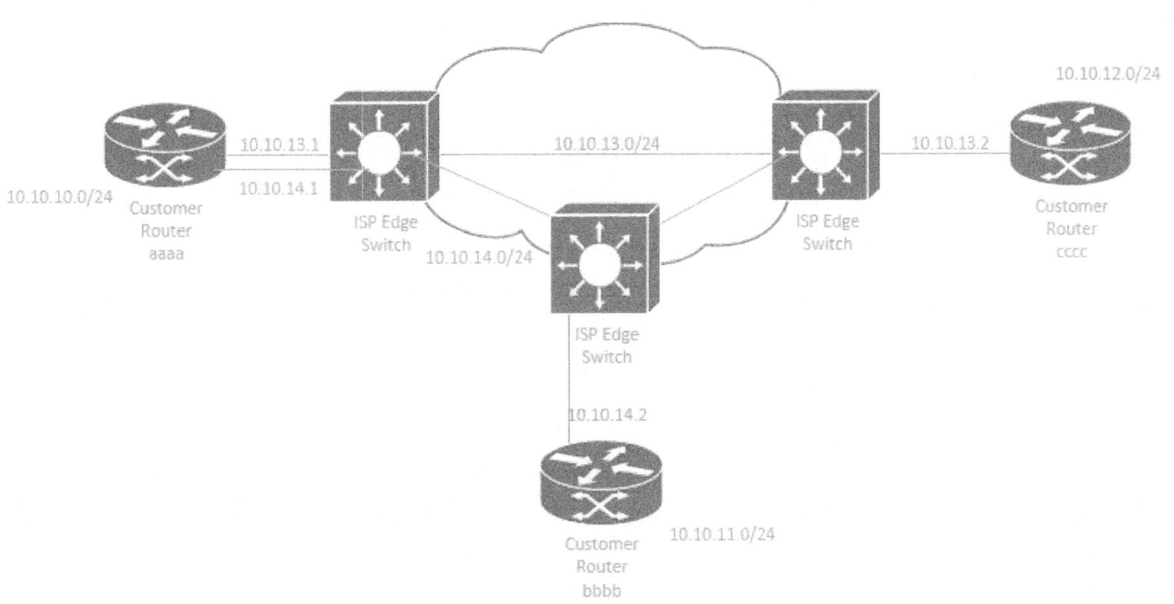

Router aaaa's routing table might look like this (I picked Physical Interfaces randomly).

Subnet	Physical Interface	Next-Hop Router IP Address
10.10.10.0/24	G0/1	Local
10.10.11.0/24	G0/2	10.10.14.2
10.10.12.0/24	G0/3	10.10.13.2
10.10.13.0/24	G0/3	Local
10.10.14.0/24	G0/2	Local

Why?

- 10.10.10.0/24 is Router aaaa's local network. It is directly connected to Router aaaa, so Router aaaa automatically learns it.
- 10.10.13.0/24 is Router aaaa's local network on the WAN between itself and Router cccc, so Router aaaa automatically learns it.
- 10.10.14.0/24 is Router aaaa's local network on the WAN between itself and Router bbbb, so Router aaaa automatically learns it.

- 10.10.11.0/24 is Router bbbb's local network. Router aaaa learns this from Router bbbb. Router aaaa sends the traffic destined for this network to Router bbbb, via Router bbbb's WAN IP address – 10.10.14.2.
- 10.10.11.0/24 is Router cccc's local network. Router aaaa learns this from Router cccc. Router aaaa sends the traffic destined for this network to Router cccc, via Router cccc's WAN IP address – 10.10.13.2.

An Ethernet Virtual Connection, or EVC is a Point-to-Point connection that determines which devices can communicate. A Point-to-Point connection is not practical when there are many sites because each router would need many physical interfaces and connections to connect to all the other locations over a full mesh.

In an Ethernet LAN Service, we create a full mesh.

I created five subnets

Subnet Name	Description
10.10.10.0/24	The local subnet for Router aaaa
10.10.11.0/24	The local subnet for Router bbbb
10.10.12.0/24	The local subnet for Router cccc
10.10.13.0/24	The local subnet for Router dddd
10.10.14.0/24	The WAN subnet for all of the routers • 10.10.14.1 is Router aaaa's external IP address on this WAN • 10.10.14.2 is Router bbbb's external IP address on this WAN • 10.10.14.3 is Router cccc's external IP address on this WAN • 10.10.14.4 is Router dddd's external IP address on this WAN

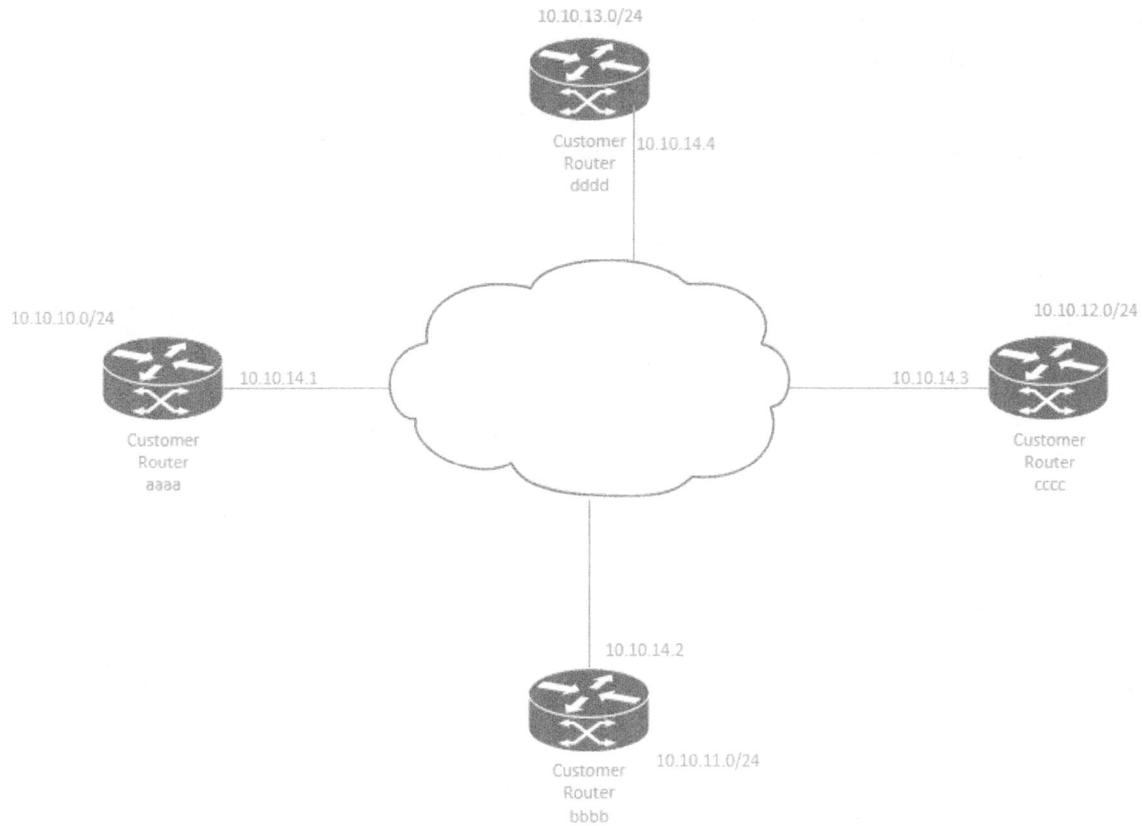

All the routers have an interface in the same subnet. Router aaaa's routing table might look like this (I picked Physical Interfaces randomly).

Subnet	Physical Interface	Next-Hop Router IP Address
10.10.10.0/24	G0/1	Local
10.10.11.0/24	G0/2	10.10.14.2
10.10.12.0/24	G0/2	10.10.14.3
10.10.13.0/24	G0/2	10.10.14.4
10.10.14.0/24	G0/2	Local

Why?

- 10.10.10.0/24 is Router aaaa's local network. It is directly connected to Router aaaa, so Router aaaa automatically learns it.
- 10.10.11.0/24 is Router bbbb's local network. Router aaaa learns this information from Router bbbb.
- 10.10.12.0/24 is Router cccc's local network. Router aaaa learns this information from Router cccc.

- 10.10.13.0/24 is Router dddd's local network. Router aaaa learns this information from Router dddd.
- 10.10.14.0/24 is the WAN's subnet. All the routers connect to it. Since it is directly connected to Router aaaa, then Router aaaa automatically learns it.

The Ethernet Tree Service is less expensive and is good when there are many smaller sites. Each remote site connects to a central site.

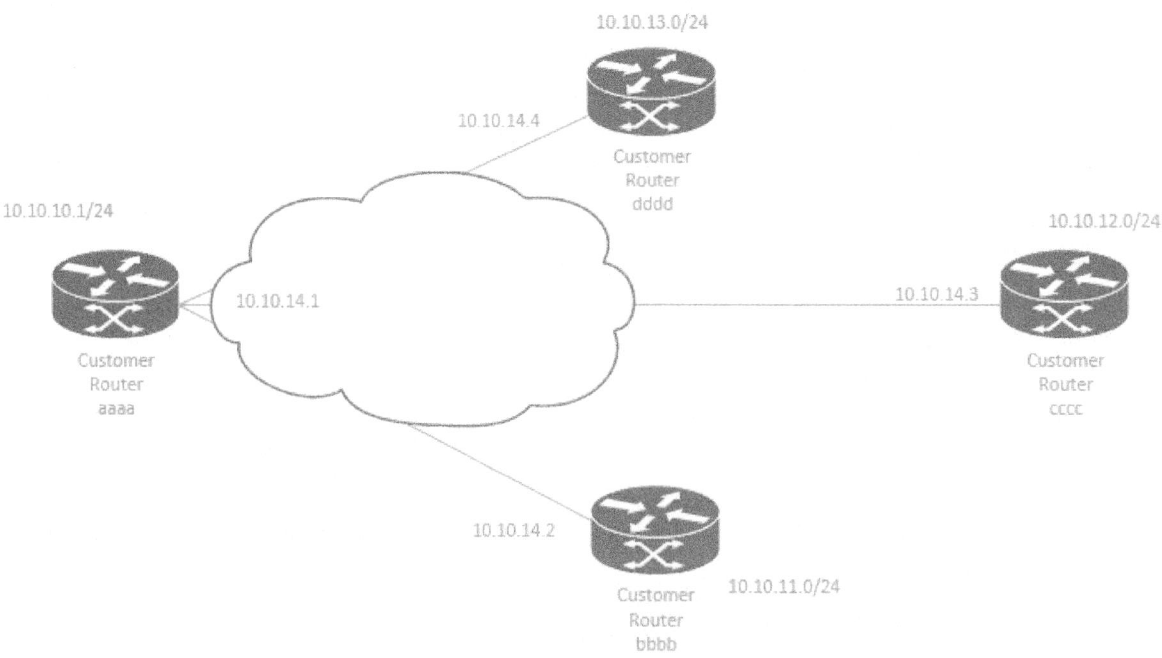

Router aaaa's table probably looks the same like in the previous example, and for the same reasons. It is directly connected to the other routers.

Subnet	Physical Interface	Next-Hop Router IP Address
10.10.10.0/24	G0/1	Local
10.10.11.0/24	G0/2	10.10.14.2
10.10.12.0/24	G0/2	10.10.14.3
10.10.13.0/24	G0/2	10.10.14.4
10.10.14.0/24	G0/2	Local

The other routers are not directly connected to each other. If we look at router dddd, it has only two directly connected routes – its own subnet (10.10.13.0) and the connection to router aaaa (10.10.10.0) It must learn about the other two subnets (10.10.11.0 and 10.10.12.0) from router aaaa.

Subnet	Physical Interface	Next-Hop Router IP Address
10.10.10.0/24	G0/1	10.10.10.1
10.10.11.0/24	G0/2	10.10.10.1
10.10.12.0/24	G0/2	10.10.10.1
10.10.13.0/24	G0/2	Local
10.10.14.0/24	G0/2	Local

The problem with all these scenarios is that they are not efficient. An ISP will not build a massive Ethernet network for a single customer. They will need to sell it to multiple customers. But they also need to keep customer traffic separated, even though many customers will use the same IP address schemes, subnets, and VLANs.

The ISP equipment on the MetroE edge is a switch because we want to forward Layer 2 Ethernet frames, not Layer 3 IP packets.

A good technology to support MetroE is called **Multiprotocol Label Switching** or **MPLS**. An MPLS creates a separate tunnel for each customer's traffic without leaking any data. It operates on the ISPs network.

The router at the edge of each customer site is called an **edge router**. An MPLS forwards Layer 3 packets. The edge router is usually provided by the ISP.

The **customer edge** or **CE** is the router that is installed at the **customer site** and the **provider edge** or **PE** is the router that is installed at the edge of the provider's network. One advantage of using a router is that the ISP can support many customers regardless of the type of data link that they are using. We can even access an MPLS network via a broadband connection if we can't use a data link.

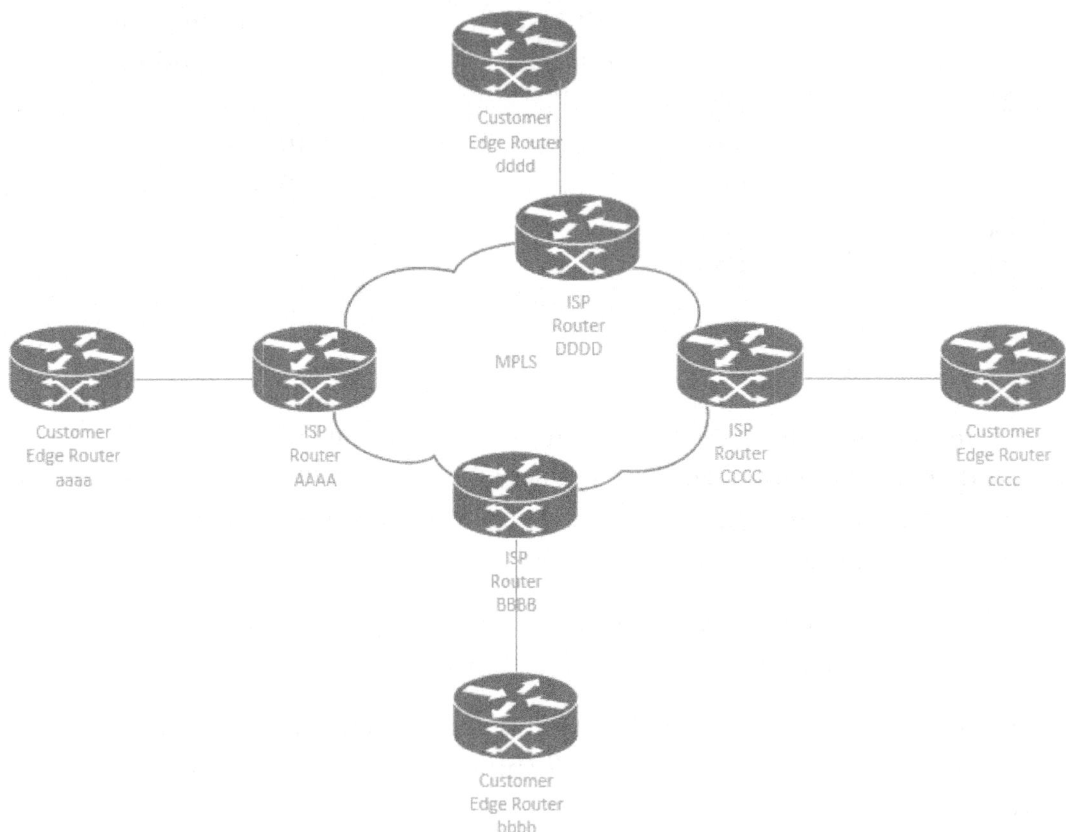

At the edge of each network, the router will add an MPLS header to the data packet and send it over the ISPs network. This header is called an **MPLS label**. The packet travels over the ISPs network until reaches the edge router on the other side. The edge router removes the MPLS header.

For example

- A device connected to Customer Edge Router aaaa's LAN wants to send a packet to a device connected on Customer Edge Router cccc's LAN
- Customer Edge Router aaaa receives the packet and adds an MPLS header to it
- Customer Edge Router sends the packet to ISP Router AAAA
- ISP Router transports the packet to ISP Router CCCC. The actual route might be complicated and pass through several ISP routers.
- ISP Router CCCC transports the packet to the Customer Edge Router cccc.
- Customer Edge Router cccc removes the MPLS header and sends the packet to the device

The service provider uses a routing protocol to learn routes between each of the customer's edge routers and advertises those routes to all the other edge routers. That allows all the customer's edge routers to learn all the necessary routes.

We can use **Quality of Service** or **QoS** on an MPLS network. The customer can mark high-priority traffic (such as those containing VoIP calls) and the MPLS network will forward them faster. The customer edge router is responsible for marking each packet, but the customer and the ISP must agree on a marking scheme.

All the edge devices (customer edge and provider edge) need to learn routes between each other. The customer can use any routing protocol that is available. The Customer edge router becomes a neighbor with the provider edge router. All the provider edge routers advertise their routes with each other so that all the customer edge routers can learn the network.

For example Customer Edge router aaaa knows about

- A directly connected route to its own local area network
- A directly connected route to ISP Edge Router AAAA
- Indirect routes to Customer Edge Routers bbbb, cccc, and dddd through ISP Edge Router AAAA (and therefore, indirect routes to ISP Edge Routers BBBB, CCCC, and DDDD through ISP Edge Router AAAA)

I didn't put any actual IP addresses here because they aren't as relevant, and we don't know what the ISP's network looks like. But router aaaa might have a routing table that looks like this.

Subnet	Physical Interface	Next-Hop Router IP Address
Local aaaa subnet	G0/1	Local
Local bbbb subnet	G0/2	ISP Edge Router AAAA's IP
Local cccc subnet	G0/2	ISP Edge Router AAAA's IP
Local dddd subnet	G0/2	ISP Edge Router AAAA's IP
ISP Edge Router AAAA	G0/2	ISP Edge Router AAAA's IP (directly connected)
ISP Edge Router BBBB	G0/2	ISP Edge Router AAAA's IP
ISP Edge Router CCCC	G0/2	ISP Edge Router AAAA's IP
ISP Edge Router DDDD	G0/2	ISP Edge Router AAAA's IP

If the ISP network or if other parts of the customer network use a different routing protocol, the router uses a tool called a **route redistribution** to take routes from one protocol and advertise them on another protocol.

In particular, the ISP uses a tool called **Multiprotocol BGP** to readvertise routing protocols between the provider edge routers. MBGP is useful because it can separate routes between different customers. Remember that the ISP is using their network to support a WAN service for multiple customers and doesn't want the routes or the data to mix.

If Goldman Sachs and Morgan Stanley buy WANs from AT&T, and each of them has offices in New York, New Jersey, Connecticut, and Florida, the data will probably travel over the same physical equipment, at least for part of the journey. Goldman Sachs shouldn't learn about routes into Morgan Stanley's network and Morgan Stanley shouldn't learn about routes into Goldman Sachs' network.

MBGP can label each route with the customer that it belongs to so that a Customer Edge will only learn or see the routes that belong to it.

1.12 Explain virtualization fundamentals (virtual machines)

Everything we talked about so far involves physical hardware. But organizations are moving to virtual hardware.

Cisco's server offering is called the Cisco Unified Computing System (UCS). There are many UCS models available, including blade servers and rack servers. You might buy servers from another vendor such as HP, Dell, or Lenovo.

Consider an organization that has four servers: a web server, a database server, an e-mail server, and a file server. That's four physical servers that must be powered on, configured, maintained, and connected to the network. Each server may only be used at 10% or 20% of its capacity. What can we do to make our infrastructure more efficient?

We get rid of the servers and set up a single physical server. We install an application on this server called a **hypervisor**. The hypervisor allows us to create multiple "virtual" servers on the same physical server. We install a server operating system on each virtual server. These are known as **Virtual Machines** or **VMs**. Each virtual server's operating system talks to the hypervisor, and the hypervisor talks to the server's physical hardware. The operating system doesn't know that it's running on a hypervisor; it thinks that it is running on a physical server.

The advantage is that we can reduce the number of physical server devices required – this reduces maintenance costs, power consumption, and the number of servers required.

Common hypervisors include VMWare and Microsoft Hyper-V (which is included with Windows Server operating systems).

Each virtual server thinks it has its own RAM, hard disk space, and processor. The hypervisor figures out how to proportion the hardware to meet the needs of each VM. But what happens when the physical server has only one physical network connection and all the VMs need to share it? And what happens when the different VMs need to talk to each other?

We create a **virtual NIC** (Network Interface Card) that connects to each VM. The hypervisor sees traffic from each VM and sends it out the physical server's network interface. The physical server's network interface also receives traffic destined for the VMs, which the hypervisor forwards appropriately.

We can also create a **virtual switch**, **virtual router**, and **virtual firewall** inside the hypervisor. Each virtual NIC connects to the virtual switch. These virtual devices communicate with each other using the same concepts as their physical counterparts, but all forwarding decisions are made by the software of the hypervisor.

We can set up a virtual Cisco switch like a Cisco Nexus virtual switch, which runs the Cisco switch operating system inside a software application. The benefit of installing a virtual Cisco switch inside a hypervisor is that we can configure it the same way as with a physical switch.

A virtual network has the same vulnerabilities as a physical network because the physical hardware does not provide any protection. Some of the problems include

- Traffic that moves from one virtual machine to another is entirely inside the physical host device and cannot be monitored by external security devices
- Virtual machines may have direct access to the internet
- A user on one virtual machine may be able to access other virtual machines on the same virtual network
- A virtual machine may have access to network resources on the physical network
- A user with access to the physical machine's hard disk drive can move a virtual machine to another physical machine
- It is easy to create or destroy an unauthorized virtual machine without being detected

A virtual firewall monitors traffic produced by the virtual machines. When operating in **bridge mode**, a virtual firewall operates exactly like a physical firewall, as part of the network infrastructure. When operating in **hypervisor mode**, the virtual firewall exists on a higher layer in the hypervisor. It monitors all virtual machine activity, but none of the VMs can see it. A hypervisor mode firewall is better because it cannot be seen or modified by users who only have access to the virtual environment.

In an organization that maintains physical servers, if a user or department needs a new server, they must place a procurement request and justify the expense. The IT department would purchase a physical server, install it, set it up, connect it to the network, and configure it.

In a VM setup, the IT department maintains several large physical servers with spare capacity. When a user or department needs a new a server, they must still place a procurement request. The IT department sets up a virtual machine on one of the physical servers, meeting the specifications requested by the department. The IT department may bill the other department for the use of the virtual server.

If we take virtualization one step further, we have a cloud.

A defining characteristic of the cloud is **on-demand self-service**. Any authorized user can log in to the cloud and create a virtual server without having to go through the IT department. The cloud automatically creates the VM without any of the users having to worry about the underlying physical hardware. If a physical server begins to fail, the cloud moves the VM to another physical machine. The cloud software also creates the virtual networking hardware and connects it. A user can stop and start the cloud server any time they want.

The cloud also offers **resource pooling**. That means that the cloud does not allocate any specific hardware to any specific virtual machine. All the physical components of the cloud are allocated to all the virtual machines. The cloud automatically allocates any necessary physical component to any virtual machine that requires it.

Rapid elasticity allows the cloud to grow or shrink almost instantly in response to user demand. For example, if we need ten new servers, we can have them up in a matter of minutes.

A cloud service is available over the internet from many types of internet connections and locations. This is known as **broad network access**.

The cloud also provides a **measured service**. That means that we can monitor how much use we the cloud. In many cloud services, the use of a virtual server is billed per hour, and the hourly rate depends on the operating system and type of hardware.

The two major **public cloud** service providers are Amazon Web Services (AWS) and Microsoft Azure. A public cloud is available to anybody. AWS and Azure offer many types of cloud services, not just servers. Cloud services include e-mail marketing, DNS, and artificial intelligence.

When we subscribe to a public cloud service, we can connect our network to it via a WAN or VPN. Then the cloud resources appear like they are physically connected to our local network.

If we don't want to outsource our cloud services, we can build our own **private cloud**. It is quite difficult to build a true private cloud that can provide on-demand self-service and rapid elasticity. A large organization may consider a private cloud if they have a substantial number of server resources that they can pool together, or the physical security requirements justify it. For example, a city can pool the servers from its public works department, police department, and fire department to create a private cloud.

The cloud service provider must create a **catalog**, which lists all the products that it offers. Connected to each product inside the catalog is a workflow or script that automatically generates the underlying system. For example, if I offer a server with the Windows Server 2019 operating system in my catalog, the work flow might be as follows

- Locate a physical server in the cloud that has available resources

- Allocate the correct amount of physical resources (hard disk drive, RAM, processor) for the new virtual machine
- Create a new virtual machine on the physical server
- Install the operating system on the virtual machine
- Configure the virtual machine with a username, password, hostname, etc.
- Create a virtual network adapter on the virtual machine and connect it to the virtual switch
- Assign the virtual network adapter an IP address

The workflow must accomplish these tasks by communicating with the virtual machine software via an **API**, or **Application Programming Interface**. That means that the VM software publisher creates a connector (called an API) in its software to allow requests from automated scripts in addition to human interaction.

The cloud appears to work seamlessly, but behind the cloud are many people who create, monitor and maintain it. We must watch the consumption of the cloud's physical resources. When demand on the cloud is high, we must add more physical resources. We must also replace any physical devices that fail. It is important to ensure that the cloud's physical resources are redundant, so that there is no single point of failure.

The cloud is not limited to hardware.

SaaS or **Software as a Service** is a concept where we pay for the right to use a software application. Somebody else takes care of writing the software, hosting the software, and backing up the data. Our only responsibility is to use the software. We don't have to think about the physical hardware. Examples of SaaS include Salesforce, Microsoft Exchange Online, and Office 365. SaaS is typically billed on a per user per month basis.

IaaS or **Infrastructure as a Service** is a concept where we pay for the right to use different hardware components. For example, we can rent different server types from Amazon Web Services' EC2, or we could rent DNS services from Route 53. IaaS is charged on a per device per hour (or per month) basis. For example, a large server might cost $0.35 per hour. If I buy an EC2 server it may come with a license for an operating system, such as Windows Server 2019. The cloud allows us to mix and match different hardware components so that we can build exactly the type of infrastructure that we require. IaaS allows us to pay for only what we use. If we use a server for five hours, we pay for five hours.

PaaS or **Platform as a Service** is a hybrid between the SaaS and IaaS. In PaaS, we don't have to worry about the hardware. We simply upload the applications we want, and the cloud provisions the necessary hardware to run them. We are still responsible for configuring the applications and backing up their data. An example is Amazon Hadoop. PaaS is typically billed on a per hour per resource basis. For example, we could be billed for each GB of data we store each month, or we could be billed for processing capacity we use. We can reduce our costs by using more efficient applications.

A PaaS may also offer software development tools so that we can write code inside the cloud and automatically have it executed.

We can connect to the cloud via the internet. For many SaaS applications, connecting to the cloud via the internet is great. For example, accessing Salesforce or Office 365 over a direct internet connection allows users to work remotely without having to use a VPN or WAN. That means that we can start using the cloud without having to worry about the internet connection or where our users are located.

Accessing the cloud via a normal internet connection can be bad because the internet does not provide any Quality of Service. Therefore, more important traffic is not prioritized. Also, the internet does not provide any encryption or authentication. For example, a server in the cloud will be accessible over the internet but won't act like it is connected to the enterprise network.

There are several ways to create a WAN connection with our cloud

- We can create a site-to-site VPN (Virtual Private Network) connection. A VPN is like a tunnel between us and the cloud. Our data travels over a normal internet connection, but over a tunnel
- We can create a virtual router inside the cloud's virtual network and establish a VPN back to our physical network. Cisco offers a virtual router called the **Cloud Services Router** or **CSR**.
- We can obtain an **MPLS** or **Ethernet WAN** connection. This requires cooperation between the ISP and the cloud provider. Cooperation with the larger service providers is expected, because they have many data centers in many countries. For example, AWS has data centers in Montreal, California, Oregon, Virginia, Frankfurt, and Tokyo (among others). That means that the WAN service provider can find a nearby connection back to the cloud, no matter where the customer is located.

A WAN has better security than an internet connection. It also provides **Quality of Service**. But a WAN is more expensive than a normal internet connection. Prior to purchasing a WAN, we should think about the speed and capacity that we need.

An **Intercloud Exchange** is a WAN connection between one service provider and another. We might choose to move our cloud services from one cloud provider to another. Or we might purchase some services from one service provider and other services from another service provider.

For example, we might purchase Office 365 and Active Directory from Microsoft Azure Active, because no other service provider can offer it. We might purchase database servers from AWS, because they are cheaper. Then we connect both services together.

In many setups, we install a broadband internet connection and a WAN connection. A broadband connection is cheaper and has a higher capacity.

Traffic that can travel over a broadband internet connection goes over the broadband, and the rest of the traffic goes over the WAN.

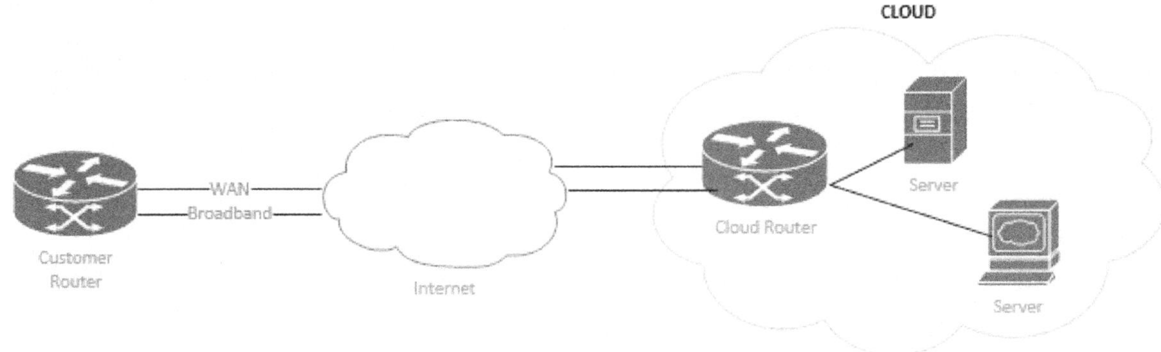

2.0 Network Access

2.1 Configure and verify VLANs (normal range) spanning multiple switches

2.1.a Access ports (data and voice)

2.1.b Default VLAN

2.1.c Connectivity

The first part of this book gave you some background information about networks and a general idea of how they communicate. We are going to learn more about those concepts later. But now it is time to start configuring Cisco equipment. Let's get a few facts out of the way

- Cisco calls each physical port on a switch or router an **interface**.
- The operating system on a Cisco device is called **IOS**, or Internetwork Operating System
- We talk to the switch or router through a Command Line Interface (CLI). There are three options
    - Telnet (by knowing the device's IP address). You shouldn't use Telnet because it is not secure. But we will learn Telnet anyways because Cisco wants us to.
    - SSH (by knowing the device's IP address)
    - Console cable (physically connect to the switch or router)
        - If you have a USB console port on the switch or router, you can connect a USB cable from the switch or router to your computer. Newer switches and routers have USB console ports.
        - If you have a serial console port on the switch or router, you can connect a console cable (known as a rollover cable) from the switch or router to the serial port on your computer.
        - If you have a serial port on the switch or router, but you don't have a serial port on your computer, you can connect a serial-to-USB cable on your computer

The console port on a switch or router says Console and is usually blue. Newer devices usually have both a USB and a serial console port. The console port is serial, but it is in the shape of an RJ-45.

To talk to the device, you must run a program called a terminal emulator. The most popular program is called PuTTY. The settings that you should configure in PuTTY

- 9600 bit rate
- No Flow Control
- 8-bit ASCII
- No parity bits
- 1 stop bit

These settings are usually default in PuTTY (except for the flow control).

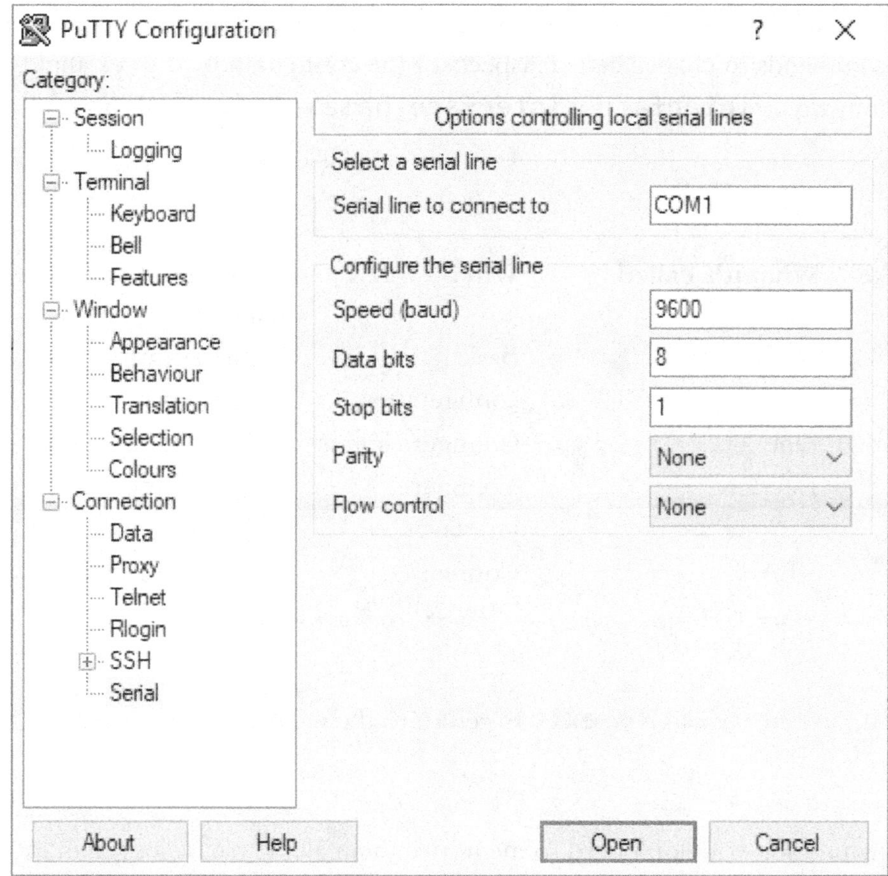

When we first console in to the switch or router, it will put us in the **user EXEC mode**. We can view settings but can't change any configuration.

We are in user mode if the prompt looks like

`Switch>`

If we type the **`enable`** command, we enter the **enable** mode. We can enter more commands in the enable mode. We still can't change the configuration. We can exit enable mode by typing **`disable`**.

We are in enable mode if the prompt looks like

`Switch#`

To change the configuration, we must enter the configuration mode. That is entered by typing **`configure terminal`**. We can exit the configuration mode by typing **`end`**. We can't enter configuration mode from user mode; we must be in enable mode first.

Even when we're in the configuration mode, we can only configure certain aspects of the device. We need to enter additional commands to change certain aspects of the configuration. For example, to configure an interface, we must type **`interface <interface name>`**. Summary of the configure modes

What the prompt looks like	What it's called	Why?	Command to get there?
Switch(config)#	Global	Basic configuration	**`configure terminal`**
Switch(config-line)#	Line	Configure logins	**`line console 0`**
Switch(config-if)#	Interface	Configure interfaces	**`interface <name>`**
Switch(config-vlan)#	VLAN	Configure VLANs	**`vlan <number>`**

From the config-line, config-if, or vlan, we can type **`exit`** to return to the main config prompt.

Some things to remember

- There are many commands and you don't need to memorize them all. If you're logged in to the switch, and you're not sure, type **`?`**
- If you're not sure about a specific command, type **`<command>?`**, where **`<command>`** is the name of the command.
- In enable mode, there are many commands that allow us to see the status of the device or certain aspects of it. These commands usually start with **`show`**. For example, the **`show ip interfaces`** command gives us a detailed status of the interfaces on a router.
- Many commands can accept a modifier at the end. A common modifier on the show commands is **`brief`**. The brief modifier gives us summary information. For example, the **`show ip interfaces brief`** command gives us a summary table containing the status of the interfaces on a router.
- Many configuration commands have modifiers as well. Going forward, I will write any command in **`this font`**. The parts of the command that you might need to change will have **`<>`** around them. For example **`ip address <IP address>`** requires you to enter an IP address in place of **`<IP address>`**. You might type **`ip address 192.168.0.1`**.

  When you have a choice of what to type, I might separate the options with a |. For example, **`switchport mode [trunk|access]`**, means that you must choose either trunk or access. You might enter **`switchport mode trunk`** or **`switchport mode access`**.

- In the configuration mode, many commands can be reversed by typing **no** in front of the command. For example, we can shut down an interface by typing **shutdown**. We can turn the interface back on by typing **no shutdown**.
- The switches and routers are smart. If we type only part of a command and there are no other matching commands, the device will execute the command.

  For example, we don't have to type the full command **write memory**. We can type **write mem**, or **wr memory**, or **wr mem**. There are no other commands that start with wr or mem, so the device knows what we are trying to type.

The console remembers the last ten commands that you typed. If you want to view a previous command, press the Up arrow. You can also press the down arrow. To edit, you can move the cursor left and right.

The configure terminal mode remembers the last ten commands that you typed in configure terminal mode, and the enable mode remembers the last ten commands that you typed in the enable mode. If you type some commands into the enable mode, and then enter configure terminal, you won't see those commands in your history.

We can view the commands we previously typed with **show history**. We can type **terminal history size <length>** to change size of the history buffer just for the session that we are in.

From the configure terminal mode, we can type **history size <length>** to change length of the history buffer for all sessions. For example, if I want to keep the buffer at a length of 40 commands, I would type **history size 40**.

The switch or router has three types of memory

- **Flash Memory** – the flash memory is where the switch stores its operating system and back up configuration files
- **ROM** – this is **Read Only Memory**, which helps the switch boot up and load its operating system
- **NVRAM** – the switch stores its main configuration file in the NVRAM. When the switch boots up, it loads its configuration from the NVRAM
- **RAM** – when the switch boots up, it loads its operating system into the RAM. Then it loads its configuration into the RAM.

There are two types of configuration files

- The **startup-config** is the configuration file that loads when the switch is powered on
- The **running-config** is the configuration file that the switch is using while it is powered on. The running-config comes from the startup-config (when the switch boots it copies the startup-config into the running-config).

  If we change the config, only the running-config is updated. Any change to the config is **live immediately**; there is no need to save changes, but if we reboot the switch, the startup-config returns and all of our changes are lost.

  Therefore, we need to save the running-config (overwrite the startup-config with the running-config) so that the changes are saved.

If I want to see the config on the device, I can type

- **`show startup-config`** to view the startup-config
- **`show running-config`** to view the running-config

The device will only show the first few lines of the configuration (or of any lengthy output). If we want to see more, we just press Enter.

If I want to save my configuration changes, I can type **`copy running-config startup-config`**, which means that I want to copy my running-config (which I just changed) overtop of the startup-config. I could also type **`write memory`**.

To erase the existing configuration, I can type

- **`write erase`**
- **`erase startup-config`**
- **`erase nvram:`**

and then reboot the device. When the device reboots, its configuration will be blank. I can reboot the device by typing **`reload`**.

If I want to change the name of the device (the hostname), I type **`hostname <name>`**

If I want to add some security, I have three options

- Security to protect the user mode with a password (through the console)
    - **line console 0** – now I've entered the login configuration mode (for the console only; this doesn't apply to users who connect over Telnet or SSH)
        - **login** – this tells the switch/router to prompt for a password for the user mode
        - **password <password>** - where <password> is the password I want to use
- Security to protect the user mode with a password (through the Telnet/SSH)
    - **line vty 0 15** – now I've entered the login configuration mode (for the Telnet/SSH only)
        - **login** – this tells the switch/router to prompt for a password for the user mode
        - **password <password>** - where <password> is the password I want to use
- Security to protect the enable mode. I configure the following
    - **enable secret <password>** - this requires us to enter a password when we enter the enable mode
    - I could also write **enable password <password>**- but this is less secure
    - If I wanted to remove the password, I could type **no enable password**

We will look at security in more detail in Section Five.

A few things to note

- If we are logged in to a device via a console cable, then every time a status changes, the switch or router posts a message in the console. These messages can get annoying. We can suppress the messages by typing **no logging console**
- The device will log you out of the enable mode times out after five minutes of in activity. **exec timeout <minutes> <seconds>** can change the timeout. If we wrote **exec timeout 0 0**, the switch would never timeout.
- In exec mode, if you type in an unknown command, the switch or router thinks that you are trying to Telnet into another device. It performs a DNS lookup and fails, which forces you wait about a minute. You can suppress this behavior by typing **no ip domain-lookup**

On a switch, we can troubleshoot connected devices

- I can see the MAC address table by typing **show mac address-table**. If I want to search for a specific MAC address, I type **show mac address-table address <address>**

```
Switch>show mac address-table
          Mac Address Table
-------------------------------------------

Vlan    Mac Address       Type        Ports
----    -----------       --------    -----
1       0001.2222.3333    DYNAMIC     Fa0/1
1       0001.2222.3334    DYNAMIC     Fa0/2

Switch>
```

  For example, **show mac address-table address 0001.2222.3334** will only show entries with the MAC address 0001.2222.3334. This is useful for when the MAC Address Table has many entries and we can't read through all of them.

- If I want to filter MAC addresses based on the interface that it was learned on, I can type **show mac address-table dynamic interface <interface name>**, where interface name is the interface name.

  For example, **show mac address-table dynamic interface Fa0/1** will only show entries on port Fa0/1.

- If I want to filter MAC addresses based on the VLAN that it was learned on, I can type show **mac address-table dynamic vlan <VLAN number>**, where VLAN number is the VLAN number.

  For example, **show mac address-table dynamic vlan 1** will only show entries on VLAN 1.

The entries in the table stay there for 300 seconds (5 minutes). If the traffic comes in, the timer is reset to zero. We can change the aging time to something else

- **mac address-table aging-time <time>** - we can change the aging time globally
- **mac address-table aging-time <time> vlan <VLAN number**> - we can change the aging time per VLAN

If the table fills up, the oldest entries are removed, even if they were seen after than the aging time. We can fit about 8000 entries in the table. We can manually clear the table of the entries, by typing

- **`clear mac address-table dynamic vlan <vlan number>`** - clears all the MAC addresses associated with a specific VLAN
- **`clear mac address-table dynamic interface <interface number>`** - clear all the MAC addresses associated with a specific interface
- **`clear mac address-table dynamic address <MAC address>`** - clear entries associated with a specific MAC address
- **`clear mac address-table dynamic`** – clears the entire table

If I want to see the status of each interface, I can type **`show ip interface brief`**. If I want to see more details, I can type **`show ip interfaces`**. Below is the output of my interface command, showing that all the interfaces are down.

```
Switch>show ip interface brief
Interface              IP-Address      OK? Method Status                Protocol
FastEthernet0/1        unassigned      YES manual down                  down
FastEthernet0/2        unassigned      YES manual down                  down
FastEthernet0/3        unassigned      YES manual down                  down
FastEthernet0/4        unassigned      YES manual down                  down
FastEthernet0/5        unassigned      YES manual down                  down
FastEthernet0/6        unassigned      YES manual down                  down
FastEthernet0/7        unassigned      YES manual down                  down
FastEthernet0/8        unassigned      YES manual down                  down
FastEthernet0/9        unassigned      YES manual down                  down
FastEthernet0/10       unassigned      YES manual down                  down
FastEthernet0/11       unassigned      YES manual down                  down
FastEthernet0/12       unassigned      YES manual down                  down
FastEthernet0/13       unassigned      YES manual down                  down
FastEthernet0/14       unassigned      YES manual down                  down
FastEthernet0/15       unassigned      YES manual down                  down
FastEthernet0/16       unassigned      YES manual down                  down
FastEthernet0/17       unassigned      YES manual down                  down
FastEthernet0/18       unassigned      YES manual down                  down
FastEthernet0/19       unassigned      YES manual down                  down
FastEthernet0/20       unassigned      YES manual down                  down
FastEthernet0/21       unassigned      YES manual down                  down
FastEthernet0/22       unassigned      YES manual down                  down
FastEthernet0/23       unassigned      YES manual down                  down
FastEthernet0/24       unassigned      YES manual down                  down
GigabitEthernet0/1     unassigned      YES manual down                  down
GigabitEthernet0/2     unassigned      YES manual down                  down
Vlan1                  unassigned      YES manual administratively down down
Switch>
```

On a switch, by default, each interface is enabled. When the interface is disabled, we say that it is shutdown. On a router, by default, each interface is disabled.

When we run the show ip interface brief command, we can see the "status" and "protocol" columns. The status tells us whether the interface is physically connected to another device and receiving an electrical signal. The protocol tells us whether the interface is receiving traffic.

The status might be down if there is no cable connected to it, there is a cable connected to it but the cable is damaged, there is a cable connected to it and to another device, but the other device is powered off or its port is shutdown.

We type **shutdown** to disables an interface. The status of the interface becomes "administratively down". We type **no shutdown** to enable the interface.

In the below example, I configured **no shutdown** on Interface F0/1. I first had to enter the configuration mode, and then I had to enter the Interface F0/1 configuration mode.

```
Switch#conf t
Enter configuration commands, one per line.  End with CNTL/Z.
Switch(config)#interface f0/1
Switch(config-if)#no shutdown
Switch(config-if)#exit
Switch(config)#exit
Switch#
%SYS-5-CONFIG_I: Configured from console by console
```

When we connect two devices together, they will agree on a speed and duplex setting through a process called auto-negotiation. We can manually change the speed and duplex setting on an interface.

- **duplex [auto | full | half]** will adjust the interface's duplex setting. Choosing auto allows it to automatically negotiate the speed. For example, **duplex half** will set the interface to half duplex.
- **speed [auto | 10 | 100 | 1000]** will adjust the interface's speed setting. For example, **speed 100** will set the interface speed to 100 mbps.

We can add a description to an interface by typing **description <text>**. This command is useful for human viewers of the configuration but has no effect on the device.

In the below example, I set the description to "connection to router", the speed to 100 and the duplex to auto.

```
Switch#conf t
Enter configuration commands, one per line.  End with CNTL/Z.
Switch(config)#interface f0/1
Switch(config-if)#no shutdown
Switch(config-if)#speed 100
Switch(config-if)#duplex auto
Switch(config-if)#description connection to router
Switch(config-if)#exit
Switch(config)#exit
Switch#
```

I checked the configuration after making these changes. Notice that "no shutdown" is missing. When we configure a shutdown or no shutdown command, it doesn't appear in the configuration of the interface, but it does appear in the status of the switch interface.

Also, notice that "duplex auto" is missing. When we set the speed or duplex to auto, the switch doesn't list the setting in the configuration.

```
!
interface FastEthernet0/1
 description connection to router
 speed 100
!
```

A switch has 24 or 48 interfaces. If I don't want to configure each one manually, I can type **interface range <Interface Type> <first port> - <last port>**. Then I can enter the configuration for all the ports in the range at the same time. The switch automatically creates configurations for each interface in the range.

The switch is very picky about this command. A switch will have ports named something like FastEthernet0/1, FastEthernet0/2, FastEthernet0/3, etc. Usually the port numbers start with "0/". We can normally write FE0/1, FE0/2, FE0/3, etc. We could even write F0/1, F0/2, F0/3, etc. and the switch would understand.

If we had a Gigabit Ethernet switch, our ports would be called GigabitEthernet0/1, GigabitEthernet0/2, GigabitEthernet0/3, etc. We can normally write GE0/1, GE0/2, GE0/3, etc. We could even write G0/1, G0/2, G0/3, etc. and the switch would understand.

With this command, we must type the interface type in full, and we must add the "0/" in front of the first port in the range, and we must type the dash with a space before and after it.

```
Switch#conf t
Enter configuration commands, one per line.  End with CNTL/Z.
Switch(config)#interface range FastEthernet 0/10 - 0/20
                                                    ^
% Invalid input detected at '^' marker.

Switch(config)#interface range FastEthernet 10 - 20
                                               ^
% Invalid input detected at '^' marker.

Switch(config)#interface range FastEthernet 0/10 - 20
Switch(config-if-range)#speed 10
Switch(config-if-range)#duplex full
Switch(config-if-range)#exit
Switch(config)#exit
Switch#
```

If I want to remove a setting from an interface, I must first enter the configuration for that interface. I could also enter a range of interfaces and remove a setting from all of them.

- **no duplex** – removes the duplex setting

- **`no speed`** – removes the speed setting
- **`no description`** – removes the description

When two devices are connected and try to auto-negotiate, they choose the best speed that each can handle (10, 100, or 1000 mbps). They also choose the best duplex that both can handle (full or half).

If we configure the speed and duplex manually, auto-negotiation is disabled. What if one device has auto-negotiation and the other device is hardcoded with a specific speed or duplex? The side that has auto-negotiation will default to the slowest speed – 10, 100, or 1000. It will default to half duplex (if the speed is 10 or 100) or full duplex (if the speed is 1000).

If one side is set to 10 mbps full duplex, or 100 mbps full duplex, the switch with auto-negotiation will set itself to 10 half duplex and the link won't work.

A Cisco switch will always try to detect the link speed and use that. If it doesn't work, then the switch will default to a speed of 10. A speed of 1000 is always full duplex, so the connection won't fail if one side is hardcoded for 1000 full duplex and the other side is set to auto-negotiate.

We can type show interfaces status to view the speed, duplex, and connection status of an interface. Notice that the speed says "a-100". If the interface is set to auto-negotiate, it will display an "a-" before the speed or duplex.

```
Switch#show interfaces status
Port      Name                Status       Vlan       Duplex  Speed Type
Fa0/1                         notconnect   1          auto    a-100 10/100BaseTX
Fa0/2                         notconnect   1          auto    auto  10/100BaseTX
Fa0/3                         notconnect   1          auto    auto  10/100BaseTX
Fa0/4                         notconnect   1          auto    auto  10/100BaseTX
Fa0/5                         notconnect   1          auto    auto  10/100BaseTX
```

Going back to my earlier example,

```
Switch>show ip interface brief
Interface              IP-Address      OK? Method Status                Protocol
FastEthernet0/1        unassigned      YES manual down                  down
FastEthernet0/2        unassigned      YES manual down                  down
FastEthernet0/3        unassigned      YES manual down                  down
FastEthernet0/4        unassigned      YES manual down                  down
FastEthernet0/5        unassigned      YES manual down                  down
FastEthernet0/6        unassigned      YES manual down                  down
FastEthernet0/7        unassigned      YES manual down                  down
FastEthernet0/8        unassigned      YES manual down                  down
FastEthernet0/9        unassigned      YES manual down                  down
FastEthernet0/10       unassigned      YES manual down                  down
FastEthernet0/11       unassigned      YES manual down                  down
FastEthernet0/12       unassigned      YES manual down                  down
FastEthernet0/13       unassigned      YES manual down                  down
FastEthernet0/14       unassigned      YES manual down                  down
FastEthernet0/15       unassigned      YES manual down                  down
FastEthernet0/16       unassigned      YES manual down                  down
FastEthernet0/17       unassigned      YES manual down                  down
FastEthernet0/18       unassigned      YES manual down                  down
FastEthernet0/19       unassigned      YES manual down                  down
FastEthernet0/20       unassigned      YES manual down                  down
FastEthernet0/21       unassigned      YES manual down                  down
FastEthernet0/22       unassigned      YES manual down                  down
FastEthernet0/23       unassigned      YES manual down                  down
FastEthernet0/24       unassigned      YES manual down                  down
GigabitEthernet0/1     unassigned      YES manual down                  down
GigabitEthernet0/2     unassigned      YES manual down                  down
Vlan1                  unassigned      YES manual administratively down down
Switch>
```

Below is a summary of what the combination of status and protocol means for the connection

Status	Protocol	Meaning
Administratively down	Down	Disabled by the administrator
Down	Down	Not connected physically
Up	Down	Connected physically, but there may be a communication error
Down	Down (err-disabled)	Err-disabled for security reasons (more on this later)
Up	Up	Connected and functioning

When the status is up and the protocol is up, the interface is working. We might say that the interface is "**up/up**", or "**up and up**". It is common to write the interface status and protocol as status/protocol.

If we want more information about an interface, we can type **show interface**. What can we learn from the **show interface** command?

```
Switch>show interface
FastEthernet0/1 is down, line protocol is down (disabled)
  Hardware is Lance, address is 0003.e42b.1601 (bia 0003.e42b.1601)
  Description: connection to router
 BW 100000 Kbit, DLY 1000 usec,
     reliability 255/255, txload 1/255, rxload 1/255
  Encapsulation ARPA, loopback not set
  Keepalive set (10 sec)
  Full-duplex, 100Mb/s
  input flow-control is off, output flow-control is off
  ARP type: ARPA, ARP Timeout 04:00:00
  Last input 00:00:08, output 00:00:05, output hang never
  Last clearing of "show interface" counters never
  Input queue: 0/75/0/0 (size/max/drops/flushes); Total output drops: 0
  Queueing strategy: fifo
  Output queue :0/40 (size/max)
  5 minute input rate 0 bits/sec, 0 packets/sec
  5 minute output rate 0 bits/sec, 0 packets/sec
     956 packets input, 193351 bytes, 0 no buffer
     Received 956 broadcasts, 40 runts, 30 giants, 0 throttles
     10 input errors, 10 CRC, 10 frame, 0 overrun, 0 ignored, 0 abort
     0 watchdog, 0 multicast, 0 pause input
     0 input packets with dribble condition detected
     2357 packets output, 263570 bytes, 0 underruns
     20 output errors, 10 collisions, 10 interface resets
     0 babbles, 10 late collision, 0 deferred
     0 lost carrier, 0 no carrier
     0 output buffer failures, 0 output buffers swapped out
```

- Speed and duplex of the interface
- Whether the speed and duplex are set automatically
- Statistics
    - Packets input – number of packets (frames) received on the interface
    - Packets output – number of packets (frames) sent on the interface
- Error Statistics

- Runts – number of frames that arrived too small. Runts are usually due to collisions
    - Giants – number of frames that arrived too big.
    - CRC – number of frames that did not pass the FCS (Frame Check Sequence). CRC errors could be caused by a bad cable.
    - Frame – number of frames that arrived in an illegal format.
    - Errors – total number of frames that arrived as runts, giants, or with CRC or other errors.
- Output Errors – total number of frames that could not be forwarded due to an error
- Collisions – total number of collisions that happened while the interface was forwarding a frame
- Late Collisions – total number of collisions that happened after the 64th byte. If the duplex settings on both devices (the switch and whatever is connected to the switch) match, there shouldn't be any late collisions because they will be detected.

Okay, now we can get to the real topic of VLANs. Remember that on a typical network, every device connects to a switch, kind of like the one in the photo below?

All these devices make up the LAN (Local Area Network). That makes the entire switch was a broadcast domain – if I send a broadcast frame from one device, it is broadcast to every device connected to the switch.

What if we wanted to plug a bunch of devices into the switch but we didn't want them to see each other's traffic? For example, we have some surveillance cameras on our network but we don't want any random users to access them.

We could create a **VLAN** or **Virtual Local Area Network**. A VLAN segments the broadcast domain into multiple domains. Each port on the switch is assigned to a single VLAN. Whatever device we plug into the switch assumes the VLAN configured on its port.

For example, we create a VLAN and call it VLAN 20. Ports 10 through 19 are assigned to VLAN 20. Now any device that is connected on ports 10 through 19 are on VLAN 20 and can communicate with each other. If we connect a device to Port 30, it won't be able to communicate with the devices connected on Ports 10 through 19.

If a device connected on Port 10 for example sends a broadcast message, the switch doesn't flood that message on all its ports – only on Ports 10 through 19. That is because the VLAN is also a broadcast domain.

The benefit of VLANs is clear: without VLANs, we would have to build a different physical network for each set of devices that we wanted to keep separate. That may not be physically possible in a large network or in an older building.

- We are reducing the amount of work that the switch must perform, because each broadcast domain becomes smaller
- We are improving security because less hosts can see broadcast data
- We can increase security by separating users and other types of devices into different VLANs

Simple switches do not support VLANs. These are commonly known as unmanaged switches. On an unmanaged switch, all the ports belong to VLAN 1 and there is no option to add additional VLANs.

On a managed switch, the default VLAN is VLAN 1, but we can create additional VLANs.

2.2 Configure and verify interswitch connectivity

2.2.a Trunk ports

2.2.b 802.1Q

2.2.c Native VLAN

What if we have a large network with multiple switches? We want to connect the switches together. We choose a port on switch one, and a port on switch two, and connect them with a patch cable. On each switch, these ports are known as Trunk ports.

A **Trunk** port carries traffic for multiple VLANs. Each frame is tagged with its VLAN while being transferred between trunk ports.

Other ports are known as **Access** ports. An Access port belongs to a single VLAN. We need access ports because devices such as computers can't tag their own data with a VLAN (and if they could it would be a major security risk because a rogue device can change the VLAN that it's on)

The switch assumes that traffic passing through an access port belongs to the VLAN assigned to the port. The standard for VLANs is called **802.1Q** – it allows switches from different manufacturers to understand each other's VLANs.

The Cisco standard is called **Inter-Switch Link** (**ISL**), but it is not popular. Let's take another look at the Ethernet header

Ethernet Header						**Data**	**Ethernet Trailer**
Preamble	SFD	Destination	Source	Tag	Type		FCS

With 802.1Q, between the source and type, we add a **Tag** field, which contains additional fields

- Type
- Priority
- Flag
- VLAN ID

The VLAN IDs range from 1 to 4096. VLAN 1 is the default VLAN that comes with every switch. VLANs 1002, 1003, 1004, and 1005 cannot be used or deleted, but nobody knows why.

When we pass traffic over a trunk port, we must tag it with a VLAN ID so that the other switch knows which VLAN it belongs to and can send it to the correct destination. An access port does not tag frames with VLANs.

Each trunk port can be configured to transfer data for one or more VLANs. We don't have to transfer data for all the VLANs on every trunk port. For example, we might have VLANs 1, 2, 3, and 4 on our switch. If we set Port 48 to be our trunk port, we might choose to transfer only VLANs 1 and 2 over it. We might also set Port 47 as a trunk port and choose to transfer only VLANs 3 and 4 over it.

Every trunk port must have one VLAN called the native VLAN. Data travelling over the native VLAN is not tagged. The native VLAN must be the same on all switches that connect to each other. We need a native VLAN in case we connect a switch to another switch that doesn't understand VLANs – the switch that doesn't understand VLANs will not tag any data but will transfer it.

This brings us to our next point: Tagging and Untagging ports. An access port is known as an **untagging port** or **untagged port**, because it strips the VLAN tags off any traffic it receives and because traffic passes through the port untagged. A trunk port is known as a **tagging port** or a **tagged port**, because it adds VLAN tags to any traffic it receives, and because traffic passes through the port tagged. The receiving switch removes the tag.

If I didn't have a trunk port, I would need to connect a cable from each VLAN to each switch.

For example, if I have two 48 port switches, and I created the following VLANs on each switch

- Ports 1 through 12 are on VLAN 1
- Ports 13 through 24 are on VLAN 2
- Ports 25 through 36 are on VLAN 3
- Ports 37 through 48 are on VLAN 4

I would need four cables to connect the VLANs. Maybe I connect the following

- Port 1 on Switch 1 to Port 1 on Switch 2 transfers VLAN 1 data
- Port 13 on Switch 1 to Port 13 on Switch 2 transfers VLAN 2 data
- Port 25 on Switch 1 to Port 25 on Switch 2 transfers VLAN 3 data
- Port 37 on Switch 1 to Port 37 on Switch 2 transfers VLAN 4 data

This wastes eight ports. If I have more than four VLANs, it would waste even more ports. But if I configure Port 48 on each switch as a trunk port, I can transfer all the VLAN data over it.

Access ports on a Cisco switch can be configured with two VLANs. Why? In a large organization using VoIP, the VoIP phones are connected on one VLAN and the computers are connected on another VLAN. In many cases, a user connects a VoIP phone to a switch and a computer to the

VoIP phone. This is known as **IP Passthrough** because the phone passes the computer's traffic through to the switch. The main advantage is that the organization only requires one physical cable per user. The Cisco switch knows how to separate VoIP and user traffic.

Before we connect switches, we need to make sure that the same VLANs are configured on all the switches and that they are correct.

For example

- VLAN 1 is for users
- VLAN 2 is for management
- VLAN 3 is for VoIP phones
- VLAN 4 is for surveillance cameras

Our VLAN scheme must be the same on all the switches in our organization. If we mess up and use VLAN 2 for VoIP phones on another switch for example, the network will malfunction, and the phones won't be able to connect to the network. This also introduces security risks.

We must make sure that VLAN 1 on Switch 1 is VLAN 1 on Switch 2, VLAN 2 on Switch 1 is VLAN 2 on Switch 2, etc.

The switches can learn the VLANs automatically through **VLAN Trunking Protocol**, or **VTP**.

When you create a VLAN on one switch, it advertises the VLAN to other switches so that they automatically configure themselves. VTP can add or delete VLANs.

We can type **`vtp mode transparent`** to turn it on and **`vtp mode off`** to turn it off. When we use VTP, we configure the VLAN on 'server' switches. Client switches copy the VLAN data from server switches.

I said that each VLAN is a separate subnet. Each VLAN is like a separate physical network. How does traffic get from a device on one VLAN to a device on another VLAN? We can connect a router to our switch and route traffic between VLANs. Or we can use a **Layer 3 Switch**, also known as a **multilayer switch**.

Consider the following. I have device aaaa and cccc on VLAN 1 and bbbb and dddd on VLAN 2. They can't talk to each other.

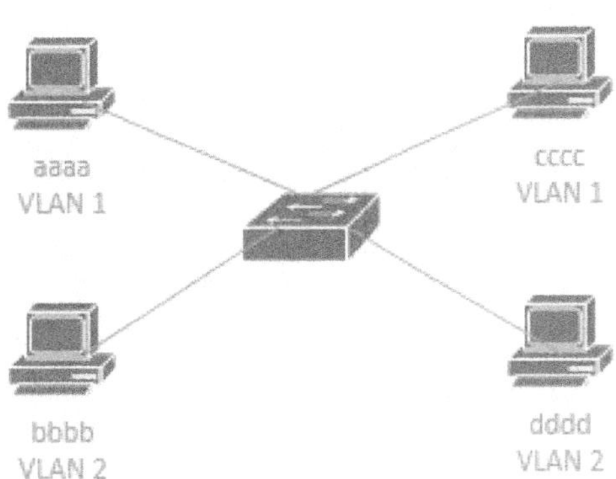

I need to add a router so that the devices can transfer data between VLANs. But I would need to connect the router to all the VLANs. I could either connect a physical cable from the router to a switch port on each VLAN, or I could connect the router to a trunk port on the switch. Sometimes this setup is called **Router on a Stick** or **ROAS**.

Or I could avoid using a router by using a Layer 3 switch.

How do we configure a VLAN on a switch?

- Enter the configuration mode
    - Type **`vlan <VLAN number>`**
        - **`name <name>`** - we can give the VLAN a descriptive name, but this is optional. Spaces aren't allowed in the name.
- Go back to each interface
    - **`interface <interface number>`**
        - **`switchport access vlan <VLAN number>`** - this gives the port its default VLAN. The default is 1.
        - **`switchport voice vlan <vlan number>`** - if we have a voice VLAN, we can add an additional VLAN for a VoIP phone.
        - **`switchport mode access`** – this tells the switch that the port is in access mode instead of trunking mode

In this example, I configured interface F0/4 as an access port. I added it to VLAN 4. I also added it to voice VLAN 5. Neither VLAN 4 nor VLAN 5 existed, so the switch informed me that it created them once they were added to the port.

Then I created VLAN 7 and tried to call it "Hazim said so", but the switch rejected this description because it had a space in it. I settled with calling it "Hazim".

```
Switch>enable
Switch#conf t
Enter configuration commands, one per line.  End with CNTL/Z.
Switch(config)#interface F0/4
Switch(config-if)#switchport access vlan 4
% Access VLAN does not exist. Creating vlan 4
Switch(config-if)#switchport voice vlan 5
% Voice VLAN does not exist. Creating vlan 5
Switch(config-if)#switchport mode access
Switch(config-if)#exit
Switch(config)#vlan 7
Switch(config-vlan)#name Hazim said so
                               ^
% Invalid input detected at '^' marker.

Switch(config-vlan)#name Hazim
```

Remember, we can configure a range of interfaces with a VLAN, all at the same time.

If we add a port to a VLAN that doesn't exist, the switch automatically creates the VLAN, and then adds the ports to it.

Packets in the voice VLAN are tagged by the phone. An access port with a voice VLAN is like a mini-trunk port, but we don't need to think about it as a real trunk. The switch won't list it as a trunk port.

We can view the VLANs on a switch by typing **`show vlan brief`**. We can also see each port assigned to each VLAN. If we type **`show vlan id <VLAN number>`** we can view more details about a specific VLAN.

When I ran **`show vlan brief`** on my switch, it showed me that VLANs 1, 3, 4, 5, and 7 are active on my switch. All the ports are on VLAN 1, which is the default VLAN (according to its name), except for Port 4. Port 4 is on VLANs 4 and 5.

VLANs 3 and 7 exist but aren't assigned to any ports.

```
Switch#show vlan brief

VLAN Name                             Status    Ports
---- -------------------------------- --------- -------------------------------
1    default                          active    Fa0/1, Fa0/2, Fa0/3, Fa0/5
                                                Fa0/6, Fa0/7, Fa0/8, Fa0/9
                                                Fa0/10, Fa0/11, Fa0/12, Fa0/13
                                                Fa0/14, Fa0/15, Fa0/16, Fa0/17
                                                Fa0/18, Fa0/19, Fa0/20, Fa0/21
                                                Fa0/22, Fa0/23, Fa0/24, Gig0/1
                                                Gig0/2
3    VLAN0003                         active
4    VLAN0004                         active    Fa0/4
5    VLAN0005                         active    Fa0/4
7    Hazim                            active
1002 fddi-default                     active
1003 token-ring-default               active
1004 fddinet-default                  active
1005 trnet-default                    active
```

How do we configure a trunk port on a switch? We go back to the interface configuration and type **`switchport mode trunk`**, then the port becomes a trunk.

Cisco switches use **DTP** or **Dynamic Trunking Protocol** to communicate. When we connect an interface on one switch to an interface on another switch, the two switches decide if they should negotiate a trunk. They decide how they are going to communicate the trunking data.

When configuring a trunk port, we can choose what protocol to use – either 802.1Q or ISL. Remember that many switches only support 802.1Q. If the two switch supports both protocols, they can decide what protocol to use. The use of the protocol might be known as encapsulation.

We can also choose the port's administrative mode. There are three choices – always trunk (the port will always be a trunk port), never trunk (the port will never be a trunk port), or negotiate (the port will turn on trunking when connected to a trunk port on another switch; otherwise it will operate as an access port).

How do we configure the trunking settings? We enter the interface configuration.

- **`switchport trunk encapsulation [dot1q | isl | negotiate]`**. This lets us choose whether the port must use 802.1q encapsulation, ISL encapsulation, or will negotiate encapsulation with another switch.

- **`switchport mode [access|trunk|dynamic desirable|dynamic auto]`**. This lets us choose the type of port
    - **`access`** – always operate as an access port

- **trunk** – always operate as a trunk port
- **dynamic desirable** – sends a negotiation message to the other switch to create a trunk and listens for negotiation messages from the other switch. If messages are received, it will create a trunk.
- **dynamic auto** – only listens for negotiation messages from the other switch to create a trunk. If messages are received, it will create a trunk.

Why do we bother with a dynamic auto setting? Maybe we want the switch to connect to another switch over a single VLAN and not trunk. If ports on two different switches are set to dynamic auto, and are connected, they won't establish a trunk.

In the example below, I configured port 24 to be a trunk port and to use 802.1Q encapsulation.

Notice that the switch didn't accept my trunk encapsulation command. Why? The proprietary ISL trunking protocol is not supported on many switches – Cisco is taking it out. If the switch doesn't support ISL, then by default the only trunking protocol available is 802.1Q and there is no way (or need) to configure it.

```
Switch>enable
Switch#conf t
Enter configuration commands, one per line.  End with CNTL/Z.
Switch(config)#Interface F0/24
Switch(config-if)#switchport mode trunk
Switch(config-if)#switchport trunk encapsulation dot1q
                                   ^
% Invalid input detected at '^' marker.

Switch(config-if)#
```

When we want to turn off negotiation, we type **switchport nonegotiate**

show interfaces <interface name> switchport tells us about the VLAN status of a particular switch port.

Looking at the VLAN status of port 24, I can see that it is set to trunk, its encapsulation is 802.1Q, and its native VLAN is 1.

```
Switch#show interfaces F0/24 switchport
Name: Fa0/24
Switchport: Enabled
Administrative Mode: trunk
Operational Mode: down
Administrative Trunking Encapsulation: dot1q
Operational Trunking Encapsulation: dot1q
Negotiation of Trunking: On
Access Mode VLAN: 1 (default)
Trunking Native Mode VLAN: 1 (default)
Voice VLAN: none
Administrative private-vlan host-association: none
Administrative private-vlan mapping: none
Administrative private-vlan trunk native VLAN: none
Administrative private-vlan trunk encapsulation: dot1q
Administrative private-vlan trunk normal VLANs: none
Administrative private-vlan trunk private VLANs: none
Operational private-vlan: none
Trunking VLANs Enabled: All
Pruning VLANs Enabled: 2-1001
Capture Mode Disabled
Capture VLANs Allowed: ALL
Protected: false
Unknown unicast blocked: disabled
Unknown multicast blocked: disabled
Appliance trust: none
```

Looking at the VLAN status of port 24, I can see that it is set to access, its encapsulation is 802.1Q, its default VLAN is 4, and its voice VLAN is 5. Notice also that it has a native VLAN of 5.

```
Switch#show interfaces F0/4 switchport
Name: Fa0/4
Switchport: Enabled
Administrative Mode: static access
Operational Mode: down
Administrative Trunking Encapsulation: dot1q
Operational Trunking Encapsulation: native
Negotiation of Trunking: Off
Access Mode VLAN: 4 (VLAN0004)
Trunking Native Mode VLAN: 1 (default)
Voice VLAN: 5
Administrative private-vlan host-association: none
Administrative private-vlan mapping: none
Administrative private-vlan trunk native VLAN: none
Administrative private-vlan trunk encapsulation: dot1q
Administrative private-vlan trunk normal VLANs: none
Administrative private-vlan trunk private VLANs: none
Operational private-vlan: none
Trunking VLANs Enabled: All
Pruning VLANs Enabled: 2-1001
Capture Mode Disabled
Capture VLANs Allowed: ALL
Protected: false
Unknown unicast blocked: disabled
Unknown multicast blocked: disabled
Appliance trust: none
```

In summary, the command shows

- Administrative Mode – what the port is configured for (trunk or access).
- Operational Mode – if the port is configured to negotiate a trunk, then this tells us whether the port successfully configured a trunk, is operating in access mode, or is down.
- Administrative Trunking Encapsulation – what kind of encapsulation the port is set to.
- Operational Trunking Encapsulation – if the port is configured to negotiate an encapsulation, and is operating in trunk mode, this tells us the encapsulation protocol that the port chose to use.

Just like interfaces, we can shutdown VLANs. We just go to the VLAN interface configuration and type **`shutdown`**. We can turn the VLAN back on by typing **`no shutdown`**.

A switch will not forward a frame belonging to an unknown VLAN or to a shutdown VLAN. For example, my switch has VLANs 1, 3, 4, and 5 configured, but 5 is shut down. If my switch receives traffic on its trunk port that is tagged with VLAN 5, it will drop the traffic. If my switch receives traffic on its trunk port that is tagged with VLAN 6, it will drop the traffic.

In the example below, I tried to shutdown VLAN 4, but the switch gave me an error. We can't shutdown the VLAN from the VLAN configuration – only from the VLAN interface configuration. Notice that there are two separate configurations – one to configure the VLAN's settings and one to configure it as an interface.

Notice also that as soon as I entered the VLAN 4 interface configuration, the switch changed VLAN 4's status to up. By default, when we create a VLAN its status is set to down, not up. We don't want to create a VLAN and have it transmit data right away – we might need to configure some settings first.

```
Switch(config)#vlan 4
Switch(config-vlan)#shutdown
                    ^
% Invalid input detected at '^' marker.

Switch(config-vlan)#exit
Switch(config)#interface vlan 4
Switch(config-if)#
%LINK-5-CHANGED: Interface Vlan4, changed state to up

Switch(config-if)#shutdown

Switch(config-if)#
%LINK-5-CHANGED: Interface Vlan4, changed state to administratively down

Switch(config-if)#exit
Switch(config)#exit
Switch#
%SYS-5-CONFIG_I: Configured from console by console
```

We can type **show vlan** to view the VLAN status.

```
Switch#show vlan

VLAN Name                             Status    Ports
---- -------------------------------- --------- -------------------------------
1    default                          active    Fa0/1, Fa0/2, Fa0/3, Fa0/5
                                                Fa0/6, Fa0/7, Fa0/8, Fa0/9
                                                Fa0/10, Fa0/11, Fa0/12, Fa0/13
                                                Fa0/14, Fa0/15, Fa0/16, Fa0/17
                                                Fa0/18, Fa0/19, Fa0/20, Fa0/21
                                                Fa0/22, Fa0/23, Fa0/24, Gig0/1
                                                Gig0/2
3    VLAN0003                         active
4    VLAN0004                         active    Fa0/4
5    VLAN0005                         active    Fa0/4
7    Hazim                            active
1002 fddi-default                     active
1003 token-ring-default               active
1004 fddinet-default                  active
1005 trnet-default                    active
```

Notice that the VLAN 4 is still "active". To see whether it is up or down, I need to type **`show ip interface brief`**.

```
Switch#show ip int brief
Interface              IP-Address      OK? Method Status                Protocol
FastEthernet0/1        unassigned      YES manual down                  down
Vlan1                  unassigned      YES manual administratively down down
Vlan4                  unassigned      YES manual administratively down down
Vlan5                  unassigned      YES manual up                    down
Switch#
Switch#
```

Two switches won't form a trunk if

- One switch has the port on access and the other switch has the port on trunk – only frames tagged with the native VLAN will be forwarded
- Both switches use dynamic auto – only frames tagged with the native VLAN will be forwarded; tagged frames will be dropped.

If we type **`show interfaces trunk`**, the switch will show details about all the established trunk interfaces.

- VLANs allowed on the trunk – all the VLANs are allowed by default unless we have specified a specific set of VLANs

- VLANs allowed and active – VLANs allowed, except for VLANs we learned about from other switches and VLANs we shut down
- VLANs allowed in STP and not pruned – VLANs allowed, except for VLANs we learned from other switches or shut down or in an STP blocking state

```
Switch# show interfaces trunk
Port        Mode    Encapsulation    Status    Native vlan
Fa0/3       on      802.1q           trunking  1
Port        Vlans allowed on trunk
Fa0/3       1, 2, 3
Port        Vlans allowed and active in management domain
Fa0/3       1, 2, 3
Port        Vlans in spanning tree forwarding state and not pruned
Fa0/3       1, 2, 3
```

If we type **show interface <interface name> switchport**, it will give us details about a specific physical trunk port

```
Switch#show interface f0/24 switchport
Name: Fa0/24
Switchport: Enabled
Administrative Mode: trunk
Operational Mode: down
Administrative Trunking Encapsulation: dot1q
Operational Trunking Encapsulation: dot1q
Negotiation of Trunking: On
Access Mode VLAN: 1 (default)
Trunking Native Mode VLAN: 1 (default)
Voice VLAN: none
Administrative private-vlan host-association: none
Administrative private-vlan mapping: none
Administrative private-vlan trunk native VLAN: none
Administrative private-vlan trunk encapsulation: dot1q
Administrative private-vlan trunk normal VLANs: none
Administrative private-vlan trunk private VLANs: none
Operational private-vlan: none
Trunking VLANs Enabled: All
Pruning VLANs Enabled: 2-1001
Capture Mode Disabled
Capture VLANs Allowed: ALL
Protected: false
Unknown unicast blocked: disabled
Unknown multicast blocked: disabled
Appliance trust: none
```

By default, all VLANs are forwarded on all trunk ports. In the trunk port configuration, I can limit the VLANs by typing **switchport trunk allowed vlan <beginning of range>-<end of range>**.

For example, I have decided to allow only VLANs 5 through 20 on Interface F0/24 (port 24).

```
Switch(config-vlan)#exit
Switch(config)#interface f0/24
Switch(config-if)#switchport trunk allowed vlan 5-20
Switch(config-if)#exit
Switch(config)#exit
Switch#
```

Now we can see that the trunking VLANs that are approved are from 5 to 20.

```
Switch#show interface f0/24 switchport
Name: Fa0/24
Switchport: Enabled
Administrative Mode: trunk
Operational Mode: down
Administrative Trunking Encapsulation: dot1q
Operational Trunking Encapsulation: dot1q
Negotiation of Trunking: On
Access Mode VLAN: 1 (default)
Trunking Native Mode VLAN: 1 (default)
Voice VLAN: none
Administrative private-vlan host-association: none
Administrative private-vlan mapping: none
Administrative private-vlan trunk native VLAN: none
Administrative private-vlan trunk encapsulation: dot1q
Administrative private-vlan trunk normal VLANs: none
Administrative private-vlan trunk private VLANs: none
Operational private-vlan: none
Trunking VLANs Enabled: 5-20
Pruning VLANs Enabled: 2-1001
Capture Mode Disabled
Capture VLANs Allowed: ALL
Protected: false
Unknown unicast blocked: disabled
Unknown multicast blocked: disabled
Appliance trust: none
```

switchport trunk native vlan <VLAN number> sets the native VLAN on a physical interface.

How do we troubleshoot a VLAN?

- Make sure that the same VLANs are configured on all the switches

- Make sure that the trunk ports are physically connected
- Make sure that the encapsulation is the same on both switches
- Make sure that the trunk mode is configured on both switches
- Make sure that the VLANs are not shut down
- Make sure that the native VLAN is the same on both switches
- Make sure that the VLAN is allowed on the trunk port of both switches

2.3 Configure and verify Layer 2 discovery protocols (Cisco Discovery Protocol and LLDP)

CDP or **Cisco Discovery Protocol** and **LLDP** or **Link Layer Discovery Protocol** allow different network devices to automatically discover each other. CDP is proprietary while LLDP is open source.

What can a device learn about another device through CDP?

- **Device Identifier** – the hostname of the remote device
- **Address** – the IP and MAC address of the remote device
- **Port** – the port on the remote device that we are connected to
- **Capabilities** – the capabilities of the remote device
- **Platform** – the model and IOS version running on the remote device

I can ask a router or switch to tell me about the neighbors it learned about through CDP by typing **`show cdp neighbors`**. I can view more details by typing **`show cdp neighbors detail`**.

```
Switch>enable
Switch#show cdp neighbors
Capability Codes: R - Router, T - Trans Bridge, B - Source Route Bridge
                  S - Switch, H - Host, I - IGMP, r - Repeater, P - Phone
Device ID    Local Intrfce    Holdtme    Capability   Platform    Port ID
Switch2      Gig 0/0/23        155          S I       C2960      Gig 0/0/20
```

The Local Interface is the port on the local device that connects to the neighboring device. The Port ID is the interface of the neighboring device that connects to the local device. We can also see the capabilities of the neighboring device.

In this case, our Switch connects from Port G0/0/23 to the neighboring Switch 2 Port G0/0/20. We also know that the neighboring switch model is a C2960.

CDP Neighbors only tells us about directly connected devices. A Cisco device won't forward details about a neighbor to its other neighbors. For security reasons, we should disable CDP on any interface that doesn't need it.

How do we check CDP?

- We can check if CDP is running by typing **`show cdp`**.
- We can check if cdp is running on an interface by typing **`show cdp interface <interface name>`**.

- We can check statistics by typing **show cdp traffic**.

```
Router#show cdp
Global CDP information:
    Sending CDP packets every 60 seconds
    Sending a holdtime value of 180 seconds
    Sending CDPv2 advertisements is enabled
Router#show cdp interface
Vlan1 is administratively down, line protocol is down
  Sending CDP packets every 60 seconds
  Holdtime is 180 seconds
GigabitEthernet0/0/0 is up, line protocol is down
  Sending CDP packets every 60 seconds
  Holdtime is 180 seconds
GigabitEthernet0/0/1 is administratively down, line protocol is down
  Sending CDP packets every 60 seconds
  Holdtime is 180 seconds
GigabitEthernet0/0/2 is administratively down, line protocol is down
  Sending CDP packets every 60 seconds
  Holdtime is 180 seconds
```

Our router tells us that CDP runs every 60 seconds. That means that our router advertises itself to neighboring routers every 60 seconds.

Our router also tells us that the holdtime is 180 seconds. That means that if our router doesn't receive a new CDP message from a neighboring router after 180 seconds, it removes it from its list of neighbors.

We can change the CDP time by typing

- **cdp timer <seconds>**
- **cdp holdtime <seconds>**

To enable LLDP, we type **lldp run** in global configuration mode. By default, even after enabling LLDP, it stays disabled on all the interfaces. We must manually enable it on any interface that requires it.

If we want an interface to stop sending LLDP messages, we can type **no lldp transmit**. We can enable it by typing **lldp transmit**. If we want an interface to ignore received LLDP messages, we type **no lldp receive**, and if we want to accept LLDP messages we type **lldp receive**.

```
Router(config)#lldp run

Router(config)#interface g0/0/1
Router(config-if)#lldp transmit
Router(config-if)#lldp receive
Router(config-if)#exit
Router(config)#exit
Router#
%SYS-5-CONFIG_I: Configured from console by console
```

I have configured LLDP on Interface G0/0/1. Now the router will both send and receive LLDP messages on that interface.

We can view the LLDP status by typing **show lldp**.

```
Router#show lldp

Global LLDP Information:
    Status: ACTIVE
    LLDP advertisements are sent every 30 seconds
    LLDP hold time advertised is 120 seconds
    LLDP interface reinitialisation delay is 2 seconds
Router#
```

We can view our LLDP neighbors by typing **show lldp neighbors**. The output from **show lldp neighbors** is almost the same as the **show cdp neighbors**.

The difference between CDP and LLDP is that LLDP does not identify the neighbor's platform or IGMP capabilities. Also, CDP lists a neighbor's capabilities whether they are enabled or not, while LLDP only lists a neighbor's capabilities when they are enabled. If we want to see a device's full capabilities under LLDP, we must type **show lldp neighbors detail**.

Like CDP, LLDP has a timer to send messages and a hold time after which it removes a neighbor from its list.

We can change the LLDP time by typing

- **lldp timer <seconds>**
- **lldp holdtime <seconds>**

2.5 Describe the need for and basic operations of Rapid PVST+ Spanning Tree Protocol and identify basic operations

2.5.a Root port, root bridge (primary/secondary), and other port names

2.5.b Port states (forwarding/blocking)

2.5.c PortFast benefits

I drew this network with redundant links. Traffic from Switch 1 to Switch 3 can pass through either Switch 4 or Switch 2.

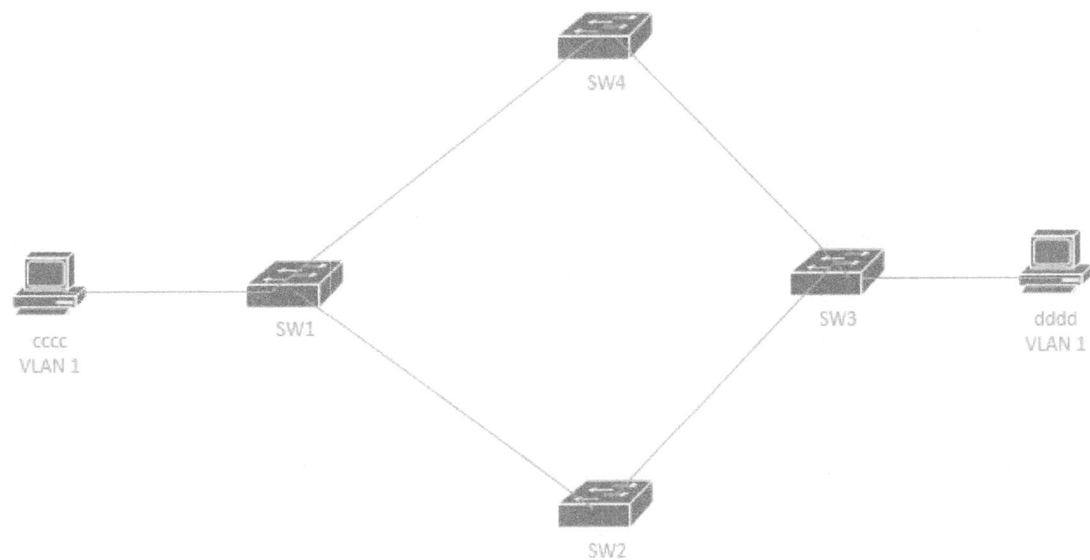

How does traffic get from "cccc" to "dddd"? It must go through SW1, and then either SW2 or SW4, and then SW3.

What would happen if SW1 doesn't know about "dddd" – it doesn't have "dddd" in its MAC address table? It would flood the frame onto Switch 2 and 4. Switches 2 and 4 would send the frame to Switch 3. Switch 3 would send the frame from Switch 2 to Switch 4 and the frame from Switch 4 to Switch 2. It also sends the frame to "dddd". Switches 2 and 4 would send to Switch 1. This would go on forever (or until one switch learned the MAC address of dddd). This is called a **broadcast storm**, and it is not good.

That frame has a from address of "cccc", and it is addressed to "dddd", but it keeps coming in through different ports. Switch 1 sees it come in from the port connected to "cccc" and then from the port connected to SW4 and then from the port connected to SW2. Each time, it updates its MAC Table with the source of the packet. This might happen hundreds of times per second. So the switch doesn't know where "cccc" is connected anymore. This is called **MAC Table Instability**.

The result of this mess is that "dddd" receives multiple copies of the same frame. This is called **multiple frame transmission**.

We should turn off the connection between Switch 1 and Switch 4 (or between Switch 1 and Switch 2). Now we can still get traffic to all the devices and we don't have any risk of creating a loop.

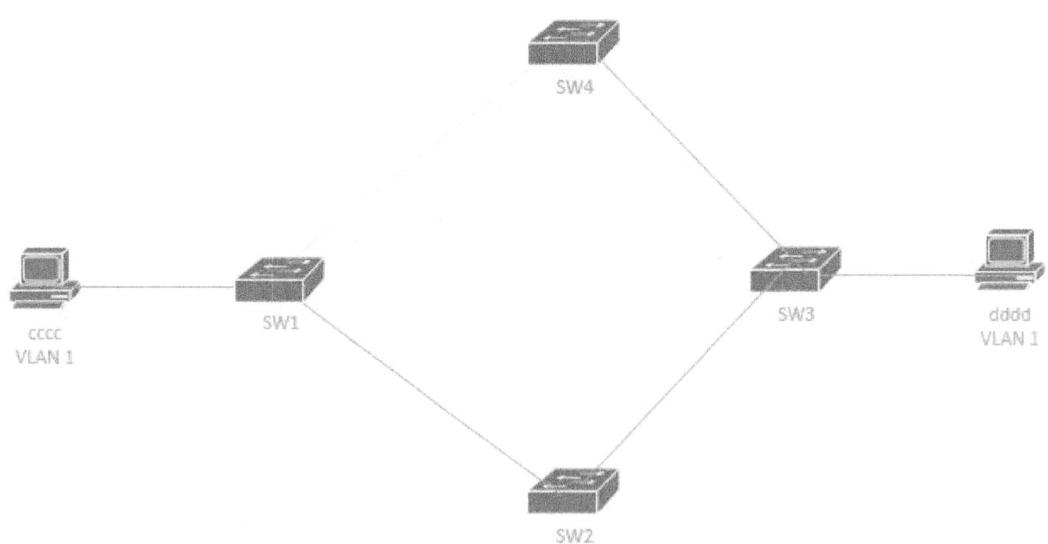

How do we decide which switch link to turn off? How do we identify redundant links like this in a large network?

We use a **Spanning Tree Protocol** (**STP**) or **Rapid STP** (**RSTP**). How does it work? The switches figure out how many connections they have amongst themselves. If two switches discover that they have multiple links (physical connections between themselves), they turn all of them off except for one. STP works on small networks of just two switches and large networks that could have dozens or hundreds of switches.

- First all the switches pick one switch to be the "**root bridge**". The root bridge is switch with the smallest bridge ID (BID).

  The bridge ID is 8 bytes

  - A 2-byte priority field – an administrator can manually configure the priority field
  - A 6-byte MAC address – this ensures that each switch has a unique bridge ID

The root bridge is the switch with the lowest priority. If multiple switches have the same priority, then the switches choose the switch with the lowest MAC address.

- The switches establish the STP by communicating through **Bridge Protocol Data Units (BPDUs)**.
- They send Hello messages, which include
    - The bridge ID of the sender
    - The bridge ID that the switch believes is the root. I said believes. When the network first starts up, every switch thinks that it is the root, because none of the switches know about the other switches' bridge IDs.

      Each time a switche receives a Hello message from another switch it decides whether to continue believing it is a root or whether another switch should be the root.

      If a switch receives a hello message from a switch with a lower bridge ID, it recognizes that switch as the root instead of itself – this other switch may not be the root either; it just has a lower bridge ID. It passes this information to other switches through subsequent Hello messages.

      Eventually, all the switches figure out which one is the root.
    - How much it costs the sending switch to access the root switch.

- The timer value

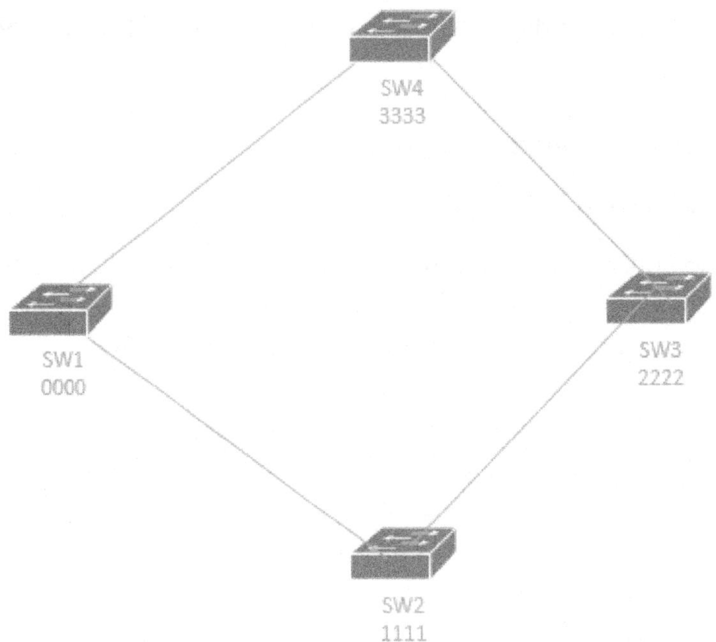

Consider this network with four switches. The switch BIDs are 0000, 1111, 2222, and 3333. When this network starts up, every switch thinks that it is root.
SW1 is the true root.
SW1 learns about SW2 and SW4, but stays as root because it has the lowest ID.
SW2 learns about SW1 and SW3, and decides that SW1 is root.
SW4 learns about SW1 and SW3, and decides that SW1 is root.
SW3 learns about SW2 and SW4, and decides that SW2 is root, which is wrong.
SW2 and SW4 tell SW3 that they think SW1 is root. SW3 checks and realizes that SW1 has a lower BID than SW2, so it now agrees that SW1 is root.
Now all the switches know that SW1 is the root.

- The interfaces on the root bridge are all set to forward traffic. They are in the **forwarding state**.
- Each of the remaining switches figures out how it is connected to the "root". If a switch has multiple connections to the root, it assigns a cost to each one. What would it cost me to get my traffic back to the root switch? The greater the bandwidth, the lower the cost. For example, a 100 Mbit/s link costs "19", while a 1 Gbit/s link costs "4". This is called the **root cost**. The switch turns off the most expensive links. The port connected to the link that stays on is called the **root port**.

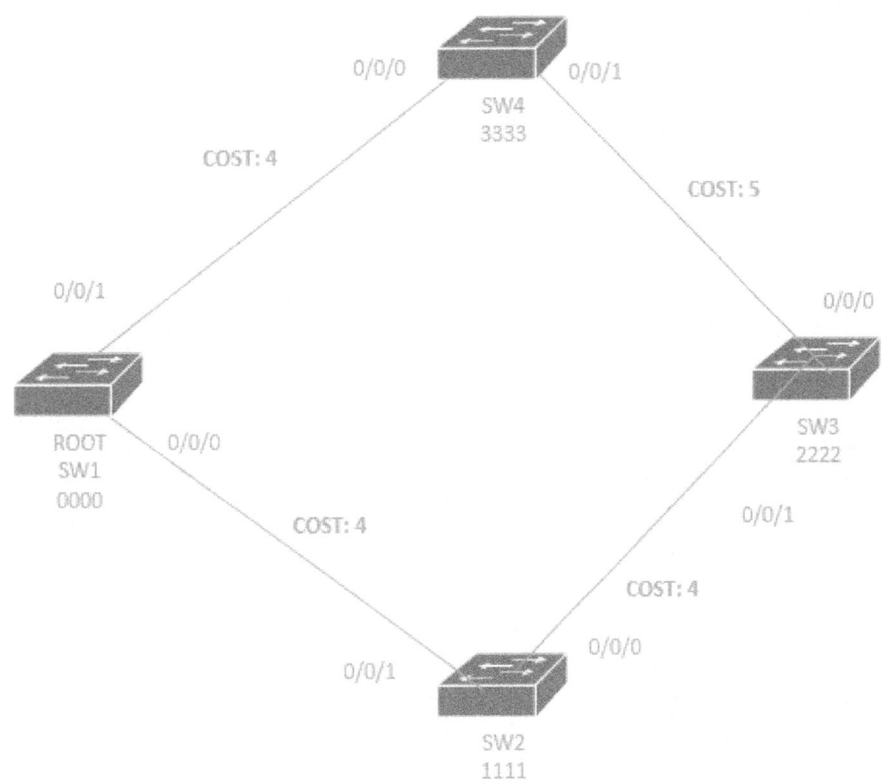

For example, SW1 is the root switch. Each of the other switch figures out the cheapest way to get the root.

SW4 and SW2 can get to the root directly. The cost is 4.

If SW4 wanted to go through the long route (through SW3 and SW2), it would cost 13 – that is the cost of all three links (5 + 4 + 4). If SW2 wanted to go through the long route (through SW3 and SW4), it would cost 13 – that is the cost of all three links (5 + 4 + 4).

Thus, SW4 keeps port 0/0/0 in a forwarding status, and SW2 keeps 0/0/1 in forwarding state.

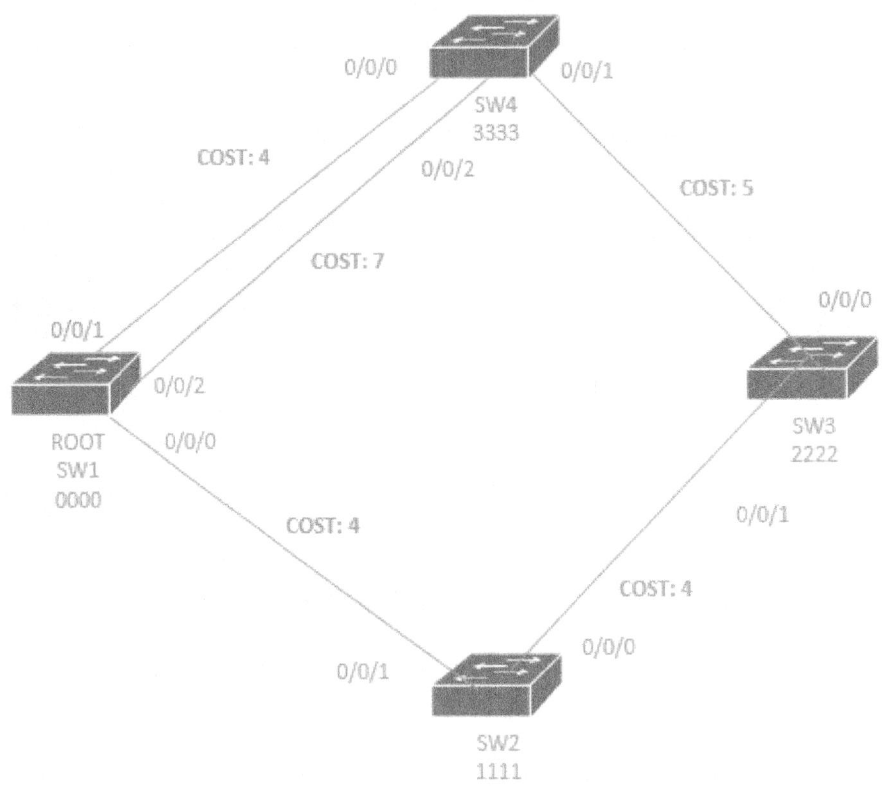

What if SW4 had two physical links to SW1? It would choose the one with the lowest cost (the one with cost of 4 and turn off the other port). That would mean that 0/0/2 on SW4 is set to a blocking state.

If the links had the same cost, it would keep the one connected to the interface with the lowest port number.

- STP only worries about ports that are working – where the status is up and up. If the cable is unplugged or if the port is administratively down, then STP doesn't consider that port in determining whether to use it.
- Remember that the topology can become complicated. There may be several switches between an edge switch and the root switch. Thus, the pathway to the root may involve several links, each of which has its own "cost".

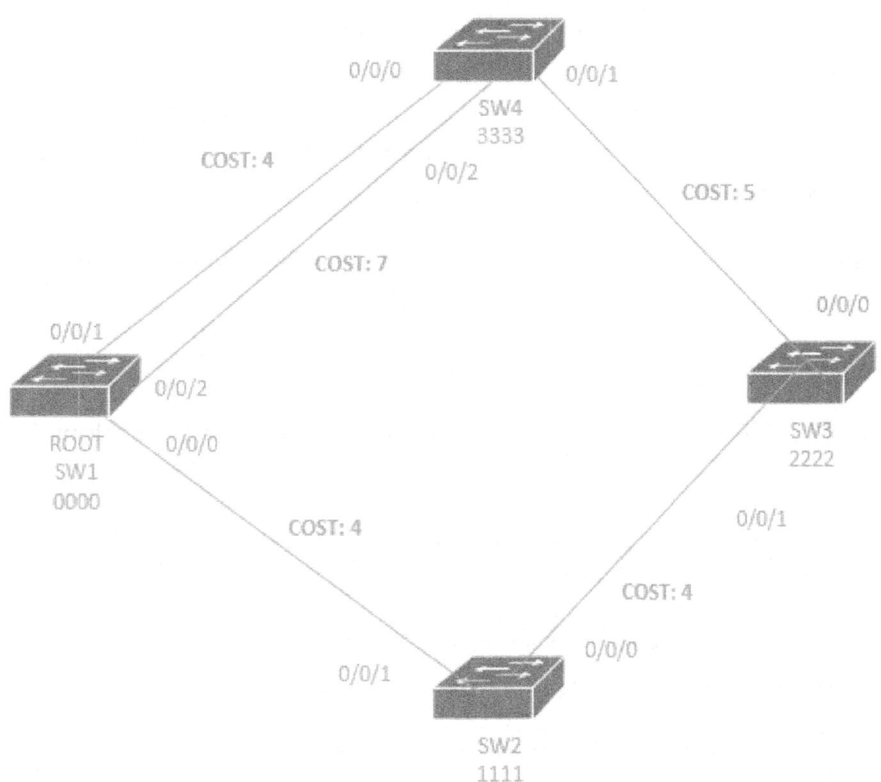

Switch 3 needs to figure out a cost. It can go through Switch 4 or Switch 2. The cost to get to the root through switch 2 is 8, and the cost through switch 4 is 9. Therefore, SW3 turns off the link between itself and SW4 (it sets port 0/0/0 to a blocking state) and sends traffic through SW3.

How did SW3 know the root cost that SW2 and SW4 have with SW1? From the Hello message. SW4 and SW2 tell SW3 what their root cost is. SW3 simply adds their root cost to its root cost to obtain the total root cost.

What if there is a tie in the root cost?

- The switch chooses a neighbor with the lowest BID
- If there is a tie in BIDs, then it chooses the neighbor with the lowest port priority
- Finally, if there is still a tie, it chooses the neighbor with the lowest physical interface number

- When there are multiple switches fighting for a connection to the root, the switch with the lowest cost connection is called the **designated switch** and the port that it uses to connect to the pathway to the root is called the **designated port**.

  SW3, port 0/0/1 is the designated port and SW2 is the designated switch, because SW2 provides SW3 with the lowest cost pathway to the switch, and SW3 is connected to SW2 through port 0/0/1.

- If multiple pathways have the same cost, then the switch chooses the pathway containing the neighboring switch with the lowest bridge ID.

- A port can have any of the following statuses:

  - **Blocking**. The switch determined that this port will cause a loop. It does not send or receive any traffic on this port, except for BPDU data.

  - **Listening**. The port does not transmit data, nor does it learn MAC addresses of devices connected to it.

  - **Learning**. The port does not transmit data, but it still learns MAC addresses of devices that could be connected to it.

  - **Forwarding**. A normally operating port. All data is transferred.

  - **Disabled**. The port was manually turned off or turned off due to a security incident. We'll talk about security incidents later. No data is transferred, not even BPDU data, and the switch does not learn MAC addresses of devices connected to it.

- The switches continually revaluate their connections and recalculate the cost of each link. Switches exchange Bridge Protocol Data Units every two seconds. In case a switch or link fails, the other switches can quickly re-establish a connection.

- The switches also continually test their data links. If a link fails, the switch sends traffic over another link. If a less expensive link starts working again, the switch returns to sending traffic over it. A switch tests its link by sending a "hello" message every two seconds. If the switch does not receive a reply after three subsequent "hello" messages (six seconds), it assumes that the link is defective and chooses a new link.

  Once STP is established, only the root switch can generate a hello. The other switches only forward the hello.

In summary, the following ports are in forwarding mode

- All the root switch ports are forwarding.

- Each non-root switch port with the lowest cost in reaching the root is forwarding.
- Each designated port is forwarding.

Any switch port that is not in forwarding is in blocking mode.

Going back to our timers

Hello	Every two seconds, the root switch sends a Hello message. The other switches expect to receive the Hello message every two seconds.
MaxAge	The MaxAge timer is ten times the Hello timer (or 20 seconds). If a switch doesn't receive a Hello message in the MaxAge time (20 seconds), it assumes that the root switch failed, and decides to change the STP
Forward Delay	The forward delay is how long a switch takes to change from blocking mode to forwarding mode, as we will see

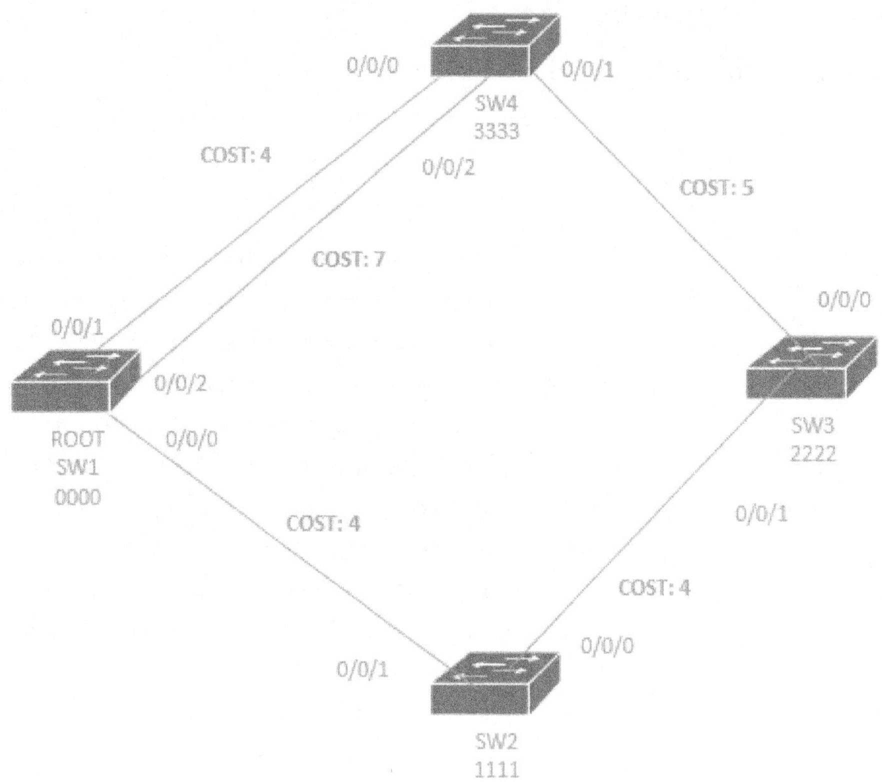

Remember that SW1 is the root, SW2 connects to SW1, SW4, connects to SW1, and SW3 connects to SW1 through SW2 because that is the route with the lowest cost.

If SW4 failed, nothing would change in STP because no other switches connect to it.

If SW2 failed, after 20 seconds, SW3 would realize that it hasn't received any Hello messages. It would start listening for Hello messages again and would send traffic through SW4. That means port 0/0/0 on SW3 would become a forwarding port.

A switch can change a port's status from forwarding to blocking immediately. But there is a 30 second delay in changing from blocking to forwarding. Why? The switch needs need to make sure it made the correct choice so that loops are not created.

There are two statuses that exist between blocking and forwarding.

- **Listening** – the switch is listening for traffic. The switch clears its MAC address table of any entry that does not send it traffic during this time. It does not forward any traffic and it does not add any new entries to the MAC address table.

- **Learning** – the switch continues to listen for traffic and adds new MAC address entries. It does not forward any traffic.

The switch remains in each state for 15 seconds. That means the total delay is 50 seconds (20 seconds waiting for a Hello message that never arrives, 15 seconds in the Listening state, and 15 seconds in the Learning state).

A better system is called **Rapid Spanning Tree Protocol** (RSTP). RSTP is an improvement over the original STP protocol. It is the same, except for the port states. In RSTP, there are three port states

- **Discarding**. The port does not send or receive any traffic. This is the same as blocking.
- **Learning**. The port does not send any traffic, but it does learn MAC addresses of devices connected to it.
- **Forwarding**. The port is sending and receiving traffic normally.

The benefit of RSTP is that we don't need to wait to change the root port or forwarding state. In RSTP, each switch designates an **alternate port** that it can use when the **root port** fails, and a **backup port** it can use when the **designated port** fails. If a switch fails, the other switches activate their alternate/backup ports as necessary.

Each switch generates its own Hello message instead of forwarding Hello messages from the root switch.

How does it work?

- The switches elect the root switch the same way as STP
- Each switch selects the root port the same way as STP
- The **alternate port** is a port on a switch that is connected to the root. A switch might have two connections to the root switch – a root port and an alternate port.
    - If the root connection fails, the root port becomes disabled, and its state is changed to discarding
    - The alternate port immediately becomes the root port and its state is changed to forwarding
    - A switch that changes its topology tells other switches so that they can flush their MAC address tables. We don't waste time with the learning/listening states.

RSTP Port Definitions

- **Point-to-Point Port** – a port that connect two switches together
- **Point-to-Point Edge** – a port that connects a switch to an endpoint (like a PC, printer, or VoIP phone)
- **Shared Port** – a port that connects a switch to a hub

How do we configure STP? We don't. STP works on a Cisco switch by default. But we could change the priority of a switch or the cost of a link.

Below is the cost of each link speed. The cost was updated in 2004 to accommodate speeds of 100 Gbps and 1 Tbps.

Speed	Cost	Cost (after 2004)
10 Mbps	100	2,000,000
100 Mbps	19	200,000
1 Gbps	4	20,000
10 Gbps	2	2000
100 Gbps	N/A	200
1 Tbps	N/A	20

The switch determines the cost based on the actual speed of the port, not its maximum supported speed.

Remember that I had two links between SW1 and SW4. If they were the same speed, I could combine them with a tool called **EtherChannel**. Then the switches pretend that both links belong to the same physical interface. This lets us double our capacity instead of turning one link off. We don't have to worry about STP, because even if one link fails, the traffic continues through the other links. We will look at EtherChannel in the next chapter.

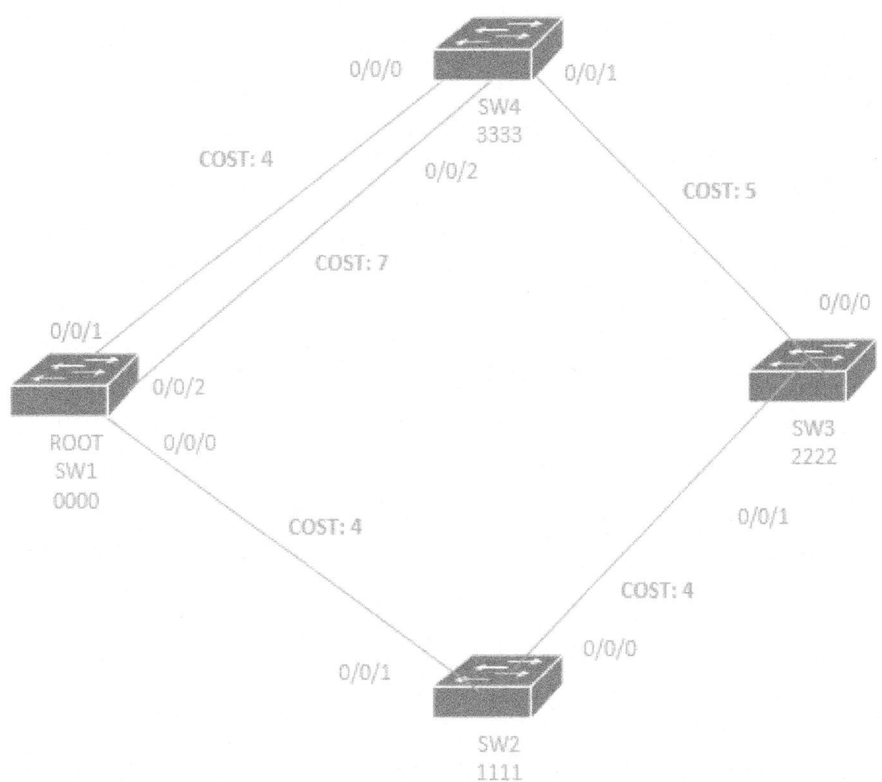

We can also turn on **PortFast** when using STP. It is on by default in RSTP. PortFast allows a port to immediately switch from blocking to forwarding, without entering the listening/learning states. We shouldn't use it on any port that is connected to a switch or hub or we could create a loop.

Why do we need PortFast? When an end user device connects to the switch, the switch must wait a few seconds to make sure that the port is a designated port. That increases the amount of time it takes for a user to establish a connection. If we turn on PortFast, an end user can connect to the switch faster.

What happens if a hacker connects a switch to a port on our network, and gives his switch a lower priority than that of the switches on the existing network? He could create a root switch and steal all the traffic. We can stop him with **BPDU Guard**. BPDU Guard is added to any port that should only be an access port. If the switch receives a BPDU message on a port with BPDU Guard, it will automatically disable the port.

Let's go back to my earlier network where I had core switches at the top (the spine leaf). I should make the core switches the root switches.

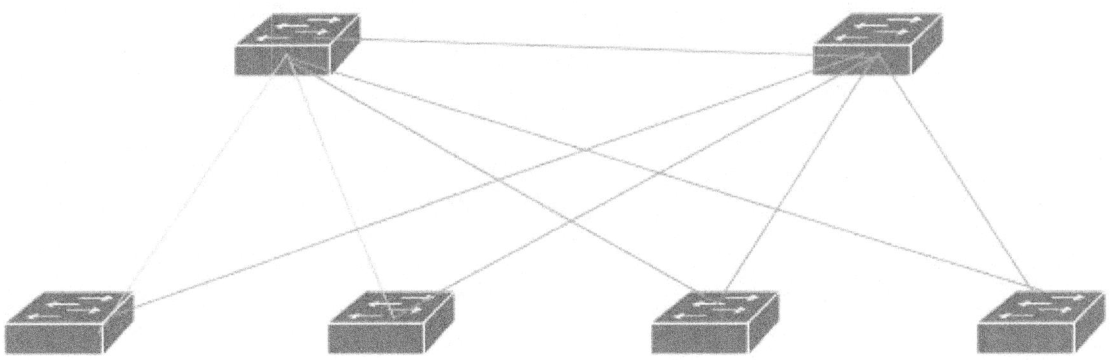

If this network had VLANs, it could get complicated. What if the pathway from some edge devices on some VLANs was cheaper than the pathway from other edge devices on other VLANs? Maybe the STP route decided that the best route for one VLAN is different from the best route for another VLAN. What do we do?

We could create multiple spanning trees

- **Spanning Tree Protocol** and **RSTP** are open protocols each of which supports only one tree
- **PVST+** or **Per-VLAN Spanning Tree Plus** protocols allows us to create a separate spanning tree per VLAN
- **Rapid PVST+** also allows us to create a separate tree per VLAN
- **MSTP** or **Multiple STP** is an open protocol, but does not necessary require one tree per VLAN

We can choose the STP mode that we want our switch to use by typing **`spanning-tree mode [pvst | rapid-pvst | mst]`**

For example, I have chosen PVST+

```
Switch>enable
Switch#conf t
Enter configuration commands, one per line.  End with CNTL/Z.
Switch(config)#spanning-tree mode pvst
```

Remember how our bridge ID was a 2-byte priority and a 6-byte MAC address? Well actually, the bridge ID is a 4-bit priority (half a byte) and a 12-bit (1.5 bytes) system ID extension, which contains the VLAN ID, and the 48-bit (6-byte) MAC address.

If I want to configure a priority for a specific VLAN, I type **`spanning-tree vlan <VLAN number> priority <priority>`**. The priority must be a multiple of 4096, between 0 and 65, 535. I tried to give it a priority of 8, but the switch rejected the command.

```
Switch(config)#spanning-tree vlan 5 priority 8
% Bridge Priority must be in increments of 4096.
% Allowed values are:
  0     4096  8192  12288 16384 20480 24576 28672
  32768 36864 40960 45056 49152 53248 57344 61440
Switch(config)#spanning-tree vlan 5 priority 4096
```

If you have a large network and any of your switches could be elected to be the root switch, then your LAN probably sucks. Instead, you should choose two switches – a primary switch and a secondary switch – that are good candidates for acting as the root switches.

We can configure a primary switch by typing **`spanning-tree vlan <VLAN number> root primary`**, and on the secondary, configure it as **`spanning-tree vlan <VLAN number> root secondary`**. In the below example, I sent my switch as primary for VLAN 5.

```
Switch>enable
Switch#conf t
Enter configuration commands, one per line.  End with CNTL/Z.
Switch(config)#spanning-tree vlan 5 root primary
```

Once configured, each switch chooses a good priority value and configures itself through the **`spanning-tree vlan <VLAN number> priority <priority>`** command. How?

- If the current root has a priority that is higher than 24,576, the primary switch chooses 24,576 as its priority
- Otherwise, the primary switch chooses a number that is 4096 less than the current root's priority.
- The secondary switch chooses a priority of 28,672.
- This command usually works because, by default, switches choose a priority of 32,768. If all the switches on the network have a priority of 32,768, then the secondary switch now has the second lowest priority, and the primary switch has the lowest.

What is the difference between RSTP and RPVST +?

- RSTP can support one tree, but RPVST+ has one tree per VLAN
- RSTP broadcasts one set of BPDU messages but RPVST + broadcasts one set per VLAN
- RSTP sends messages in the native VLAN of the trunk port but RPVST + sends each message inside the corresponding VLAN
- RSTP and RPVST+ both use a 16-bit priority, but RSTP sets the VLAN portion to 0.

Since we can set a different priority per VLAN, it follows that we can also set an interface cost per VLAN. We type **spanning-tree vlan <VLAN number> cost <cost>**. We must configure this command on each interface separately. In the below example, I set Port 6's VLAN 5 cost to 200.

```
Switch(config)#interface F0/6
Switch(config-if)#spanning-tree vlan 5 cost 200
Switch(config-if)#
```

We can verify the spanning tree settings by typing show spanning-tree. In our example, the switch is listing spanning tree data for VLAN 1.

- Under Root ID, it tells us that the Root ID on the network has a priority of 32769. It also tells us that the MAC address of the Root is 0050.0FBC.9AAC. In this case, our switch is the root – it says, "This bridge is the root".
- Under Bridge ID, it tells us the priority and MAC address for the current switch. In this case, the current switch is the Root. Therefore, the Root ID and Bridge ID would have the same values.
- The switch also tells us the Hello Time, Max Age, and Forward Delay times.
- The switch lists any interfaces that are in a forwarding state. In this case Fa0/7 is a designated port.

```
Switch#show spanning-tree
VLAN0001
  Spanning tree enabled protocol ieee
  Root ID    Priority    32769
             Address     0050.0FBC.9AAC
             This bridge is the root
             Hello Time  2 sec  Max Age 20 sec  Forward Delay 15 sec

  Bridge ID  Priority    32769  (priority 32768 sys-id-ext 1)
             Address     0050.0FBC.9AAC
             Hello Time  2 sec  Max Age 20 sec  Forward Delay 15 sec
             Aging Time  20

Interface        Role Sts Cost      Prio.Nbr Type
---------------- ---- --- --------- -------- --------------------------------
Fa0/7            Desg FWD 19        128.7    Shr
```

2.4 Configure and verify (Layer 2/Layer 3) EtherChannel (LACP)

Remember that I had two links between SW1 and SW4. If they were the same speed, I could combine them with a tool called **EtherChannel**. Then the switches pretend that both links belong to the same physical interface. This lets us double our capacity instead of turning one link off. We don't have to worry about STP, because even if one link fails, the traffic continues through the other links.

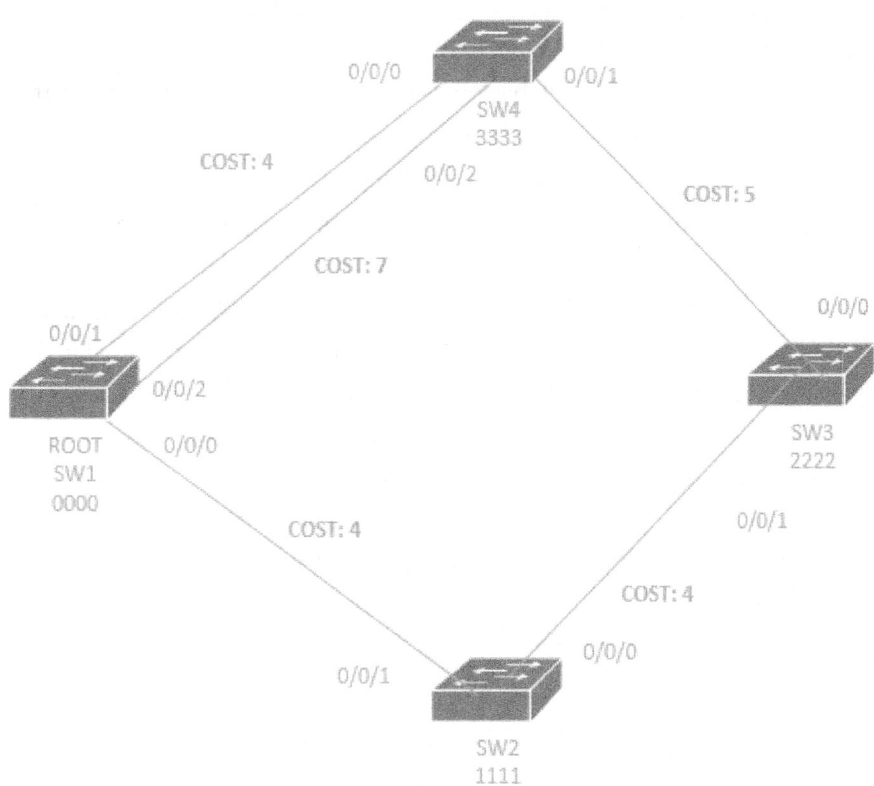

EtherChannel is also known as PortChannel or Channel-Group.

To configure EtherChannel on a set of interfaces, we first choose a channel number, and then enter the configuration for the channel by typing **`interface port-channel <channel-number>`**. If the channel didn't previously exist, the switch will create it. We don't need to manually create a channel – adding it to a physical interface will automatically create it.

We add each interface to the EtherChannel by typing **`channel-group <channel number> mode on`**. For example, I added channel group two to Port 7.

```
Switch(config)#interface F0/7
Switch(config-if)#channel-group 2 mode on
Switch(config-if)#exit
```

We can configure the channel-group mode by typing **`channel-group <channel number> mode [auto | desirable | active | passive | on]`**.

There are two EtherChannel protocols - **Cisco's Port Aggregation Protocol** (**PAgP**) or the **Link Aggregation Control Protocol** (**LACP**). PAgP has two modes – desirable and auto. LACP has two modes – active and passive.

- **Auto** – the port acts passively. It does not negotiate an EtherChannel with another switch, but it does listen for EtherChannel messages from other switches. It will establish an EtherChannel upon receipt of an EtherChannel message. This method uses PAgP.
- **Desirable** – the port acts actively. It sends EtherChannel messages to other switches and attempts to activate an EtherChannel. This method uses PAgP.
- **Active** - the port acts actively. It sends EtherChannel messages to other switches and attempts to activate an EtherChannel. This method uses LACP.
- **Passive** – the port acts passively. It does not negotiate an EtherChannel with another switch, but it does listen for EtherChannel messages from other switches. It will establish an EtherChannel upon receipt of an EtherChannel message. This method uses LACP.
- **On** – the port is configured manually. It operates as an EtherChannel and does not negotiate with the other switch.

```
Switch(config)#interface F0/7
Switch(config-if)#channel-group 2 mode auto
Switch(config-if)#exit
```

We verify the EtherChannel's settings through the following commands

- **`show etherchannel`** gives us a list of EtherChannels activated on the switch

```
Switch#show etherchannel
                Channel-group listing:
                ----------------------

Group: 1
----------
Group state = L2
Ports: 0 Maxports = 8
Port-channels: 1 Max Port-channels = 1
Protocol:    -

Group: 2
----------
Group state = L2
Ports: 2 Maxports = 8
Port-channels: 1 Max Portchannels = 1
Protocol:   PAGP

Group: 5
----------
Group state = L2
Ports: 0 Maxports = 8
Port-channels: 1 Max Port-channels = 1
Protocol:    -
Switch#
```

- **show etherchannel summary** provides this information in a summary table. In our example, it shows us that Port Channel #2 is activated on ports FastEthernet0/7 and FastEthernet0/8.

```
Switch#show etherchannel summary
Flags:  D - down        P - in port-channel
        I - stand-alone s - suspended
        H - Hot-standby (LACP only)
        R - Layer3      S - Layer2
        U - in use      f - failed to allocate aggregator
        u - unsuitable for bundling
        w - waiting to be aggregated
        d - default port


Number of channel-groups in use: 3
Number of aggregators:           3

Group  Port-channel  Protocol    Ports
------+-------------+-----------+-----------------------------------------------

1      Po1(SD)           -
2      Po2(SD)           PAgP   Fa0/7(D) Fa0/8(D)
5      Po5(SD)           -
```

For EtherChannel to function properly, the following settings must be the same on all the interfaces in the channel

- Speed
- Duplex
- Access – all interfaces must be access or all interfaces must be trunks
- VLAN (for an access port) or allowed VLANs (for a trunk)
- Native VLAN for a trunk
- STP interface settings

If the settings are not the same, the channel will not work. If a PortChannel is disabled due to an error, its physical ports will also be error disabled.

Once we've established an EtherChannel between two switches, how does a switch decide which frame should be sent out of which physical interface? We call this **load balancing**. There are several criteria that the switch can use. We can configure it by typing **`port-channel load-balance <method>`**. The method to use in the command is in brackets below.

- Source MAC (src-mac)
- Destination MAC (dst-mac)

- Source & Destination IP (src-dst-mac)
- Source IP (src-ip)
- Destination IP (dst-ip)
- Source & Destination IP (src-dst-ip)
- Source TCP/UDP Port (src-port)
- Destination TCP/UDP Port (dst-port)
- Source & Destination TCP/UDP (src-dst-port)

The main goal of load balancing is to prevent frames from arriving in a different order from how they were sent. We must think about the type of traffic flowing over each VLAN and choose the best load balancing option. For example, a video feed coming from a surveillance camera and travelling to a DVR will have the same source address. The different video packets should all take the same route.

We can ask the switch for its opinion as to what route it would send the traffic on by typing **`test etherchannel load-balance interface <etherchannel number> <load balance method>`**.

For example, if I wanted to know how the EtherChannel would send traffic to a device with the MAC address AA:BB:CC:DD:EE:FF, I could write **`test etherchannel load-balance interface 1 mac AABBCCDDEEFF`**.

The switch responds that it would choose Port 7 (FastEthernet0/7)

```
Switch#test etherchannel load-balance interface port-channel 1 mac AABBCCDDEEFF

    Would select FA0/7 of Po2
```

2.6 Compare Cisco Wireless Architectures and AP modes

You can think of a wireless access point like a switch in that it allows multiple devices to connect to it and it moves their traffic to the wired network. When an access point is equipped with both wireless and wired connections, it is considered **autonomous**.

The autonomous WAP broadcasts one or more SSIDs which are mapped to VLANs. We call each of these SSIDs a **Wireless LAN** or **WLAN**.

What really makes a WAP autonomous is that when two wireless clients are connected to the same access point and attempt to exchange traffic, the access point can directly transfer data between them. It doesn't have to route the traffic through a switch (to a switch and back).

Autonomous WAPs become a problem when we have many access points. Why?

- We need to configure a management IP address on each access point so that we can log in and configure it remotely. Failing that, we would need to connect a console cable to each access point and configure it manually, which would be a hassle.

- That means we need to create a management VLAN that each access point can access. We should put the management IP on a management VLAN so that unauthorized users cannot access it.

- Each time a client associates and disassociates (roams), it should be able to keep the same IP address. That means that if I'm walking around a large building, my wireless devices should remain connected to the Wi-Fi.

- If we create a new VLAN, we must set it up on every access point and switch. That requires us to manually reconfigure each WAP.

How do we solve these problems? In the past, the solution was to purchase a device called a wireless controller. The wireless controller is part of a set of tools called **Cisco Prime Infrastructure** and helps us configure and manage WAPs automatically.

We install the controller on our network and configure our Wi-Fi on the controller. When a WAP connects to the network, it looks for a controller. The controller configures the WAP automatically from a template.

If we log in to the controller and change the network configuration, the controller automatically changes the configuration on each connected WAP.

Controllers are less popular now – they are being replaces with **cloud-based WAPs**. The WAP management is no longer on a physical controller in your network, but in the cloud. You configure the network through a web-based control panel. Each time a WAP is connected to the network, it reaches out to a cloud server and downloads its configuration.

The Cisco cloud is called **Meraki** and it can configure more than just WAPs. The beauty of Meraki is that it allows us to configure networks across multiple buildings and countries from the same interface. When you purchase a new WAP, you register its serial number on the Meraki cloud. You tell the cloud how the WAP fits into your network. When the WAP connects to the cloud, it knows what configuration to download. We might also call this **zero-touch provisioning**.

Some things that the cloud can do

- Configure the WAPs without a management VLAN
- Upgrade the firmware on each WAP
- Upgrade the configuration on each WAP
- Change the channel and transmit power that each WAP uses based on the conditions and detected interference
- Monitor device statistics
- Monitor and report on rogue devices

The cloud does not see the actual Wi-Fi data. That passes from the WAP to the physical local network or to the internet as required. The cloud only provides the management. User data travelling over the network takes a route called the **data plane**, while configuration data and statistics take a route called the **control plane**.

Some of the tasks that the WAP does in real time

- Transmit and Receive data
- Manage MAC addresses of connected devices
- Encrypt and decrypt traffic

Some of the management tasks that the WAP must do

- Manage the power and channel use
- Allow devices to roam and associate
- Authenticate clients
- Manage Quality of Service
- Manage security

We can create a WAP that just handles the real time tasks. This type of WAP is called called the **lightweight access point**. The management tasks are then outsourced to a controller known as a **Wireless LAN Controller**, or **WLC**. It is better if these management tasks are handled centrally because they involve more than one access point. Forcing each WAP to handle these tasks would consume unnecessary resources or be inefficient.

The lightweight WAP (LAP) handles only Layer 1 and Layer 2 functions, while the other functions are handled by the WLC. Unlike an autonomous WAP, the LAP cannot function on its own. We call this a **split-MAC architecture**.

The LAP and WLC communicate through a tunnel. When I say tunnel, I mean that the LAP and WLC package all their traffic and transport it over the normal network, but they do so in a way that encapsulates all their traffic. This tunnel can operate over different networks and VLANs. We could put the controller in a central location and use it to manage LAPs that are in different physical locations.

How does the LAP communicate with the WLC? It uses the **Control and Provisioning of Wireless Access Points** protocol, or **CAPWAP**. If each LAP and WLC has a valid IP address, and the underlying network is working properly, management data is encapsulated inside an IP packet and then transported.

The CAPWAP creates two tunnels

- **CAPWAP control messages** are used to configure the LAP and manage its operation. The WLC and LAP encrypt the messages so that a rogue WLC cannot change the LAP's configuration.

  The management traffic is encapsulated, so we don't need to create a separate management VLAN.

- **CAPWAP data** travel between the clients and the LAPs. This data is not encrypted.by default but can be. Thus, the data travels from the host device to the LAP and then to the WLC and then to the destination.

  The data is encapsulated in an IP Packet. This is important because we no longer need to configure VLANs on the switches that the LAPs are connected to. We only configure the VLANs on the WLC, and the WLC configures the VLANs on the LAPs.

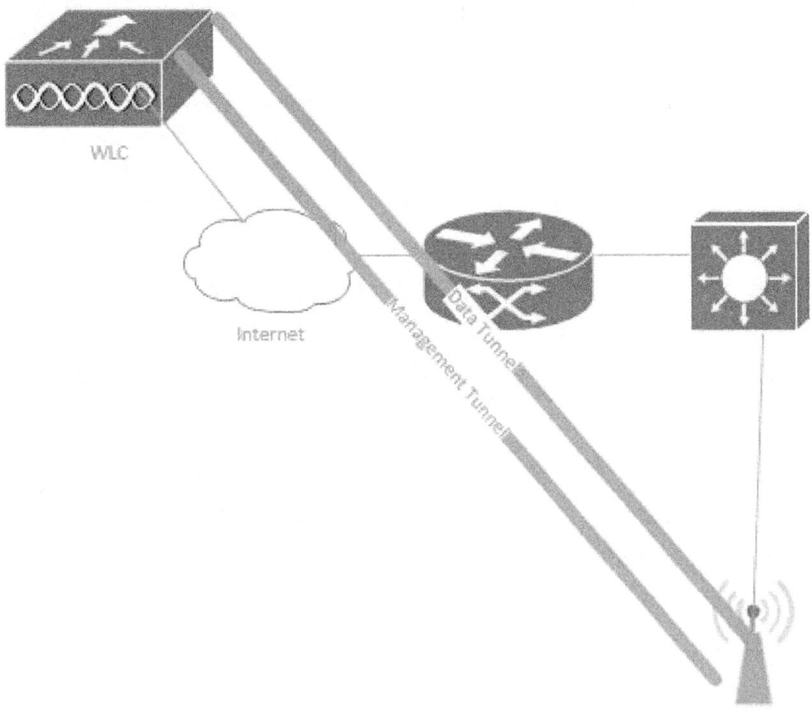

How do we ensure that the LAP and WLC trust each other? From the factory, each LAP and WLC comes with a certificate. The LAP checks the certificate on the WLC to ensure that it is legitimate, and the WLC checks the certificate on each LAP to ensure that they are legitimate. This prevents a hacker from installing a rogue LAP on your network.

Some of the things that the WLC does for us

- It automatically changes the channel each LAP is using so that neighboring LAPs have different channels
- It adjusts the transmit power of each LAP so that their signals do not interfere
- It allows a client to roam from one LAP to another without disruption to its connection
- If there are multiple LAPs in the same area and one is overloaded (has too many clients), it can force some of those clients onto another LAP. This is known as **client load balancing**.
- It monitors the radio frequencies being transmitted by devices in the coverage area. This allows it to detect rogue APs, ad hoc devices, and interference.
- It authenticates clients so that only authorized devices can connect to the network.
- It redirects clients to a DHCP server so that they can obtain an IP address before connecting to the network.

Think about the tunnels. We want each tunnel to be approximately the same length. If we put the WLC at the edge of the network, some tunnels will be short, and some will be long. Traffic over the long tunnels would experience more latency. We should install the WLC in a central location. This is called a **centralized WLC deployment**.

The WLC should connect to a switch in the core layer. We should think about how many access points we have and how many we plan to purchase in the future. We should also think about how many clients we have and how many we plan to add. That allows us to purchase a WLC that has enough capacity to support the network. We may need to purchase more than one WLC if our network is large enough or if we want to add redundancy.

It is possible to set up a WLC as a virtual machine, which can be installed in the cloud. We call this a **cloud-based WLC deployment**. We can deploy multiple virtual machines if we need multiple WLCs.

Some Cisco switches come with built in WLCs, each of which can each handle a small number of LAPs. In a small network, or a distributed network where each location has a small number of LAPs, we can install Cisco switches with built in WLCs instead of purchasing a large standalone WLC. We call this an **embedded WLC deployment**. The LAP does not have to be directly connected to the switch that is running the WLC, it just has to be reachable by the switch.

If we have a very small office, we can install one AP that has a built in WLC. Other LAPs in the office connect to this AP's controller. We call this the **Cisco Mobility Express WLC deployment**.

A WLC can support up to 6000 LAPs and 64,000 clients. A VM-based WLC can support up to 3000 LAPs and 32,000 clients. A Cisco switch-based WLC can support up to 200 LAPs and 4000 clients. An AP with a built-in WLC can support up to 100 LAPs and 2000 clients.

When the LAP powers on, it can operate in one of several modes

- **Local**. The LAP is broadcasting at least one BSS (SSID) on one channel. The LAP is also scanning the other channels and reporting the noise, interference, and rogue devices to the WLC. The LAP can only scan the other channels when it is not transmitting data.

  The Local mode is the default mode. If we change the LAP's mode to one of the other modes, the local mode is disabled, and the AP stops broadcasting the BSS.

- **Monitor**. The LAP will not transmit any data, but it is monitoring the wireless environment for noise, interference, and rogue devices. The LAP is also predicting where the other LAPs are located.

- **FlexConnect**. If we install a LAP in a site that does not physically contain a WLC, then there is a risk that the LAP loses connectivity with the WLC. When the CAPWAP tunnel loses connectivity, the LAP acts like a Layer 3 switch and moves traffic between an SSID and its respective VLAN, without having to send it to the WLC.

- **Sniffer**. A sniffer is when the LAP captures traffic that is sent from other devices. The LAP is secretly capturing wireless traffic that is being broadcast in its coverage area. This traffic can be sent to a packet analysis program or a server.

- **Rogue Detector**. The AP listens for traffic and collects the MAC addresses of devices on the network that are transmitting data. If we see a MAC address that is on the wireless network and on the wired network, then we can assume it is a rogue device.

- **Bridge**. The LAP connects two networks together. We can put multiple LAPs in bridge mode to create a mesh network, or a point-to-multipoint network. We can put two LAPs in bridge mode to create a point-to-point network (such as those in Part 1).

- **Flex+Bridge**. This combines the FlexConnect feature with the Bridge feature, so that we can enable VLAN switching on a mesh network.

- **SE-Connect**. The LAP collects wireless spectrum data to determine if there are sources of interference. We need to use a spectrum analysis program to analyse the data.

2.7 Describe physical infrastructure connections of WLAN components (AP, WLC, access/trunk ports, and LAG)

Remember that an autonomous AP can map each BSS (SSID) or WLAN to a VLAN. We connect the autonomous AP to a trunk port on our switch. The autonomous AP must tag each frame with its VLAN.

For example, the Guest Wi-Fi might be VLAN 5 and the Corporate Wi-Fi might be VLAN 10.

If we use a LAP, then we connect it to an access port, because traffic for multiple VLANs can be transported through the CAPWAP tunnel.

On the physical controller, there are several physical ports

- The **Service Port** is used for managing the system. We connect this port to an access port on the switch.
- A **Distribution System Port** handles AP data and AP management traffic. We connect this port to a trunk port on the switch.

  We can configure the distribution system ports to operate redundantly in pairs. In each pair, one port is the primary and one is the backup. We can create a Link Aggregation Group or LAG so that multiple ports can act as one larger connection. This allows the WLC and the switch to balance the traffic across multiple cables. Because WLCs don't have the ability to negotiate an EtherChannel, we must configure the switch ports with an unconditional or always-on EtherChannel configuration.
- The **Console Port** is used to configure the WLC locally.
- The **Redundancy Port** is used to connect one controller to another for redundancy. This is also known as High Availability.

To map each WLAN to a VLAN, we create a logical interface in the controller. We create one logical interface per WLAN. For each logical interface, we must specify the

- IP Address
- Subnet Mask
- Default Gateway
- DHCP Server IP Address
- VLAN ID. We can assign a VLAN to multiple WLANs.
- Physical port on the WLC. We can assign multiple WLANs to the same physical port.

What kinds of logical interfaces are available on a WLC?

- **Management Interface**. We only send management traffic over the management interface, such as SSH sessions, Network Time Protocol, user authentication, and logging. We also use this interface to establish tunnels between the LAP and the WLC.
- **Redundancy Management**. When we have two WLCs working together for redundancy, the active WLC uses the Management Interface, and the backup or standby WLC uses the Redundancy Management Interface. Each interface has a unique IP address.

  The primary WLC uses the IP address assigned to the Management Interface, and the backup or standby WLC uses the IP address assigned to the Redundancy Management Interface.

  Remember that these are not physical ports – the primary and backup traffic may travel through the same port on each WLC.
- **Virtual Interface**. This is the interface that a client connects to when it obtains a DHCP address or when it needs to authenticate. The client connects to the Virtual Interface's IP address, and the WLC relays the DHCP or authentication message to wherever it needs to go. Only clients see the Virtual Interface.

  We should assign the virtual interface a unique non-routable IP address such as a private IP address. If we have multiple WLCs, we should assign the Virtual Interface in each WLC the same IP address. That way, a client can move from one WLC to another without disrupting its connection. The client will assume that all the different WLCs are the same WLC.

- **Service Port Interface**. This interface is only used by the physical service port and can only be used for managing the WLC.
- **Dynamic Interface**. The Dynamic Interface connects a WLAN to a VLAN and is therefore used to move user traffic. We must create a different Dynamic Interface for each WLAN. Each Dynamic Interface must have its own IP address.

2.8 Describe AP and WLC management access connections (Telnet, SSH, HTTP, HTTPS, console, and TACACS+/RADIUS)

How do we access the configuration of a Cisco WAP?

- Connect to its Console port via a console cable
- Use SSH or Telnet
- Access its GUI (Graphical User Interface) via a web browser
- Configure it through the controller (if it is a LAP)

We can't make many configuration changes to a Cisco LAP because it obtains its configuration from the WLC. For example, we can tell the LAP the IP address of the WLC that it should connect to.

How do we access the configuration of a Cisco WLC?

- We can its web-based GUI via HTTP or HTTPS. We simply type the WLC's IP address into a web browser.
- We can use SSH.
- We can connect to it with a console cable. The first time we configure the WLC, we must set up a management IP address so that we can access it through a web-based GUI or through SSH. We might need to do this through a console cable.

The WLC supports the use of RADIUS or TACAS+ to authenticate users.

In an enterprise environment, when a user connects to a Wi-Fi connection, he enters a username and password (this might be the same username and password that is assigned to the user for other purposes such as e-mail, computer systems, etc.). The WLC takes these login credentials to an enterprise RADIUS or TACAS+ server and confirms that they are accurate and that the user is permitted to access the network.

We can also authenticate users with a set of local usernames and passwords.

We can also allow an administrator to log in to the controller using his enterprise username and password. The controller authenticates the user in the same manner.

2.9 Configure the components of a wireless LAN access for client connectivity using GUI only such as WLAN creation, security settings, QoS profiles, and advanced WLAN settings

A LAP advertises the SSID or Service Set Identifier so that a client can connect to the network. In the background, the WLC connects the WLAN to a VLAN. It takes traffic from the client and passes it to the network. Once we've created a WLAN on the controller, the controller will automatically configure all the LAPs.

The maximum number of WLANs on a controller is 512, but the maximum number that a LAP can broadcast is 16. Each new WLAN advertised by a LAP reduces the resources available to that LAP. The LAP must advertise each SSID on a regular interval, and the more WLANs we have, the more time the AP must spend broadcasting SSIDs, and the less time it can spend sending/receiving traffic. That means a LAP can spend more time advertising its SSIDs than it does sending and receiving traffic.

We should limit the number of SSIDs to three if possible. If we need a larger number of SSIDs, we might sort LAPs into different groups and assign some WLANs to some groups and other WLANs to other groups. For each WLAN, we must tell the controller

- The name of the SSID
- The controller interface and VLAN assigned to that WLAN
- The wireless security type we will use

The first step is to configure a security server to authenticate users who are attempting to connect to our wireless network. Each time a user attempts to connect to the wireless network, he is prompted to enter his credentials

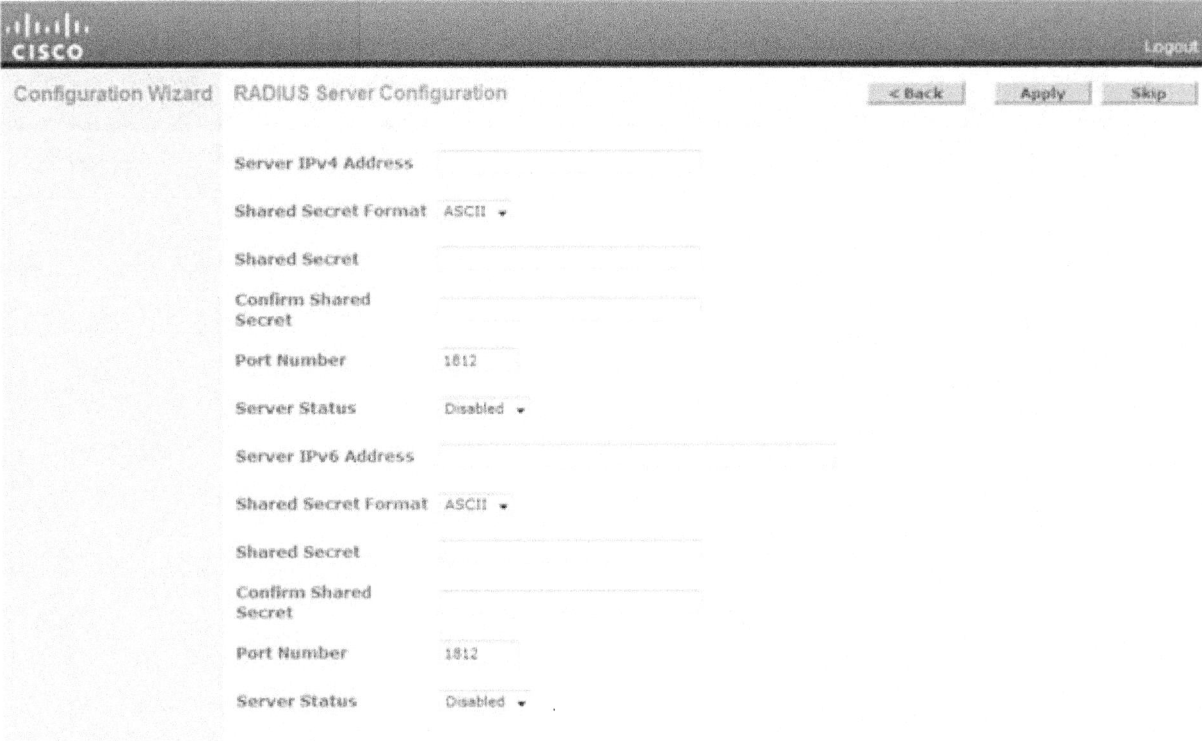

If we are authenticating users with a passcode, we don't need to do this. Otherwise, we choose **Security -> AAA -> RADIUS > Authentication**. We can set this up through the configuration wizard as well.

We must specify the server's IP address, shared secret, and port number. If we have multiple RADIUS servers, the controller will try each of them in order when attempting to authenticate a user. We can enable or disable a server from this page. When a server is disabled, the WLC won't attempt to authenticate a user through it.

Save Configuration | Ping | Logout | Refresh

CISCO MONITOR WLANs CONTROLLER WIRELESS SECURITY MANAGEMENT COMMANDS HELP FEEDBACK

Controller

General
Inventory
Interfaces
Interface Groups
Multicast
Internal DHCP Server
Mobility Management
Ports
NTP
CDP
Advanced

Interfaces

New...

Interface Name	VLAN Identifier	IP Address	Interface Type	Dynamic AP Management
management	untagged	10.0.20.103	Static	Enabled
virtual	N/A	1.1.1.1	Static	Not Supported

Second, we create a dynamic interface. Choose **Controller -> Interfaces**. The controller will show you all the existing interfaces. There will already be a management interface and a virtual interface. To create a dynamic interface, we must choose its name and assign a VLAN to it. We also assign it an IP address, subnet mask, gateway, and DHCP server address. When the interface receives a DHCP request from a client, it will forward the request to the DHCP server.

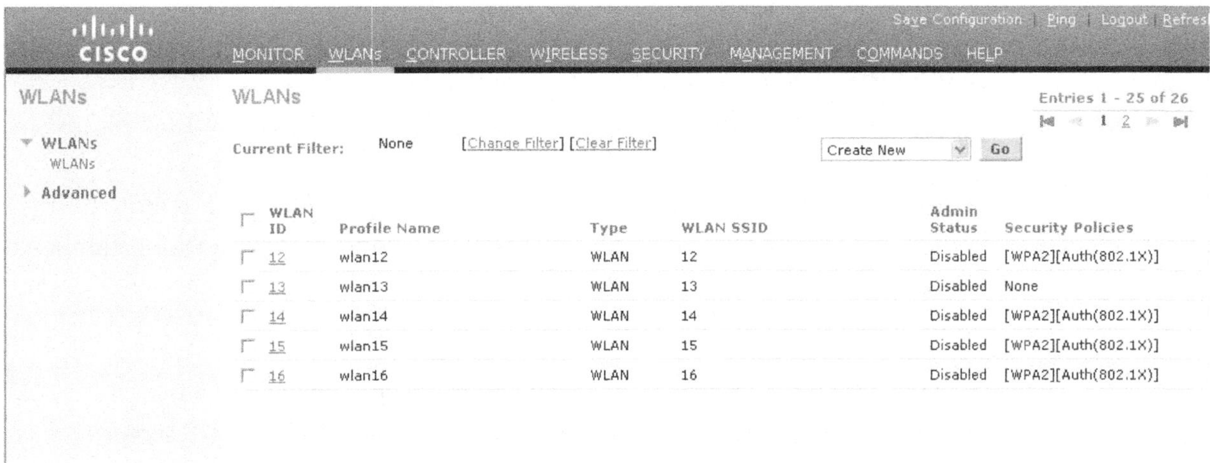

WLAN ID	Profile Name	Type	WLAN SSID	Admin Status	Security Policies
12	wlan12	WLAN	12	Disabled	[WPA2][Auth(802.1X)]
13	wlan13	WLAN	13	Disabled	None
14	wlan14	WLAN	14	Disabled	[WPA2][Auth(802.1X)]
15	wlan15	WLAN	15	Disabled	[WPA2][Auth(802.1X)]
16	wlan16	WLAN	16	Disabled	[WPA2][Auth(802.1X)]

Third, we create a new WLAN. Choose WLANs and the controller will show you all the existing WLANs. To create a new WLAN, we must specify the SSID name and a descriptive name. We also choose a WLAN ID number. There are more advanced options for each WLAN, which you can specify after it has been created

- Whether the WLAN is enabled or disabled
- The type of security enabled on the WLAN

- Whether the WLAN will be broadcasted on all LAPs or only on LAPs that support 2.4Ghz or only on LAPs that support 5Ghz. This is called the Radio Policy, and it can be specified by selecting a policy such as 802.11a, 802.11a/g, 802.11g, or 802.11b/g. By default, a WLAN will be broadcast on all LAPs.

- The dynamic interface that is connected to the WLAN. We must create a dynamic interface before we can properly configure a WLAN.

- Whether the LAPs should broadcast the SSID name or whether it should be hidden. Some administrators believe having a hidden network is a good idea, but in practice it is ineffective.

- The WLAN security type. There are several options, including some that are no longer considered secure. We should select a secure option.

  - **None**. This is also known as Open Authentication.

  - **WPA+WPA2**. This uses Wi-Fi protected access. In other words, a user must enter a static security key.

  - **802.1x**. This uses EAP authentication with dynamic WEP.

  - **Static WEP**. This uses a static WEP key that a user must enter. WEP is considered insecure.

  - **Static WEP + 802.1x**. This uses EAP authentication or a static WEP key.

  - **CKIP**. This uses the Cisco Key Integrity Protocol.

  - **None + EAP Passthrough**. This uses open authentication with remote EAP authentication. The client device can connect via open authentication, and then the user is authenticated via EAP.

Once we select a general security type, we can choose a more specific security type. Remember that we created a security server connection earlier (a RADIUS server).

If we select an option with 802.1x, then the controller will pass the user's login credentials to an external authentication server. That means that the controller doesn't decide if a user is allowed to connect – it asks another server if that user is permitted to connect. In the AAA Servers tab, we can choose up to six of the servers we specified earlier. The WLC will try each server in order when attempting to authenticate a user.

The WLC will contact each server through the management interface. We can check the Radius Server Overwrite Interface box so that the WLC can contact the server through its dynamic interface instead.

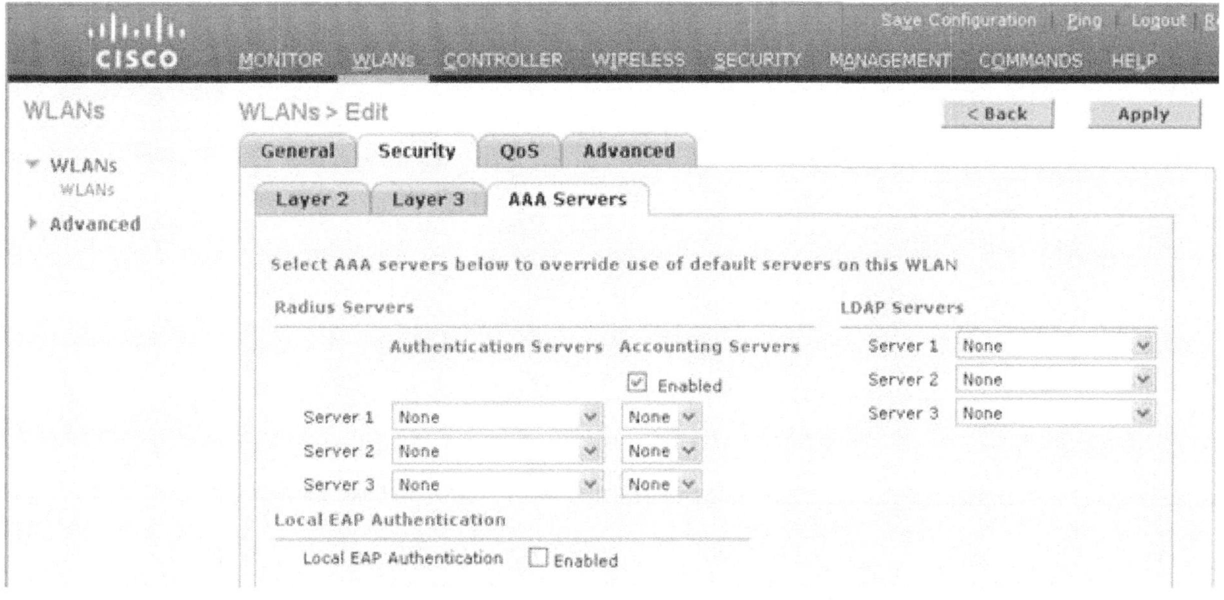

We next need to configure the Quality of Service by selecting QoS. The controller will not prioritize traffic on any WLAN by default. Each wireless frame is given the same priority. We can ask the WLC to give traffic from specific WLANs a higher priority. The following priorities are available

- Platinum for voice traffic
- Gold for video conferencing traffic
- Silver for regular traffic
- Bronze for background traffic

There are more advanced features that we can configure include detecting holes in the Wi-Fi coverage, blocking specific clients from connecting, or limiting the amount of traffic that each client can pass.

By default, a WLAN session expires after thirty minutes. The client must reauthenticate with the WLC after the time expires. That means that your Wi-Fi will disconnect every thirty minutes. We can adjust this time limit.

The WLC maintains a set of security policies, which you can view under **Security -> Wireless Protection Policies -> Client Exclusion Policies**. If a client violates one of these policies, it is blocked from connecting for 60 seconds. Possible violations include using the wrong IP address or entering the wrong password.

By default, you cannot manage a WLC from a Wi-Fi connection. The WLC blocks management traffic that originates on a Wi-Fi connection to prevent rogue users from attempting to modify settings on the controller. You must connect to the WLC through a wired connection, unless you change this.

3.0 IP Connectivity

3.1 Interpret the components of routing table

3.1.a Routing protocol code

3.1.b Prefix

3.1.c Network mask

3.1.d Next hop

3.1.e Administrative distance

3.1.f Metric

3.1.g Gateway of last resort

For a while I've been talking about switches and how we forward traffic on a local network. Let's think about routers now. A router forwards traffic from one local network to another.

I mentioned earlier that we can connect a router to another router via an Ethernet WAN or a serial connection (which users HDLC).

You will see three types of Cisco routers

- A **SOHO** (**Small Office Home Office**) router. This type of router offers basic connectivity to commercial broadband internet. It will also offer basic DHCP, firewall VPN features. It may not support WANs, HDLC, or MPLS technology.

- A standard **Enterprise** router. This type of router supports all the major enterprise features including VPN, WAN, DHCP. It will certainly support multiple WAN or serial connections.

- An **ISR (Integrated Services Router)**. The Cisco ISRs offer Enterprise features, but they also offer advanced features such as VoIP management, advanced firewalls, and threat detection. An ISR's hardware can be upgraded – we can install cards to provide the router with additional interfaces so that it can connect to a T1, a CSU/DSU, analog phones, etc.

How do we connect a router? What are the basic steps?

- Connect the router's LAN port to the switch
- Connect the router's WAN to an ISP interface (like a modem or CSU/DSU). Connect the Ethernet WAN if you have one
- Connect to the console port
- Power on the router
- Configure the router. Specifically, we should configure the router interfaces, the routing protocol, and the security settings. If we have a router with advanced features, we should configure those as well.

I already talked about the basic configuration of a router or switch in section two. Some ideas that are the same on a Cisco router and on a switch

- User, enable and configure terminal modes, and the process of logging in to them
- Console port connection and terminal settings
- Ability to access the router through Telnet or SSH
- Router hostname configuration
- Router interface configuration, including the speed and duplex
- Command to shutdown an interface or to turn it back on (no shutdown)
- Running and start up configuration and the ability to save the running config to the start up config
- Memory types and purposes

What is different about a router?

- A router does not have VLANs. We do not configure VLANs on a router.
- A router interface can be configured with a static IP address or a DHCP address. A switch port interface does not have an IP address
- All router interfaces, by default, are shutdown. They must be turned on manually.
- A router may have an auxiliary port to connect to a remote modem
- A router, by default, does not allow access via Telnet or SSH. It must be manually enabled.
- A router uses the **show ip interface brief** to tell us about the interfaces and their status.

Let's look at the **show ip interface brief** command some more.

```
Router#show ip interface brief
Interface              IP-Address      OK? Method Status                Protocol
GigabitEthernet0/0/0   unassigned      YES unset  up                    down
GigabitEthernet0/0/1   unassigned      YES DHCP   administratively down down
GigabitEthernet0/0/2   unassigned      YES unset  administratively down down
Loopback0              100.100.100.100 YES manual up                    up
Vlan1                  unassigned      YES unset  administratively down down
```

- **Line Status** or **Status** tells us if the physical layer is working (if the cable is plugged in)
    - Administratively down means that the interface was shut down. By default, an interface is shut down unless we turn it on.
    - Down means that the cable is unplugged or that there is some other communication issue on the physical layer
- **Protocol Status** or **Protocol** tells us if the Layer 2 is working (if the device is communicating)
    - If the Line is Up and Protocol is Down, then there is probably a speed or duplex mismatch between the router and another router

It's not possible for the Protocol to be up and the Line Status to be down.

We can also type **`show protocols`** to view this data.

```
Router#show protocols
Global values:
  Internet Protocol routing is enabled
GigabitEthernet0/0/0 is up, line protocol is down
GigabitEthernet0/0/1 is administratively down, line protocol is down
GigabitEthernet0/0/2 is administratively down, line protocol is down
Loopback0 is up, line protocol is up
  Internet address is 100.100.100.100/24
Vlan1 is administratively down, line protocol is down
```

How do we configure a router interface? From the configure terminal, we type **`interface <interface name>`**. We can configure the following additional settings on an interface

- **`ip address <IP address> <subnet mask>`** - most router interfaces will be configured statically, but if the router interface will receive an IP address via DHCP, we don't need to enter this command.
- **`no shutdown`** – by default, an interface will be shutdown. We must turn it on so that we can use it.
- **`description <name>`** - this command is optional and allows us to give the interface a memorable description

If we type **`show ip route`**, the router will print a list of routes that are configured on it.

```
Router#show ip route
Codes: L - local, C - connected, S - static, R - RIP, M - mobile, B - BGP
       D - EIGRP, EX - EIGRP external, O - OSPF, IA - OSPF inter area
       N1 - OSPF NSSA external type 1, N2 - OSPF NSSA external type 2
       E1 - OSPF external type 1, E2 - OSPF external type 2, E - EGP
       i - IS-IS, L1 - IS-IS level-1, L2 - IS-IS level-2, ia - IS-IS inter area
       * - candidate default, U - per-user static route, o - ODR
       P - periodic downloaded static route

Gateway of last resort is not set

     100.0.0.0/8 is variably subnetted, 2 subnets, 2 masks
C       100.100.100.0/24 is directly connected, Loopback0
L       100.100.100.100/32 is directly connected, Loopback0
S       100.100.50.0/24 [1/0] via 100.100.50.1
```

I will explain some terms briefly now, and we will learn more about them in the coming sections. Each time a router receives a packet, it needs to decide where to send it. How? It checks the routing table. The routing table has a list of routes.

Each route has a list of destination networks and where traffic addressed to that network should be sent. For example, a route might say traffic addressed to network 10.10.0.0/24 (the range would be 10.10.0.0 to 10.10.0.255) should go to router 10.10.0.1. If our router receives a packet addressed to 10.10.0.50, it would check the route table and realize that it should be sent to 10.10.0.1.

In front of each route is a letter or a code. The router displays a legend that tells us what each code means. For example, L means local, and S means static. This code is better known as **the routing protocol code**. It tells us how the router learned the route.

Next to the code is an IP address (known as a prefix) and a subnet mask (the slash followed by a number). Together, they identify a network. For example, 100.100.100.0/24 identifies the network with the range of IP addresses from 100.100.100.0 to 100.100.100.255. The router knows that any packet addressed to an address within this range must follow what this route tells us.

The last route on the list says that it is "via 100.100.50.1". That means that traffic in that route should be sent to the next router, which has an address of 100.100.50.1. This router is known as the **next hop router**. When our router sees a packet addressed to a host in the 100.100.50.0/24 network, it sends it to the 100.100.50.1 router.

We might have multiple routes to the same destination network. The router might know about a route because it is directly connected, because an administrator programmed it, or because it learned it from another router. When there are multiple routes, which one should the router use?

In brackets after the network name is the number "[1/0"]. The first number is the **administrative distance**. The administrative distance tells us how much the router trusts the route. The lower the number, the more the router trusts the route. The router will choose the route that it trusts the most.

The second number is the **metric**. The metric tells us how efficient the route is. The longer the route, the higher the metric. Again, the router will choose a route with the lowest metric.

When the router receives a packet addressed to a network, but does not have a route to that network, it sends the packet to the **gateway of last resort**. We must manually configure the gateway of last resort on the router. In my example, the gateway of last resort is not set.

A route will only appear in the routing table if the interface that it is connected to is up and up (the status and line protocol are up). When the interface goes down, the router will remove its applicable routes from the routing table. When the interface comes back up, the router will return the applicable routes to the routing table.

Let's review how a router learns the different routes so that it can forward packets

- **Connected Route** – the router automatically learns about other routes that are directly connected to it. Each router will have at least two directly connected routes – one to its LAN and one to its WAN.
- **Static Route** – an administrator can manually program the router with a route. This is known as a static route.
- **Routing Protocol** – the router learns routes to far away networks from other routers that are directly connected to it. It does so through a routing protocol. There are several types of routing protocols and we will learn how they work.

Remember that when a device wants to send a packet, it asks if the destination IP address is in the local subnet (the LAN). If so, it sends the packet to the local switch. It uses ARP to find the MAC address of the destination device, and the switch forwards it. If not, then it sends the packet to the router. It encapsulates the packet in an Ethernet frame and addresses that frame with the router's MAC address.

But what does the router do exactly when it receives a packet?

- First the router makes sure that the packet arrived without error.
- It verifies that the packet is actually addressed to the router (it is possible for the router to receive packets through a broadcast that are not addressed to it)
- The router deencapsulates the old frame headers revealing the IP packet inside
- The router looks up the destination in the routing table, based on the IP address

- It checks the ARP table for the destination router's MAC address. If it is not there, it requests it through ARP
- Encapsulate the frame with the destination router's MAC address and sends the frame

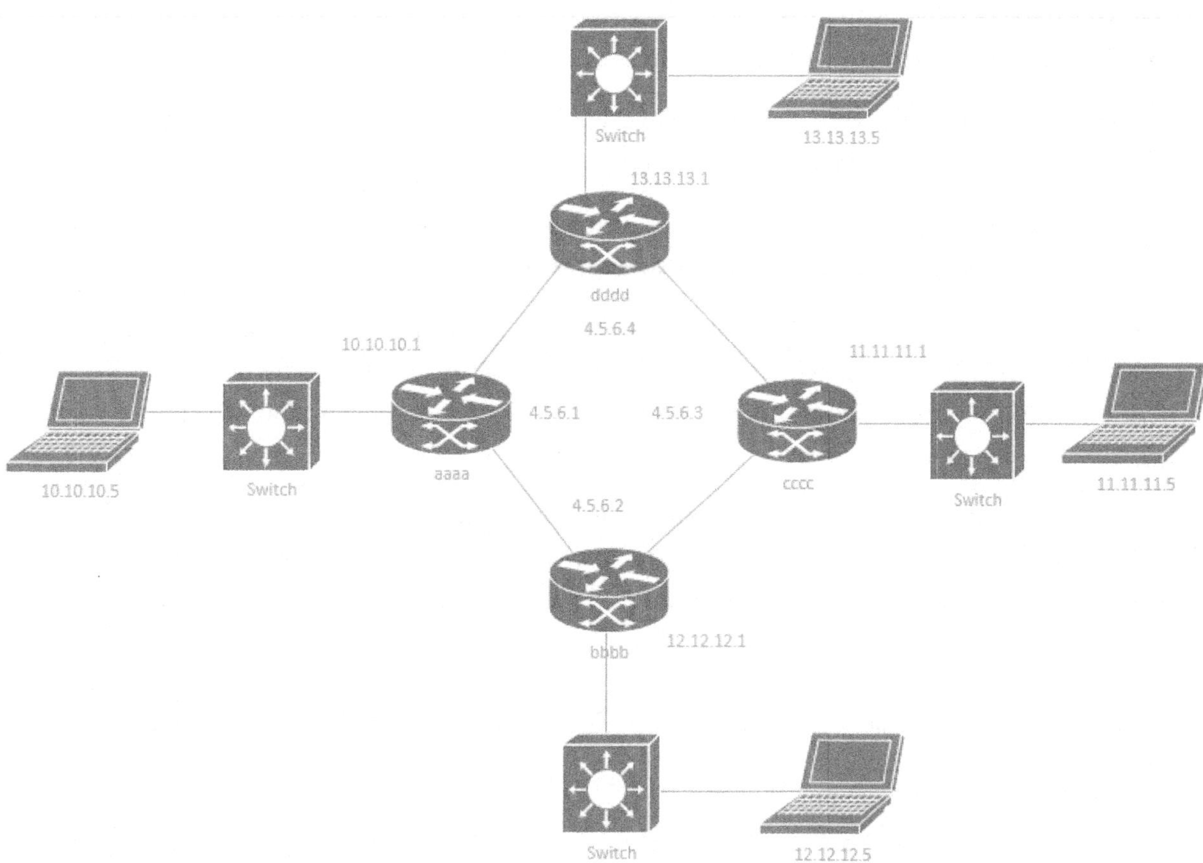

The computer on the left has an IP address of 10.10.10.5 and it wants to send a message to the computer on the right, which has an IP address of 11.11.11.5. Our router has a MAC address of aaaa, and the computer on the right is connected to a router with a MAC address of cccc.

Computer 10.10.10.5 prepares an IP packet addressed to 11.11.11.5. It realizes that 11.11.11.5 is not on its local network. Thus, it encapsulates the IP packet into a frame addressed to its local router's MAC address (aaaa). The router aaaa receives the packet and checks its routing table.

Notice that each router has a local interface in its subnet (with a local IP address), and a WAN interface in the wan subnet (that starts with 4.5.6). When a device wants to talk to its local router, it uses the local interface. When a router wants to talk with another router, it uses that router's WAN interface.

Maybe router aaaa has the following routes

- 10.10.10.0/24 via the local interface. This is the directly connected local network on the left.

- 12.12.12.0/24 via router 4.5.6.2. This router is directly connected, so our router learns it automatically.
- 13.13.13.0/24 via router 4.5.6.4. This router is also directly connected, so our router learns it automatically.
- 11.11.11.0/24 via router 4.5.6.2. This router is not directly connected, so our router learns it from router bbbb (4.5.6.2).
- 11.11.11.0/24 via router 4.5.6.4. Our router also learns this route from router dddd (4.5.6.4).

The router knows that it can send the packet to the router with the IP address 4.5.6.2 or 4.5.6.4. Let's say that the route through 4.5.6.2 is better, so the router chooses that one.

It sends an ARP message to router 4.5.6.2 and learns that its MAC address is bbbb. It encapsulates the packet in a frame with the destination MAC address bbbb, and sends it to bbbb.

The router bbbb receives the frame and dencapsulates it. The router checks its routing table and sees that it has a directly connected route to network 11.11.11.0/24. Using the same process, it obtains the MAC address to the router 11.11.11.1, which is cccc. It encapsulates the packet with an Ethernet frame and sends it to cccc.

Router cccc receives the frame and dencapsulates it. The router checks its routing table and sees that 11.11.11.5 is in the local network. It encapsulates the frame with the MAC address of the computer 11.11.11.5 and sends it to the computer.

We can configure an interface on a router by entering the interface configuration. There are several items we can configure

- **mac-address <MAC address>**. This sets a configured MAC address for an interface. It is optional because the interface will have a default MAC address from the factory that the router can use. If our interface did not have a MAC address, the router would use the MAC address of the lowest-numbered interface.

- **ip address <IP address> <subnet mask>** allows us to set an IPv4 address on the interface

- **ip address dhcp** allows the router to learn the IPv4 address via DHCP

- **ipv6 address <address/prefix length> eui-64** allows the router to generate an EUI-64 IP address on the interface. A Cisco router will understand the abbreviated address. In other words, we can type **ipv6 address <address>/64 eui-64**

- **ipv6 address dhcp** allows the router to learn the IPv6 address through DHCP

- **ipv6 address autoconfig** allows the router to use the SLAAC to configure an IP address

- **`ipv6 address <address> link-local`** tells the router to use a specific link-local address (instead of automatically generating an IPv6 address). A router will automatically generate a link local IP address on any enabled interface. It's possible to create a WAN link with only IPv6 link-local addresses.

- If a host needs to contact a service but doesn't know the IP address of the router that offers it, it sends a message to a single Anycast address. Upon receipt of a packet addressed to an Anycast address, the network forwards it to a single router that offers the applicable service (even though there may be many). Routers forward the Anycast packet until it reaches a router that can accept it. We can configure an Anycast address by typing **`ipv6 address <IP address> anycast`**.

A router won't support IPv6 out of the box. We must enable it by typing **`ipv6 routing`** in global configuration mode.

CCNA doesn't mention the ping or tracert commands explicitly, but they are important to know.

The ping command tells us if a host is reachable. Ping uses ICMP or Internet Control Message Protocol. The formal name for ping is

- **ICMP echo request** – this is the packet that we send to the host

- **ICMP echo response** – this is the packet that the host sends back

ICMP does not use TCP or UDP. It is its own Layer 3 protocol. ICMP works on most operating systems – Windows, Mac, UNIX, and it works inside Cisco IOS devices.

When we send a ping, the ping command uses default parameters. We can modify the following parameters

- How many times we should send the ping request

- Whether we shouldping an IP address or a hostname (if we ping a hostname, the operating system will find the IP address via a DNS lookup and then ping that)

- How long we should wait until we assume that the ping has timed out

- How big should each packet be

- Whether we should send the pings continually or just a few times

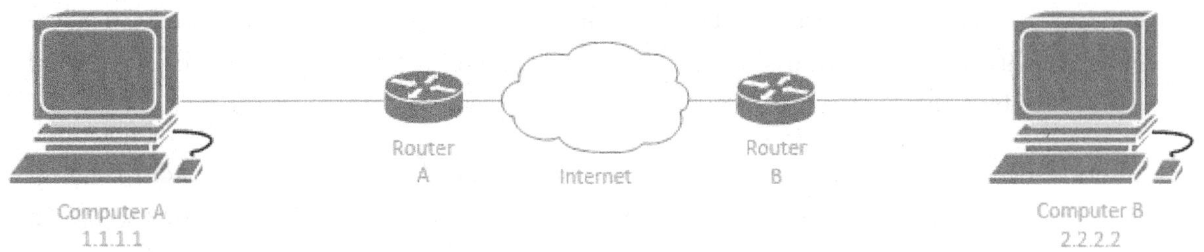

If Computer A can't reach Computer B, one of the first troubleshooting steps we can take is to ping Computer B from Computer A. There are many issues that can cause a host to become unreachable, but we should try to ping it first. If we are in a remote location and can't connect to Computer A to perform the ping, we might log in to Router A via SSH and ping Computer B from inside Router A.

By default, a Cisco router will send five pings. If the router does not receive a reply within two seconds, it assumes that the ping timed out (failed).

An example of a failed ping is below.

```
Router#ping 2.2.2.2

Type escape sequence to abort.
Sending 5, 100-byte ICMP Echos to 2.2.2.2, timeout is 2 seconds:
.....
Success rate is 0 percent (0/5)
```

An example of a successful ping is below.

```
Router#ping 2.2.2.2

Type escape sequence to abort.
Sending 5, 100-byte ICMP Echos to 2.2.2.2, timeout is 2 seconds:
!!!!!
Success rate is 100 percent (5/5), round-trip min/avg/max = 33/34/36 ms
```

The first time we ping a remote router that we haven't connected to before, we usually receive a success rate of four out of five. Upon receipt of the first ping message, the remote router will check its ARP table. It won't find the MAC address of the router that initiated the ping, and so it will be unable to reply. The remote router will an ARP request too learn the local router's MAC address. Upon receipt of the local router's MAC address, it will reply to the ping. This process takes more than two seconds, and thus the ping times out.

If we can ping Router B from Router A, that means that Router A has a route to Router B. It also means that Router B has a route back to Router A. If we are able to ping Computer B from Router A, it also means that Router B has a LAN connection to Computer B.

It goes without saying that if the ping works, then the physical connection between the routers is working. Also, the ARP is functional because Router A learned Router B's MAC address.

What IP address does Router A use when pinging Router B? It uses the external subnet IP address interface (the one that connects it to Router B), not the one that connects it to Computer A. That means that the connection between Router A and Router B is working, but it doesn't mean that Router A can send traffic back to Computer A.

For further verification, we can perform an **extended ping**. We want to send the ping from Router A, but from computer A's subnet.

The normal ping command is **ping <IP address or hostname>**.

To create an extended ping, we type **ping <IP address> source <source IP address>**.

If ping works from the external subnet, but not from the internal subnet, then we know that there is a routing issue inside our router.

We can also ping Computer A from Router A. If the ping fails, then we know that the internal network (switch) may be the issue. If not, then we know that the switch is working which means that the switch knows the router's MAC address and Computer A's MAC address.

If I can't ping Computer A from Router A

- Computer A might have the wrong static IP (in the wrong subnet) or could not access a DHCP server
- The switch is not configured with the correct VLAN
- The switch is blocking traffic to/from the router or to/from Computer A

We can also ping Computer A from Router A's external interface. If the ping from the internal interface is good, but the external interface fails, then the router is not passing traffic, or Computer A does not have the correct default gateway. Why? A ping from the internal interface will reach Computer A and receive a reply due to ARP – Computer A will figure out Router A's internal MAC address, but a ping from the external IP won't.

If we send the packet from Router A's external IP address, Computer A will try to reply. It will realize that the interface is outside the subnet, but it won't know what gateway to send its reply to.

When we have multiple routers in a pathway and one of them is the problem, we can run a tracert (traceroute). Where did traceroute come from? Here is another question. You know that switches can get rid of loops by using Spanning Tree Protocol?

How do routers get rid of loops? In each IP Packet header is a field called the **Time to Live** or **TTL**. When a device creates the packet, it usually gives it a TTL value of 30. Each time the packet reaches a router, the router deducts one from the TTL and sends it to the next router. If the TTL gets to zero, the router drops it (does not forward it). This prevents loops because a packet in a loop will eventually have a TTL of 0 and disappear Actually, the router that sets the TTL to zero sends a reply that says "TTL exceeded".

So what? If we wanted to find all the routers in a pathway, we would send a traceroute message with a TTL of 1. The first router would set the TTL to zero and reply with the "TTL exceeded" message, and we would identify it. Then we would send a traceroute message with a TTL of 2. The first router would set the TTL to one and the second router would set the TTL to zero and reply with the "TTL exceeded" message, and we would identify it. We keep doing this until we have reached the destination at the end.

That is what the traceroute command does, except that it sends three packets at a time. We measure how long it takes to receive a reply – this is called the round-trip time.

A router usually replies with its TTL exceeded message on the IP address of the source interface that received the original message and not the destination address that would be forwarding the message.

We can change the default parameters of traceroute just like we can with ping, or we can just type traceroute and use the default settings.

3.2 Determine how a router makes a forwarding decision by default

3.2.a Longest match

3.2.b Administrative distance

3.2.c Routing protocol metric

Let's say that my router has three active routes

- 10.5.5.0/24 via 11.11.11.1
- 10.5.5.0/25 via 11.11.11.2
- 10.5.5.7/32 via 11.11.11.3

These routes overlap somewhat.

- 10.5.5.0/24 has a range from 10.5.5.0 to 10.5.5.254
- 10.5.5.0/25 has a range from 10.5.5.0 to 10.5.5.127
- 10.5.5.7/32 has a range of a single IP address – 10.5.5.7

If my router receives a packet addressed to 10.5.5.253, which route will it choose? It will choose the route via 11.11.11.1 because that is the only applicable route. What if my router receives a packet addressed to 10.5.5.7? Which route will it choose? All three routes are applicable, but the router will choose the route through 11.11.11.3.

Why? When there are overlapping routes, the router will choose the most specific route. That is the route with the narrowest network. This is known as the **longest match forwarding decision** because the router is selecting the route with the longest network prefix.

The router gives each route an administrative distance. The administrative distance is a measure of how much the router trusts the source that it learned the route from.

Below is a table that summarizes the administrative distance of each route source (also known as the default distance). The router learns routes from other routers through protocols such as EIGRP, BGP, or OSPF.

Route Source	Default Distance Values
Connected interface	0
Static route	1
Enhanced Interior Gateway Routing Protocol (EIGRP) summary route	5
External Border Gateway Protocol (BGP)	20
Internal EIGRP	90
IGRP	100
OSPF	110

Intermediate System-to-Intermediate System (IS-IS)	115
Routing Information Protocol (RIP)	120
Exterior Gateway Protocol (EGP)	140
On Demand Routing (ODR)	160
External EIGRP	170
Internal BGP	200
Unknown	255

The router will choose the route with the shortest distance. A router does not believe routes that have a distance of 255 and will not route traffic to them. As we will learn, we can manually change the administrative distance. We might want a router to prioritize the use of a route learned from a neighboring router.

Going back to my active routes. Let's pretend that

- 10.5.5.0/24 via 11.11.11.1 has a distance of 1
- 10.5.5.0/25 via 11.11.11.2 has a distance of 5
- 10.5.5.7/32 via 11.11.11.3 has a distance of 20

My router receives a packet addressed to 10.5.5.7. Which route does it choose? It still chooses 11.11.11.3 (with an administrative distance of 20). Why? The router always gives priority to the route with the longest prefix. If we have multiple routes with the same prefix length, for example

- 10.5.5.7/32 via 11.11.11.1 has a distance of 1
- 10.5.5.7/32 via 11.11.11.2 has a distance of 5
- 10.5.5.7/32 via 11.11.11.3 has a distance of 20

Then it would choose the route with the shortest distance.

What if I have three routes with the same prefix length and the same administrative distance? Let's say that the router learned three different routes to the same network via the BGP protocol. Which one does the router choose?

- 10.5.5.7/32 via 11.11.11.1 has a distance of 20
- 10.5.5.7/32 via 11.11.11.2 has a distance of 20
- 10.5.5.7/32 via 11.11.11.3 has a distance of 20

Well, the protocol must assign a metric to each route. The metric tells us how efficient the route is. There are two common ways to measure efficiency – the speed of the connection or the number of routers or "hops" that a packet must pass through in order to reach its destination.

- 10.5.5.7/32 via 11.11.11.1 has a distance of 20 and a metric of 5
- 10.5.5.7/32 via 11.11.11.2 has a distance of 20 and a metric of 7

- 10.5.5.7/32 via 11.11.11.3 has a distance of 20 and a metric of 14

In this case, the router would choose the route via 11.11.11.1 because it has the shortest metric and because the prefix length and administrative distance tied with the other two routes.

We will learn more about administrative distances and routing protocols later in this section.

3.3 Configure and verify IPv4 and IPv6 static routing

3.3.a Default route

3.3.b Network route

3.3.c Host route

3.3.d Floating static

There are three types of static routes

- **Network Route** – this is a route to an entire subnet. For example, 10.5.5.0/24 is a static route to the network with a range from 10.5.5.0 to 10.5.5.255
- **Host Route** – this a route to a single IP address. For example, 10.5.5.5/32 is a route to 10.5.5.5.
- **Default Route** – this is a route that the router uses when no other routes match the destination of a packet. It is the route of last resort.

We can configure a static route by telling the router either what local interface to use or what destination to send the traffic to. For example, we can either write **`ip route <subnet name> <subnet mask> <local interface>`** or **`ip route <subnet name> <subnet mask> <destination ip>`**.

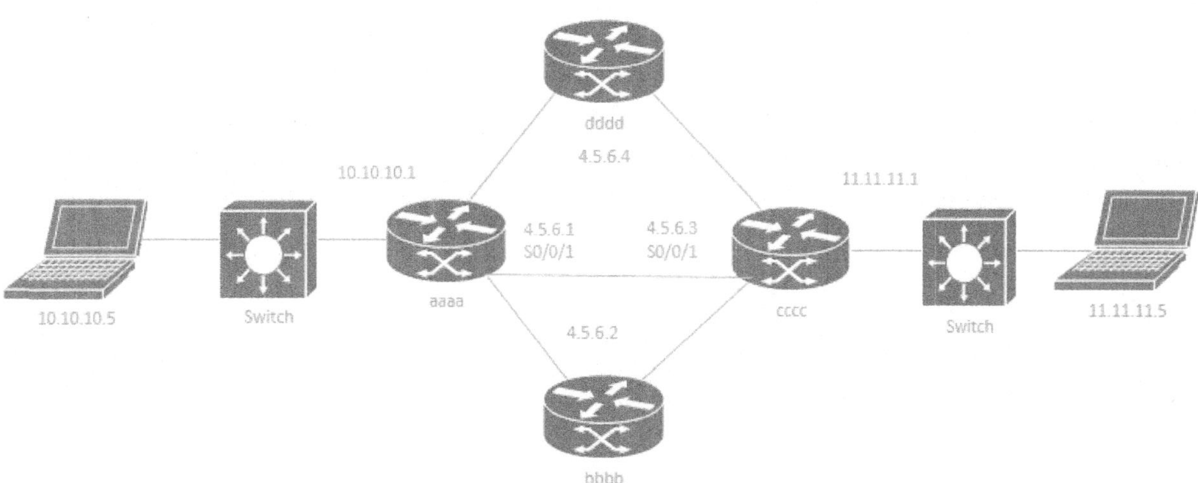

For example, I would like to program router aaaa to use a static route to router cccc's network (11.11.11.0/24). I know that router cccc is connected to router aaaa via the interface S0/0/1.

- I would write **ip route 11.11.11.0 255.255.255.0 S0/0/0**. In effect, I told my router "send packets addressed to the 11.11.11.0/24 network out via the S0/0/0 interface, and the device on the other end of that interface will take care of the rest".

- I could also write **ip route 11.11.11.0 255.255.255.0 4.5.6.3** because I know that router cccc has an IP address of 4.5.6.3. In effect, I told my router "send packets addressed to the 11.11.11.0/24 network to 4.5.6.3, and 4.5.6.3 will take care of the rest".

  If we create a route using a destination IP, the router will only use it if the destination has a route already. That means that router aaaa will only use this route if it knows of an actual route to 4.5.6.3 first. In our case, 4.5.6.3 is directly connected to interface S0/0/1. But if it wasn't – if our router couldn't reach 4.5.6.3, or if S0/0/1 wasn't configured – this command would not accomplish anything. Remember, when we enter this command, the router must guess which interface 4.5.6.3 is connected to.

```
Router(config)#ip route 11.11.11.0 255.255.255.0 S0/0/0
Router(config)#ip route 11.11.11.0 255.255.255.0 4.5.6.3
Router(config)#
```

Notice that I wrote out the full subnet mask in the command.

The router removes static routes from its routing table when they stop working. When they start working again, they are added back. If we want to keep the route in the table no matter what, we type **ip route <subnet name> <subnet mask> <local interface> permanent**.

We can verify the static routes configured inside our router by typing **show ip route static**. The first route (the one with the S0/0/0 interface will show up in the routing table as being "directly connected". The second route (the one with the 4.5.6.3 IP address) will show up in the routing table as being connected "via 4.5.6.3".

```
Router#show ip route
Codes: L - local, C - connected, S - static, R - RIP, M - mobile, B - BGP
       D - EIGRP, EX - EIGRP external, O - OSPF, IA - OSPF inter area
       N1 - OSPF NSSA external type 1, N2 - OSPF NSSA external type 2
       E1 - OSPF external type 1, E2 - OSPF external type 2, E - EGP
       i - IS-IS, L1 - IS-IS level-1, L2 - IS-IS level-2, ia - IS-IS inter area
       * - candidate default, U - per-user static route, o - ODR
       P - periodic downloaded static route

Gateway of last resort is not set


C       11.11.11.0 is directly connected, S0/0/0
S       11.11.11.0 is connected via 4.5.6.3
```

A static route is assigned a priority (administrative distance) of 1. It is always the first route used, when there are multiple routes with the same prefix length. If we want to give a static route a shorter priority, we type **ip route <subnet name> <subnet mask> <local interface> <priority>**, for example **ip route 11.11.11.0 255.255.255.0 4.5.6.3 priority 90**.

How can we troubleshoot a static route? What could go wrong?

- The router does not check to make sure that the static route is accurate when we enter it. The router cannot predict the external network topology. If we have the wrong subnet or the wrong network name or the wrong destination or the wrong interface, then the route won't work.

- If the route is configured correctly but does not appear routing table, that means we didn't add the route, or the link is down, or the router doesn't have a connected route for our static route.

- Even if the route is in the routing table, the router might not use it if another route with a shorter administrative distance or longer prefix is present.

If we type **show ip route <IP address>** the router will tell us what route it will choose to get to a particular IP address. For example, I have only three active routes in my router. I asked the router what route it would choose to reach 10.10.1.1, but it didn't have an active route. I asked the router what route it would choose to reach 100.100.100.5, and it said that it was directly connected. It matched the route with the network 100.100.100.0/24.

```
     100.0.0.0/8 is variably subnetted, 2 subnets, 2 masks
C       100.100.100.0/24 is directly connected, Loopback0
L       100.100.100.100/32 is directly connected, Loopback0

Router#show ip route 10.10.1.1
% Network not in table

Router#show ip route 100.100.100.5
Routing entry for 100.100.100.0/24
Known via "connected", distance 0, metric 0 (connected, via interface)
  Routing Descriptor Blocks:
  * directly connected, via Loopback0
      Route metric is 0, traffic share count is 1
```

We can configure an IPv6 static route by typing **ipv6 route <destination network> <next-hop IPv6 address>** or **ipv6 route <destination network> <outgoing interface>**. We can specify both the next-hop IPv6 address and the outgoing interface.

We can configure the global unicast address or the link-local address of the next router as our destination.

If we use a global unicast address, the router can determine the proper outgoing interface to get to the destination. If we use a link-local destination address, we must also specify the outgoing interface through **ipv6 route <destination network> <outgoing interface> <next-hop IPv6 address>**.

We can create a route to a single IP address instead of a network. It is just a matter of using a /128 mask. We would type **ipv6 route <destination network/128> <next-hop IPv6 address>**.

For example

- My destination router has a network of aaaa:aaaa:aaaa:aaaa:: /64,
- My destination router has an IPv6 address of aaaa:aaaa:aaaa:aaaa:bbbb:bbbb:bbbb:bbbb facing my local router's interface,
- My destination router has an IPv6 link-local address of fe80:0000:0000:0000:0000:0000:0000:0000 facing my local router's interface, and
- My destination router is connected to my local router's G0/0/1 interface

I could configure a static route with any of the following commands

- **ipv6 route aaaa:aaaa:aaaa:aaaa:: /64 aaaa:aaaa:aaaa:aaaa:bbbb:bbbb:bbbb:bbbb** – this tells the router to send traffic to the aaaa:aaaa:aaaa:aaaa:bbbb:bbbb:bbbb:bbbb router. Since this is a global unicast IPv6 address, our local router automatically detects it on the G0/0/1 interface and knows to send traffic out of that interface.

- **ipv6 route aaaa:aaaa:aaaa:aaaa:: /64 G0/0/1** – this tells the router to send the traffic out of the G0/0/1 interface. The router already knows the IPv6 address of the destination router connected to this interface.
- **ipv6 route aaaa:aaaa:aaaa:aaaa:: /64 G0/0/1 fe80:0000:0000:0000:0000:0000:0000:0000** – this tells the router to send traffic out the G0/0/1 interface, but also that it should go to the fe80:: address.

Remember that like in IPv4, a router will automatically detect directly connected IPv6 addresses and create routes for them. It won't create routes for directly connected link-local addresses.

To configure the default route, we type **ipv6 route ::/0 <outgoing interface>**. We could also type **ipv6 route ::/0 <destination>**. Remember that since this route has the widest prefix, the router will choose it last.

When we want the router to give priority to routes learned from a routing protocol, but also want it to remember some static routes in case those protocols fail, we configure a floating route. A static route has an administrative distance of one. That is the highest priority a route can have. We can give a static route a higher administrative distance by typing **ip route <destination network> <next-hop IP address> <administrative distance>** or **ipv6 route <destination network> <next-hop IPv6 address> <administrative distance>**.

We should give the route an administrative distance that is higher than the one given to the routing protocol in use.

We can verify the routes by typing

- **show ipv6 route local** to see the local routes
- **show ipv6 route static** to see the static routes

If we want to know which route a router will take, we can ask it with show ipv6 route **<IPv6 address of destination>** and the router will tell us what route it would choose.

We should always verify the static route before entering it. Verify that you chose the correct interface, next-hop IPv4 or IPv6 address, and prefix/prefix length or subnet mask. The Cisco router will accept static route commands that are poorly constructed, as long as the syntax is correct.

Routers and VLANs didn't make sense earlier because we didn't know enough about routers. But remember that if I want to pass traffic between two VLANs, I need either a router or a Layer 3 switch.

Let's say that I have a switch with four VLANs

- Ports 1 through 12 are on VLAN 1
- Ports 13 through 24 are on VLAN 2
- Ports 25 through 36 are on VLAN 3
- Ports 37 through 48 are on VLAN 4

If I want to route traffic between devices on the different VLANs, I might connect a router to Port 1, Port 13, Port 25, and Port 37. That is, I connect one router interface to a port on each VLAN. This is inefficient; it wastes ports. If I have many VLANs, it may not even be possible.

We can instead make one port on the switch an 802.1Q trunk port and connect the router to it. Packets that need to move between VLANs travel through the trunk port and up into the router. The router moves the packet to the correct VLAN and sends it back down to the trunk port. The switch now has a packet in a different VLAN. This is known as a **Router on a Stick** configuration or **ROAS** because in a network diagram, it appears like a router is connected via a single cable (a stick).

How do we configure a router on a stick? Or how do we configure a router to connect to a trunk port on a switch using a single physical interface? We must set up a sub interface for each VLAN on the router.

We can enter the sub interface configuration for any router by typing **`interface <name>.<subint>`**. If the sub interface doesn't exist, the router will create it automatically. For example, to configure the subinterface two on interface G0/0/1, I typed

```
Router#conf t
Enter configuration commands, one per line.  End with CNTL/Z.
Router(config)#interface G0/0/1.2
Router(config-subif)#
```

Notice that the router entered the "subif" or sub interface configuration.

We configure the VLAN on the sub interface with the following commands

- **`encapsulation dot1q <VLAN ID>`** - tells the router that we are using encapsulation on this sub interface and what the VLAN ID is.

- **`ip address <IP address> <subnet mask>`** - assigns an IP address to the VLAN sub interface

In this example, I configured interface G0/0/1.2 to use VLAN 2, and I set the IP address 4.5.6.7/24 on it.

```
Router#conf t
Enter configuration commands, one per line.  End with CNTL/Z.
Router(config)#interface G0/0/1.2
Router(config-subif)#encapsulation dot1q 2
Router(config-subif)#ip address 4.5.6.7 255.255.255.0
Router(config-subif)#exit
Router(config)#exit
Router#
%SYS-5-CONFIG_I: Configured from console by console
```

On the switch side, we add the switchport mode trunk command to the physical interface. We don't set an IP address or VLAN on a switch trunk port.

Technically, the sub interface number doesn't need to match the VLAN number. We could have created sub interface 5 and added VLAN 2 to it. We only need to ensure that we assign the sub interface an IP address/subnet that are in the VLAN.

If we configure an IP address on the physical interface, it is assumed to be in the native VLAN. We can set the native VLAN on a sub interface by typing **encapsulation dot1q <VLAN ID> native**.

We can see the active VLANs by typing **show vlan**

```
Router#show vlan

VLAN Name                             Status    Ports
---- -------------------------------- --------- -------------------------------
1    default                          active
1002 fddi-default                     active
1003 token-ring-default               active
1004 fddinet-default                  active
1005 trnet-default                    active

VLAN Type  SAID       MTU   Parent RingNo BridgeNo Stp  BrdgMode Trans1 Trans2
---- ----- ---------- ----- ------ ------ -------- ---- -------- ------ ------
1    enet  100001     1500  -      -      -        -    -        0      0
1002 fddi  101002     1500  -      -      -        -    -        0      0
1003 tr    101003     1500  -      -      -        -    -        0      0
1004 fdnet 101004     1500  -      -      -        ieee -        0      0
1005 trnet 101005     1500  -      -      -        ibm  -        0      0

VLAN Type  SAID       MTU   Parent RingNo BridgeNo Stp  BrdgMode Trans1 Trans2
---- ----- ---------- ----- ------ ------ -------- ---- -------- ------ ------

Remote SPAN VLANs
------------------------------------------------------------------------------
```

When we perform a shutdown on a physical interface, the router shuts down all the associated sub interfaces. For example, if we shut down G0/0/2, the router shut down G0/0/2.1 as well.

When we perform a no shutdown on a physical interface, the router starts up all the associated sub interfaces. For example, if we perform a no shutdown on G0/0/2, the router starts up G0/0/2.1 as well.

```
Router#conf t
Enter configuration commands, one per line.  End with CNTL/Z.
Router(config)#interface G0/0/2
Router(config-if)#no shutdown

Router(config-if)#
%LINK-5-CHANGED: Interface GigabitEthernet0/0/2, changed state to up

%LINK-5-CHANGED: Interface GigabitEthernet0/0/2.1, changed state to up

Router(config-if)#exit
Router(config)#exit
Router#
%SYS-5-CONFIG_I: Configured from console by console
Router#
Router#sh ip int b
Interface              IP-Address      OK? Method Status                Protocol
GigabitEthernet0/0/0   unassigned      YES unset  up                    down
GigabitEthernet0/0/1   unassigned      YES DHCP   up                    down
GigabitEthernet0/0/1.2 4.5.6.7         YES manual up                    down
GigabitEthernet0/0/2   unassigned      YES unset  up                    down
GigabitEthernet0/0/2.1 unassigned      YES unset  up                    down
Loopback0              100.100.100.100 YES manual up                    up
Vlan1                  unassigned      YES unset  administratively down down
```

If the main interface is shut down, we cannot start up one of its sub interfaces. But if the main interface is up, we can start up and shut down any of its sub interfaces. I shut down G0/0/2.1, but kept G0/0/2 up.

```
Router#conf t
Enter configuration commands, one per line.  End with CNTL/Z.
Router(config)#interface G0/0/2.1
Router(config-subif)#shutdown

Router(config-subif)#
%LINK-5-CHANGED: Interface GigabitEthernet0/0/2.1, changed state to administratively down

Router(config-subif)#exit
Router(config)#exit
Router#
%SYS-5-CONFIG_I: Configured from console by console

Router#
Router#
Router#sh ip int b
Interface              IP-Address      OK? Method Status                Protocol
GigabitEthernet0/0/0   unassigned      YES unset  up                    down
GigabitEthernet0/0/1   unassigned      YES DHCP   up                    down
GigabitEthernet0/0/1.2 4.5.6.7         YES manual up                    down
GigabitEthernet0/0/2   unassigned      YES unset  up                    down
GigabitEthernet0/0/2.1 unassigned      YES unset  administratively down down
Loopback0              100.100.100.100 YES manual up                    up
Vlan1                  unassigned      YES unset  administratively down down
```

Some ROAS troubleshooting tips

- Make sure that your VLANs are configured correctly on your LAN switches
- Make sure that you have identified every VLAN configured on each LAN switch, and created a sub interface on the router for each VLAN
- Make sure that you have created the sub interfaces under the correct router physical interface
- Check that each sub interface is configured with the correct IP address and subnet
- Check that the native VLAN has been configured on the router and on the switch
- Make sure that none of the interfaces or sub interfaces are shutdown

If we're using a layer three switch to route traffic, we must first enable routing on the switch

- Enable routing with the **sdm prefer lanbase**-routing command. We must then reload the switch for this command to activate.
- Once the switch is back up, turn on IP routing with the **ip routing** command

- Configure each VLAN interface on the switch. When we configure a VLAN on a switch, we type **vlan <VLAN ID>**. When we configure a VLAN interface, we type interface **vlan <VLAN ID>**. This is known as a **Switched Virtual Interface**, or **SVI**.
    - Assign the VLAN interface an IP address through the **ip address <IP address> <subnet mask>** command

I created VLAN 36. When I accessed it through the **interface vlan 36** command, the switch changed it state to up.

```
Switch#
Switch#conf t
Enter configuration commands, one per line.  End with CNTL/Z.
Switch(config)#vlan 36
Switch(config-vlan)#exit
Switch(config)#interface vlan 36
%LINK-5-CHANGED: Interface Vlan36, changed state to up
Switch(config-if)#ip address 5.6.7.8 255.255.255.0
```

When we create the VLAN interface, it automatically creates the VLAN as well. We can verify the VLAN by typing **show vlan**.

```
Switch#show vlan

VLAN Name                             Status    Ports
---- -------------------------------- --------- -------------------------------
1    default                          active    Po1, Po2, Po5, Fa0/1
                                                Fa0/2, Fa0/3, Fa0/5, Fa0/6
                                                Fa0/7, Fa0/8, Fa0/9, Fa0/10
                                                Fa0/11, Fa0/12, Fa0/13, Fa0/14
                                                Fa0/15, Fa0/16, Fa0/17, Fa0/18
                                                Fa0/19, Fa0/20, Fa0/21, Fa0/22
                                                Fa0/23, Fa0/24, Gig0/1, Gig0/2
3    VLAN0003                         active
4    VLAN0004                         active    Fa0/4
5    VLAN0005                         active    Fa0/4
7    Hazim                            active
35   VLAN0035                         active
36   VLAN0036                         active
1002 fddi-default                     active
1003 token-ring-default               active
1004 fddinet-default                  active
1005 trnet-default                    active
```

We can also verify the VLAN interface by typing **show interface VLAN36** or **show interface** to show all the interfaces.

```
Switch#show int vlan36
Vlan36 is up, line protocol is down
  Hardware is CPU Interface, address is 0050.0fbc.9a04 (bia 0050.0fbc.9a04)
  MTU 1500 bytes, BW 100000 Kbit, DLY 1000000 usec,
     reliability 255/255, txload 1/255, rxload 1/255
  Encapsulation ARPA, loopback not set
  ARP type: ARPA, ARP Timeout 04:00:00
  Last input 21:40:21, output never, output hang never
  Last clearing of "show interface" counters never
  Input queue: 0/75/0/0 (size/max/drops/flushes); Total output drops: 0
  Queueing strategy: fifo
  Output queue: 0/40 (size/max)
  5 minute input rate 0 bits/sec, 0 packets/sec
  5 minute output rate 0 bits/sec, 0 packets/sec
     1682 packets input, 530955 bytes, 0 no buffer
     Received 0 broadcasts (0 IP multicast)
     0 runts, 0 giants, 0 throttles
     0 input errors, 0 CRC, 0 frame, 0 overrun, 0 ignored
     563859 packets output, 0 bytes, 0 underruns
     0 output errors, 23 interface resets
     0 output buffer failures, 0 output buffers swapped out
```

On a layer three switch, the VLAN interface state is the same as the actual VLAN state. For the VLAN to be up

- The VLAN must be defined on the switch – either explicitly or learned through VTP
- At least one access interface on the switch is assigned to the VLAN and is up, or a trunk interface on that switch has the VLAN assigned to it
- The VLAN is not shutdown
- The VLAN interface is not shutdown

You can think of a Layer 3 switch as a switch with a built-in router. The VLAN interfaces belong to the router part. Since they operate separately, they must both be up for routing to work.

The physical interface ports on the switch belong to the switch. But we can make a physical interface act like a router interface. We call this a **routed port**.

Any frame that arrives on the routed port is handled like a packet instead

- The switch (the router part of the switch) strips the ethernet header/trailer from the frame, exposing the destination IP address

- It checks the routing table on the switch and determines where the packet goes. Remember that we configured an IP address for each VLAN interface.

- It encapsulates the packet in a new ethernet frame and send it back to the switch part of the switch. The switch sends the packet to its destination.

We only use the routed port when we have a single port connected to a subnet. When we have multiple ports, we should use the SVI configuration

In the interface configuration, we type **no switchport** to create the routed port. If we want to go back to a switchport, we just type **switchport**.

Enter the interface configuration

- Type **no switchport**

- Assign the port an IP address through the **ip address <IP address> <subnet>** command

```
Switch#conf t
Enter configuration commands, one per line.  End with CNTL/Z.
Switch(config)#interface F0/2
Switch(config-if)#no switchport
Switch(config-if)#ip address 3.4.5.3 255.255.255.0
Switch(config-if)#exit
Switch(config)#show interfaces status
```

We can verify the settings by typing

- **show interfaces** – gives us many details about each interface, including the VLAN interfaces

- **show interfaces status** – provides a summary about each interface in a table. The routed ports say "routed" under the VLAN; only physical ports are shown through this command

```
Switch#show interfaces status
Port      Name               Status       Vlan       Duplex  Speed Type
Fa0/1                        notconnect   1          auto    auto  10/100BaseTX
Fa0/2                        notconnect   routed     auto    auto  10/100BaseTX
Fa0/3                        notconnect   1          auto    auto  10/100BaseTX
Fa0/4                        notconnect   1          auto    auto  10/100BaseTX
Fa0/5                        notconnect   1          auto    auto  10/100BaseTX
Fa0/6                        notconnect   1          auto    auto  10/100BaseTX
Fa0/7                        notconnect   1          auto    auto  10/100BaseTX
Fa0/8                        notconnect   1          auto    auto  10/100BaseTX
Fa0/9                        notconnect   1          auto    auto  10/100BaseTX
Fa0/10                       notconnect   1          auto    auto  10/100BaseTX
Fa0/11                       notconnect   1          auto    auto  10/100BaseTX
Fa0/12                       notconnect   1          auto    auto  10/100BaseTX
```

In a tiered design, the ports on the core switches are usually routed ports. This is an important configuration because core switches are connected to multiple VLANs

What happens when we want to use a Layer 3 protocol over redundant links through EtherChannel? EtherChannel over Layer 3 allows a switch can balance the Layer 3 traffic over multiple links.

To configure the EtherChannel on Layer 3

- We must first configure the PortChannel interface (this is the separate virtual interface)
    - **interface port-channel <number>**
        - **no switchport**
        - **ip address <IP address> <subnet mask>**
- Configure each interface to be part of an EtherChannel as before
    - **no switchport** – configures the port as a routing port
    - **no ip address** – this is added to the interface automatically when we add the no switchport
    - **channel-group <number> mode on** – adds the port to the PortChannel

It is important to follow the above commands in order. I tried to add Channel-Group 4 on to interface F0/4 before creating Channel-Group 4. The result is that the switch automatically created the Port-Channel 4 virtual interface. When I ran the no switchport command it failed.

```
Switch(config)#
Switch(config)#interface F0/4
Switch(config-if)#channel-group 4 mode on
Switch(config-if)#
Creating a port-channel interface Port-channel 4

Switch(config-if)#no switchport
Command rejected (Port-channel): Either port is L2 and port-channel is L3, or vice-versa
Switch(config-if)#
Switch#
%SYS-5-CONFIG_I: Configured from console by console
```

I went back and configured the Port-Channel 4 virtual interface as a routed port and added an IP address to it.

```
Enter configuration commands, one per line.  End with CNTL/Z.
Switch(config)#interface port-channel 4
Switch(config-if)#no switchport
Switch(config-if)#ip address 5.5.5.5 255.255.255.0
Switch(config-if)#exit
Switch(config)#interface F0/4
```

Then I added the no switchport and port-channel commands to the interfaces.

```
Switch(config)#interface F0/5
Switch(config-if)#no switchport
Switch(config-if)#channel-group 4 mode on
Switch(config-if)#exit
```

We can verify these settings by typing **`show etherchannel`**. The switch will provide us with a list of active etherchannels and the number ports in each one.

```
Switch#show etherchannel
              Channel-group listing:
              ----------------------

Group: 4
----------
Group state = L3
Ports: 2 Maxports = 8
Port-channels: 1 Max Port-channels = 1
Protocol:    -
```

If we type **show etherchannel summary**, we can see additional details such as the ports added to each etherchannel.

```
Switch#show etherchannel summary
Flags:  D - down        P - in port-channel
        I - stand-alone s - suspended
        H - Hot-standby (LACP only)
        R - Layer3      S - Layer2
        U - in use      f - failed to allocate aggregator
        u - unsuitable for bundling
        w - waiting to be aggregated
        d - default port


Number of channel-groups in use: 1
Number of aggregators:           1

Group  Port-channel  Protocol    Ports
------+-------------+-----------+----------------------------------------------

4      Po4(RD)          -      Fa0/4(D) Fa0/5(D)
Switch#
```

For EtherChannel to work, remember that the speed and duplex must be the same on all ports and that routing must be enabled on each port.

3.4 Configure and verify single area OSPFv2

3.4.a Neighbor adjacencies

3.4.b Point-to-point

3.4.c Broadcast (DR/BDR selection)

3.4.d Router ID

We will now look at **dynamic routes**. The internet is massive and there are millions of routers on it. There is usually more than one way to get to a destination. Routers and links fail all the time. How can a router determine the best route in real time as it changes?

We use a **routing protocol**. A routing protocol is a set of rules for learning and updating routes. The main routing protocol that we will look at is **OSPFv2**

A **routed** or **routable protocol** is one that allows a router to forward packets. IPv4 and IPv6 are routable protocols. IPv4 allows a router to send packets, but it does not help the router figure out where to send the packets.

The idea behind the routing protocol

- A router can learn routing information from its neighbors (routers that are directly connected to it)
- It can teach a neighbor about routes that it knows and that it has learned from other neighbors
- It can pick the best route to a destination when more than one route is available
- It can detect failed routes and select new best routes. This is called convergence.

When a router receives a packet, the only decision it makes is which router to send it to next. It doesn't need to plan out the packet's entire route. Each router decides on the packet's next destination. But collectively, the routers use routing protocols to figure out the best route.

There are two types of routing protocols. To understand how they work, we need to understand what an **autonomous system** or **AS** is. It is a network that is under the control of one organization. For example, the network at your office is a single AS. The internet is not an AS because there are thousands of ISPs, each with control of their own network. These networks work together, but each one is controlled by a different party.

- **Interior Gateway Protocols**, or **IGPs**. An IGP works inside a single autonomous system or AS. An IGP allows packets to be routed inside the system.

- **Exterior Gateway Protocols**, or **EGPs**. An EGP works between multiple autonomous systems. An EGP allows packets to be routed between different systems. The only EGP that we will learn about is **Border Gateway Protocol**, or **BGP**.

Each AS is assigned a unique number, called an **AS Number** (**ASN**). It is kind of like an IP address and is unique for that AS worldwide.

In the diagram below, we have three ASNs – ASN 5 belonging to Dave, ASN 6 belonging to Alice, and ASN 7, belonging to Bob. Each ASN has its own internal network, which could consist of multiple routers. Each router may maintain its own local network (LAN). Thus each ASN could consist of multiple LANs.

Notice that there is a router at the edge of each ASN. This edge router gives the ASN connectivity to other ASNs.

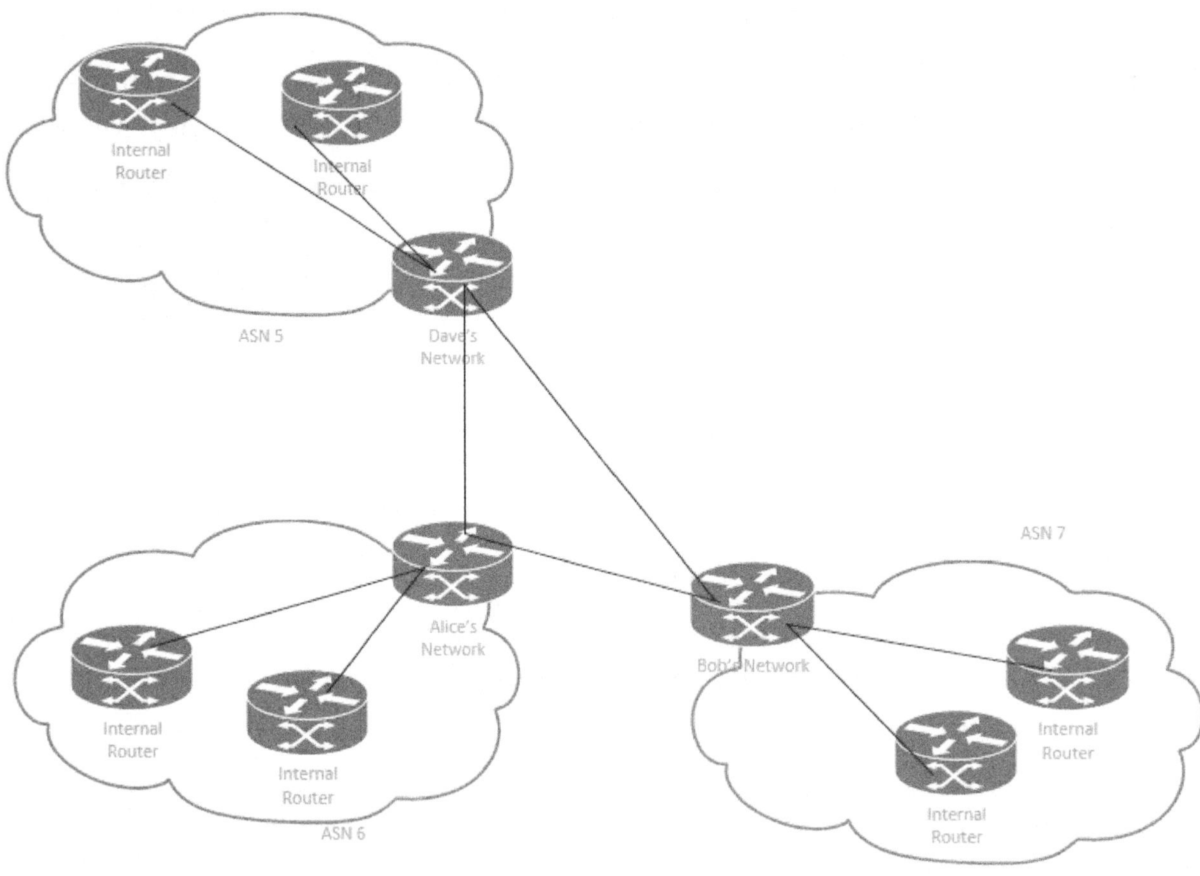

.

There are many different EGPs available and you can choose the one that is right for you. The two most popular ones are OSPFv2 and EIGRP (Enhanced Interior Gateway Routing Protocol), but the CCNA only focuses on OSPFv2.

Inside the routing protocol is an algorithm (a kind of artificial intelligence or set of rules) that figures out how to learn the routes and choose the best one. There are three categories of algorithms

- **Distance Vector** – The distance vector calculates the distance that a packet must travel from its source to its destination. The distance vector usually calculates the number of routers or "hops" that the packet must pass through. These algorithms are not popular because they are slow to update when the network topology changes.
- **Link State** – this type of algorithm calculates the distance to the packet's destination based on the cost (or speed) of each link.
- **Advanced Distance Vector** – This type of algorithm uses both the distance vector and the link state algorithms. EIGRP is an example of an advanced distance vector.

How does each routing protocol work?

- **RIPv2** – How many hops (routers) does a packet have to travel through? RIPv2 is considered a Distance Vector algorithm. RIPv2 selects the route with the lowest cost. It has slow convergence (it takes a long time to update when the network topology changes.
- **OSPF** – How much does each route cost? We assign a cost to each link based on its bandwidth and add them up. OSPF selects the route with the lowest cost. OSPF is considered a link state algorithm.
- **EIGRP** – EIGRP factors in the cost of each link, the amount of delay in each interface and the number of links. It's considered an advanced distance vector algorithm.

RIP might choose a route with a single hop even though the connection is slower, whereas OSPF might choose a route with multiple routers (and potentially high latency) even though the connection speed is faster.

What if we have multiple routing algorithms in use? What if we connect a network using OSPF with one using EIGRP? We can take routes learned from one protocol and advertise them through another protocol. This is called **route redistribution**.

What happens when the router learns about the same destination (route) through multiple algorithms? We assign each algorithm an **administrative distance**. The distance is how much weight we should give to each algorithm. The lower the weight, the more likely we are to use it.

The table below (repeated from earlier) summarizes the distance associated with each route source.

Route Source	Default Distance Values
Connected interface	0
Static route	1

Enhanced Interior Gateway Routing Protocol (EIGRP) summary route	5
External Border Gateway Protocol (BGP)	20
Internal EIGRP	90
IGRP	100
OSPF	110
Intermediate System-to-Intermediate System (IS-IS)	115
Routing Information Protocol (RIP)	120
Exterior Gateway Protocol (EGP)	140
On Demand Routing (ODR)	160
External EIGRP	170
Internal BGP	200
Unknown	255

Clearly, a connected or static route has the highest priority, followed by BGP (external route) and then an internal route. We can change the administrative distance, but we must do so on each router.

We can give an individual static route a larger administrative distance by typing **`ip route <network ID> <subnet mask> <destination> <distance>`**.

Now let's look at how OSPF works. Each router is busy gathering information about its routes like the static and directly connected routes.

The router maintains a database called the **Link State Database** or **LSDB**, which contains its idea of how the internet is organized and connected. Each time the router learns a new route, it sends out a message called the **Link State Advertisement** (**LSA**) telling the neighboring routers what it learned. The other routers put the data from the LSA into their databases. The neighboring routers flood the LSA to other routers. But a router will only accept and reflood an LSA if it doesn't already have it. This prevents the LSA from flooding in an endless loop. By default, the LSA expires after 30 minutes.

After a while, all the routers that are connected (directly or indirectly) have the same LSDB – they learned about the network topology from other routers and updated it accordingly, but they still don't know about the best pathway to each network. What is the relationship between the LSDB and the routing table?

Well, the router analyses the LSDB and creates routes by calculating the best ones. We will see how.

Two routers are considered OSPF neighbors if

- They are directly connected. They can be directly connected over an ethernet WAN, a serial link, or a switch. They must be on the same VLAN.
- They use OSPF
- The two routers exchange OSPF messages
- They agree to become neighbors because of the OSPF messages

A router can have multiple OSPF neighbors. We can see a router's neighbors by typing **`show ip ospf neighbor`**.

A new router can connect to the network and send **OSPF Hello messages**. Other routers with OSPF will be listening for the message and create a neighbor relationship. The Hello contains the router's unique router ID (a 32-bit number that is by default the router's IPv4 interface address). We can configure a different RID if we want.

A router sends the Hello message in a packet to 224.0.0.5 which is a multicast IP address that all the OSPF routers listen on. In summary

- We connect two routers to each other
- They don't know anything about each other
- One router sends the Hello to 224.0.0.5. The Hello contains the RID
- The other router replies acknowledging the Hello, and sends its own RID in reply
- Each router verifies that the Hello messages are sent without error

When two routers agree to become neighbors, they do not automatically exchange the entire contents of their LDSB. Instead each router tells the other router which LSAs it has in its database. Each router then determines which LSAs are missing and requests them from the other routers.

Each router continues to send the other router Hello messages at regular intervals so that the other router can verify that it is still operational.

Each router maintains two timers

- The **Hello Interval** is how often a hello message is sent

- The **Dead Interval** is how long a router will wait without receiving a hello message. By default, it is four times the hello interval. Once the hello messages stop coming in, the router assumes that the neighbor has died.

When we have multiple routers on the same VLAN, one is elected to be the **Designated Router** (**DR**) and a second one is elected to be a **Back-Up Designated Router** (**BRD).** The DR is responsible for providing other routers with a copy of the LSDB. If the DR fails, the BDR takes over, and a new router is selected to be the BDR.

It is better to have a DR and a BDR when there are multiple routers. Otherwise, each router will attempt to share its LSDB with all the other routers.

The IP address 224.0.0.5 is a multicast address that the DR can use to send messages.

The IP address 224.0.0.6 is a multicast address that a router can use to send a message to the DR

The routers that aren't a DR or BDR are called **DROthers**. They do not establish a full OSPF state.

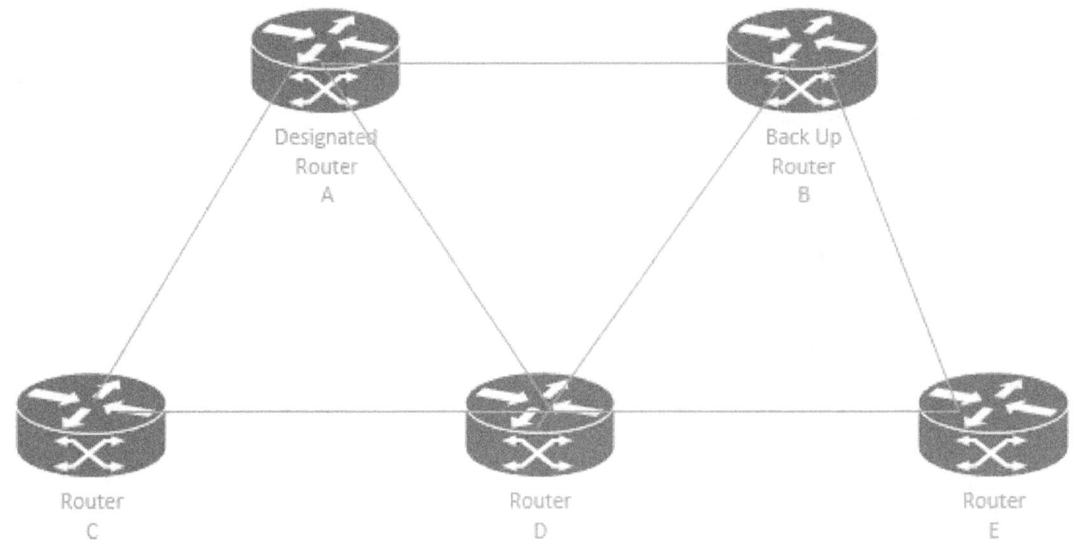

I have five routers – A, B, C, D, and E. Router A is the designated router and Router B is the Back-Up Designated Router.

On a DROther router, if we type `show ip ospf neighbor`, we see

- **Fully adjacent neighbors** for the DR and BDR. Two routers that are on the full state are adjacent neighbors, also known as **fully adjacent neighbors**. That is, they have exchanged the link state database.

Routers A and B are fully adjacent with each other and with routers C, D, and E. That is, we have the following fully adjacent neighbor relationships: A-B, A-C, A-D, A-E, B-C, B-D, and B-E.

- **2-way state neighbors** for the other DROthers. Two routers are neighbors if they have the 2-way state and are on the same link.

  We have the following 2-way state neighbor relationships: C-D, C-E, and D-E.

But how does OSPF rank each route? Under OSPF, the metric is – what is the sum of the cost of each **outgoing interface** in the route? Whichever route is the cheapest is best. OSPF only looks at the outgoing interfaces.

That means that the router on the other end of the route may choose a different way back.

In the following example, Bob's Network and Dave's Network want to communicate. There are 5 routers in between – A, B, C, D, and E. What are all the routes from Bob's Network to Dave's Network? The cost of each outgoing interface is in brackets.

- Bob's Network (3) – Router A (6) – Router B (4) – Dave's Network. The total cost is 13.
- **Bob's Network (3) – Router B (4) – Dave's Network. The total cost is 7. This is the best route.**
- Bob's Network (3) – Router C (5) – Router D (6) – Dave's Network. The total cost is 14.
- Bob's Network (3) – Router C (5) – Router D (6) – Router B (4) – Dave's Network. The total cost is 18.

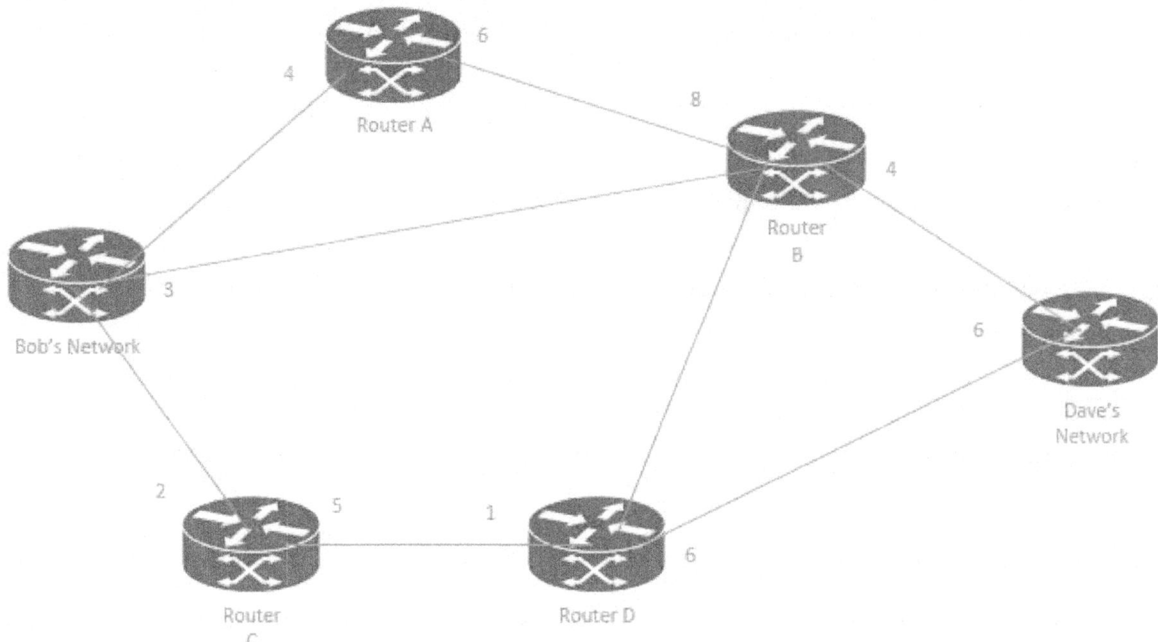

On the way back

- Dave's Network (6) – Router B (8) – Router A (4) – Bob's Network. The total cost is 18.
- Dave's Network (6) – Router B (8) – Bob's Network. The total cost is 14.
- Dave's Network (6) – Router B (8) – Router D (1) – Router C (2) – Bob's Network. The total cost is 17.
- **Dave's Network (6) – Router D (2) – Router C (3) – Bob's Network. The total cost is 11. This is the best route.**

What happens when we have many routers and subnets? The routers must keep track of thousands of other routers in the memory. The LSDB will be massive and the computing power to search it will be massive. If a single router stops working, all the other routers must recalculate the entire algorithm and routes.

To solve this, we break down the system into OSPF areas. We can group our routers into different areas. When we use multiple areas, a router must think about the route in its own area and no others. When we have more than 50 routers, we should use areas.

How do we decide which routers belong to which areas?

- The interfaces in the same subnet should be the same area
- Each area should be contiguous
- There will be several types of routers

- We might choose a large router to be the Backbone Router. The Backbone router connects to all the areas and controls the **backbone area**.
- A router can be considered "internal" if all its interfaces connect to routers that are in the same area
- An **Area Border Router** (**ABR**) has some interfaces in the backbone area and some in the non-backbone area

- A non-backbone area must be able to reach the backbone area by having an ABR that connects to both the backbone area and the non-backbone area
- Any router that connects to the backbone area is a backbone router – an ABR can also be a backbone router
- An **intraarea route** is one that goes between routers in the same area
- An **interarea route** is one that goes between routers in different subnets

In my diagram, I have two areas. At the top is my backbone router, which resides in the backbone area. Below are two Area Border Routers. Each ABR connects to the Backbone Router. We also have Internal Routers A, B, F, and G.

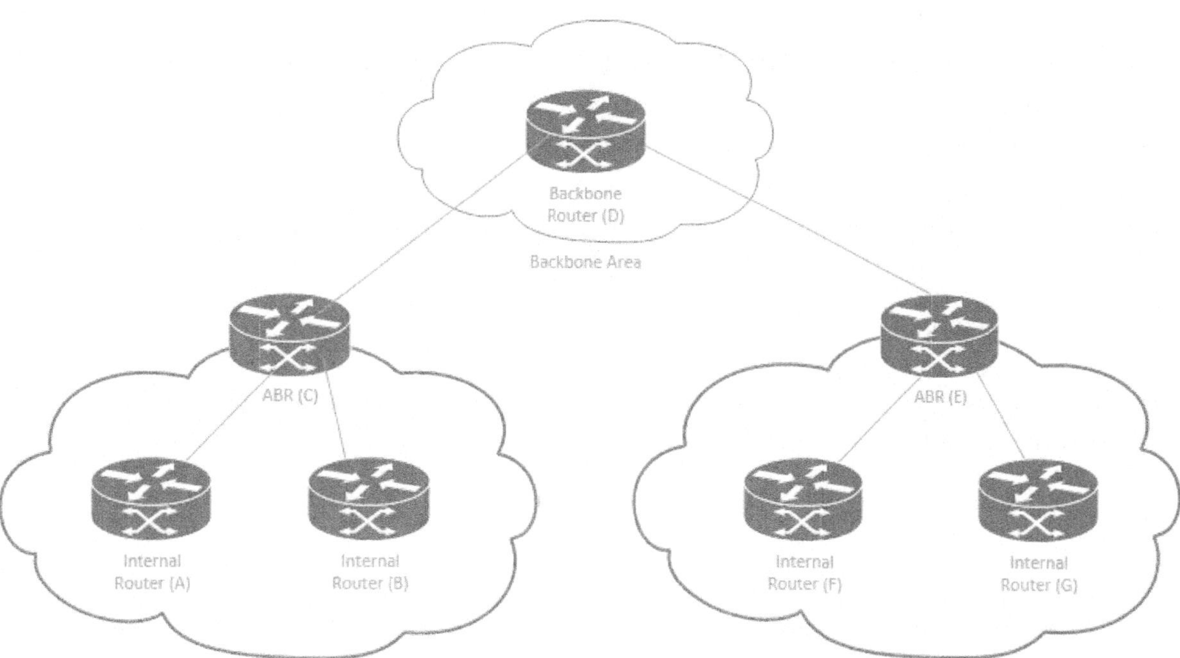

The internal routers on the left (A and B) don't need to know the route all the way to internal routers F and G. But a router must still know that there are other subnets in other areas so that it can send them traffic. It only needs limited information – the subnet. It doesn't need to know how routers in other area are connected.

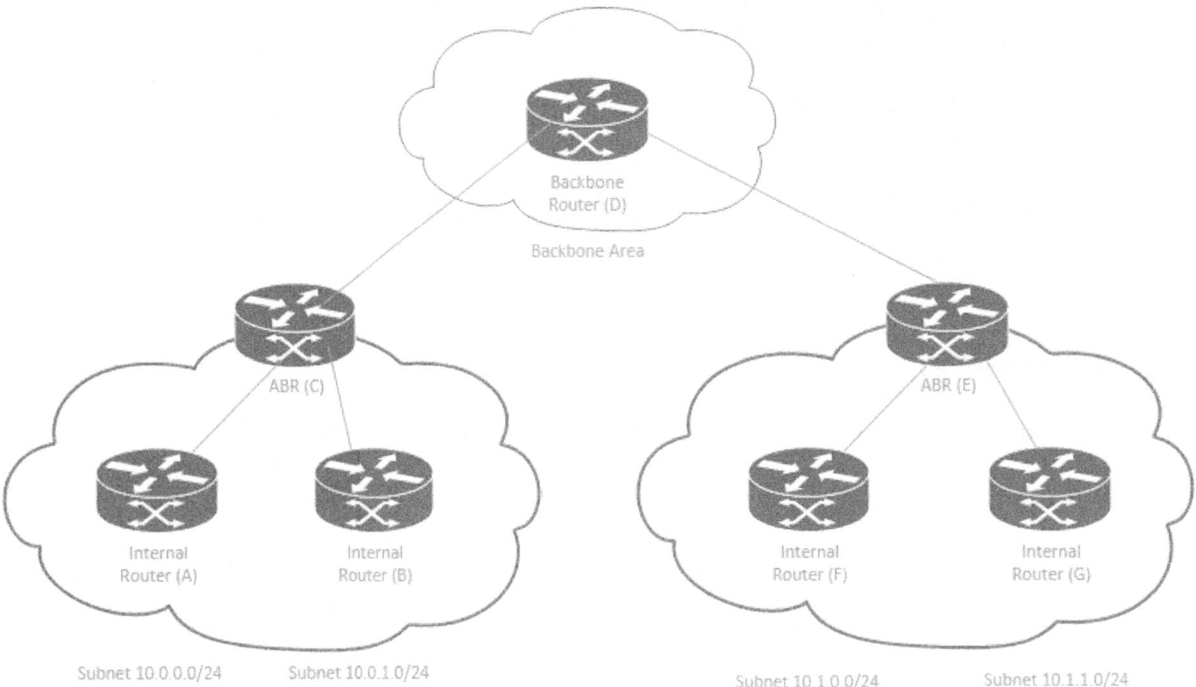

On the left, we have subnets 10.0.0.0/24 and 10.0.1.0/24. Router A and Router B need to know the exact routes to those subnets. On the right, we have subnets 10.1.0.0/24 and 10.1.1.0/24. Router A and Router B do not need to know the exact routes. Instead they just say that those networks are connected router C, the Area Border Router. Router C can figure out how those packets get to the ABR E, and ABR E can figure out how packets addressed to those networks can get to Routers F and G.

What does the LSDB look like?

- There is one router LSA for each router in our area. This is called a **Type 1 LSA**. It contains the following information
    - Router ID
    - Router Interfaces
    - IP address/netmask
    - Router Interface Status
    - What neighbors the other router knows

- There is one network LSA for each network that contains a DR if the DR has at least one neighbor that is connected to our router. This is called a **Type 2 LSA**. A Type 2 LSA always stays within the area that created it. It contains the following information
    - DR address
    - BDR address
    - Subnet ID and mask
- There is one summary LSA for each subnet in a different area. This is called a **Type 3 LSA**. It contains the following information.
    - Subnet ID and Mask
    - RID of the ABR that advertised the LSA

Now for the fun part. How do we configure OSPF?

- Type **`route ospf <process ID>`** to enter the OSPF configuration mode. The process ID allows us to have multiple OSPF processes on a single router. The process ID is between 1 and 65535 and can be different on every router.
    - Configure the OSPF router ID. OSPF will use the router ID. If a router ID is not configured, OSPF will use the IP address of the loopback interface or of a physical interface.
        - Type **`router-id <ID>`** to give the router an ID number. The ID must be in the format of an IP address.
        - Create a loopback interface by typing **`interface loopback <number>`**. This will automatically create a loopback interface and enter its configuration.

          Add an IP address to the interface by typing **`ip address <IP address> <subnet mask>`**.

          If there are multiple loopback interfaces, the router will choose the largest IP address as the OSPF Router ID.
        - Assign an IP address to a physical interface. The router will choose the highest IP from the interfaces that are up.

    If we change the router ID while the router is running, it won't take effect until the router is rebooted.

- Type **network <IP address> <wildcard mask> area <OSPF Area ID>** to enable the OSPF on any interface that matches the IP address and wildcard mask. There are five wildcards
  - Wildcard 0.0.0.0 – the IP address must match exactly
  - Wildcard 0.0.0.255 – first three octets must match
  - Wildcard 0.0.255.255 – the first two octets must match
  - Wildcard 0.255.255.255 – the first octet must match
  - Wildcard 255.255.255.255 – this wildcard matches everything

  For example

  - IP address 5.5.5.5 and wildcard 0.0.0.0 will only match IP address 5.5.5.5
  - IP address 5.5.5.5 and wildcard 0.0.0.255 will match any IP address that starts with 5.5.5, which is the range of IP addresses 5.5.5.0 to 5.5.5.255
  - IP address 5.5.5.5 and wildcard 0.0.255.255 will match any IP address that starts with 5.5, which is the range of IP addresses 5.5.0.0 to 5.5.255.255
  - IP address 5.5.5.5 and wildcard 0.255.255.255 will match any IP address that starts with 5, which is the range of IP addresses 5.0.0.0 to 5.255.255.255
  - IP address 5.5.5.5 and wildcard 255.255.255.255 will match any IP address

  If you enter a network IP address and doesn't match the wildcard, then it will be changed. The octet in the IP address will be set to 0 when the octet in the wildcard is 255. For example, if I write 252.342.432.4 wildcard 0.0.0.255, the router will change my IP address to 255.342.432.0

Notice that we didn't configure OSPF on a physical interface. We just configured a network IP address with an area ID. The router automatically interprets the OSPF configuration and applies it to any applicable interface.

Router OSPF is a process, not just a configuration. Therefore, OSPF will not start unless there is at least one working physical interface.

```
Router(config)#router ospf 1
OSPF process 1 cannot start. There must be at least one "up" IP interface
```

In my example, I have three routers in my OSPF area (area 1).

- Router A controls subnet 10.1.0.0/24
  - Interface 0/0/0 connects to Router B
  - Interface 0/0/1 connects to Router C
- Router B controls subnet 10.1.4.0/24
  - Interface 0/0/0 connects to Router C
  - Interface 0/0/1 connects to Router B
- Router C controls subnet 10.2.0.0/24
  - Interface 0/0/0 connects to Router A
  - Interface 0/0/1 connects to Router B

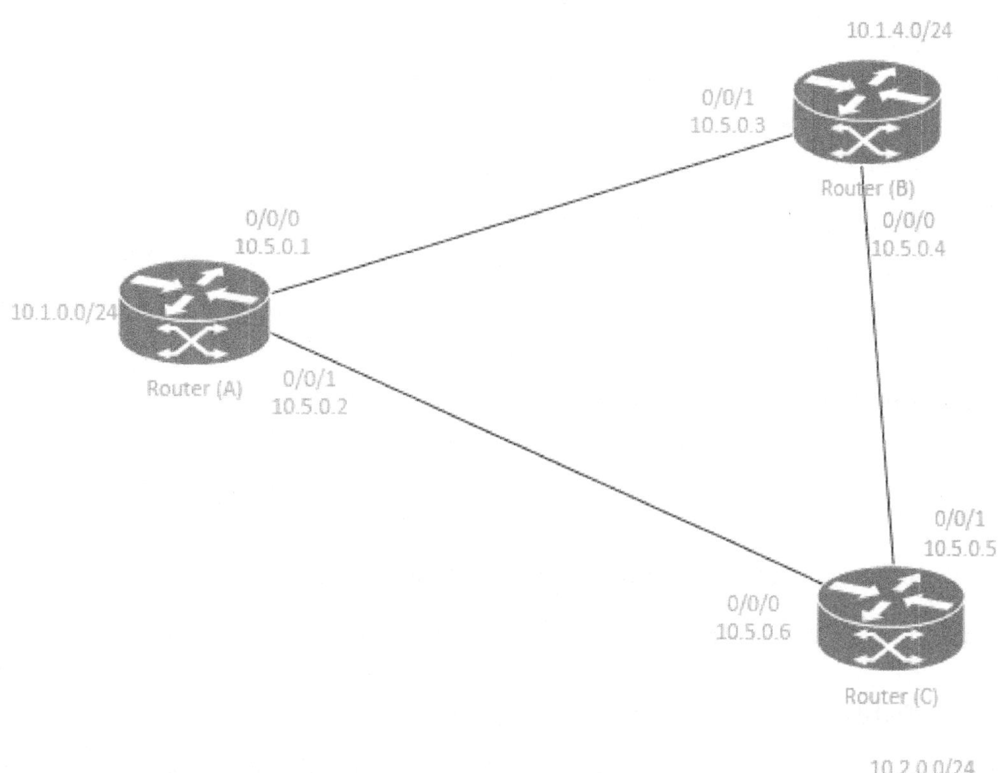

If I enable OSPF on Router A with the **`network 10.0.0.0 0.255.255.255 area 1`**, it will match the networks that are controlled by Router B and Router C. Therefore, the router will enable OSPF on both interfaces 0/0/0 and 0/0/1.

If I enable OSPF on Router A with the **`network 10.2.0.0 0.0.255.255 area 1`**, it will match the network that is controlled by Router C. Therefore, the router will enable OSPF on interface 0/0/1.

We can verify OSPF with the following

show ip ospf interface to see if the interfaces are enabled with OSPF. Only an OSPF enabled interface is listed

- **show ip ospf interface brief** to see one line per interface
- **show ip ospf interface <interface name>** to see details about just one interface

```
Router#show ip ospf interface
GigabitEthernet0/0/0 is up, line protocol is up
IP address 10.5.0.1, Process ID 1 VRF RemoteOfficeVRF, area 0.0.0.10
Enabled by interface configuration
State DOWN, Network type BROADCAST, cost 4
Index 1, Transmit delay 1 sec, Router Priority 1
No designated router on this network
No backup designated router on this network
0 Neighbors, flooding to 0, adjacent with 0
Timer intervals: Hello 10, Dead 40, Wait 40, Retransmit 5
No authentication
Number of opaque link LSAs: 0, checksum sum 0
switch#
```

show ip ospf neighbor to see the neighbor relationships

```
Neighbor ID      Pri    State       Dead Time    Address      Interface
10.5.0.3         1      FULL/DR     00:00:36     10.5.0.1     GigabitEthernet0/0/0
```

The output from the **show ip ospf neighbor** command tells us the following

- Neighbor ID – the neighbor's IP address or ID
- Priority – the priority of the neighboring router
- State – the state tells us the status of the neighboring router. We want the state to be FULL. The state also tells us if the router is a DR, BDR, or DROTHER.
    - FULL/ - the state is full
    - FULL/DR – the state is full, and the neighboring router is a Designated Router
    - FULL/BDR - the state is full, and the neighboring router is a Back Up Designated Router
    - FULL/DROTHER - the state is full, and the neighboring router is a DROTHER (neither a designated router nor a back up designated router). That means that our router is probably a DR or a BDR.

  - 2WAY/DROTHER – the state is two-way. That means that both routers are DROTHER, which is why they didn't reach a full state.

- Address – the address of the neighboring router's interface
- Interface – the local interface of the router that is connected to the neighbor

show ip ospf database to see the LSAs received from our neighbors. Our router has learned routes from the other two routers. The ADV Router is the IP address of the router that is advertising the LSA. The Link ID is the ID (IP address) of the router that we learned the LSA from.

If we learn the LSA from a router that advertised it, then both the Link ID and ADV Router will be the same. If the router we learned the LSA from received it from another router, then they would be different.

```
Router# show ip ospf database
OSPF Router with id(10.5.0.1) (Process ID 1)
                    Displaying Router Link States(Area 0.0.0.0)
  Link ID          ADV Router      Age          Seq#       Checksum  Link count
10.5.0.3        10.5.0.3        1731     0x80002CFB     0x69BC         8
10.5.0.6        10.5.0.6        1112     0x800009D2     0xA2B8         5
10.1.4.0        10.5.0.3        1112     0x800009D2     0xA2B8         5
10.2.0.0        10.5.0.6        1112     0x800009D2     0xA2B8         5
```

show ip route to see the routes that the router figured out from the database. We can see that our router learned two routes – a route to 10.1.4.0/24 via G0/0/0 and a route to 10.2.0.0/24 via G0/0/1.

```
Router#show ip route
Codes: L - local, C - connected, S - static, R - RIP, M - mobile, B - BGP
       D - EIGRP, EX - EIGRP external, O - OSPF, IA - OSPF inter area
       N1 - OSPF NSSA external type 1, N2 - OSPF NSSA external type 2
       E1 - OSPF external type 1, E2 - OSPF external type 2, E - EGP
       i - IS-IS, L1 - IS-IS level-1, L2 - IS-IS level-2, ia - IS-IS inter area
       * - candidate default, U - per-user static route, o - ODR
       P - periodic downloaded static route

Gateway of last resort is not set

O      10.1.4.0/24 [110/2] via 10.5.0.3, GigabitEthernet0/0/0
O      10.2.0.0/24 [110/2] via 10.5.0.6, GigabitEthernet0/0/1
```

If we run the **show ip ospf database** command on multiple connected routers, we should see the same data. Why? All connected routers share the same LSDB data. If there is a mismatch, it could indicate that the OSPF Hello messages

If OSPF is our only routing protocol, and if we know how many subnets there are in our area and how many are directly connected, we can subtract them to determine how many we should learn via OSPF

I can enable the OSPF on a per-interface basis

- Enter OSPF configuration. Type **`no network <network ID> area <area ID>`** to remove OSPF networks from the OSPF configuration
- Enter the interface configuration mode for each interface we want to enable OSPF on. Type **`ip ospf <process ID> area <area ID>`** to enable OSPF

If we type **`show ip ospf interface`**, it will show up as "attached via interface" instead of "attached via network".

A passive interface is one that does not have a router connected to it. The router will not send Hello messages or accept Hello messages on this interface. It will still advertise the subnet connected to this interface via OSPF.

We can make an active interface into a passive interface. This is a good idea when we are using a router to connect multiple VLANs on the same physical LAN.

- The **`passive-interface <interface name>`** in the main configuration changes that interface to passive
- The **`passive-interface default`** makes all interfaces passive
- The **`no passive-interface <interface name>`** in the main configuration returns that interface to passive

We can verify the interface status by typing **`show ip ospf interface brief`**.

When we have a large network, and in that network, we have a single default route to the internet, the router with the connection to the internet should teach all the other routers about it. Remember that the default route is the route that a router uses when no other routes match the destination of the packet. By default, a router won't advertise its default route. In the OSPF configuration, we type **default-information originate** to tell the router to advertise its default route over OSPF (in the OSPF configuration). The router will advertise this route whether it is working or not. Now internal routers will know to pass their traffic to the internet-connected router when they have traffic that needs to reach the internet.

At the beginning of this chapter, I said that OSPF chooses the cheapest route, and that it bases the cost on the outbound interface. But how does it know how much an interface costs?

The cost of an interface is based on its speed. By default, a router has a reference speed of 100,000. What the router does is divide the interface speed by the reference speed to obtain the cost.

For example, a Fast Ethernet interface has a speed of 100,000. The cost is 100,000 / 100,000 = 1. A 10 mbps interface has a speed of 10,000. The cost is 100,000 / 10,000 = 10.

A Gigabit Ethernet interface speed is 1,000,000. The cost is 100,000 / 1,000,000 = 0.1. But the router won't accept a speed that is less than 1. As a result, all interface speeds that are 100 mbps or greater have a cost of 1.

A better system would be to set the reference to a higher value, but OSPF was developed before higher speeds existed, and the reference has not been updated.

We can change the cost or the interface or the reference value

- On a specific physical interface, we can manually set the cost by typing **ip ospf cost <cost>**. This only changes the cost on a single interface.
```
Router#conf t
Enter configuration commands, one per line.  End with CNTL/Z.
Router(config)#int G0/0/0
Router(config-if)#ip ospf cost 5
```
- We can change the interface's bandwidth by typing **bandwidth <speed>**, where speed is in Kbps. Remember that the router calculates the cost from the interface's bandwidth setting. It is generally a bad idea to change the bandwidth.
- Change the reference bandwidth by typing **auto-cost reference-bandwidth <speed>** in Mbps. On some routers, the speed is in Gbps. This command is entered in the OSPF configuration mode. This affects calculations for all interfaces.
```
Router(config)#router ospf 1
Router(config-router)#auto-cost reference-bandwidth 1000000
% OSPF: Reference bandwidth is changed.
        Please ensure reference bandwidth is consistent across all routers.
```

When the router has multiple routes to the same destination network with the same OSPF cost, it chooses the one with the lowest Router ID. We might want the router to maintain multiple routes for redundancy. We can permit a router to maintain multiple paths by typing **maximum-paths <maximum number of routes>**. Now the router will maintain multiple routes and balance the traffic on all of them. The router will balance the traffic.

If we are having trouble with OSPF, we can reset it by typing **clear ip ospf process**. The router will forget about all its neighbors and re-establish relationships and routes.

Let's take another look at the Designated Router and Back-Up Designated Router. How does a group of routers pick one to be the DR and another to be the BDR?

By default, the router with the highest priority setting will become the DR, and the router with the second highest priority will be the BDR. If there is a tie (there usually is because the default priority for a router will be one), then the router with the highest router ID will become the DR, and the router with the second highest router ID will become the BDR.

We can change a router's priority by typing **ip ospf priority <priority>** on each interface that has OSPF. This ensures that the router with the highest priority wins. We could also change its router ID, but this is not a good idea because we might want to use the router ID to identify the router.

```
switch#configure terminal
switch(config)#interface G0/0/0
switch(config-if)#ip ospf priority 11
```

Once a DR and BDR are elected, if the DR fails, then the BDR becomes the DR and the remaining routers elect a new BDR. If a new router enters the subnet, the DR and BDR do not change, even if the new router is better than the existing DR or BDR.

There are two types of OSPF networks: broadcast networks and point-to-point. Most networks are broadcast networks. In a broadcast network, the router advertises its Hello message by sending an Ethernet broadcast frame to the other connected devices.

A Point-to-Point connection can operate as an Ethernet WAN or Ethernet Private Wire, where ethernet frames are transmitted from one router to another through a service provider. On a Point-to-Point connection, we can have OSPF but we will not elect a DR or BDR.

How can we troubleshoot an OSPF connection?

- Make sure that the necessary interfaces are Up/Up – check the interface with the **show ip interface** command

- Verify that all interfaces are in the same subnet. All routers on a subnet should become neighbors and reach the 2-way state, if not the full state. A router should reach the full state with a DR or BDR.
- Ensure that OSPF is running on both routers.
- Verify that each router has a unique Router ID.
- Verify that there is no firewall or Access Control List that is blocking the traffic and that neighbor authentication is working.
- Ensure that the OSPF enabled interfaces are in the same OSPF area.
- Verify that the Hello and Dead timers are the same on each router.
- When all the settings are correct, and the routers are fully adjacent, they will exchange their LSDBs. If the settings are not correct, the routers will not become neighbors.

  One weird exception is that if the network type is different on each router – one router thinks that the network is Point-to-Point while the other router thinks that the network is a broadcast network – the routers will become neighbors and exchange LSDBs, but they won't add routes to their routing table. That is because one router is expecting to see a DR/BDR and the other router isn't.

3.5 Describe the purpose of first hop redundancy protocol

The **First Hop Redundancy Protocol**, or **FHRP**, allows us to use redundant links to keep a network functional in the event of a failure.

If our network was connected to a WAN or internet via a single router, and the router failed, we would lose all connectivity. This is known as a **single point of failure**. A good design – a redundant design – avoids single points of failure.

What happens when two routers are connected to the same LAN subnet? We have a redundant connection, but external routers will have two routes to the subnet and can't decide which one to use.

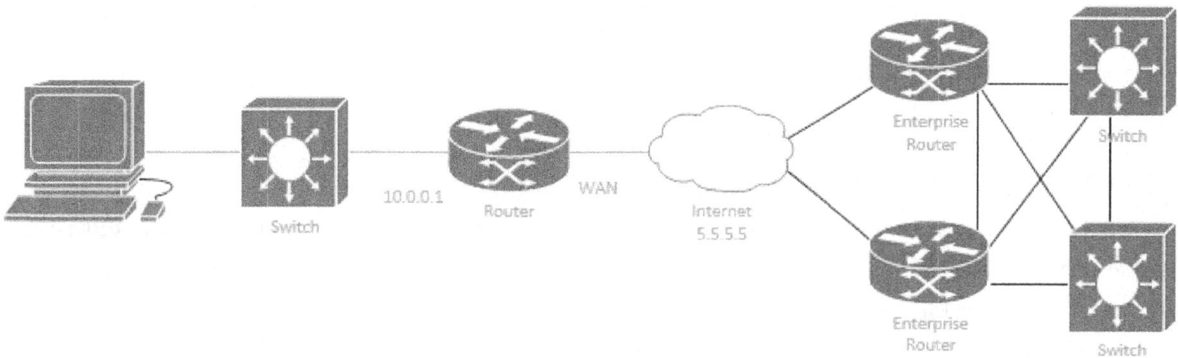

In this diagram, our router on the left side is connected to the internet via a WAN link, which is a single point of failure. On the right side, our enterprise routers each have a connection to the internet, but they also have a connection between themselves, thus there is no single point of failure. Each enterprise router also has a redundant connection to the switches on the far right.

The problem with a redundant network is that it is expensive. The cost of purchasing and configurating additional routers or WAN connections may be more than the cost of downtime resulting from the failure of the existing equipment.

In our network, we have two redundant routers. How do hosts know which router to use? They have three choices

- Everybody can use Router 1 as their default router and configure their gateway for 10.0.0.1. If Router 1 fails, everybody can manually switch to Router 2 and configure their gateway for 10.0.0.2.
- Everybody can use Router 2 as their default router and configure their gateway for 10.0.0.2. If Router 2 fails, everybody can manually switch to Router 1 and configure their gateway for 10.0.0.1.

- Half the hosts use Router 1 as their default router and half use Router 2. If Router 1 fails, the hosts that used Router 1 change to Router 2. If Router 2 fails, the hosts that used Router 2 change to Router 1.

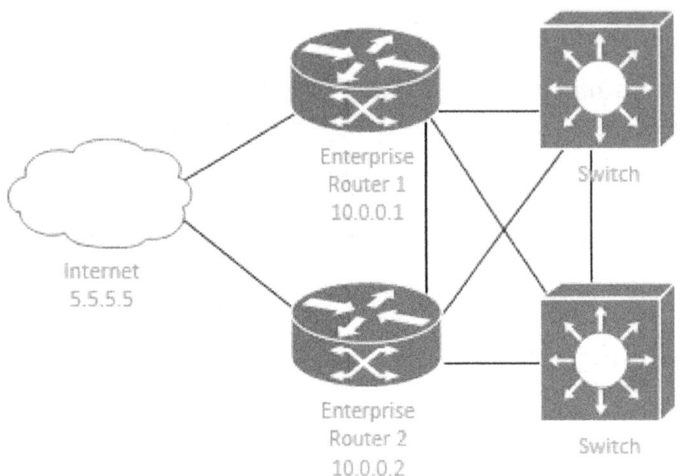

None of these options are good because they are not "seamless". We must wait until the router stops working and then manually change our settings. With FHRP, we create a virtual default router that everybody connects to. The two physical routers pretend like they're part of the same virtual router. If one router fails, the other router takes over.

FHRP is a framework, but the underlying protocol can depend on the network. There are three main protocols

- **HSRP** or **Hot Standby Router**. This was the original Cisco protocol.
- **GLBP** or **Gateway Load Balancing Protocol**. This is a newer Cisco Protocol.
- **VRRP** or **Virtual Router Redundancy Protocol**. This is an open source protocol.

In HSRP, one router is active, and the remaining routers are standby. The active router assumes a virtual IP address and a virtual MAC address, which we create through the HSRP configuration. The virtual IP address must be in the same subnet as the router's local interface.

The hosts on our local network use the virtual IP address as their default gateway. The standby routers are aware of the virtual IP address and MAC address. The routers use HSRP messages to communicate with each other and to decide which router is the active one and which router is on standby.

When a router fails, the other router takes over and assumes the virtual IP and MAC address. IP address configuration and ARP entries on the hosts do not change.

But remember that a switch forwards packets based on the MAC address of each connected device. Since a new router is assuming the virtual MAC address, the switch port pointing to the active router will have changed. The new router sends a frame to the switch that its connected to using the virtual MAC address that it just assumed. Now the switch updates the MAC address table to reflect the port connected to the newly active router.

When we have a network with multiple VLANs, we can keep both routers active, but use one router for some VLANs and the other router for the other VLANs. We can configure FHRP on a set of Layer 3 switches as well as on a router.

For the purposes of the CCNA, we do not need to learn how to configure FHRP. FHRP can function with a combination of interfaces on the same router or interfaces across multiple routers. On any interface that is a member of a FHRP group, we would configure the following commands. We must first choose a group number for our FHRP protocol.

- **`standby <group number> priority <priority>`** - this command sets the priority for the interface. The router will use the interface with the highest priority

- **`standby <group number> pre-empt`** – this tells the router that this interface must be used as the primary router when it is available. If I have a primary router and a standby router, and the primary router fails, the standby router will take over.

  When pre-empt is set, as soon as the primary router is available, it becomes the primary router again. This can be bad in a large network because routes might take time to converge. If the primary router takes over immediately, it will cause some downtime.

  To avoid this, we create a delay by typing **`standby <group number> pre-empt delay minimum <time in seconds> reload < time in seconds>`**. This gives the new primary router time to build its routing table before it takes over.

  The minimum time is the amount of time the router waits before taking over. The reload time is the amount of time the router waits before taking over if the router had been reloaded. The reload timer starts when the first interface is up.

- **`standby <group number> ip <IP address> secondary`** – this allows us to configure the virtual IP address that the group will use

4.0 IP Services

4.1 Configure and verify inside source NAT using static and pools

NAT or **Network Address Translation** was a tool created to help the world conserve the very scarce IPv4 addresses until IPv6 was invented.

Three tools were developed to slow the consumption of IPv4 addresses

- NAT
- Private IP addresses
- **CIDR** or **Classless Interdomain Routing**

NAT works with private IP addresses.

Think about how massive the internet is. Now imagine that there are some central routers that must send traffic to any part of the internet. Imagine how big their routing tables must be. Those routers need a lot of processing power and a lot of memory to search the table and process every packet, which is not possible.

Thus, we invented CIDR, which allows us to aggregate the different routes. It all started with **IANA**, or the **Internet Assigned Numbers Authority**. IANA decided to cut the IP address space into chunks and give each chunk to a different regional ISP.

For example, IANA gave the IP addresses that started with 201 to AT&T. In other words, AT&T is assigned addresses from 201.0.0.0 to 201.255.255.255. AT&T took this address space and subdivided it among its customers. For example, one customer received the network called 201.1.1.0/24, which gave them the addresses between 201.1.1.0 and 201.1.1.255. A second customer received the network called 201.1.2.0/24, which gave them the addresses between 201.1.2.0 and 201.1.2.255, and so on.

The point is that there are 16,777,216 IP addresses in AT&T's range. In addition, since AT&T is allocating each customer a Class C network, there are 65,536 separate Class C networks in AT&T's address space.

With CIDR, a major internet router doesn't need to learn the route to every network, just the major ones. For example, Verizon's router doesn't need to learn routes to all 65,536 AT&T networks. If the destination IP address begins with 201, Verizon knows to send the packet to AT&T. AT&T's router can take that packet and find the appropriate route to the customer's network.

Remember that IPv4 addresses are scarce. AT&T doesn't need to give every customer an entire /24 network (256 IP addresses) unless they need it. That might be a waste. Instead of giving them a classful network (an A, B, or C network), AT&T can give them a CIDR block.

For example, we can assign a customer the 201.1.1.32/28 network, which allows them to use IP addresses 201.1.1.33 to 201.1.1.46. Thus, AT&T can split its network into small chunks.

The purpose of NAT is to allow a device without a public unique IP address to communicate over the Internet. NAT works with private IP addresses.

NAT works through a router. In my network, my ISP assigned me only one IP address – 201.201.201.201. This address is given to the public facing interface on my router. I have multiple computers that need to access the internet through the router, but their addresses start with 10. How can they communicate?

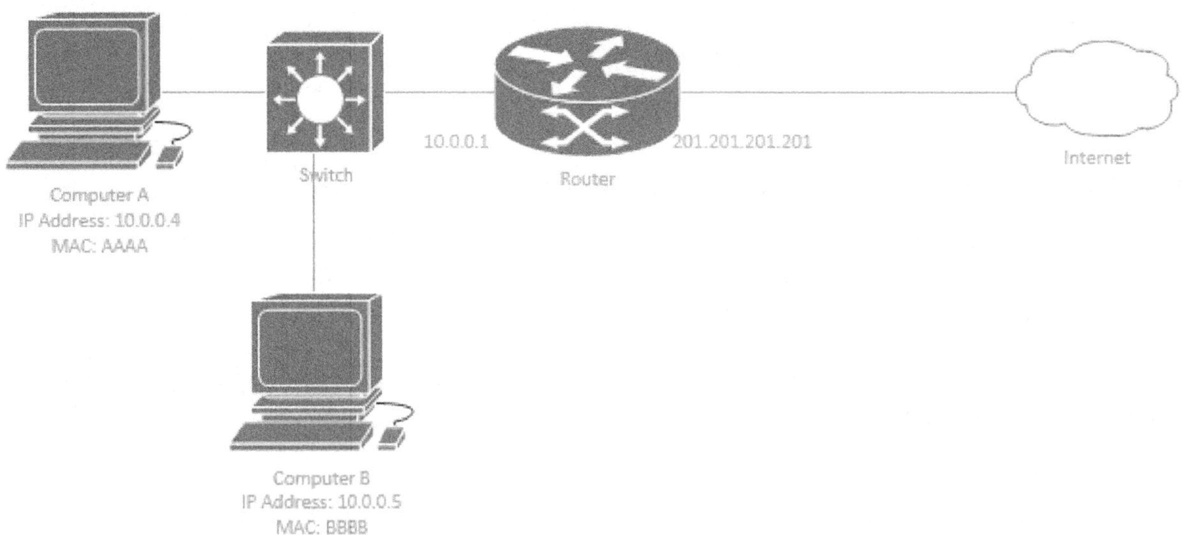

Well, the router must map each external IP address with an internal IP address. Now, if the router had many external IP addresses (enough to provide each internal device with one), we would create a **static NAT**.

In the following example, I have three internal devices and three external IP addresses assigned to the router. They are trying to access a host on the internet with the IP address 5.5.5.5. Inside the router, I can create a Static NAT Table

Public IP Address	Private IP Address
201.201.201.201	10.0.0.4
201.201.201.202	10.0.0.5
201.201.201.203	10.0.0.6

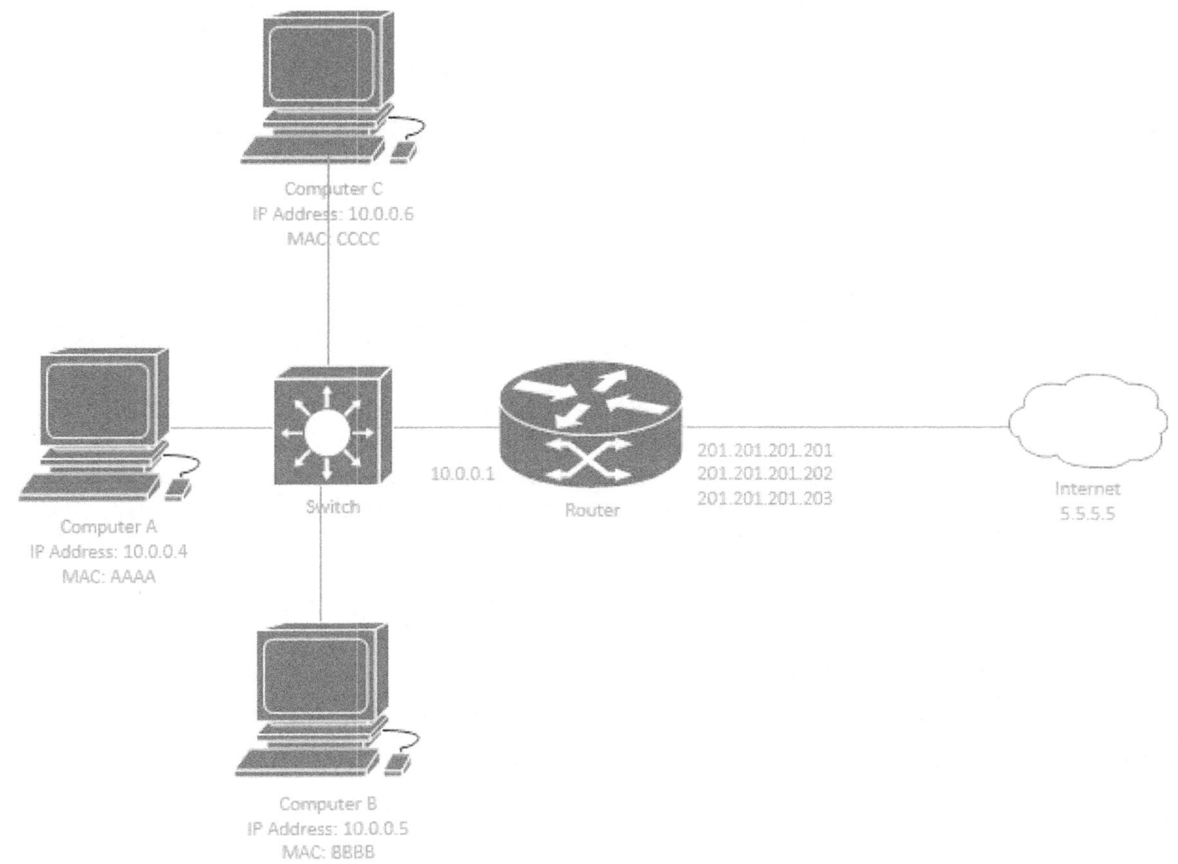

Let's look the process when Computer A wants to send a message to a device on the internet with the IP address 5.5.5.5?

- Computer A realizes that its IP address is 10.0.0.4 and that 5.5.5.5 is in a different subnet. Therefore, it sends its packet to the router's LAN IP address, 10.0.0.1. We already learned how frames are routed through a local network.
- The source IP on the packet is 10.0.0.4 and the destination IP is 5.5.5.5
- The router checks the Static NAT Table. It finds out that public IP 10.0.0.4 is mapped to 201.201.201.201.
- The router changes the source IP address to 201.201.201.201 and forwards it out of its external interface. We already learned how the router finds the route to an external network.
- The server at 5.5.5.5 receives the packet.
- The server replies to Computer A, but it puts the destination address as 201.201.201.201, because it doesn't know about the 10.0.0.4 IP address. It has no visibility inside the 10.0.0.0/24 network on the left.

- The router receives the reply on its external interface.
- It checks the table and finds that 201.201.201.201 is mapped to 10.0.0.4.
- It changes the destination IP address to 10.0.0.4 and forwards the packet to Computer A through its internal interface.

Cisco calls the private IP addresses **inside local IP addresses**, and the public IP addresses **inside global IP addresses**. The external device IP addresses are called **outside global IP addresses**.

We are only worried about changing the IP address of our internal devices, not the external ones. It is possible to create a NAT for external devices but that isn't a concern in the CCNA.

We must configure the static NAT on each interface that will see traffic involving the NAT. We need at least two interfaces – an inside and an outside.

Enter the interface configuration and type **`ip nat inside`** or **`ip nat outside`** depending on whether the interface is inside or outside the local network.

Go back to global configuration mode and type **`ip nat inside source static <inside local IP address> <inside global IP address>`** for each static IP mapping.

My configuration would look like this

```
Router(config)#interface GigabitEthernet0/0/1
Router(config-if)#ip nat inside
Router(config-if)#exit
Router(config)#interface GigabitEthernet0/0/2
Router(config-if)#ip nat outside
Router(config-if)#exit
Router(config)#ip nat inside source static 10.0.0.4 201.201.201.201
Router(config)#ip nat inside source static 10.0.0.5 201.201.201.202
Router(config)#ip nat inside source static 10.0.0.6 201.201.201.203
```

I can verify the NAT static mappings by typing **`show ip nat translations`**. I can verify the statistics by typing **`show ip nat statistics`**.

```
Router#show ip nat translations
Pro  Inside global      Inside local       Outside local      Outside global
---  201.201.201.201    10.0.0.4           ---                ---
---  201.201.201.202    10.0.0.5           ---                ---
---  201.201.201.203    10.0.0.6           ---                ---

Router#show ip nat statistics
Total translations: 3 (3 static, 0 dynamic, 0 extended)
Outside Interfaces: GigabitEthernet0/0/2
Inside Interfaces: GigabitEthernet0/0/1
Hits: 854  Misses: 0
Expired translations: 0
Dynamic mappings:
```

The hits tells us how many packets have been translated by NAT.

The problem with this example is that IPv4 addresses are scarce. We might have hundreds of computers, but our ISP is unwilling to provide us with hundreds of IP addresses. Thus, we can use a **dynamic NAT**. How does it work?

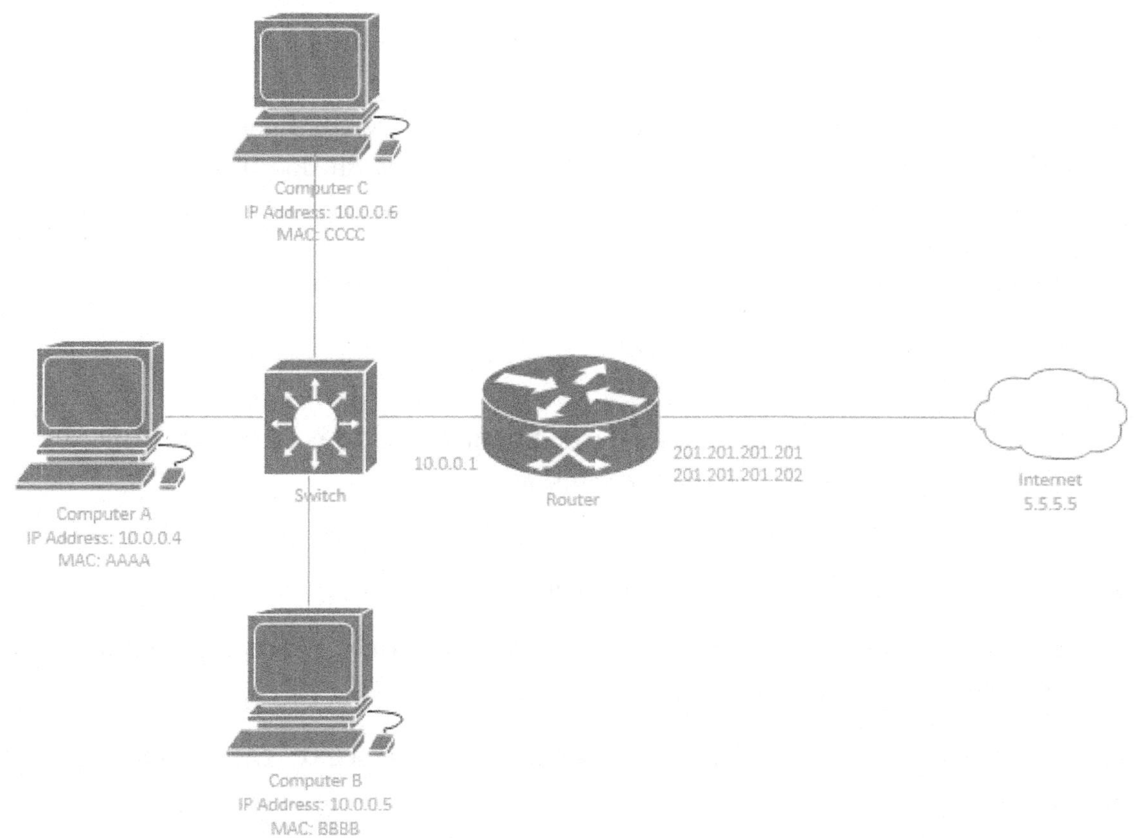

I only have two public IP addresses, but at least three internal devices. Thus, I don't map any IP addresses to any devices.

I instead create a NAT Pool, which contains my available public IP addresses.

Pool
201.201.201.201
201.201.201.202

My NAT table is empty

Public IP Address	**Private IP Address**

- If computer A wants to send a message to 5.5.5.5, it again realizes that the destination is not in its subnet. It creates a packet and sends it to the router.
- The router realizes that Computer A needs a public IP address. It chooses an IP address from the pool and assigns it to Computer A. Now my NAT table has an entry and there is one IP address left in the pool.

Public IP Address	**Private IP Address**
201.201.201.201	10.0.0.4

- Like before, the router changes the source IP address of packets coming from Computer A to the public IP of 201.201.201.201. It also changes the destination IP address of packets travelling to Computer A from 201.201.201.201 to 10.0.0.4 and forwards them out of its local interface.

We can configure a dynamic NAT like a static NAT.

Again, we enter the interface configuration and type **`ip nat inside`** or **`ip nat outside`** depending on whether the interface is inside or outside.

We must create an ACL (Access Control List) that matches the local IP addresses whose traffic should be translated by NAT. We will learn more about ACLs later.

We establish a NAT Pool by typing **`ip nat pool <Pool Name> <First IP Address> <Last IP Address> netmask <subnet mask>`**.

Finally, we create the NAT by typing **`ip nat inside source list <ACL Number> pool <Pool Name>`**, where ACL Number is the number of the ACL we created earlier, and the Pool Name is the name of the Pool we created earlier.

In my example, we set G0/0/1 as the inside NAT interface, and G0/0/2 as the outside NAT interface. We created ACL 1 to permit access to 10.0.0.4 through 10.0.0.6. The router recognizes that internal devices with IP addresses 10.0.0.4 through 10.0.0.6 match ACL 1.

Then we created a NAT pool with the range of 201.201.201.201 to 201.201.201.202 and called it mainpool.

Then we told the router to use ACL 1 and the NAT pool mainpool. Now the router knows that traffic entering G0/0/1 from devices 10.0.0.4 through 10.0.0.6 should be assigned an IP address from the range of 201.201.201.201 to 201.201.201.202 if it is leaving the G0/0/2 interface.

```
Router(config)#interface GigabitEthernet0/0/1
Router(config-if)#ip nat inside
Router(config-if)#exit
Router(config)#interface GigabitEthernet0/0/2
Router(config-if)#ip nat outside
Router(config-if)#exit
Router(config)#access-list 1 permit 10.0.0.4
Router(config)#access-list 1 permit 10.0.0.5
Router(config)#access-list 1 permit 10.0.0.6
Router(config)#ip nat pool mainpool 201.201.201.201 201.201.201.202 netmask 255.255.255.252
Router(config)#ip nat inside source list 1 pool mainpool
```

I can verify the NAT dynamic mappings by typing **`show ip nat translations`**. I can verify the statistics by typing **`show ip nat statistics`**.

Note that until the router begins to exchange traffic, there will be no dynamic mappings and the **`show ip nat translations`** command will return nothing.

The statistics show two misses counters. The first counter tracks missed packets across all forms of NAT in the router, while the second counter tracks missed packets among the specific NAT dynamic pool we created.

```
Router#show ip nat statistics
Total translations: 0 (0 static, 0 dynamic, 0 extended)
Outside Interfaces: GigabitEthernet0/0/2
Inside Interfaces: GigabitEthernet0/0/1
Hits: 0  Misses: 0
Expired translations: 0
Dynamic mappings:
-- Inside Source
access-list 1 pool mainpool refCount 0
 pool mainpool: netmask 255.255.255.252
       start 201.201.201.201 end 201.201.201.202
       type generic, total addresses 0 , allocated 0 (0%), misses 0
```

After we start exchanging traffic, we see that our router assigned both IP addresses in the pool, and that it exchanged some traffic.

```
Router#show ip nat translations
Pro  Inside global      Inside local       Outside local      Outside global
---  201.201.201.201    10.0.0.4           ---                ---
---  201.201.201.202    10.0.0.5           ---                ---

Router#

Router#show ip nat statistics
Total translations: 2 (0 static, 1 dynamic, 0 extended)
Outside Interfaces: GigabitEthernet0/0/2
Inside Interfaces: GigabitEthernet0/0/1
Hits: 440  Misses: 2
Expired translations: 0
Dynamic mappings:
-- Inside Source
access-list 1 pool mainpool refCount 0
 pool mainpool: netmask 255.255.255.252
       start 201.201.201.201 end 201.201.201.202
       type generic, total addresses 0 , allocated 2 (100%), misses 0
```

Notice that I have two misses in the first counter but none in the second counter. The first time 10.0.0.4 sent a packet, the router received the packet but didn't have a NAT IP address allocated to it, so it dropped the packet and created a mapping. Thus, it registered a miss. The first time 10.0.0.5 sent a packet, the router did the same thing. The second time 10.0.0.4 and 10.0.0.5 sent packets, the router already had a mapping, so it was able to forward their traffic.

If the router notices that an IP address from the pool hasn't been in use for a while, it returns it to the pool so that it can be given to another device. But if all the addresses are in use and another device wants to send traffic out to the internet, it must wait until an address becomes available. This could take seconds or minutes or even days. What if we have a large office with hundreds of employees who need to access the internet, and only two IP addresses?

We can use **NAT Overload** also known as **Port Address Translation**, or **PAT**.

In my next example, I only have one public IP address and three computers that want to talk at the same time.

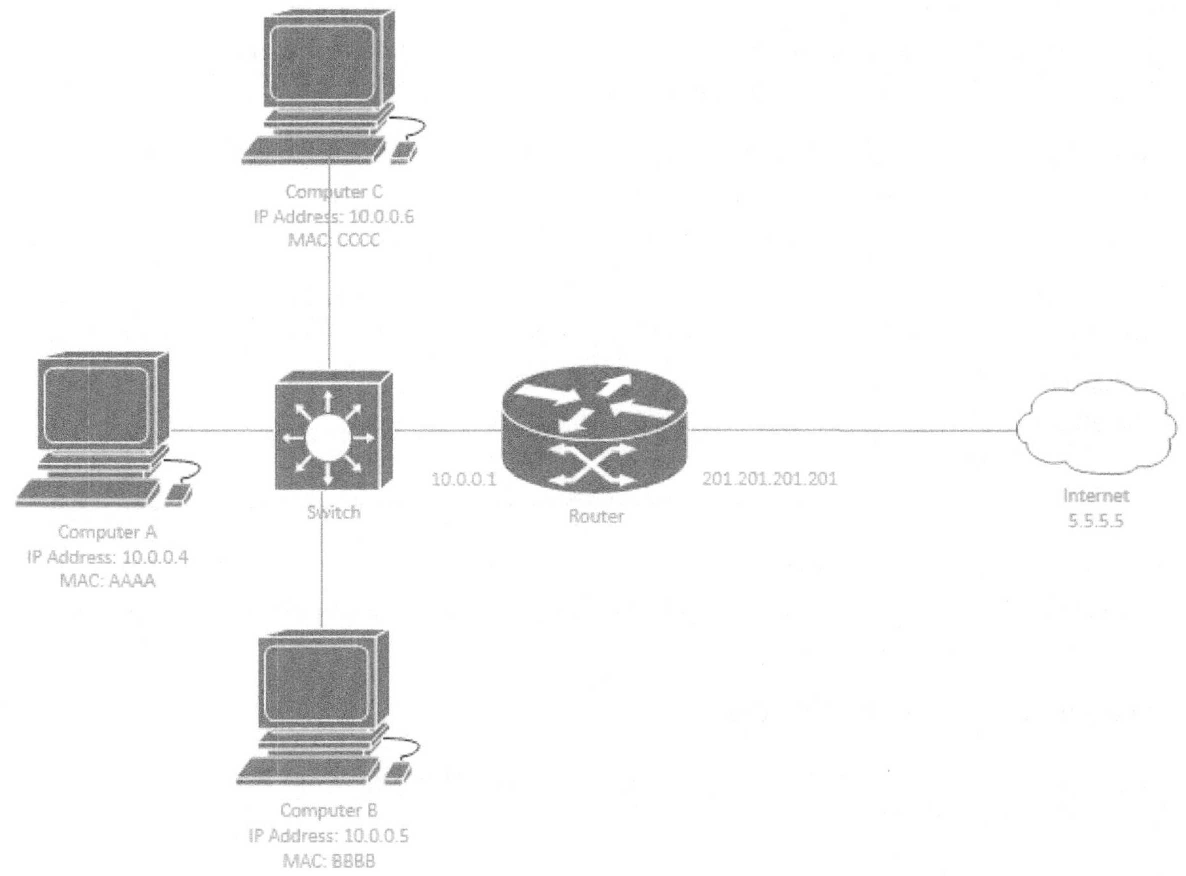

Now I need to look at the IP port used by each device. Let's say that each computer is attempting to access a website on Port 80. The full address of the website is 5.5.5.5:80.

Computer A, B, and C realize that 5.5.5.5 is not in their subnet so they send their traffic to the router. Their addresses are

- Computer A – 10.0.0.4:80
- Computer B – 10.0.0.5:80
- Computer C – 10.0.0.6:80

The router only has one address – 201.201.201.201. Thus, it creates the following mapping

Public IP Address & Port	Private IP Address & Port
201.201.201.201:49501	10.0.0.4:80
201.201.201.201:49502	10.0.0.5:80
201.201.201.201:49503	10.0.0.6:80

The router gave each local device the same IP address but a different port. It chose ports 49501 to 49503, which are ports that aren't used for common applications. The actual port numbers aren't too important.

When the router receives traffic from 10.0.0.4:80, it knows to change its source IP address/port to 201.201.201.201:49501, and when the router receives traffic with a destination of 201.201.201.201:49501, it changes its destination/port to 10.0.0.4:80.

What if Computer A is also sending traffic over HTTPS (port 443)? The router assigns it the same external IP address and another port. Remember, the router assigns a port when it sees traffic that requires it. It doesn't do so proactively. Now our table looks like this.

Public IP Address & Port	Private IP Address & Port
201.201.201.201:49501	10.0.0.4:80
201.201.201.201:49502	10.0.0.5:80
201.201.201.201:49503	10.0.0.6:80
201.201.201.201:49504	10.0.0.4:445

Using NAT Overload, we can map tens of thousands of ports to one IP address. A single computer on our local network might use between 5 and 15 ports. Thus, we can support thousands of computers with one public IP address.

We can configure NAT overload like dynamic NAT.

Again, we enter the interface configuration and type **`ip nat inside`** or **`ip nat outside`** depending on whether the interface is inside or outside.

We must create an ACL that matches the local IP addresses whose traffic should be translated by NAT.

Finally, we create the NAT by typing **`ip nat inside source list <ACL Number> interface <Interface> overload`**, where ACL Number is the number of the ACL we created earlier, and the Interface is the external interface that NAT will operate on. NAT will automatically use the IP address of the interface that it is assigned to.

```
Router(config)#interface GigabitEthernet0/0/1
Router(config-if)#ip nat inside
Router(config-if)#exit
Router(config)#interface GigabitEthernet0/0/2
Router(config-if)#ip nat outside
Router(config-if)#exit
Router(config)#access-list 1 permit 10.0.0.4
Router(config)#access-list 1 permit 10.0.0.5
Router(config)#access-list 1 permit 10.0.0.6
Router(config)#ip nat inside source list 1 interface GigabitEthernet0/0/2
```

I can verify the NAT overload mappings by typing **`show ip nat translations`**. I can verify the statistics by typing **`show ip nat statistics`**.

```
Router#show ip nat translations
Pro  Inside global          Inside local       Outside local      Outside global
---  201.201.201.201:49501   10.0.0.4:80           ---                ---
---  201.201.201.201:49502   10.0.0.5:80           ---                ---
---  201.201.201.201:49503   10.0.0.6:80           ---                ---
---  201.201.201.201:49504   10.0.0.6:443           ---                ---

Router#show ip nat statistics
Total translations: 4 (0 static, 0 dynamic, 4 extended)
Outside Interfaces: GigabitEthernet0/0/2
Inside Interfaces: GigabitEthernet0/0/1
Hits: 0  Misses: 0
Expired translations: 0
```

What could possibly go wrong?

- We have the wrong inside and outside commands applied to each interface. For example, we set our inside interface as an outside interface. Or we set an interface as inside but it isn't connected to the LAN.
- We don't have the correct range of IP addresses configured.
- We don't have the correct ACL configured, or an internal address that should have its packets translated is not part of the ACL.
- The pool has run out of IP addresses in dynamic NAT.
- We configured PAT but did not choose the correct interface.
- We have another ACL that is blocking the traffic.
- We created the NAT correctly, but no traffic is coming to the router for some other reason.

First make sure that the packet is leaving the user's computer and reaching the correct internal interface on the router. Then make sure that the router has a correct NAT translation using the show commands. Then make sure that the router is transporting the packets out of the correct interface.

4.2 Configure and verify NTP operating in a client and server mode

NTP or **Network Time Protocol** makes sure that every device on the network has the same time, even when they are in different time zones.

If routers and switches don't synchronize their clocks, then their messages will have the wrong time stamp and none of them will be able to determine when a message was sent or received. When two network devices communicate, they exchange NTP messages and synchronize their clocks. Eventually, as more and more devices exchange NTP messages, their clocks get closer to the real time.

The first thing we must do is set the correct time zone and daylight savings time.

- **`clock timezone <Time Zone Name> <UTC Time Offset>`**
  - The Time Zone Name can be any meaningful name we choose.
  - The UTC Time Offset is between -12 and +12 depending on the time zone that we are in. For example, Pacific Time is -8. If we are in the Pacific time zone, we type **`clock timezone PST -8`**.
- **`clock summer-time <Time Zone Name> recurring`**
  - The Time Zone Name can be any meaningful name we choose.
  - We type recurring to make sure that the router changes the time based on daylight savings time each spring and fall.

We can set the time with **`clock set <time> <date>`**.

We can view the time with **`show clock`**. The switch will accept the time that we entered in 24-hour format as UTC time, and then convert it to the local time zone. Notice that I entered "20" for the hour, but the switch converted it to "12 PST", which is the eight-hour time difference.

```
Switch>enable
Switch#conf t
Enter configuration commands, one per line.  End with CNTL/Z.
Switch(config)#clock timezone PST -8
Switch(config)#clock summer-time PST recurring
Switch(config)#
Switch#
%SYS-5-CONFIG_I: Configured from console by console

Switch#clock set 20:20:20 02 May 2020
Switch#show clock
12:20:24.271 PST Sat May 2 2020
```

Now that we've configured a reasonably correct time, we need to set up the Network Time Protocol.

There are two methods

- **NTP Master**. A device that is an NTP Master has an internal clock. It tells other devices what time it is, but other devices can't tell it what the time is.

  We configure it with **`ntp master <level>`**. This level is known as a stratum.

- **NTP Server**. A device that is an NTP Server tells other devices what time it is, but other devices can tell it what time it is. It can accept a time update from a device with a more accurate time, and then it can send time updates to other devices.

  We configure it with **`ntp server <IP address or hostname>`** and specify the IP address or hostname of an external server that can provide us with the time. Cisco recommends that we configure at least three external servers so that we can obtain an accurate time.

We can verify the status by typing **`show ntp status`**.

```
Router(config)#ntp master 1
Router(config)#exit
Router#
%SYS-5-CONFIG_I: Configured from console by console
Router#show ntp status
Clock is synchronized, stratum 1, reference is 127.127.1.1
nominal freq is 250.0000 Hz, actual freq is 249.9990 Hz, precision is 2**24
reference time is AF34136F.00000037 (3:7:27.055 UTC Wed Mar 17 1993)
clock offset is 0.00 msec, root delay is 0.00  msec
root dispersion is 0.00 msec, peer dispersion is 0.01 msec.
loopfilter state is 'CTRL' (Normal Controlled Loop), drift is - 0.000001193 s/s system poll
interval is 4, last update was 10 sec ago.
```

The status tells us that the Clock is synchronized and provides the reference. The reference is the IP address of the source of the time (typically another router). In this case, our router is the master, so the source of the time is itself (127.127.1.1).

If we type **`show ntp associations`**, we can obtain a list of other NTP servers that the router is attempting to connect to.

```
Router#show ntp associations

address         ref clock       st   when     poll    reach  delay          offset
 disp
*~127.127.1.1   .LOCL.          7    29       64      377    0.00           0.00
 0.24
 * sys.peer, # selected, + candidate, - outlyer, x falseticker, ~ configured
```

A * in front of an entry indicates that the router was successful in obtaining a time stamp from the server.

The stratum level is the hierarchy of the NTP server. A level of one is the highest. The most master server has a stratum of one. A server with a stratum of one gets its time from its own internal hardware. The higher the stratum, the more accurate the time is assumed to be.

Any client that obtains its time from a server adds one to the level. For example, if our server has a stratum of two, when our clients obtain the time from it, they change the stratum level to three. Any devices obtaining the time from those clients change the stratum level to four, and so on.

Each time a device obtains a time from another server, the accuracy of the time decreases. A time stamp with a stratum of four has been passed through three routers, so it is considered less accurate than a time stamp with a stratum of two or three. The stratum level helps us determine how accurate a time stamp is.

The stratum level can be between one and fifteen. A time stamp with a level of 16 or higher cannot be trusted. The default stratum is eight.

The government runs some NTP servers that are available for the public to use. We don't need to run our own time server unless we have an air-gapped network.

We type **`ntp server <external server name>`** to use an external NTP server.

For example, **`ntp server time-a-b-nist.gov`** allows our device to obtain the time from the NIST server.

A better solution is to create a master NTP server on our network. The server can be a device such as a router or switch.

- This server is synchronized with the external clock by typing **`ntp server <external server name>`**, which is very accurate.
- We also synchronize it with the internal clock by typing **`ntp master <level>`**, so that our network continues to maintain an accurate time if access to the external NTP server fails.
- We must make sure that the NTP master level is higher than that of the external server so that the internal server relies on the external server for its time first.

A router **loopback interface** is an internal interface that exists if the router is up, and the loopback is not shutdown.

We can configure a loopback interface by typing **interface loopback <number>**. We can pick any number for the interface. As soon as we enter the loopback interface configuration, the router creates the interface.

Why do we want to configure a loopback? We can give it an IP address and pretend that it's a physical interface. But it's a physical interface that doesn't shut down because it doesn't physically connect to anything.

A router might be reachable through more than one physical interface. If an NTP client (another device on the network that wants to know what time it is) uses a specific interface to reach the router, and that interface fails, the NTP client won't be able to obtain a timestamp from the router, even if other interfaces remain reachable.

One benefit of creating a lookback interface inside the router is so that we can always reach it as long as one physical interface is working. After we create the interface we then change the NTP Source inside the router to the loopback IP interface with the **ntp source loopback <loopback number>** command.

```
Router(config)#interface loopback 0

Router(config-if)#
%LINK-5-CHANGED: Interface Loopback0, changed state to up

%LINEPROTO-5-UPDOWN: Line protocol on Interface Loopback0, changed state to up

Router(config-if)#ip address 100.100.100.100 255.255.255.0
Router(config-if)#exit
Router(config)#ntp master 4
Router(config)#ntp source loopback 0
Router(config)#exit
Router#
%SYS-5-CONFIG_I: Configured from console by console
```

After we created the loopback interface with an ID number of 0, the interface automatically came up. We then specify an IP address (100.100.100.100) for the interface. Finally, we set the NTP source to be the loopback 0.

On our client, we reference the NTP loopback IP address by typing **ntp server 100.100.100.100**. Now we can reach the router via NTP regardless of which interface is active. Why does this work? The router creates an internal route to the loopback IP from all of its external physical interfaces. Thus, we can always reach the loopback interface.

4.3 Explain the role of DHCP and DNS within the network

Remember that a computer understands addresses in numeric format (like 8.8.8.8) and a human understands text (like google.com). We use the **DNS (Domain Name Service)** to convert the human-readable address into a computer-readable address.

When I try to visit google.com, my computer calls up the nearest DNS and asks it to provide information about google.com. google.com is known as a **domain name**. A DNS will contain a set of records about each domain name, which are provided by the owner. What kind of information can it provide?

- **A or AAA**. The **A (Address Mapping)** record tells us the IPv4 address of the server that is hosting the website. The AAA record tells us the IPv6 address.
- **TXT (SPF, DKIM)**. The **TXT (Text)** record tells us some text. Two common uses of TXT records
    - **SPF** or **Sender Policy Framework**. Think of an e-mail like a letter. It has a "to" address and a "from" address. I could send a fake letter and use a fake "from" address because nobody can verify that the "from" address is correct. An e-mail is the same. A spammer could spoof the "from" address and make it look somebody legitimate sent the e-mail. How can we stop this?

      The sender must use an e-mail server to send the e-mail. This server has a unique IP address. If the legitimate sender has control over his domain name and server, he can create a Text entry called the SPF and put the IP address of his e-mail server in there.

      When a recipient receives a message, he checks the IP address in the SPF belonging to the legitimate sender. If it matches the actual sender, then he knows that the e-mail is legitimate.
    - **DKIM** or **DomainKeys Identified Mail** is another way to identify an e-mail's legitimate sender. A user of DKIM creates a unique signature via public key cryptography. It's essentially a signature that can't be forged – it has two parts, a private key that only the sender knows, and a public key that recipients can use to verify his identity. The legitimate sender places a copy of the public key in DKIM. He uses the private key to digitally sign every e-mail he sends. When a recipient receives an e-mail, he verifies that the signature matches the public key in the record.
- **SRV**. The **SRV (Server)** record tells us about the location of servers that operate specific processes. The server location includes an IP address or domain name and a port number. The domain name in an SRV record must itself have an A record or else it won't be located.

- **MX**. The **MX (Mail Exchanger)** record tells us the IP address or domain name of the mail server that receives e-mail on behalf of the domain. If my e-mail is hazim@hsmservices.ca and I host my own e-mail, then the record may point to my own server. If my e-mail is hosted by Gmail, my MX record may point to gmail.com.

  When you send an e-mail, your e-mail program (or SMTP server) will query the MX records for each recipients' address so that it knows where to send the message.

  The domain name in an MX record must have its own record, or else it won't be located.
- **CNAME** or **Canonical Name** points one domain name to another. The purpose of a CNAME record is to point one name to another. The CNAME record must itself have an A name record.

  For example, foo.example.com can point to bar.example.com. bar.example.com must have an A record or else it won't be located.

  When a computer receives a CNAME reply, it must then look for the corresponding A record.
- **NS** or **Name Server**. The NS record tells us which DNS server is **authoritative** for the domain. The owner of a domain name maintains DNS records for his name on an authoritative name server. The authoritative name server has the most accurate records.

  Since the internet is distributed, DNS servers operated by other users might copy the records from the authoritative name server and respond to queries. When you access a website, your computer won't necessarily query the authoritative name server for that site. It may query a local nameserver operated by your organization or ISP.
- **PTR** or **Pointer Record**. A Pointer is like a CNAME, but the computer does not look further for the A record.

  For example, foo.example.com can point to bar.example.com. bar.example.com must have an A record or else it won't be located.

Each record can contain multiple entries for load balancing. We can give each entry a different priority. For example, we might have multiple servers to handle our e-mail or website hosting.

An **internal DNS** is one that is operated by an organization for use on its internal network. A network might have devices that are accessible internally such as servers, switches, and printers. Each device is assigned a unique hostname on the network. The internal DNS server provides users with DNS records corresponding to these internal devices. A user may need to access both internal devices and external hosts. Therefore, the user may need to program his computer to query both an internal DNS server and an **external DNS** server. The external DNS provides information about hosts that are available to the public (on the internet). It is possible for an internal DNS to also be an external DNS.

An organization may choose to host its DNS with a third party. Examples of **third-party DNS** include Amazon (AWS) Route 53 and CloudFlare. A third-party DNS is scalable and can provide inquiries to many users at the same time. In addition, a third-party DNS is centrally located so that updates to the DNS propagate across the internet quickly.

The hierarchy of a DNS starts at the **authoritative server**, which is maintained by the owner of the domain name. Below the authoritative server are servers operated by national internet service providers. They aggregate DNS records from the different authoritative servers. Below them are servers operated by local ISPs. Below them are servers operated by organizations for local networks.

When we query a DNS server, we might start at the local level. If the local server doesn't have an answer, we check at the next level. If it doesn't have an answer, we continue working our way to the top until we reach the authoritative server.

A **Reverse DNS lookup** is when we have an IP address and want to know which domain name it belongs to. An IP address may belong to multiple domain names. The PTR record is used for the Reverse DNS lookup.

We can obtain the domain name corresponding to an IP address by querying the domain name **in-addr.arpa**. If we want to know the domain name for the IP address 1.2.3.4, we would query the name:

4.3.2.1.in-addr.arpa

Notice that we prepended the IP address in reverse to the front of the in-addr.arpa domain name.

Each DNS record has a **TTL** or **Time To Live**. This is a number that tells the non-authoritative DNS servers the length of time (in seconds) until a record expires. For example, if a TTL is 3600, then the DNS record expires after one hour. If my local DNS server obtains authoritative DNS records from google.com's DNS, and the TTL is one hour, then it should check again for updated records after one hour.

If we make the TTL long, then any changes will take a long time to propagate across the entire internet. If we make the TTL short, then changes will propagate quickly, but our DNS server will receive more queries.

I covered DHCP earlier but let's look at a few more details. Remember that when a computer joins a network, and doesn't have a static IP address, it gets one through DHCP.

If I want a specific device to obtain the same IP address each time, I create a **MAC Reservation**. I must know the device's MAC address. If I don't know the MAC address, I can check my switch or DHCP server. I program my DHCP server with the device's MAC address and corresponding DHCP address. When the device joins the network and requests a DHCP address, the server checks if its MAC address is on the list. If so, it offers it the corresponding IP address.

A **pool** is a group of IP addresses that can be assigned to devices requesting addresses over DHCP. An administrator should make the range wide enough to accommodate all the devices that would request addresses, taking the lease time into consideration. An **IP Exclusion** is a list of IP addresses that should not be assigned via DHCP.

The **Lease Time** is the length of time that an IP address is assigned to a device. A common lease time is seven days. Once the lease time expires, the device must obtain a new IP address. Once a DHCP address is assigned, the server reserves that address for the entire length of the lease time, even if the device disconnects from the network. If the device rejoins the network during the lease time, it will be assigned the same address. A device can give up its DHCP address during the lease time by sending the server a **Release** message, but in practice devices rarely do so.

When we have a network with many guests (such as a guest Wi-Fi), we should make the lease time short. Otherwise, we will have many thousands of leased IP addresses for devices that are no longer connected. Think about the Wi-Fi at an airport. You might connect for a few hours and then get on your plane. If the lease time was seven days, the airport's network would continue to reserve your IP address for seven days, which would be six days and 22 hours longer than necessary.

The DHCP **Scope Options** provide options such as gateway and DNS servers. When a client device receives a DHCP address, the DHCP server also tells it about the default gateway and DNS servers on the network.

The DHCP server is usually part of the router or is somewhere on the local network (subnet). When a client joins the network and requests an address via DHCP, its request will not travel past the router. Remember that a DHCP message is a broadcast message and that routers do not forward broadcast messages.

What if I have a large distributed network with multiple routers but I only have one central DHCP server? I use a tool called a DHCP Relay. The **DHCP Relay** lives in the router. It listens for DHCP messages and forwards them to an external DHCP server. It also receives DHCP reply messages from the external server and forwards them to requesting devices on the internal network. On a Cisco router, this is known as an **IP Helper Address**.

We can configure the IP Helper address on a Cisco router by entering the applicable interface's configuration and typing **`ip helper-address <IP address>`**.

4.4 Explain the function of SNMP in network operations

SNMP, or **Simple Network Management Protocol** is an open source framework for collecting data about different network devices. That data includes statistics, configuration, and network status.

An **SNMP manager** is a server that collects data from the different devices. We might call this device a **Network Management Station**, or **NMS**.

Each device that reports to the server has a software program known as a **SNMP agent**. The agent collects data from the device and sends it to the manager via an SNMP protocol.

The agent stores the variables for its device in a **Management Information Base** (**MIB**). For a single device, this MIB could contain hundreds or thousands of variables.

Each variable is known as an **object ID** or **OID**. The OIDs can be open-source or vendor proprietary. They are organized into a hierarchy. Variable names can be complicated, so it is easier to manage the devices via an NMS.

The SNMP agent can send data to the NMS regularly, or the NMS can regularly query the SNMP agent on each device. When an abnormal issue is detected, the NMS can notify an operator via e-mail or an on-screen alert. The NMS can also reconfigure the affected device.

NMS uses a **Get message** to request information from the agent. These Get messages may be called SNMP Get, GetNext or GetBulk. The device replies with a **Get Response message**. A server can send a device a **Set message** to change its configuration.

It also uses an SNMP Set message to change the configuration on the device.

The SNMP agent can be configured to send an alert when a variable reaches a certain level. In that case, the SNMP agent sends a **Trap message** or an **Inform message** to the NMS. Trap messages were created in the first version of SNMP. They are sent via UDP and the agent doesn't keep track of whether the message is received. Inform messages use UDP, but the NMS must send a response to acknowledge receipt.

We should use an ACL to secure our SNMP so that only an authorized NMS can send or receive messages with our network device. We can also secure our SNMP with a password.

SNMPv1 and SNMPv2 used communities. A **community** was defined by a **community string**. The agent and the manager needed to belong to the same community, by knowing the community string. The Get and Set messages include the community string in plain text. The community string is kind of like a password. An agent won't accept a message with the wrong community string (the wrong password).

A community could be **read-only** (**RO**) where the NMS can't change anything on the device or **read-write** (**RW**) where the agent accepts both Get and Set messages from the NMS.

SNMPv3 introduced security and removed communities. It has three features. First, it provides encryption so that a message cannot be read by an unauthorized user. Second it provides authentication so that a manager can authenticate with a client device via a username and password, which are not sent in plain text. Third, it provides message integrity so that we can verify that the SNMP message was not modified during transmission.

4.5 Describe the use of syslog features including facilities and levels

When we're logged in to a switch or a router via console, we can see different logging messages appearing. By default, "logging console" is enabled.

If we find the messages annoying, we can turn them off in our session by typing **`no logging console`**. This is only valid for the session that we are in.

A user logged in to a switch or router via Telnet or SSH will not see the logging messages unless we do two things

- Activate the logging through the global **`logging monitor`** command
- Each user must activate the logging in his individual Telnet or SSH session by typing the **`terminal monitor`** command after he logs in.

After a logging message is sent to the user, it is gone forever. If nobody was logged in to the switch or router when the message was generated, it is also gone forever.

We can store the messages in the RAM by typing **`logging buffered`** in the global configuration. If we come back later and want to check the messages, we type **`show logging`**.

We can also tell the device to send the messages to a central server. A central server for logging messages from network devices is called a **syslog server**. We do this by typing **`logging host <syslog server IP address or hostname>`** in the global configuration.

Each IOS log message has looks like this

```
*May 2 18:30:15.113: %LINEPROTO-1-UPDOWN: Line protocol on Interface
GigabitEthernet0/0/1, changed state to up
```

This message tells us the following

- The timestamp: May 2 18:30:15.113
- The router program that created the message: %LINEPROTO
- The severity of the message: in this case it is 1
- The name of the message: UPDOWN
- A human readable description of the message: Line protocol on Interface GigabitEthernet0/0/1, changed state to up

Some things we can do

- We can disable the time stamp by typing **`no service timestamps`**.

- We can give each message a sequence number so that it can be referenced later, by typing **`service sequence-numbers`**.

The message severity is from 0 to 7 as shown in the following table

Message Number	Severity
0	Emergency
1	Alert
2	Critical
3	Error
4	Warning
5	Notification
6	Informational
7	Debug

We should deal with any message with a severity of 0 or 1 immediately. A message that has a severity of 2, 3, or 4 should be dealt with as soon as possible.

We might want to ignore messages that are of a low severity. We can do that by typing a number or severity after the logging command. The switch will stop logging or sending messages above the designated severity level. The commands are

- **`logging console <number or severity>`**
- **`logging monitor <number or severity>`**
- **`logging buffered <number or severity>`**
- **`logging trap <number or severity>`**. This is an exception for the logging host command.

For example, if we don't want to view messages below the Warning level in our console, we can type **`logging console warning`** or **`logging console 4`**.

We can verify the logging by typing **`show logging`**.

```
Switch>enable
Switch#show logging
Syslog logging: enabled (0 messages dropped, 0 messages rate-limited,
          0 flushes, 0 overruns, xml disabled, filtering disabled)

No Active Message Discriminator.


No Inactive Message Discriminator.


    Console logging: level debugging, 8 messages logged, xml disabled,
          filtering disabled
    Monitor logging: level debugging, 8 messages logged, xml disabled,
          filtering disabled
    Buffer logging:  level warnings, xml disabled,
          filtering disabled

    Logging Exception size (4096 bytes)
    Count and timestamp logging messages: disabled
    Persistent logging: disabled

No active filter modules.

ESM: 0 messages dropped
    Trap logging: level informational, 8 message lines logged
        Logging to 10.5.5.5
```

We can see the Console logging, Monitor logging, Buffer logging, and Trap (syslog) Logging levels. We can also see the IP address of the syslog server.

The switch or router will list each logging level by name not by number.

We can erase any logs by typing **clear logging**.

The router will not show any messages of a debug severity unless we log in and type **debug**. The debug command stays active until we type **no debug**. We turn on debug to monitor activities in the router. For example, I can turn on ICMP debugging by typing **debug ip icmp**. If I want to turn it off, I must type **no debug ip icmp**.

```
Switch#debug ip icmp
ICMP packet debugging is on
Switch#
```

The generation of debug messages consumes a substantial amount of router resources and should only be enabled when necessary. That is why it is disabled by default.

4.6 Configure and verify DHCP client and relay

How do we set up DHCP or Dynamic Host Configuration Protocol? Remember that if a host connects to our network, it must be assigned an IP address (unless it has a static IP). A DHCP server assigns IP addresses.

There are four messages that are sent from the client to the server

- **Discover**. This is the first message that the client sends to the server. It is the equivalent of "hey, I'm new here and I need an IP address".
- **Offer**. This is a message that the server sends to the client, offering it an IP address. It is the equivalent of "hey, here is an IP address that you can use".
- **Request**. This message is sent by the client to the server. In this message, the client asks to lease the IP address that the server offered. It is the equivalent of "I received your offer and I accept".
- **Acknowledgement**. This message is sent by the server to the client. The server confirms that it has assigned the address to the client. It also confirms the subnet mask, gateway, and DNS server IP addresses. It is the equivalent of "I confirm that you accepted my IP address and I won't offer it to anybody else. By the way, our network uses the following settings for the gateway and DNS".

A host without an IP address uses the IP address 0.0.0.0 until it receives one from the DHCP server. A host that is looking for a DHCP address sends messages to 255.255.255.255, which is the local broadcast IP address that any host can use to send a message to all the other hosts on the same local network. Packets sent to 255.255.255.255 are not forwarded by routers, but they are flooded by switches.

How can we send a broadcast message to all the devices on our local subnet? Normally, we need to know the MAC address of the recipient in order to send it a message. Well, the broadcast IP address 255.255.255.255 translates into the broadcast MAC address of FF:FF:FF:FF:FF:FF. A switch will flood traffic addressed to FF:FF:FF:FF:FF:FF across all of its interfaces (in the same VLAN).

Thus, a host without an IP address uses 0.0.0.0 as its IP address and sends a Discover message to 255.255.255.255. This message travels across the entire LAN, and hopefully to the DHCP server on the LAN.

When the DHCP server receives the Discover message, it sends its Offer reply to 255.255.255.255 as well, because it knows that the client doesn't have an IP address yet. This message is seen by everybody, but it is encapsulated in the client's ethernet MAC address. Thus, the requesting client knows that this message was intended for it, and other clients know that the message was not intended for them.

I mentioned earlier that if our DHCP server is far away, we can use the helper address on the router to send requests to it. It is recommended to create a central DHCP server, but it is technically possible to establish a separate DHCP server on each LAN's router.

On a Cisco router, we type **`ip helper-address <DHCP server IP address>`** to configure a helper IP address. Now our router listens for DHCP Discover messages and forwards them to the DHCP server. We must configure this address on any interface connecting to a LAN that doesn't have a DHCP server and needs it.

The router changes the message's source IP address to its own IP address and changes the destination IP address from 255.255.255.255 to that of the DHCP server. That way, the DHCP server can reply directly to the router, and the router can forward that reply to the requesting client.

In the example below, our external DHCP server has an address of 10.10.10.10 and our router has an IP address of 10.0.0.0. Computer B sends a Discover message, which the router receives. Since the router has a helper IP address, it changes the source IP address to its own IP address and destination address to the DHCP server's IP address.

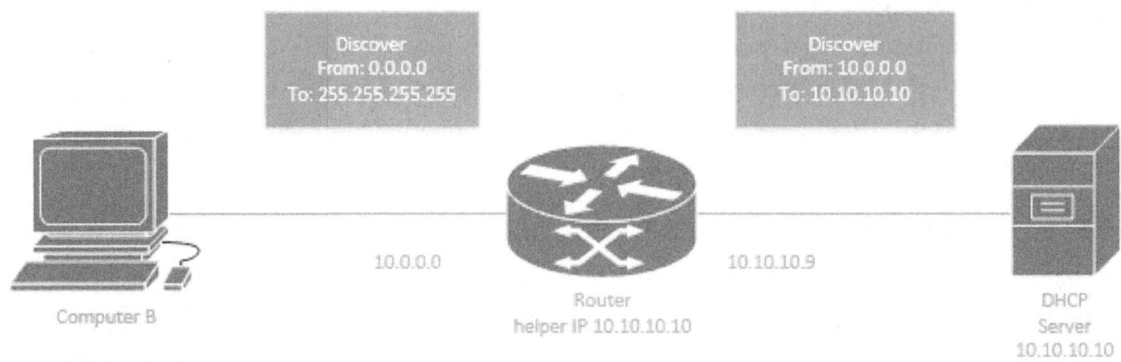

On the way back, the router receives the Offer message, but it doesn't know who it should go to. The client doesn't have an IP address anyways. It changes the destination IP address to 255.255.255.255 and broadcasts it all over the local network.

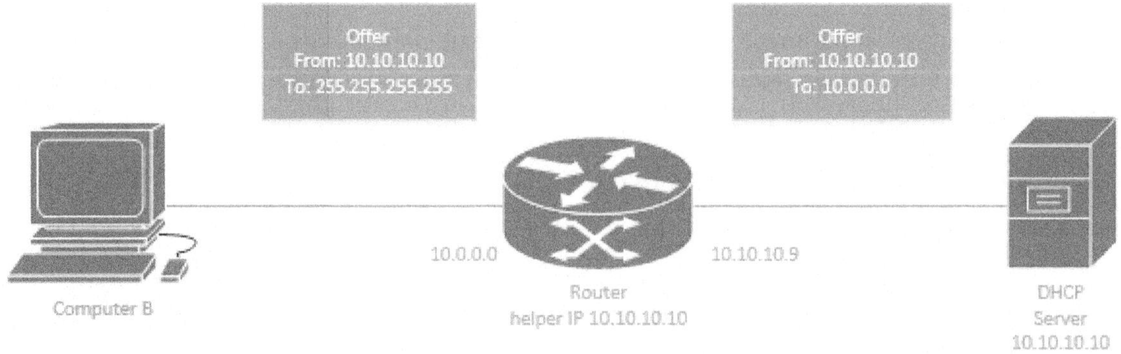

Notice that the Discover message comes from the Router's LAN IP address 10.0.0.0, so that the DHCP server replies to the Router's LAN IP address 10.0.0.0. This is important, because if the router has multiple LAN connections, it needs to know to forward the DHCP packet out of the correct interface.

We should configure the DHCP Server with the following information

- **Subnet** – the range of IP addresses that the DHCP server can issue
- **Reserved IP addresses** – IP addresses that the DHCP server cannot issue
- **Subnet mask** – the mask assigned to the network where the IP addresses come from
- **Default gateway** – the gateway that DHCP clients should use
- **DNS Server IP addresses** – the DNS Server addresses that the clients should use
- **Lease time** – the amount of time that a DHCP address is valid after being issued to a client. The client may be able to renew the IP address before it expires.

There are three ways to allocate a DHCP IP address

- **Dynamic Allocation**. The server picks the first available address from the range and assigns it to the device. If I have a large Wi-Fi network such as in an airport, with thousands of different devices connecting to it each day, I might choose to allocate DHCP addresses dynamically.
- **Automatic Allocation**. The server remembers which address it assigned to each device in the past. It tries to assign the device the same IP address each time, if available. If I had an office with users who bring their laptops to work, I would try to allocate the same IP address to each device. I wouldn't make it mandatory because devices are replaced, and new devices are added all the time. I would need the option to allocate IP unused IP addresses to new devices.
- **Manual Allocation**. The administrator manually programs a relationship between a MAC address and an IP address. If a device with a matching MAC address joins the network, it is automatically assigned the same IP address each time. The network will reserve this IP address and never assign it to any other device. I would use this when I have specific devices like printers and surveillance cameras, which are better off accessible at the same address each time, and I'm not able to program a static IP address into each device.

By default, the Windows Operating System uses DHCP. We can configure DHCP on a Cisco switch by typing **`ip address dhcp`**. Now our switch will request an IP address by DHCP. This command must be configured inside each VLAN that requires it.

```
Switch>enable
Switch#conf t
Enter configuration commands, one per line.  End with CNTL/Z.
Switch(config)#interface vlan 1
Switch(config-if)#ip address dhcp
Switch(config-if)#exit
Switch(config)#
Switch#
```

Once the VLAN is up, we can check that the DHCP is working by checking with **show interfaces vlan <VLAN ID>**. If the VLAN or interface is down, then the switch obviously won't obtain an IP address.

```
Switch#show interfaces vlan 1
Vlan1 is up, line protocol is up
  Hardware is CPU Interface, address is 0050.0fbc.9aac (bia 0050.0fbc.9aac)
  Internet address is 10.10.1.5/28
  MTU 1500 bytes, BW 100000 Kbit, DLY 1000000 usec,
     reliability 255/255, txload 1/255, rxload 1/255
  Encapsulation ARPA, loopback not set
  ARP type: ARPA, ARP Timeout 04:00:00
  Last input 21:40:21, output never, output hang never
  Last clearing of "show interface" counters never
```

We can also type **show dhcp lease** to see the details about the IP address. What do we see?

- 10.10.1.5 is the IP address we were assigned
- 10.10.10.10 is the DHCP server IP address
- 10.10.1.1 is the default gateway IP address
- 255.255.255.0 is the subnet mask

```
Switch#show dhcp lease
Temp IP addr: 10.10.1.5 for peer on Interface: Vlan1
Temp sub net mask: 255.255.255.0
   DHCP Lease server: 10.10.10.10 , state:
   DHCP Transaction id:
   Lease: 0 secs,  Renewal: 0 secs,  Rebind: 0 secs
Temp default-gateway addr: 10.10.1.1
   Next timer fires after: 00:00:00
   Retry count: 0  Client-ID:cisco-0050.0FBC.9AAC-Vlan
   Client-ID hex dump: 636973636F2D303035302E304642432E
                       94141432D566C616E
   Hostname: Switch
```

A router interface will normally be assigned a static IP address, but it is possible to assign it a DHCP address. We use the same command as the switch, but we do so through the physical interface configuration.

```
Router#conf t
Enter configuration commands, one per line.  End with CNTL/Z.
Router(config)#
Router(config)#interface gigabitethernet0/0/1
Router(config-if)#ip address dhcp
Router(config-if)#end
Router#
%SYS-5-CONFIG_I: Configured from console by console
```

We can verify the DHCP IP address on a router by checking **show ip route static**. When the router learns a DHCP IP address, it adds it to the routing table as a static route with an administrative distance of 254. Remember that DHCP routes have an administrative distance of 254, while normal static routes have an administrative distance of 1.

```
Router# show ip route static

S*     0.0.0.0/0 [254/0] via 10.10.0.5
```

A host on a network must have the following

- **IP address** – it needs to know who it is
- **Subnet Mask** – it needs to know the size of its network
- **Gateway** – it needs to know which router to send traffic to, when the destination is outside its local network
- **DNS Server** – it needs to know who to ask when it has a domain name that needs to be translated into an IP address

4.7 Explain the forwarding per-hop behavior (PHB) for QoS such as classification, marking, queuing, congestion, policing, shaping

Quality of Service or **QoS** is a tool that allows our network to prioritize certain types of traffic. The actions apply when the data is inside the device – that is between the time that it enters a device and the time that it leaves. These actions are called **per-hop behaviors** or **PHBs**.

We want our traffic to arrive on time and we want it to arrive accurately. There are four things we monitor

- **Bandwidth**. That is how fast our connection is. It's the capacity of our connection. We should divide our bandwidth among different types of traffic so that each one gets its fair share instead of allowing some forms of traffic to overwhelm our internet connection. We can assign a different proportion of bandwidth to each type of traffic.

- **Delay** is the time that it takes for a packet to get from its sender to its destination. We can measure the one-way delay, or the round-trip delay. Delay is also known as **latency**.

- **Jitter** is the difference in the one-way delay between different packets. If we send some packets, 1 second apart, we expect them to arrive on the other side one second apart. If they arrive too far apart, we will experience a drop in the connection quality. If they arrive too close together, we might overload the buffer.

- **Loss** is the number of packets that do not arrive at their destination. It is typically expressed as a percentage.

Imagine a highway from New York to Los Angeles. The bandwidth is like the number of lanes on the highway. The speed limit is fixed, so if we want to increase the number of cars arriving per minute, we must add more lanes.

The delay is the time it takes for a car leaving New York to arrive in Los Angeles. The delay could be affected by traffic jams, congestion, accidents, etc.. If part of the road is blocked or has fewer lanes open, the cars don't arrive on time. In a computer network, if some equipment has failed or is overloaded, the packets don't arrive on time.

The jitter is the delay between car arrivals. If the cars leave New York one minute apart, we expect them to arrive in Los Angeles one minute apart, and in the same order.

Loss is the number of cars that don't arrive at all.

We want to provide each user with the best possible experience, but we also want to make sure that business-critical applications are given priority. This is known as **Quality of Experience** or **QoE**.

Delay and Jitter are more important in interactive applications such as Remote Desktop Connections, websites, and VoIP. They are less important for non-interactive applications such as file transfers, which may require more bandwidth.

Think about a file transfer like sending a book through the mail. We rip out every page and send it as a separate packet. The recipient doesn't care if the pages arrive in the wrong order because they have page numbers and he can put them back together when they all arrive. The recipient can't do anything with the book until every page arrives. If any pages go missing, the sender can resend them.

Now think about a video call or a phone call. Every word is sent as a separate packet. The recipient's computer must play the packets back in real time, as they arrive. If the packets arrive in the wrong order, then the words that you say will be played back in the wrong order. If the packets arrive late, then there will be a delay when you are speaking. If the packets don't arrive at all, then the recipient won't be able to hear some of your words. The recipient can't wait until all the packets arrive and then try to play them back in the correct order, and the recipient can't ask the sender to send them again because the phone call is live.

VoIP and video applications do have some error correction mechanisms, but they can only go so far.

For a VoIP call, we need

- 80 kbps of bandwidth
- A one-way delay of less than 150 ms
- 30 ms or less of jitter
- A 1% packet loss or less

For a Video call, we need

- Between 384 kbps and 20 Mbps of bandwidth depending on the quality, type of video, and compression. Videos with lots of movement require more bandwidth.
- A one-way delay of less than 200 ms to 400 ms
- 30 ms or less of jitter
- A 1% packet loss or less, and ideally a 0.1% packet loss

The first thing that a network device does is it examines the packet's header to determine what kind of data is inside. This is called **classification**. The network device maintains several queues, one for each type of traffic. It puts each packet in the appropriate queue and transmits them based on their priority.

For example, we have a VoIP queue that support 100 packets/second, and a data queue that supports 10 packets/second. If 100 VoIP packets, and 50 data packets arrive, the VoIP packets are sent out immediately, but the data packets get stuck in the data queue for up to five seconds (the first ten are sent out immediately, ten more in the next second, etc.).

Every time the packet enters or exits a device it can be classified. But a packet might pass through dozens of interfaces along its journey. A more efficient solution is to classify the packet once, as close to its creation as possible and mark it. **Marking** is the process of changing the packet's header so that other devices know what level of service to apply to it.

The marking is called the **DSCP** or **Differentiated Service Code Point**. Other devices downstream read the DSCP value and understand what level of service to provide it.

Inside the IPv4 header is a portion called the **Type of Service**, or **ToS**, and that is where the DSCP goes. We can give it a number from 0 to 63. We mark the IP header because it stays with the packet from the beginning of its journey to the end, unlike the Ethernet header

In IPv6, the marking location is called the **Traffic Class**.

The other area that we can use to mark a packet is the Ethernet Frame. Inside the Ethernet Frame is a field called the 802.1Q section. We call this the **Class of Service** (**CoS**) or **Priority Code Point** (**PCP**). We only use the 802.1Q section on an ethernet frame that is being passed over a trunk port. Thus, the CoS only stays on frames that are travelling through a trunk.

QoS can work with an ACL. If traffic from specific devices such as VoIP phones or video conferencing equipment must be prioritized, and those devices sit in specific ranges of IP addresses, we can configure an ACL.

If an ACL doesn't fit our needs, we can use **Cisco Network Based Application Recognition**, or **NBAR**. The second variation of NBAR is called **NBAR2**, which can look inside the contents of each packet to determine the type of traffic it is carrying. NBAR can match over 1000 types of applications because each one has a unique **application signature**.

On a router, we can enter NBAR configuration by typing **`class-map matchingexample`**.

The problem is that just because your network trusts a QoS marking in a header doesn't mean that others will too. Otherwise, an end user could mark all his packets as having a high priority and override the wishes of the network administrator. Thus, we create a **trust boundary** that determines where we start to trust QoS markings. The trust boundary typically starts at an edge switch in our internal network (after traffic has left the end user devices).

When we use IP passthrough with a VoIP phone, the VoIP phone acts like a mini switch and can perform the marking. Thus, we would set the VoIP phone as the trust boundary.

What one network considers "priority 1" could be "priority 2" or "priority 3" in a different network. For multiple networks to be able to understand each other's QoS markings, **DiffServ** was developed.

DiffServ is an architecture with recommended DSCP values for different types of traffic, allowing multiple networks to create consistent markings. There are several sets of DSCP values

- **Expedited Forwarding** or **EF** is a marking for packets that require low delay, low jitter, and low loss. The DSCP value is 46. Voice traffic is typically marked as EF. By default, a Cisco IP Phone will mark voice traffic with EF. EF is the highest priority of traffic.

- **Assured Forwarding or AF** is a set of 12 DSCP values that fit into a table. There are four separate queues, and three separate drop priorities. When combined, we get 12 different values.

  AF41, AF41, and AF43 (known as AF4x) are used for video conferencing.
  AF31, AF32, and AF33 (known as AF3x) are used for streaming video.
  AF21, AF22, and AF23 (known as AF2x) are used for data that requires low latency.

  To the left of each bracket is the DSCP value and to the right is the AF value. The drop priority is how likely a router is to drop the packet when it is too busy.

	Best Drop	**Moderate Drop**	**Worst Drop**
Best Queue	34 (AF41)	36 (AF42)	38 (AF43)
Moderate Queue	26 (AF31)	28 (AF32)	39 (AF33)
Lower Queue	18 (AF21)	20 (AF22)	22 (AF23)
Worst Queue	10 (AF11)	12 (AF12)	14 (AF13)

- **Class Selector** or **CS** values. The ToS is a 3-bit IP Precedence field or IPP. DiffServ uses the ToS field to hold a DSCP value called the Class Selector. The CS values are from CS0 to CS7. CS values are used for normal data.

DiffServ values are open source, but Cisco encourages us to use them. Cisco devices use the DiffServe standard by default.

I mentioned queues earlier. A queue is a line up of packets that are waiting to be sent. We make the packets line up just like at the airport, in different classes. Regardless of the queue, all the packets must leave through the same interface. But we let more packets out of the higher priority queues than out of the lower priority queues. This is called **prioritization**. There are several prioritization algorithms

- **Round Robin**. In the round robin, the router takes a packet from the first queue and then one from the second queue and then a packet from the third queue, and then so on. The router takes a packet from each queue in order, and no queue is given priority.

- **Weighted Round Robin**. We can give each queue a weight. For example, we take five packets from the first queue (the VoIP queue), and then two packets from the second queue (video queue), and then one packet from the third queue (data queue). This ensures that more important traffic is given priority and but also that each type of traffic is given an opportunity to transmit.

A tool that helps with ensuring that all traffic is given a share of the bandwidth is called the **Class-Based Weighted Fair Queuing** or **CBQFQ**. We configure each queue to have a specific percentage of the bandwidth. For example, the VoIP queue is given 50% of the bandwidth, the video queue is given 30% of the bandwidth, and the data queue is given 20% of the bandwidth.

- The problem with a Weighted Round Robin is that some types of packets can't wait in a queue, even if all the packets are eventually sent out. For example, the router should send out voice traffic as soon as it receives it. We can use **LLQ** to specify some queues as **priority queues**. Traffic from a priority queue is always sent out as soon as it is received, no matter how full the other queues are. When the router is not sending traffic from a priority queue, it runs the round robin on the other queues.

  If the priority queues occupy all the bandwidth on the interface, then the router will never get to the other queues. This is called **queue starvation**. We can avoid queue starvation by using **queue policing**. We simply limit the amount of bandwidth a priority queue can use so that other queues have a chance. This could cause the router to discard some of the priority traffic. If we discard only a small portion of the priority traffic, the end users may not notice.

- **Call Admission Control** or **CAC** is another tool that helps us send out the priority traffic as it arrives, without discarding any of the traffic.

How can we create a good QoS strategy?

- If we don't have enough bandwidth to support all our applications, we must separate each type of traffic into a separate queue.
- We give more important types of traffic higher priority.
- We use a priority queue for voice and video traffic so that the packets are sent out as soon as they arrive. Voice traffic should have a separate queue from video traffic.
- The voice and video traffic should be given enough bandwidth so that the router does not drop any of their packets.
- We use a round-robin queue for other types of data.
- Use the CAC tool to prioritize voice and video traffic if necessary.

Traffic **policing** and **shaping** helps us limit traffic by setting a rate for each type of traffic. The router monitors the rate of traffic. Each time a new packet arrives, the router determines whether it will cause the router to exceed the rate that was set.

If the rate will not be exceeded, the router lets the packet through.

If the rate will be exceeded, and traffic shaping is enabled, the router queues the packet. If the rate will be exceeded, and traffic policing is enabled, the router drops the packet.

With policing, the traffic isn't allowed to exceed a specific rate. Policing might allow the traffic to exceed the specified rate for a brief period (this is called bursting).

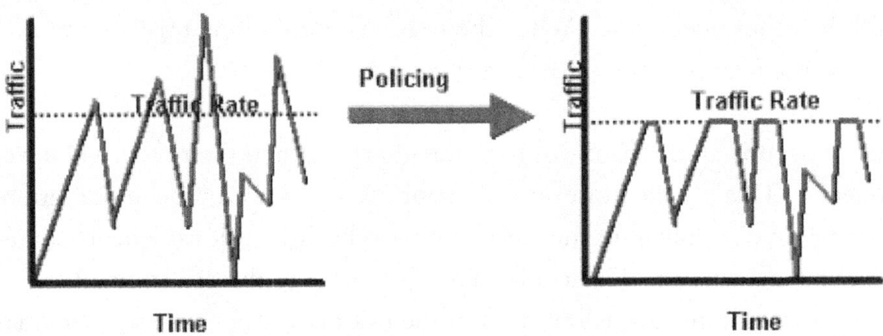

Traffic Policing is used by Internet Service Providers to limit the amount of bandwidth a customer can send over a connection. For example, if we are paying for a 10 Mbps connection, the service provider might drop any traffic that exceeds that rate unless we paid for more bandwidth.

Instead of dropping the extra packets, we might choose to mark them as low priority and let them through. If the network has ample resources, we transport the packets received above the policing limit because it doesn't cost us anything. When the network gets congested, we drop any packets that are marked as low priority so that other clients can pass their traffic.

With shaping, we set a specific data rate. When additional packets arrive that would cause us to exceed the rate, we put them in a queue and hold them until they can be sent. For example, if our rate is 10 Mbps, and we're receiving traffic at a rate of 11 Mbps, some of it is stored in the queue until the rate drops below 10 Mbps. If we're receiving traffic at a rate of 9 Mbps, we don't need to make any changes.

Traffic shaping causes jitter and delays while some packets are waiting. We can configure the traffic shaper to apply on less important traffic so that voice and video traffic is unaffected.

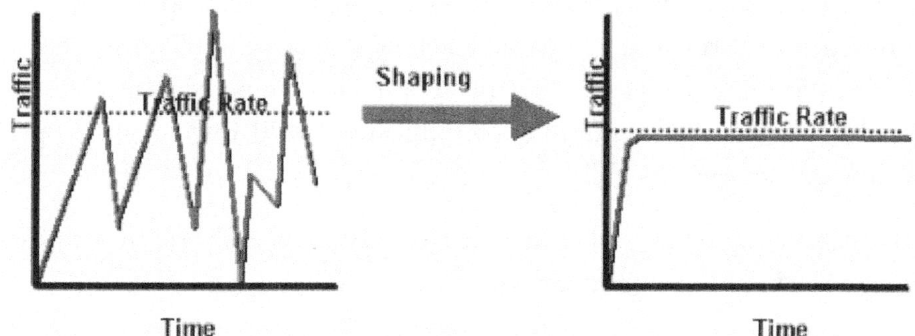

Over time, the traffic shaper is designed to maintain traffic at a specific rate, called a **time interval**. If our rate is 10 Mbps, then we can only send 10 Megabytes every second. What if our interface speed is 100 Mbps? The traffic shaper would send the 10 Megabytes at the beginning of each second. It would take 0.1 seconds to send 10 Megabytes out of a 100 Mbps interface. That means that the interface is idle for the next 0.9 seconds. Then it is ready to send traffic out again.

This would be a problem for voice traffic because the maximum delay is 150 ms, and our traffic could be delayed up to 1 second (1000 ms). It is recommended that we use a time interval of 10 ms or less for traffic shaping when voice or video applications are involved. That means that a voice packet won't be slowed down by more than 10 ms because of traffic shaping. Instead of setting our rate as 10 Megabytes per second, we would set it as 0.1 Megabytes per 10 ms. Now our interface sends traffic 100 times per second instead of one time per second.

TCP has a tool called **windowing**, as mentioned earlier. During a TCP connection the recipient gives the sender a window size. The window size tells the sender how many packets he can send before having to wait for the recipient to acknowledge receipt. If the window size is five, then the sender sends five packets and waits. The sender won't send any more packets until the recipient acknowledges receipt of the first five.

Each time a recipient acknowledges receipt of a message, it also sends a new window size to the sender. If the transmissions are going well, the recipient continues to increase the window size. Eventually, the window size is so big that the data flows in a continuous stream and the sender never stops sending.

If the transmissions are not going well (if packets are being lost), the recipient begins to decrease the window size to slow it down.

The problem is that a queue in a router has a limited capacity. If we experience congestion, the queue fills up with data and the router has no more place to put the data, so it starts dropping the additional traffic. This is called a **tail drop**.

We can use a congestion avoidance tool like windowing to reduce the amount of traffic coming in to the router. Downstream that lets us avoid filling up the router queues.

When the queues are empty, we operate like normal. When the queues are full, we drop all new traffic. This is known as the **maximum threshold**. To avoid reaching a state with full queues, we begin dropping a percentage of traffic when the queues have filled past a certain percentage. This is known as a **minimum threshold**. For example, if our minimum threshold is 70%, we might drop 10% of incoming traffic when the queues are 70% full.

We do not drop all packets at the same rate. Remember that we have classified each packet with its DSCP value. We can drop a higher rate of less important traffic.

4.8 Configure network devices for remote access using SSH

I mentioned router and switch security earlier. You can access a router or switch remotely via Telnet or SSH, but only SSH is secure. Do not use Telnet.

You can protect access to a device's configuration by entering the security configuration.

Type **line vty 0 15** to enter the login configuration mode (for the Telnet/SSH only), then use the following commands

- **login** – this tells the switch/router to prompt for a password for the user mode
- **password <password>** - where <password> is the password I want to use

In the above example, I only have one user password. If I have multiple users, they each must know the password. I could instead create multiple user accounts. I would type

- **username <username> secret <password>** - where <username> is the username, and <password> is the password I want to use. The username is a global command; it isn't applied inside the line console command.
- **line console 0** – now I've entered into the login configuration (for the console only; this doesn't apply to users who connect over Telnet or SSH)
    - **login local** – this tells the switch/router to prompt for a username and password for the user mode, and to do so from the local configuration, instead of an external server

If we have a large organization, we could connect our switch to an external server, such as a RADIUS server. The external server handles authentication and user accounts. This would be better than manually configuring usernames and passwords on every device.

To configure SSH,

- **hostname <switch name>** - this configures the name of the switch; it should have been set earlier. We should choose a unique name for each switch/router in our organization.
- **ip domain-name <domain name>** - this is the domain name for our organization
- **crypto key generate rsa** – the switch user the hostname and domain name to generate an RSA key (for encryption). When you enter this command, the switch will ask you for a modulus size.

We could also disable Telnet or other types of logins with the transport input command. **transport input <parameter>** determines which connection method the switch supports.

- **transport input all** – Telnet and SSH are supported
- **transport input telnet ssh** - Telnet and SSH are supported
- **transport input none** – Neither Telnet nor SSH are supported
- **transport input ssh** – Only SSH is supported
- **transport input telnet** - Only Telnet is supported

If we're curious about who is connected, we can type **show ssh**.

But how do we connect to the switch via SSH? What is its IP address?

If we have a static IP

- We enter the VLAN configuration mode by typing **interface vlan <VLAN number>**. We should choose a VLAN to configure the IP address on. We issue the following command to configure an IP address
  - **ip address <IP address> <subnet mask>** - this provides the interface with an IP address
  - **no shutdown** – just in case the interface was shut down.
- We issue the following commands in the main configuration
  - **ip default-gateway <default gateway IP address>** - this provides the switch with a default gateway
  - **ip name-server <DNS IP address #1>** - this is optional, but allows the switch to use a DNS server

Below, I have configured VLAN 40 to use an IP address of 5.5.5.5/24, and configured the switch to use a default gateway IP address of 5.5.5.1, and a DNS server of 4.4.4.4.

```
Switch(config)#interface vlan 40
Switch(config-if)#ip address 5.5.5.5 255.255.255.0
Switch(config-if)#exit
Switch(config)#ip default-gateway 5.5.5.1
Switch(config)#ip name-server 4.4.4.4
```

If we have a dynamic IP (DHCP)

- We enter the VLAN configuration mode by typing **interface vlan <VLAN number>**
    - **ip address dhcp** – this tells the switch that the interface is using DHCP. The switch sends out a DHCP request.

Below, I have configured VLAN 40 to use DHCP.

```
Switch(config)#interface vlan 40
Switch(config-if)#ip address dhcp
Switch(config-if)#exit
```

How can we verify the IP address is configured correctly? We can use one of the following commands

- **show running-config** – under the VLAN interface, this will show us the VLAN's static IP address, and under the global configuration, this will show us the switch's default gateway and DNS

- **show interfaces vlan <VLAN number>** - this will list details for the VLAN. We can see if the VLAN has an IP address.

- **show dhcp lease** – if DHCP is enabled, this command will show us the IP address obtained by the switch.

```
Switch#show dhcp lease
Temp IP addr: 0.0.0.0 for peer on Interface: Vlan40
Temp sub net mask: 0.0.0.0
   DHCP Lease server: 0.0.0.0 , state:
   DHCP Transaction id:
   Lease: 0 secs,  Renewal: 0 secs,  Rebind: 0 secs
Temp default-gateway addr: 0.0.0.0
   Next timer fires after: 00:00:00
   Retry count: 0  Client-ID:cisco-00E0.B0B3.5A01-Vlan
   Client-ID hex dump: 636973636F2D303045302E423042332E
                       54130312D566C616E
   Hostname: Switch
```

We can Telnet or SSH from one router into another. A good reason for this is when there is a routing issue preventing us from accessing a router directly, but the router is still connected to our network indirectly. We can use the following commands

- **ssh <username> <ip address of router>**

- **telnet <ip address of router>**

Once we have connected, the prompt changes to the hostname of the router that is connected. We can exit the session by typing **`exit`** or **`quit`**.

We can Telnet or SSH from one router to another to another to another.

4.9 Describe the capabilities and function of TFTP/FTP in the network

FTP is an important protocol for transferring files over the internet. An FTP server holds files and accepts incoming connections from FTP clients. FTP clients connect to the FTP server and download files. During the connection, the client and the server complete a three-way handshake. The client and server authenticate with each other. Once the FTP server has authenticated the client and the client has optionally authenticated the server, they can issue commands to each other.

The FTP protocol has a standard set of commands that allow us to do the following

- List the contents of a directory or move to a new directory (folder).
- Create a new directory.
- Delete an existing directory.
- Transfer a file from the server to the client (via a Get command).
- Transfer a file from the client to the server (via a Put command).

Once a connection has been established, the client can perform these commands on the server and the server can perform these commands on the client.

It is possible to access an FTP server via a command line, but most people prefer to use an FTP client application with a graphical user interface. The GUI provides an interface like Windows Explorer/Mac Finder so that we can browse directories and drag/drop files.

The FTP server is built in to Windows Server Operating systems but must be enabled and configured. We can also install a commercial FTP server application that provides advanced features such as logging and user authentication.

When configuring an FTP server, it is important to ensure that each user only has access to the specific files and directories that he requires.

During an FTP session, there are two sub-connections. A **Control Connection** is used to exchange FTP commands. A **Data Connection** is used to send and receive data. This data includes lists of files and directories and the actual transfer of files.

The Control Connection is created when the client connects to the FTP server. An FTP connection's three-way handshake is like that of any other TCP Connection.

- The client sends a TCP SYN message to the server.
- The server acknowledges the TCP SYN with a TCP ACK and sends its own TCP SYN to the client.
- The client replies with a TCP ACK message to the server.

Once the handshake is established, the client chooses a port to communicate over. The FTP server uses Port 21. The client can choose any dynamic port that is not in use. It must inform the server of the port that it selected via the FTP PORT command. For example, if our client selected port 49876, it would tell the FTP server that it wants to communicate on 49876.

Once the server receives the FTP PORT command, it tries to establish a connection with the client over port 49876. This system is called **Active FTP**.

If the FTP server is on a local network, Active FTP can operate without any issues. If the FTP server and FTP client are separated by a router and/or a firewall, the connection might be blocked due to the strange port selected by the client. The firewall will typically block incoming connections.

We can get around this issue with **Passive FTP**. The client doesn't know that a firewall is blocking the connection. But if it doesn't receive a connection from the FTP server, after successfully establishing a connection, it assumes that something is blocking it.

The client sends the server an **FTP PASV** command. The server chooses a dynamic port to listen on. For example, the server might choose port 49876. The FTP server tells the client that it chose port 49876 with the FTP PORT command. The client connects to the FTP server over port 49876. The firewall will probably not block this connection because it originated inside the network.

FTP is not secure. Usernames, passwords, and files are sent over the internet in plaintext. But we can implement a secure FTP called **FTP over TLS** or **FTP Secure** (**FTPS**). We create the same three-way handshake as before. During the handshake, the client informs the server that it would like to use TLS by providing the **FTP AUTH** command. When the client chooses to send data to the FTP server, it does so via port 21 over TLS.

TFTP, or Trivial **File Transfer Protocol** is a stripped-down version of FTP that uses port 69. TFTP is used on devices that have limited resources. We can use the Get and Put commands to download and upload files, but we can't authenticate with the server or list directories. That means that a client must know the exact name of the file that it wants to download and sends the server a command telling it to provide it with a specific file.

Since anybody can access the TFTP server without a password, we should only use it to store files that are available to the public.

One use of FTP and TFTP is to transfer a copy of the IOS operating system. Unlike Windows, IOS (the Cisco router and switch operating system) is stored as a single file.

Some background on Cisco file storage systems. A Cisco router or switch stores data on a flash memory, which has no moving parts, and can continue to store data even after the router has been powered off. Some Cisco devices allow you to remove the flash memory.

Some Cisco devices also include USB ports. When we have a USB port, we can store data on a removable USB flash drive.

We can view the device file system by typing **show file systems**. A Cisco device will have multiple file systems. The main types of file systems are

- **Disk**. The disk is the flash memory and is present in every device.
- **Usbflash**. The USB Flash drive that may be inserted into the device (if the device has this capability)
- **NVRAM**. A portion of the flash memory that stores the startup-config file.
- **Opaque**. An internal file system that the router uses to run internal processes.
- **Network**. External file systems that are located on external servers, if the device can connect to them.

I can type **show flash** to view the files in the flash file system. I can also type **dir flash**. Both commands tell us the amount of space in use and the amount of space available.

```
Router#show file system
File Systems:

       Size(b)       Free(b)      Type  Flags  Prefixes
*   3249049600    2761893909     flash     rw  flash:
         29688         23590     nvram     rw  nvram:
Router#show flash

System flash directory:
File  Length   Name/status
  3   486899872isr4300-universalk9.16.06.04.SPA.bin
  2   28282    sigdef-category.xml
  1   227537   sigdef-default.xml
[487155691 bytes used, 2761893909 available, 3249049600 total]
3.17338e+06K bytes of processor board System flash (Read/Write)
```

Remember again that if I type **show running-config**, I can view the contents of the configuration in the memory. If I type **show startup-config**, I can view the contents of the startup configuration.

If we make changes to the device configuration, the running-config is updated, not the startup-config. When the router or switch reboots it reloads the startup-config and copies it into memory.

The startup-config becomes the running-config. If we want changes to our running-config to become permanent, we should save them to the startup-config.

It is technically possible to store the Cisco IOS on an external server. Each time the router or switch boots, it loads the IOS over the network. But this is a bad idea because if the external server is inaccessible, the router won't be able to boot. A better approach is to store the operating system on the Flash.

To upgrade the IOS, we can obtain a new version from the Cisco website. We can copy it to an external server or to a USB flash drive. Then, we copy it to the router by typing **copy <source> <destination>**. The Cisco device will ask us more questions when we type this command.

For example, to copy a file from an TFTP server to the Flash, we type **copy tftp flash**. The router will ask us about the IP address of the TFTP server and the filename. By default, the destination filename will be the same as the source, but we have the option to enter a new name. If we want to use the name in [], we can just press Enter.

```
Router#copy tftp flash
Address or name of remote host []? 10.10.1.1
Source filename []? cisco-ios-111.bin
Destination filename [cisco-ios-111.bin]?

Accessing tftp://10.10.1.1/cisco-ios-111.bin......
```

Before the router copies the file, it checks the file size and verifies that it has enough space to copy it. If the Flash has a file with the same name, the router will ask us to overwrite the existing one.

We should make sure that our TFTP server is accessible to our router or switch.

After we have downloaded the file, we should verify that it is legitimate. Cisco publishes an MD5 hash for each IOS file on its website. We can recalculate the MD5 hash on the router. If the hash calculated by the router matches the hash on the Cisco website, we know that the file is legitimate and that no errors occurred in transmission.

We can type **verify /md5 <filename>** to calculate the hash.

```
R2# verify /md5 flash0: ciscoiosfile.bin
...........................................................................
...........................................................................
MD5 of flash0: ciscoiosfile. bin Done! (flash0: ciscoiosfile.bin) =
a8238djhsd8978sfjsdf889sd
```

Instead of using TFTP, we can copy a file via FTP or SCP.

To copy a file over FTP, we use a similar command as TFTP, by typing **copy ftp flash**. It is important to note that the TFTP command expects an IP address for the TFTP server, while the

FTP command allows us to enter a URL or hostname. Note that the switch or router must have a DNS server configured for us to successfully be able to use a URL or hostname in the command.

```
Router#copy ftp flash
Address or name of remote host []? 10.10.10.1
Source filename []? ciscoiosfile.bin
Destination filename [ciscoiosfile.bin]?
Ftp username Or password is not set !, Please set and try again...
```

Before we run the FTP command, we should set a username and password in the global configuration; otherwise, we will see the above error.

We set the FTP Username via the **ip ftp username <username>** command and the FTP Password via the **ip ftp password <password>** command.

```
Router(config)#ip ftp username Hazim
Router(config)#ip ftp password Hazim
```

5.0 Security Fundamentals

5.1 Define key security concepts (threats, vulnerabilities, exploits, and mitigation techniques)

The key to a good security policy is to keep the bad people out, but also to avoid inconveniencing the legitimate users. The cost of the security should not be greater than the risk caused by a lack of security. We must always remember that if the security policy stops a business from operating efficiently, it will not be effective.

An enterprise network is complicated

- We have thousands to hundreds of thousands of users and thousands to hundreds of thousands to millions of different devices spread across multiple locations.
- Users have different roles, and each role requires access to different resources.
- Some users want to work from home or from the road, but they need to connect to the enterprise network.
- Users might want to use their personal devices on the network, including laptops and smartphones.
- The enterprise network may need to exchange data with other networks such as the government, vendors, or customers.
- There are many different network devices from many different vendors.
- Parts of the network are in different states or countries. Each state or country may have different laws about how data is stored or transmitted.

A weakness in our network is called a **vulnerability**. Somebody can take advantage of a vulnerability to penetrate our network. They do so with a malicious tool called an **exploit**. An exploit is a tool that is used against a vulnerability. The scenario where a person uses an exploit to take advantage of a vulnerability is called a **threat**.

We can reduce the risk that a threat poses by using a **mitigation technique**. But first, we must identify the threat.

For example, if a router has a flaw in its firmware that might be a vulnerability. A tool that can be used to enter the router without permission, by taking advantage of the firmware flaw is an exploit. If a hacker uses this tool, that is a threat. We might install a firewall or upgrade the router's operating system as a mitigation technique.

How can we secure the whole network when we have

- Different types of equipment such as Routers, Switches, Wireless Access Points and Controllers
- Different models of equipment
- Different ages of equipment each of which may be running a different version of the firmware or operating system

We might not even know what all the different threats are. Before we can secure the network, we must first understand what all the components are and where the vulnerabilities lie. That means

- Identify the physical location of every device and how it connects to other devices
- Identify the logical connections of every device including IP addresses, virtual ports, and VLANS
- Identify the make, model, and serial number of every device. Identify the operating system version running on every device. If a vulnerability arises in an operating system that we are using, we can patch it.

There are many types of attacks. For the CCNA, it is important to understand them in general terms, but for the real world, it is important to know exactly what they are. This chapter goes into a lot more detail than you're expected to know.

One type of threat is called **spoofing**. Each device within the network assumes that the other devices are who they say they are. If a device says that it has a specific IP address and MAC address other devices assume that it is telling the truth.

In a spoofing threat, a rogue device can change its IP address or MAC address so that it matches that of a legitimate device and then send traffic as that device. Devices receiving the traffic will assume that it originated from a legitimate device.

Recall that each network device is assigned a unique IP address. Two network devices can communicate over a WAN or public network if they know each other's IP addresses. A hacker can intercept their communication by changing his machine's IP address to match that of one of the devices. This method takes special skill and control/modification of network routers, because

- Most network devices/computers will detect the IP address conflict.
- The device whose IP address is spoofed will not receive any traffic because it is being intercepted by the hacker's computer. The hacker's computer must pretend to be the legitimate computer and carry on the communication.

- To remain undetected, the hacker will have to intercept the IP traffic through the router and then forward it to the legitimate recipient.

A broadcast IP address is a special type of IP address that exists in every network. The broadcast address allows a device to send a single message to all the IP addresses on that network. One type of broadcast message is known as an "echo". Devices receiving the "echo" message reply to the sending device.

In a Smurf Attack, the hacker forges the "from" portion of the echo message so that it appears to have come from another system. The device whose address appears in the "from" portion will receive all the replies. Depending on the size of the network, and the number of echo messages sent, that device could receive hundreds or thousands of replies.

There are millions of web servers operating on the internet (which host websites). If a hacker wants to bring down a web server, the hacker would flood that server with massive amounts of traffic. The web server would then be unable to respond to legitimate traffic, and ordinary users would be unable to visit the website. This is known as **denial of service**. Services other than websites exist on the internet (credit card processing, databases, etc.), and all are vulnerable to DoS.

There are many types of DoS attacks

- **SYN flooding**. When a user wants to connect to a web server, a three-way handshake (SYN, SYN/ACK, ACK) process occurs between the two computers.
    - The user sends a SYN message to the server; the server responds with a SYN/ACK message to the user, and the user responds with an ACK message to the server
    - In SYN flooding, the hacker imitates a legitimate user and sends more SYN requests than the web server can handle. The web server responds with the SYN/ACK response, but the hacker does not complete the third part by sending the SYN.
    - The server keeps a connection open waiting for an ACK message that never arrives. The server can only keep a limited number of connections open. If all of them are waiting for ACK messages that will never arrive, then the server won't be able to establish connections with legitimate users

- **Fragmenting**. When data travels over the internet, the sending computer breaks it down into pieces known as packets. The packets may take different routes to reach their destination. The receiving computer puts the packets back together. The data in each packet should not overlap.
    - In a fragmenting attack, the hacker send data to the server, but puts overlapping data into each packet
    - The server attempts to put the data back together but can't. If the operating system isn't equipped to recognize this attack and discard the bad packets, then it will crash.

How to prevent Denial of Service

- Most DoS attacks are preventable now. Why? A hacker will not have enough bandwidth to bring down a large web service. Major websites such as Google, Facebook, eBay, etc. use distributed server farms consisting of millions of servers, with redundant pathways to the internet. A hacker will not have enough capacity to overload their systems.
- Most enterprise systems contain firewalls that can easily detect and block DoS attacks. If a substantial amount of illegitimate traffic appears to be originating from a single source, it can simply be turned off.
- For a small monthly fee, services such as CloudFlare offer large-scale cloud-based firewalls to protect smaller websites from DoS attacks (which they normally could not afford).
- A company should never be a victim to the same attack twice. After the first attack, they must investigate and configure their systems so that it never happens again. The most common types of attacks are well documented, and systems are available to prevent them.

Distributed Denial of Service was invented after DoS stopped working (due to improvements in internet infrastructure).

With DDoS, a hacker infects thousands (or hundreds of thousands) of computers (or other IP devices such as cameras) and uses all of them to send traffic to a web server that he wants to crash. These computers are known as **bots** and together they form a **botnet**. Since the traffic appears legitimate (and is in fact originating from hundreds of thousands of different sources, in different geographic locations, with different internet service providers, and different computer types), it is difficult to filter or prevent.

The botnet operator will continue to acquire additional bots, to grow his botnet. The operator might lease his network of bots to a person or organization that wants to bring down a website (for revenge, competition, or other reasons).

An **Amplified DDoS** attack happens when the hacker's request is much smaller than the victim's response. For example, the hacker is requesting a copy of a webpage. The request may be a few bytes in size, but the response is the entire webpage, which may be several megabytes. If the hacker has a way to divert the response to another destination, he can launch an attack with little bandwidth.

A **Reflective DDoS** attack is when the hacker forges the destination address of his request to that of the victim. The victim server sees requests for web pages that are coming from itself. Therefore, the victim begins sending traffic back to itself.

In a **Man-in-the-Middle** attack, a hacker inserts himself between the sender and recipient of an electronic communication. Keep in mind that more than 60% of internet traffic is machine generated (one computer talking to another with no human interaction).

Consider that Alice and Bob are two hypothetical internet users having an encrypted conversation. They could be two humans, or it could be that Alice is an online banking user and Bob is the bank. The purpose of the communication is irrelevant. Consider that the hacker, Eve, wants to spy on them.

Alice and Bob's messages pass through a central server. Depending on Alice and Bob's geographical locations, the messages may pass through many servers, routers, switches, fiber optic cables, and copper lines. The internet is fragmented, and different parts are owned by different companies. If Alice is in New York and Bob is in Los Angeles, the traffic must pass through many states, and many internet service providers.

- If the traffic between Alice and Bob is unencrypted, and Eve can obtain access to one of the servers, routers, switches, or physical connections, then Eve can spy on the conversation.

- If the traffic is unencrypted, but Alice does not have access to one of the servers that the connection travels through, Eve could trick Alice into sending messages addressed to Bob to her instead (by corrupting/modifying Alice's address book). Eve would do the same to Bob. In Alice's address book, Eve replaces Bob's address with her own. In Bob's address book, Alice replaces Alice's address with her own. Alice sends messages to Eve thinking she is sending them to Bob, and Bob sends messages to Eve thinking he is sending them to Alice. Now Eve can read Alice's messages and forward them to Bob. Eve can also read Bob's messages and forward them to Alice. Neither Alice nor Bob is aware that Eve is reading their communications.

- If the communication is encrypted and uses public key cryptography (such as Apple iMessage), a man-in-the-middle attack is more difficult. Users encrypt messages with public keys (which they obtain from a central directory). If Alice wants to send a message to Bob, she obtains Bob's public key from Apple, encrypts the message, and sends it to Bob. Bob uses his private key (which only he knows) to decrypt the message. If Eve can intercept the message, she could perform a man-in-the-middle attack
    - We will discuss public key cryptography in more depth later, but in general consider this
        - A private key can only decrypt a message. A user keeps his private key secret.
        - The user generates a public key from his private key. He gives the public key to everybody who wants to send him a message. The public key can only encrypt a message.
    - Eve generates her own public and private keys
    - She hacks into the central directory and changes Bob's public key to her own
    - Alice decides to send a message to Bob. She checks the directory for Bob's public key, and receives what she thinks is Bob's public key (but is in fact Eve's public key)

- Alice sends the message to Eve (thinking she is sending it to Bob)
- Eve decrypts the message, reads it, and then encrypts it with Bob's public key
- Eve sends the message to Bob
- Bob receives the message, thinking it came from Alice and decrypts it with his own private key
- Eve does the same thing with Alice's public key so that she can intercept messages that Bob is sending to Alice

A hacker can use a Man-in-the-Middle attack to poison the ARP. The hacker must send the last ARP message to be successful.

Computer A has IP address 10.0.0.4 and MAC address AAAA. It wants to learn the MAC address of Computer B, so it sends an ARP Request, which is broadcast over the entire network. The ARP message says, "if you're IP address is 10.0.0.5, what is your MAC address". The hacker's computer is on the bottom and has an IP address of 10.0.0.6 and a MAC address of HHHH.

Computer B will respond to tell Computer A that it's IP address is 10.0.0.5, but Computer H (the hacker's computer) will respond afterwards to tell it that the MAC address is HHHH. Computer B won't know that Computer H did this. Computer A will address traffic intended for Computer B to Computer H.

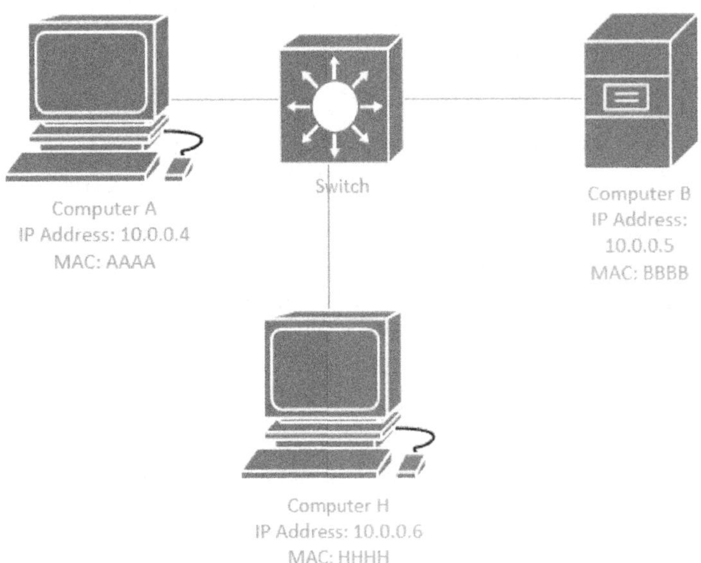

If a hacker wants to identify areas to attack, he can perform a **reconnaissance attack**. Many legitimate tools such as nslookup and ping can also be used by a hacker to discover open ports and other vulnerable systems. Once a hacker has discovered the vulnerabilities, he can plan a further attack.

What is a **buffer**? The buffer is kind of like a lineup at airport security. The flow of passengers is not steady. When there are more passengers than security guards, a long lineup develops. If the airport doesn't have enough room to hold all the passengers, they might have to wait outside.

The buffer is the same. Consider a web server or other computing device. Information is coming in over a wire. Sometimes the information is coming in quickly, and sometimes it is coming in slowly. The server must take each piece of data and process it somewhere. When the levels of traffic are high, the server can't process all of it in real time. Thus, all data first enters a buffer, where it lines up to be processed. The server takes data from the buffer at a steady rate.

- For example, the traffic ranges from 0.5GB/s to 2GB/s
- The server can process data at 1GB/s
- If the traffic is 1GB/s or less, the server can process the traffic in real time. The traffic passes through the buffer but doesn't spend any time there.
- If the traffic is more than 1GB/s, the server can't process the traffic in real time. The buffer starts to fill up.

The buffer has limited capacity. If the buffer fills up, then it should reject additional data. For example, if the buffer has a capacity of 10GB, and data comes in at a rate of 2GB/s, but the computer can only process 1GB/s, then after 10 seconds, the buffer will be full.

The buffer may be designed to hold specific sizes of data. For example, a buffer may be designed to store IP addresses. Recall that an IP address is 12 digits. If a hacker sends a piece of data that is larger than what the buffer expects, a buffer overflow results. For example, if the IP address is 12 digits, and the hacker sends 14 digits, a buffer overflow could result.

In 2014, a major exploit known as Heartbleed caused security vulnerabilities across millions of websites, including Facebook, Google, and Revenue Canada. How did it work?

- Websites encrypt their data with an algorithm known as SSL
- A developer created an app called OpenSSL, which makes it easy for web developers to implement SSL in their website, using minimal code
- Millions of websites, including millions of the worlds largest websites used the OpenSSL app
- When a user visits a website, a connection is created. The user's computer and the web server keep the connection open for as long as necessary (but for no longer than necessary). To preserve resources, the server closes the connection when it is no longer required. It checks if the user is still present through a method known as a "heartbeat", which is the electronic equivalent of asking the user "are you there?" ever minute. If the user says "yes", the connection stays open. If the user doesn't reply, the server closes the connection.
    - Every minute, the user's computer sends a small random amount of data to the web server. The user's computer sends the web server the length of the data as well.
    - For example, the user's computer might send "sdkjfasfjksdlfskldflskdf" length:24

- The web server sends the data back. Thus, the web server and the user's computer know that both are still online and agree to keep the connection active.
- In fact, the server stores the data in a buffer and gives it an address (the address is the spot where the data starts). To return the data to the user, the server locates the data at that address, and counts the number of spaces based on the length it was provided. If the data's address starts at position 40 in the buffer, then the server will start reading at position and count another 23 position. Thus, the server will return the data from position 40 to position 63.
- A hacker found out that OpenSSL didn't verify the accuracy the length that the user's computer provided.
- Thus, a hacker could send a small amount of data such as "aaa" and a large length such as length:4523
- The server would store "aaa" in memory and then send back 4523 bits of data, starting with "aaa". If aaa started at position 40, the server would reply with the data from position 40 to position 4562. What kind of data is stored in the other positions? Anything is possible.
- If the hacker repeated these steps, eventually he would receive most of the contents of the server's memory, which could include encryption keys and private banking information.
- This bug could have been easily prevented with a few lines of code to verify the length of the data.
- Once discovered, it was quickly patched. But hackers had been using the security hole to steal data undetected for over two years.

How to prevent

- Proper code and error handling in programs. The buffer overflow happens because the computer receives data in an unexpected format and doesn't know what to do. Buffer overflows can be prevented by writing good code that checks for errors and refuses to accept data that does not meet the required format. A program shouldn't crash when it receives invalid data; it should simply reject it.
  - The correct data has an expected format (length, character type, contents, format, etc.)
  - In pseudocode, write an "if" statement. If the data doesn't match the expected format, then reject the data.

Malware is any type of malicious application. There are many types of malware.

A **virus** is an unauthorized program that causes undesired activity. A virus is not a standalone program, but instead it latches on to another legitimate program. When the legitimate program runs, so does the virus.

Viruses typically infect executable programs such as programs with extensions of .exe. Viruses can also infect documents, such as Microsoft Word documents or Microsoft Excel spreadsheets. These are known as macro viruses. Current versions of Microsoft Office disable macros by default (a user can open a Microsoft Office document file without allowing the macro to execute).

Viruses can enter automatically through backdoors. A user could inadvertently introduce a virus by clicking on attachments or downloading files from the internet.

The damage that a virus does is called the **payload**. Viruses can cause a wide range of effects from being simply a nuisance to deleting files. Viruses that infect industrial control systems can cause millions of dollars in damage. Viruses that infect medical equipment can put lives at risk.

A virus can be detected and prevented using an **antivirus program**. An antivirus program has two methods of detecting viruses

- **Definitions**: A definition is a specific "fingerprint" of the virus. An antivirus program may contain hundreds of thousands of virus definitions. It scans each new file introduced into the computer against the definitions. If the attributes of a file match a definition, then the antivirus program knows that it has located a virus (and knows which virus it has located).

  To develop the antivirus definitions, the antivirus software manufacturer must first obtain copies of the virus and create the definition. That means that some computers have already been infected with the virus by the time the definition has been created. Thus, definitions do not provide complete protection against viruses.

  A **polymorphic virus** is one that attempts to change its code. Each time the virus runs, the code changes slightly, but the damage that it causes remains the same. A polymorphic virus attempts to hide from antivirus definitions.

- **Heuristics**. A heuristic is a type of artificial intelligence. It allows the antivirus program to determine whether a specific program is legitimate or not, based on its behavior. For example, a program that attempts to modify critical system files is likely not legitimate.

  The latest generation antivirus programs share data with the cloud. For example, Norton Antivirus automatically collects data regarding suspicious applications from users. This data is sent to a response center for further analysis. Norton Antivirus then updates all user programs with the results. By sharing data with the cloud, antivirus programs can detect viruses faster.

The most famous computer viruses have been

- ILOVEYOU. Released in 2000, ILOVEYOU was transmitted via e-mail with a subject line of "I love you". It overwrote system files and personal files, before spreading through e-mail. It caused $15 billion in damage.
- MyDoom. Similar, to ILOVEYOU, MyDoom spread via e-mail in 2004. It is estimated that 25% of all e-mails sent in 2004 were infected with MyDoom. It caused $38 billion in damage.
- Stuxnet. Stuxnet is a special kind of virus because it infected the firmware of a USB drive. The firmware of a USB drive is not typically accessible to the computer or to an antivirus program – it's considered "read only" memory and allows the USB drive to read/write data from/to the computer.

  The Stuxnet virus contained a second virus inside of it. When the USB drive was inserted into a PLC (an industrial control system), the second virus infected the PLC. Stuxnet only infected Siemens S7 PLCs.

  Stuxnet was used to infect industrial control systems that were "air gapped" (not connected to the internet or to any network).

  Stuxnet was unusual because
    - It took advantage of multiple zero-day exploits (security holes that are unknown to the software manufacturers). A zero-day exploit is considered valuable to a virus manufacturer/hacker, and to use several in the same virus is highly unusual. Zero-day exploits are quickly patched by manufacturers once discovered and can't be reused. A zero-day exploit could be worth up to a million dollars. To use several million dollars worth of zero-day exploits in a virus that brings the creator no financial reward is highly unusual.
    - It limited its infection to only specific types of computers and PLCs. Most virus manufacturers do not want to limit the damage that they cause.
    - It is estimated that Stuxnet took between three man-years and fifteen man-years to prepare. Development of Stuxnet required advanced knowledge of the Windows operating system, USB firmware, and Siemens PLCs.

Crypto-malware and **ransomware** are closely related. Crypto-malware is a type of virus or malicious program that encrypts data on a computer.

The malware can be introduced through e-mail or downloaded files. The malware usually encrypts user documents, videos, photos, and music. It does not usually encrypt system files.

The distribution of crypto-malware is usually automated, although people or organizations can be specifically targeted. It should be noted that after the crypto-malware has infected the computer, then the author is able to view the contents of the computer. At that point, he can make an assessment as to how high of a ransom to charge. For example, if an ordinary person was targeted, the ransom might be low, but if a hospital was targeted, then the ransom might be high.

After infection, the computer operates as normal, but the user is provided with a message that their files have been encrypted. The malware usually instructs the user to pay a ransom to unlock the files. The ransom must typically be paid in bitcoin.

There are two types of crypto-malware

- Crypto-malware that pretend to encrypt the files. They change the file extension to something random, but do not encrypt the file. When the extension is changed back to the original, the files revert to normal. These forms of crypto-malware are extremely rare.
- Crypto-malware that encrypt the files. After the files are encrypted, the key is sent to a central server. The user receives the decryption key after paying the ransom. Some forms of crypto-malware do not provide the option to decrypt the files, either because they are misconfigured or because the intention is to prevent a user from accessing his files.

Ransomware is an extension of crypto-malware, in that it instructs the user to pay a ransom in exchange for unlocking the files.

Typically, the user is instructed to visit a TOR website, where they are provided further instructions. TOR websites are generally able to hide their location, although law enforcement agencies have developed methods to identify them. The user is instructed to pay the ransom with cryptocurrency (untraceable currency) such as bitcoin.

In most cases, the hackers provide the victim with the tool to decrypt their files upon receipt of payment. In some cases, the hackers do not.

The ransom amounts have ranged from the equivalent of $500 to $20,000 depending on the person or organization that was affected. Many organizations pay the ransom and don't publicly admit that they have been hacked.

How to prevent ransomware

- Proper user education to teach users how to identify potential ransomware delivered via e-mail, and to not open unusual attachments.
- Block e-mail attachments that contain macro-enabled Microsoft Word and Excel documents.
- Regularly install Windows operating system security updates

How to defeat ransomware once infected

- Attempt to restore data from backup or from the Volume Shadow Copy. This only works if the organization has backed up their data, and only the data that was backed up can be restored. This is not effective against newer versions of ransomware, which delete the Volume Shadow Copy.

- Attempt to decrypt the ransomware. Police forces in the EU have been able to provide victims with assistance in decrypting some forms of ransomware. Some versions of ransomware use weak encryption that can be broken through brute force or other techniques.
- Pay the ransom. In earlier cases, it was almost certain that the hackers would automatically (or manually) provide the decryption key upon payment of the ransom. In more recent cases, this is not guaranteed because there are many copycat ransomware viruses created by people with very little knowledge or infrastructure. Ransomware developers have franchised their operation to "script kiddies" who are simply distributing the ransomware and collecting payments. There are also versions of ransomware that have been put out by nation-states to cause political disruption; this type of malware only destroys data but is disguised as ransomware.

Notable infections

- In 2019, Jackson County, Georgia paid $400,000 to remove ransomware from their computers.
- University of Calgary paid $20,000 to decrypt computers infected by ransomware in 2017. The FBI later charged two people in Iran with spreading the virus, which infected computers at health care providers and other organizations.

Notable ransomware

- CryptoLocker was transmitted over e-mail as a ZIP file. Inside the e-mail was an executable disguised as a PDF. The decryption key was sent to a remote server. A victim could pay a ransom and receive a decryption key automatically. The creators of CrytoLocker made an estimated $27 million. In 2014, security firm FireEye was able to obtain the database of decryption keys, allowing victims to decrypt their files for free.
- WannaCry took advantage of a zero-day exploit in the Windows Server Message Block. WannaCry infected computers that had not patched the Windows Server Message Block vulnerability. The average ransom amount was $600. Over 200,000 computers were infected, with losses estimated at over $4 billion.
- Unlike other forms of ransomware, Petya encrypted the master boot record of a Windows computer. This caused the entire computer hard drive to be encrypted. Another version, known as NotPetya was targeted towards Ukrainian government entities and critical infrastructure. NotPetya quickly spread to other computers worldwide and could not be decrypted. It is believed that NotPetya was created by the Russian government.

The difference between a **worm** and a virus is that the worm replicates by itself, whereas the virus must attach itself to a legitimate file. The virus only runs when the legitimate file runs.

Worms can generally spread over a network from computer to computer, by themselves. They take advantage of security holes.

Examples of worms

- SQL Slammer took advantage of a buffer overflow bug in Microsoft SQL Server. The worm would randomly generate IP addresses and then send itself to those IP addresses. If the IP addresses belonged to computers that were running an unpatched version of SQL Server, then the worm would be successful in infecting them. The worm caused many internet routers to crash, and reboot. Each time the routers rebooted, they would resend routing updates to each other, which would cause internet traffic congestion. SQL Slammer was exceptional in that it fit inside a single data packet.

A **trojan** is a legitimate program that hides an illegitimate program. A user must install the trojan and/or give it permission before it can take effect. Trojan is named after the Trojan horse.

Trojans can hide in many programs including toolbars, screensavers, games, and other applications.

Examples of Trojans

- FinFisher (FinSpy), which is developed by Lench IT Solutions plc. This trojan is used to infect Windows computers and all brands of phones. It travels through e-mail, links, and security flaws in popular programs. Many antivirus programs are unable to detect it.

  FinFisher is sold to law enforcement agencies and dictatorships, some of which are accused of numerous human rights violations.

A **rootkit** provides unauthorized administrative level access to a computer by changing its operating system and attempting to bypass its security functions.

There are five types of rootkits

- **Firmware**. A firmware rootkit hides inside the device firmware (such as the BIOS, video card controller, router, network card, or hard drive controller). The device firmware is not typically scanned by (and is out of reach of) antivirus programs. While manufacturers such as HP have introduced BIOS integrity features that check for changes to the BIOS firmware, rootkits can infect other components such as the graphics card or hard drive.

- **Virtual**. A virtual rootkit is also known as a hypervisor rootkit. It operates between the processor and the operating system. It intercepts calls made by the operating system, like a "man-in-the-middle" attack. The result is that the processor believes that it is talking to the operating system and the operating system believes that it is taking to the processor, but, both are talking to the rootkit. The rootkit sends everything it learns to a central server.

- **Kernel**. A kernel rootkit runs on a computer with the highest privileges (the same privileges as the operating system) by replacing parts of the operating system core and device drivers. A kernel rootkit can't be detected by an antivirus program because the rootkit is acting like part of the legitimate operating system.

- **Library**. A library level rootkit replaces legitimate operating system DLLs with fake ones. A library is a set of code/functions that an application can reference (a software developer will include different DLLs with their application so that they don't have to rewrite thousands of lines of code). When an application references code in an infected DLL, the rootkit will also run.

- **Application Level**. An application level rootkit replaces application files with fake versions. The application may need to run at an elevated level in order to cause damage.

Examples of rootkits

- LoJack. LoJack is a legitimate rootkit that comes preinstalled in the BIOS of some laptops. If the laptop is lost or stolen and later connected to the internet, LoJack will report the location of the laptop to a server. LoJack is designed to remain on the laptop even if its hard disk drive is erased or replaced.

- Sony BMG. In 2005, Sony installed a rootkit known as XCP (Extended Copy Protection) on music CD's that it released. When users attempted to play the CD's through their computer, the rootkit created security vulnerabilities. The intention of the rootkit was to prevent people from copying music off the CD's, but the rootkit created security holes and hid in the background.

  Sony was forced to recall all unsold music CDs and faced multiple class-action lawsuits.

A **keylogger** records each key that a user presses. It may also take screenshots, activate the webcam, or activate the microphone without the knowledge or consent of the user.

The keylogger reports all data back to a central source or records the data on the computer for further retrieval. Data may be sent via

- Email
- FTP
- Wireless/Bluetooth to a nearby receiver

A keylogger may have legitimate purposes if installed by an employer or law enforcement agency. Some antivirus programs will detect keyloggers created by law enforcement and some will deliberately ignore them.

A keylogger may be used to invade the privacy of another person (stalking) or it may be used for financial gain (the logged data is analysed to obtain online banking passwords, e-mail passwords, etc.).

The keylogger may be introduced into a system through another type of malware such as a virus or trojan.

Whether the keylogger can be detected by an antivirus program depends on where it runs. Keyloggers that run in the operating system kernel or through a hypervisor may be undetectable.

Keyloggers can also be hardware-based

- Keyboard keylogger device (USB device that sits between the keyboard cable and the computer). A keyboard's circuitry can be covertly modified to include a keylogger.
- Wireless keyboard sniffer (device that can intercept signals between a wireless keyboard and the dongle; this device functions when the connection is not encrypted or where the encryption method can be easily broken)

How to prevent keyloggers

- It is difficult, if not impossible to detect a hardware based keylogger, especially one that is embedded into the device circuitry. Keeping computer hardware physically secure is the best defense. In addition, the use of multi-factor authentication methods can keep accounts secure even when the usernames and passwords are compromised.
- Most software-based keyloggers are detectable by antivirus programs. Some software-based keyloggers that take advantage of zero-day exploits or that operate on the firmware, kernel, or hypervisor level cannot be detected.

Adware is software that shows advertisements. The advertisements may appear as pop-ups, videos, or audio. Adware may be included in legitimate software programs such as games, music applications, or other applications. Typically, adware is bundled with low-quality applications. The advertisements are also of low quality as most legitimate advertisers do not want to be associated with this type of exploitation.

Adware can also be installed without the user's consent when introduced as part of a computer virus or trojan.

Adware can hijack legitimate website advertisements. When a user visits a legitimate website, the adware swaps advertisements placed by the website owner with advertisements sold by the adware publisher. Thus, the revenue from the advertisements is diverted to the adware publisher without the knowledge of the user or website owner.

It may be difficult or impossible to remove adware. Adware may spy on a user's activity or browsing history. The adware publisher may sell this data to market research firms or use it to show the user more relevant advertising.

It is illegal to install or distribute adware without the consent of the user. In addition, the user must have an opportunity to remove the adware. There is no specific anti-adware law, but Section 5 of the Federal Trade Commission Act prohibits "unfair or deceptive acts". The Federal Trade Commission (FTC) is empowered to commence civil actions against publishers who distribute adware.

Spyware is software that spies on a user's activity. Spyware can include keyloggers but can also include components that take screenshots or videos, activate the webcam or microphone, and/or copy files.

The distribution of spyware can be prosecuted under the Computer Fraud & Abuse Act, as further discussed in this book. It can be further prosecuted under harassment and stalking laws if the behavior amounts to such.

A **logic bomb** is a program that is installed by a legitimate user. The logic bomb appears to be legitimate. The logic bomb remains dormant until activated by a specific date/time or event. In Windows, the logic bomb can be programmed to activate in the Event Scheduler.

The logic bomb can steal data, delete data, or cause other harmful actions. Logic bombs are commonly installed by disgruntled system administrators. After the system administrator is fired or quits, the logic bomb activates and damages the company's systems.

Social engineering is the attempt to use psychological methods to manipulate individuals into providing confidential information or access to systems.

Unlike malware, social engineering relies on human emotion

- Wanting to be liked
- Fear
- Wanting to help
- Intimidation
- Familiarity
- Hostility

A good book on social engineering is *Social Engineering: The Art of Human Hacking* by Christopher Hadnagy.

Why do social engineering attempts work? There are many reasons.

- **Authority**
  - The person on the other end of the phone call/in person acts with authority. People are afraid to challenge those who appear to be in a position of authority (such as members of senior management).
  - Authority can be established by confidence, tone of voice, clothing, and/or uniforms.
  - People are afraid to challenge authority because of perceived negative consequences (getting fired)
  - The consequences do not have to be explicitly stated by the thief. They can be implied, or the user might simply assume what they are based on the alleged authority.
  - Social engineering authority attacks can be prevented by enforcing policy against all users, regardless of their position. The company must create a culture where verifying the identity of another person is encouraged, regardless of that person's position.
  - For example, the thief could pretend to be a member of senior management and convince the victim that she could lose her job if she does not comply. The thief could demand that the victim provide him with corporate financial information, or wire money to a third party.

- **Intimidation**
  - Intimidation uses the threat or idea of negative consequences if the person fails to comply.
  - The thief does not have to make any direct threats, but instead may cause the victim to believe that negative consequences will occur (or the victim may assume that negative consequences will occur if they fail to comply).
  - For example, the thief could pretend to be a police officer and convince the victim that she will be arrested if she does not comply. The thief demands that the victim disclose sensitive data relevant to an investigation.

- **Consensus**
  - Consensus involves a group-decision.
  - If a social engineer is unable to convince a specific person to perform an action, he could attempt to convince others in that person's social circle. Those other people could convince the victim to proceed.

  - For example, the thief could convince the victim that her co-workers completed the same action.

- **Scarcity**
  - Scarcity means that something is unavailable or in limited supply.
  - If the victim values something that is scarce, they may forgo normal procedures and fall into the trap to obtain that item.
  - For example, the victim wants a rare (sold out) toy at Christmas time. The thief convinces her that he can supply the toy if she provides him with her credit card/banking information (which he uses fraudulently). The victim never receives the toy.

- **Familiarity**
  - The victim feels familiar with the situation and proceeds because nothing seems out of place.
  - The thief can convince the victim to focus on ideas that are familiar, by dropping names, projects, or other tasks into the conversation.
  - Although the victim does not know the thief, she is led to believe that he is a legitimate co-worker.

- **Trust**
  - The victim trusts the thief and proceeds with their own free will.
  - The victim believes that the person they are talking to or the site that they have visited is legitimate.
  - The thief may take time to build this trust, especially with a high-value target. The greater the victim trusts the thief, the more the victim will be willing to do.

- **Urgency**
  - Urgency is like scarcity
  - Urgency builds on the idea that there is a limited time to act.
  - People hate losing money more than they hate not making money.
  - For example, the victim could be told that money is about to be withdrawn from their bank account and they only have a few minutes to stop it (by providing their banking information to the thief). Normally, the victim would take their time to check that the person they are speaking with is legitimate but bypasses these risk controls because of the urgency.

Phishing is the attempt to obtain sensitive data by pretending to be a trusted entity. Phishing usually occurs through e-mail or telephone. Phishing is usually sent as a mass e-mail to thousands or millions of people.

Typically, a user will receive an e-mail asking them to sign in to their bank account or other account (PayPal, eBay, Amazon). The e-mail is fake, and the website that the e-mail leads to is fake (but appears to be real).

Typical phishing e-mails will say

- Your account has been compromised and you must log in to correct the issue
- Your account will be suspended if you don't log in
- You have received a large payment (Interac eTransfer) and you must log in to accept the money

The hacker may register a domain that looks like the legitimate one. For example, the user may register www.paypa1.com instead of www.paypal.com. Or the hacker may register a domain that is completely unrelated to the original website and attach a subdomain that looks like the legitimate site. For example, the hacker registers fakewebsite.com and attaches the "www.paypal" subdomain to it, making www.paypal.com.fakewebsite.com. The users will see the first part of the URL "www.paypal.com" and think they are on a legitimate site, even though the user's browser went to fakewebsite.com.

Update Required!!

Recently, there's been activity in your PayPal account that seems unusual compared to your normal account activities. Please log in to PayPal to confirm your identity.

This is part of our security process and helps ensure that PayPal continue to be safer way to buy online. Often all we need is a bit more information. While your account is limited, some options in your account won't be available.
How to remove my limitation?
You can resolve your limitation by following these simple steps:

- **Log in here.**

- Provide the information needed. The sooner your provide the information we need, the sooner we can resolve the situation.

"If this message sent as Junk or Spam, its just an error by our new system, please click at Not Junk or Not Spam"

Sincerely,

PayPal

How do we prevent phishing?

- Proper user education to identify suspicious e-mails.
  - Knowledge that legitimate e-mails from banks and other sites will contain the user's full name while phishing e-mails will not (unless the sender has access to the user's data)
  - Phishing e-mails and/or websites may (but not always) contain poor grammar or spelling
  - Phishing websites will not contain the correct URL. Users should always check that they have visited the correct URL.
- Automated systems that detect and filter phishing e-mails. These systems are built into most web browsers and e-mail systems and verify that the e-mails originated from legitimate sources and that the websites are legitimate.

Spear Phishing is like phishing, but it targets specific groups or people. The more precise the targeting, the higher the response rate.

A normal phishing attack could target millions of users. For example,

- A hacker could send a fake e-mail appearing to be from Bank of America to 1,000,000 e-mail addresses
- From those 1,000,000 addresses, only 250,000 might work
- The SPAM filter would block 200,000 from those 250,000
- From the 50,000 only 10,000 might have accounts at Bank of America
- 80% of those users might be smart enough to detect the phishing scam, in which case only 2,000 people respond
- The attack is shut down early on, and many users are unable to respond, so the hackers only collect data from 500 users
- The success rate is about 0.005%. Although it is low, the return on investment might be high. It may cost the hackers a few hundred dollars out the e-mail, but they might be able to collect at least $100 from each user (for a total of $50,000).

In spear phishing, the hackers identify specific customers of Bank of America for example. They may use a list stolen from the bank. The hackers customize the e-mail to include the name and other personally identifying information of each recipient. As a result, the SPAM filter will be less likely to identify the e-mail as SPAM, and the user will be more likely to respond.

Whaling is like Phishing, but targets high-value individuals such as celebrities, CEOs or other executives. Whaling is specifically targeted to the high-value individual. Whaling takes more effort to execute, but the response rate is higher, and the amount of money stolen from each user is higher. Many high-net worth individuals have access to credit cards with high limits.

Another scheme involves a scammer visiting a store such as Best Buy and attempting to illegally purchase expensive electronics in the name of a celebrity on credit. The scammer disappears with the electronics and the store is never paid. The store should have verified that the buyer legitimately represents the celebrity.

How do we prevent whaling?

- Proper user education
- 100% identity verification of the person who is seeking information.
- A high-net worth individual should understand that he is at much higher risk of exploitation either through fraud or extortion schemes. This person should employ people who specialize in detecting and preventing these threats.

Vishing or **VoIP Phishing** and **Smishing** or **SMS Phishing** are forms of phishing that use a VoIP phone or SMS messages. Smishing is particularly dangerous, because although we can block many types of malicious e-mails, it is difficult to block SMS messages – they contain very little metadata (except for the date and sender, all SMS messages look the same).

Pharming is a form of phishing where we redirect a legitimate website's traffic to an illegitimate website.

In a **watering hole attack**, a thief plants a form of malware on a frequently visited website. The users visit the website and download the malware.

A watering hole attack typically takes advantage of a zero-day exploit. It allows malware to download in the background without any indication to the user.

How to prevent

- Proper antivirus can prevent many watering hole attacks
- Website operators should ensure that their servers and code are up to date
- Watering hole attacks that take advantage of zero-day exploits cannot be prevented

In **cross-site scripting**, a user includes script as part of their input in a web form or link. There are three types

- Non-persistent XSS attack, where the script is executed by the web server immediately and sent back to the browser
    - For example, a hacker sends a user a link to a legitimate online banking website, but the link includes some code that executes (through the website) in the user's browser. The script copies the user's login credentials and sends them to the hacker.
- Persistent XSS attack, where the script is stored by the web server and executed against others
    - For example, a hacker posts a YouTube comment and includes some HTML (which includes links and photographs to an ecommerce site). The HTML executes in each visitor's web browser, and all visitors see the comment (including the links and photographs). This is unlikely to happen on YouTube because data is sanitized, but it is certainly possible on other websites.
- DOM-based XSS attack, where the script is executed by the browser

How to prevent

- Proper input validation in web forms both on the web browser side and on the server side
- Remove or filter all script characters from web forms, including “<”, “;”, and “|”
- Use anti-XSS libraries such as ANTIXSS

- Use Content Security Policy in the website

In **cryptography** the data is encrypted. Hackers try to decrypt it. There are many ways, but all cryptographic attacks can be prevented. Some of the attacks include

- **Birthday**. Consider a set of values (not necessarily unique values), k. In any set k, the possibility that at least two values are identical is $1.25k^{1/2}$. If we have a set of two values, then the possibility that they are identical is $1.25(2)^{1/2} = 1.75\%$. As the set grows, the possibility that two entries will be identical also grows. This idea came from the fact that in a room of 30 people, there is at least a 50% chance that two of them share a birthday.

- **Known Plain Text/Cipher Text**. If the hacker can intercept a portion of the plain text communication and the corresponding portion of the cipher, he can use cryptanalysis to decrypt the algorithm. The hacker does not require the entire communication, only a portion. Good encryption algorithms can mitigate this threat because they use large keys.

- **Rainbow Tables**. Recall that it is bad security practice to store passwords in plain text. Passwords are typically hashed, and the hash is stored (the hash is not reversible).

  But a hacker could generate a dictionary of passwords (common and uncommon) and calculate the corresponding hash for each one. This dictionary is known as a rainbow table. The hacker could then steal a hash and look up the corresponding password for each one.

  Rainbow tables are readily available on the internet for passwords up to eight characters (every possible combination!) and rainbow tables of even longer passwords can be computed.

  To prevent the use of rainbow table attacks, modern password hash functions incorporate a 'salt'. The salt is a random set of characters appended to the end of each password before the hash is calculated. The hash and the salt are stored in plain text. If the hash database is compromised, the hacker would have to regenerate each rainbow table incorporating the salt into every password to make any sense of it. This would be practically impossible.

- **Dictionary**. A Dictionary attack uses a list of predetermined passwords and brute force to guess the password. The dictionary could consist of common words in the English language, especially common passwords such as "password", "12345678", and "abcd".

  A hacker could create a custom dictionary based on the user account that he is trying to hack into. For example, the dictionary could be customized to include the names of the user's children, pets, vehicles, etc..

Many organizations force users to choose complex passwords. Password complexity could include

- o Not reusing the same password
- o Including upper case letters, lower case letters, numbers, and special characters
- o Ensuring that the password meets a minimum length
- o Not using a person's name, address, or username in the password

Yet, it is still possible to create a custom dictionary based on the password complexity requirements. For example, if the user's password was 'donkey', then a complicated password might be 'D0nkey!'. Users tend to substitute @ for a, 0 for o, 1 for l, and so forth in a predictable manner.

A dictionary attack can be prevented by limiting the amount of password attempts a user has before his account is locked out. Of course, the dictionary attack could occur offline, or the hacker may have a way to bypass the incorrect password attempt count.

- **Brute Force**. A brute force attack is like a dictionary attack, except that the system attempts every password combination possible (based on the character set), starting from the letter a and working its way up until the password is guessed. For example, the system will guess the password 'sdfsfgdgsdfsdfd', and then the next password would be 'sdfsfgdgsdfsdf*e*'

  The length of time for a brute force attack to be successful depends on the computing power available (how many passwords can be attempted every second) and the length of the password (how many passwords need to be attempted).

  An online brute force attack is when the brute force occurs against a live computer. For example, consider Active Directory, a Microsoft system that stores user accounts on a central server. When a user attempts to log in to an Active Directory-based computer, the computer validates the login credentials with the server. On a successful login, the computer caches the correct credentials on the local computer. If the computer is later offline (or off the local network), the user can still log in (the computer validates the login with the cached credentials).

  - o In an **online attack**, the hacker would brute force the computer's login while it is connected to the Active Directory server. This attack would likely be unsuccessful because the server would notice the incorrect logins and disable the account.
  - o In an **offline attack**, the hacker would brute force the computer's login while it is not connected to the Active Directory server. This attack may or may not be successful depending on the length and complexity of the password.

How to prevent

- Offline attacks can't be prevented. Where possible, secure equipment so that it is not stolen. Stolen equipment is more susceptible to offline attacks.
- Enforce stronger password requirements (including special characters, numbers, upper/lower case letters).
- Enforce a timer that delays the entry of passwords. This can be accomplished at the software or hardware level, by hashing the password multiple times.
- Offline data can be encrypted with a strong algorithm that takes several seconds to validate the password. This would be a minor inconvenience to a user entering an incorrect password, but would substantially slow down a brute force attack.

5.2 Describe security program elements (user awareness, training, and physical access control)

Users are not experts at security and hackers are always looking for new ways to exploit them. We need to train people so that they can recognize and report security threats.

The best security program has

- **User Awareness** – We make users aware that threats exist so that they can be vigilant.
- **User Training** – We teach users how to formally detect threats. A user training policy should apply to any user who has access to our network. Users must be encouraged to report potential security threats.

  One new way that organizations train users is to send them fake phishing e-mails and see if they respond or provide their credentials. If they do, then they are warned that they clicked on a link that could have come from a hacker, so that they learn how to recognize similar threats in the future.

  Even the most highly trained security analysts are vulnerable to phishing attacks, especially when the attacker is sophisticated. We are all human, and social engineering is designed to work on weak human emotions.

- **Physical Access Control** – We keep people out of the places that they shouldn't be. Keeping network and server infrastructure physically secure is important because a person with physical access can
  - Physically damage the equipment by powering it off or removing the hard disk drives
  - Gain console access to network equipment. Most Cisco switches and routers can be physically reset by a user with physical access, regardless of the type of security on the device.
  - Connect unauthorized devices such as USB drives to servers, routers, and switches.

  With a physical access control system, we use an electronic system to keep track of who entered, where they entered, and what time they entered. We can restrict the areas that each person can access, and we can restrict the time of day that they can access an area.

Tailgaiting is an attempt to obtain unauthorized access to a physical facility.

Many offices, industrial facilities, and data centers are controlled via electronic proximity card and/or biometric locks. When a legitimate user unlocks an entrance with their access card and/or biometric lock, an intruder can follow them into the building. Tailgaiting works because

- A person might hold the door open for a person who is walking behind him (doing otherwise might be considered rude)
- A person might not wait to verify that the door closed and locked behind him, and another person might follow him. The door lock might not work properly, in which case the door does not fully close.

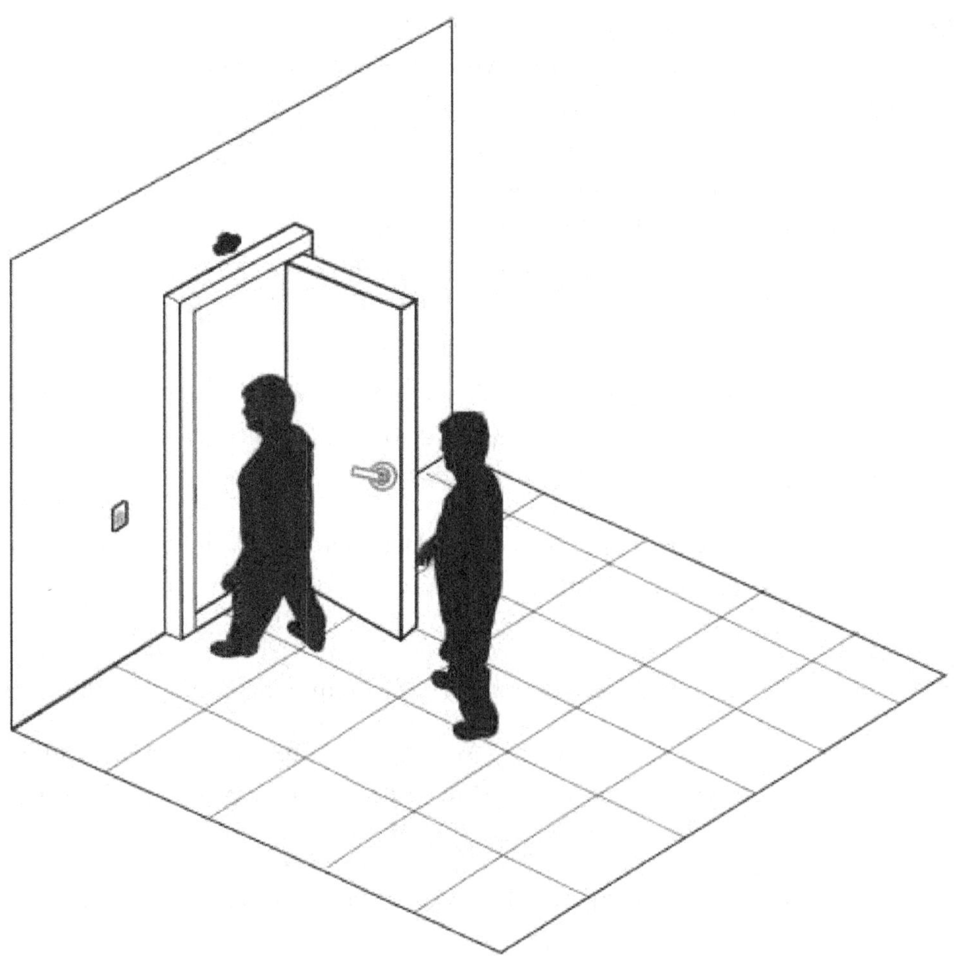

How to prevent

- Proper user education to enforce the use of access cards and prohibit tailgating. Users should know that not holding the door is not considered rude.
- Install a security guard at each entrance or monitor entrances with security cameras
- In more extreme cases, installation of man trap doors might be necessary. A man trap door allows only one person to enter at a time. The man trap door contains cameras with artificial

intelligence to detect the number of people inside and permits entry to only one individual at a time.

A **Fence** or **Gate** or **Cage** keeps people out or keeps people in. For example, a tool storage area inside a building/warehouse might be fenced in.

Consider

- Who you are trying to stop. A chain-link fence can be cut with wire cutters easily. Even a barbed wire fence can be cut. Fences are good for slowing down random people who are trying to climb over but are not so good for vehicles or sneaky people. In those cases, a concrete wall may be required.
    - An electric fence is more effective at keep people out but may introduce unwanted legal liability. An electric fence must have clear signage that identifies it as such. It should also be separated from the public by a normal fence so that people cannot inadvertently contact it.
- Whether the fence is opaque or transparent (chain link). The fence may need to be opaque so that people can't see inside.
- The height of the fence. A tall fence may stop people from climbing or seeing over it, but it is irrelevant if people can cut through the fence or fly drones into the facility.
- Fences can be used in combination. The fence provides a buffer zone. It slows people down. By the time a person has penetrated the fence, security will have been able to intercept them. The fence can be monitored with cameras, security patrols, and sensors.

Inside a building, chain link fencing can be used to set up cages for controlled physical access. It is cheaper to build a cage than a physical room.

A **security guard** is a human who provides security. The security guards may be stationed in key areas, may walk around, or may drive patrol vehicles.

Proper training is important. A security guard who is not vigilant will not be effective. Security guards who use excessive force, are disrespectful, or are perceived to be incompetent, will cost the company money, introduce legal liability, and damage its reputation.

Security guards may be outsourced from a company like G4S or Guarda. There is no good reason to outsource, except for cost. When renting security guards, it is important to ensure that the security company sends the same people each time, so that they become familiar with the premises. Many companies outsource security so that they do not have to risk legal liability in the event that a security guard acts inappropriately.

A larger organization may be able to better train an internal security force, even with as few as 50 security guards.

The security guard's most important tool is his brain. Security guards also have other tools like guns, handcuffs, batons, and pepper spray, depending on the state/province that they are in. The organization must decide if it should risk the liability and cost of training to supply security guards with weapons.

Artificial intelligence is no substitute for a human brain. It is important to ensure that the security guard is aware of his surroundings. A security guard who is complacent may be worse than no security guard at all. Security guards are human and can be manipulated through social engineering techniques.

In general, a security guard is not a law enforcement officer. A security guard is entitled to

- Enforce the law when seeing an actual commission of a crime on the organization's property
- Use reasonable force to protect himself or another human being from physical harm or death
- Use reasonable force to protect the physical property of his organization
- Detain an individual who the security guard knows has committed a felony (an indictable offense in Canada), and promptly turn him to a law enforcement agent
- Use reasonable force to prevent a trespasser from entering a secured facility

Security guards may also have dogs that can detect for food, drugs, or explosives. Like a weapon, the use of a dog can also subject the organization to serious legal liability.

A security guard also keeps track of visitors

- Signs visitors in and out
- Verifies that the visitors are legitimate

- Ensures that visitors have been briefed on the organization's security and safety policies and that they are wearing appropriate personal protective equipment (PPE), if required
- Escorts visitors to the appropriate locations

An **alarm** is necessary to protect critical assets. The two main types of alarms

- Intruder alarm – detects intrusions
- Environmental alarm – detects a fire, flood, high temperatures, etc.

The alarm will have multiple components

- **Sensor**. The sensor detects an event
    - Motion Sensor detects motion, which could indicate the presence of an unauthorized person
    - Glass Break Sensor detects if glass has been broken based on the specific sound frequency that broken glass makes
    - Door/Window Contact detects if a door/window is closed or if has been opened. The sensor consists of a magnet that sits on the door/window and a contact that sits on the door/window frame. This creates a closed circuit. When opened, the door/window breaks the circuit, and an alarm activates
    - Smoke Detector detects for the presence of smoke but can also sound a false alarm. It can be triggered by dusty conditions.
    - Flood Detector detects moisture content. This may be installed in a server room.
    - Thermostat detects temperatures that are too high or too low. High temperatures can lead to equipment damage. Cold temperatures can cause water pipes to burst.
- **Controls**. The controls allow the alarm to be programmed. The controls collect data from the sensors and decide if an abnormal event has occurred, in which case the alarm is triggered. The controls send an alert to another device.
- **Alerts**. The alarm must make an alert, or else it will have no purpose. It must notify somebody that an abnormal condition is present. Some forms of alerts
    - Siren/Flashing Lights can scare intruders but are by themselves just a nuisance. Some intruders will ignore the alarms, especially when there are many false alarms. A police department will probably not respond to an audible alarm unless they are specifically notified that a crime is in progress.
    - Alert on a control panel. The alarm can notify a monitoring station so that the responsible people can verify that the alarm is real and take additional action such as calling the police, calling for emergency services, or dispatching a security guard to investigate.
    - Automated phone call/email/SMS alert to the responsible people

When an alarm is triggered, a security guard might first review the surveillance cameras in the relevant areas to determine if there is a problem. The security guard would then physically investigate the areas and act as appropriate. If nothing out of the ordinary is present, the security guard may turn off the alarm and record his findings.

An alarm system can be divided into multiple zones. Each zone is subject to its own rules. For example, a zone can be always armed, or it can be armed at night. A server room might always be armed unless somebody needs to access it. An office might only be armed at night when nobody is present.

When an alarm is in an armed state, any sensor activity will trigger an alarm.

The control system for an alarm must be in a physically secure room. The control system must itself be alarmed (connected to a tamper-detecting sensor), so that any attempt to disable it is detected.

5.6 Configure and verify access control lists

An **ACL** or **Access Control List** is most commonly used by routers to filter traffic and to prioritize different types of packets.

We can apply the rules of an access control list on an incoming interface (where the packet enters the router) or on an outgoing interface (where the packet leaves the router). That means we can decide to apply an access control list before we make a routing decision or after.

We must enable the access control list on each router interface that processes a packet, and in the same direction that the packet travels.

On a Cisco router, there are only two options for what we can do with a packet: **permit** or **deny**. Permit allows a packet to continue to its destination while deny discards the packet.

The ACL looks at the source IP address, destination IP address, source port, and/or destination port to determine whether to permit or deny the packet. Essentially, an ACL is a list of rules. When the router receives a packet, if an ACL applies to an interface where the packet was received or is about to be sent out of, the router checks each rule in the ACL, one-by-one, against the packet. The router applies the first rule in the ACL that matches the packet, and then stops processing.

For example, if my ACL says

- Rule #1: Permit all traffic from 192.168.0.1
- Rule #2: Deny all traffic from the range 192.168.0.1 to 192.168.0.255
- Rule #3: Permit all traffic from the range 192.168.0.0 to 192.168.255.255

A packet from 192.168.0.1 will match Rule #1 and will be permitted. Technically, it will also match Rule #2 and Rule #3, but the router will stop processing after Rule #1.

A packet from 192.168.0.2 will not match Rule #1, but will match Rule #2, and will be denied. Technically, it will match Rule #3, but the router will stop processing after Rule #2.

A packet from 192.168.2.1 will not match Rule #1 and will not match Rule #2 but will match Rule #3 and will be permitted.

A packet from 192.170.0.0 will not match any rules and will therefore be denied. By default, you can assume that at the end of each ACL is a hidden rule that denies traffic to any packet that didn't match the previous rules.

Each ACL must be given a name or a number. There are two types of ACLs

- **Standard Numbered ACLs** (1 to 99 and 1300 to 1999)

- **Extended Numbered ACLs** (100 to 199 and 2000 to 2699)

An ACL can be named or numbered.

- **A Standard Named ACL** matches the packet based on its source IP address only. It applies only in subcommands and is identified by its name.
- **A Standard Numbered ACL** matches the packet based on its source IP address only. It applies in the router's global configuration and is identified by its number.
- **An Extended Named ACL** matches the packet based on its source IP address, destination IP address, source port, and/or destination port. It applies only in subcommands and is identified by its name.
- **An Extended Numbered ACL** matches the packet based on its source IP address, destination IP address, source port, and/or destination port. It applies in the router's global configuration and is identified by its number.

How do we configure an ACL?

We type **`access-list <#> <action> <parameters>`**

- The # is the number of the access control list that we want to configure from 1 to 99 or from 1300 to 1999
- The action is either to **permit** or **deny** the traffic
- The parameters tell the router us what properties of the traffic to match. In a standard ACL, the parameter is the source IP address.

If we want to stop any traffic from the address 4.4.4.4, we would type **`access-list 1 deny 4.4.4.4`**.

In older versions of IOS, we would add the word host before the IP address, **`access-list 1 deny host 4.4.4.4`**.

If we want to match a range of IP addresses, we can use a **wildcard mask**. The wildcard mask looks like a subnet mask, in that it contains four octets. If an octet is all "0", then the router will compare it with the source IP address. If the octet is "255", then the router will ignore it.

In IPv4, that means that I have five possible decimal wildcard masks.

- 0.0.0.0 – this means that we should match the exact IP address. We don't need to use a wildcard if we want to match the exact IP address.
- 0.0.0.255 – this means that we should match IP addresses with the same first three octets.

- 0.0.255.255 – this means that we should match IP addresses with the same first two octets.
- 0.255.255.255 – this means that we should match IP addresses with the same first octet.
- 255.255.255.255 – this means that we should match all IP addresses. It is like not using an access control list.

For example, if I want my ACL to apply to addresses in the range of 192.168.0.0 to 192.168.0.255, I am trying to match the first three octets (192.168.0). I would use a wildcard of 0.0.0.255, so I could write **`access-list 1 deny 192.168.0.0 0.0.0.255`**.

Notice that I wrote 192.168.0.0 as the IP address that I wanted to match. I could have written any valid IP address in that range, such as 192.168.0.10, but the preferred method is to set the matching octets to 0. If we don't, IOS will automatically change them to 0 when saving the command.

The wildcard masks I mentioned were called **decimal wildcard masks**. If I want to get more granular, I can use a **binary wildcard mask**. We can use a binary mask to match a specific subnet that is not /8, /16, /24, or /32. How do we do this?

- We figure out the subnet that we want the ACL to apply to
- We figure out the subnet mask of the subnet
- We calculate a wildcard mask by subtracting the subnet mask from 255.255.255.255

For example, if my subnet is 10.10.2.0 and my subnet mask is 255.255.255.128, then I would subtract 255.255.255.128 from 255.255.255.255. The result is 0.0.0.127.

I would configure my ACL as **`access-list 1 deny 10.10.2.0 0.0.0.127`**.

If I was given **`access-list 1 deny 10.10.2.0 0.0.0.127`** as a command to reverse engineer to determine the range of addresses implied by the wildcard mask, I would just add the wildcard mask to the IP address.

10.10.2.0 + 0.0.0.127 = 10.10.2.127

Therefore, my network range is from 10.10.2.0 to 10.10.2.127. Addresses with sources inside this network are denied by my list.

As I said, by default the router denies any packet that doesn't match any rules in the list. We can override this by creating a list with the word "any" and type **`access-list 1 permit any`**. This would be useful if we want to allow all traffic except for those from a few sources. We would create several specific deny rules followed by one "any" rule.

We could also create an **access-list 1 deny any rule** to block traffic. This rule would be redundant, but it would allow us to keep track of the number of packets that had been denied. An ACL will log the number of packets that it denies, but the hidden deny rule doesn't keep track of anything.

In my examples, I used the number "1" for my list. That means that all my rules belong to List #1. I don't have to create a List, I just create multiple rules using the access-list command and give each of them the same number.

The best practices for configuring an ACL

- The ACL should be created as close to the packet's destination as possible. That means it is better to create it on an outgoing interface instead of an incoming interface. This avoids the risk of accidentally dropping packets.
- The extended ACL should be created as close to the packet's source as possible. Extended ACLs must match many parameters and there is less risk that a packet will be dropped accidentally. By placing the extended ACL close to the source, we avoid having to process packets that will be dropped.
- We should be able to determine each packet's source IP address.
- Remember that the router will apply all the rules sequentially until it finds one that matches. Then it will stop applying rules. We should configure the rules so that they are sequential in an order that makes sense.
- We should place the most specific rules at the top of the ACL.
- The router will deny any traffic that doesn't match any rules.
- For security reasons and to avoid disruption to the network, we should disable an ACL before making changes to it.

We can apply an ACL to each interface by entering the interface configuration

Type **ip access-group <ACL number> <direction>**. The ACL number is the list number. The direction is either "in" or "out" and determines whether the rule will apply to traffic entering or leaving the interface. The interface will now apply all the rules that belong to the ACL number.

In my router configuration, I might choose to permit traffic from 9.9.9.9, and 4.4.4.4, and deny traffic from 10.0.0.0 coming in through interface G0/0/0.

Below, I configured my router

```
Router>enable
Router#conf t
Enter configuration commands, one per line.  End with CNTL/Z.
Router(config)#access-list 1 deny 10.0.0.0
Router(config)#access-list 1 permit 9.9.9.9
Router(config)#access-list 1 permit 4.4.4.4
Router(config)#interface G0/0/0
Router(config-if)#ip access-group 1 in
Router(config-if)#^Z
Router#
%SYS-5-CONFIG_I: Configured from console by console
```

When we check the router configuration, we see that the GigabitEthernet0/0/0 interface has the command "ip access-group 1 in"

```
interface GigabitEthernet0/0/0
 no ip address
 ip access-group 1 in
 duplex auto
 speed auto
 shutdown
!
```

Further down in the configuration, we see the access-list

```
access-list 1 deny host 10.0.0.0
access-list 1 permit host 9.9.9.9
access-list 1 permit host 4.4.4.4
!
!
!
!
```

If we want to see a list of our IPv4 ACLs, we can type **show ip access-lists**. If we want to see all our ACLs, including IPv6 ACLs, we type **show access-lists**.

The router lists each access list along with its rules and number of matches for each rule. If there are no matches, then the router does not list anything next to the rule.

```
Router#show access-lists
Standard IP access list 1
    10 deny host 10.0.0.0 (2034 matches)
    20 permit host 9.9.9.9 (8 matches)
    30 permit host 4.4.4.4
```

If we look at the relevant router interface, it will tell us the number of the outbound and inbound ACL. If there is no ACL, it will say "not set".

```
Router#show ip interface G0/0/0
GigabitEthernet0/0/0 is up, line protocol is up
...
Outgoing access list is not set
Inbound access list is 1
```

Some ACL troubleshooting tips

- Are the ACL rules being applied in the correct order?
- Do the IP addresses and wildcard masks match the traffic?
- Is the ACL applied to the correct interface?
- Is the ACL applied in the correct direction?
- If I run a tracert or ping on my router, it will not be filtered by the router ACL, so don't worry. We can run the tracert or ping as required.
- We can perform some advanced troubleshooting by enabling logging on a specific rule. We would type **access-list <number> permit <IP address> <wildcard mask> log**. Notice that we added "log" at the end.

  Now the router will list each packet, its source IP address, its destination IP address, and what happened to it.

  For example, I created a rule to deny traffic from the address 10.0.0.5. I received a packet headed towards 10.10.10.10 and my router decided to deny it on April 30 at 11:11 AM. The router outputs this data.

  ```
  Router(config)# access-list 2 deny 10.0.0.5 log

  ...

  Apr 30 11:11:30 list 2 denied 10.0.0.5 -> 10.10.10.10
  ```

When configuring an extended ACL, we would type **access-list <list number> <action> <protocol> <source IP address and wildcard> <source port> <destination IP address and wildcard> <destination port>**

- The list number is the same as before, but the range can be from 100 to 199 or 2000 to 2699. When we specify a number in this range, the router understands that we are configuring an Extended ACL and expects to see additional parameters.
- The action is either **permit** or **deny**
- The protocol can be IP, TCP, UDP, or ICMP
- The source IP address and wildcard are configured as before.
- We now have a destination IP address and wildcard as well. The same wildcard rules apply.
- We also have a source port and a destination port. We have several options here
    - **eq <#>**. This matches traffic equal to #. For example, eq 21 matches traffic on port 21.

      If we don't want to write the port number, we could also write a keyword. For example, 'eq www' matches traffic on the WWW port, which is port 80.

      The router converts the most popular port numbers to their keywords. For example, if you typed "eq 21', the router would change it to "eq ftp'
    - **ne <#>**. This matches traffic that is not equal to #. For example, ne 21 matches traffic that is not on port 21.
    - **lt <#>**. This matches traffic that is less than #. For example, lt 1000 matches traffic that is on ports between 1 and 1999.
    - **gt <#>**. This matches traffic that is greater than #. For example, gt 1000 matches traffic that is on ports greater than 1000.
    - **range <#> to <#>**. This matches traffic in a range. For example, range 2000 to 3000 matches traffic on ports between 2000 and 3000.

For an extended ACL, if we configure a source IP address or destination IP address without a wildcard (that is, we are matching a single IP address), we must add the word "host" before the IP address.

All the parameters specified by the rule must match a packet for the rule to be applied.

For example, **`access-list 101 deny tcp host 5.5.5.5 gt 1000`** will deny any traffic that is TCP based, with a source IP address of 5.5.5.5 and a source port that is greater than 1000. Notice that if we only have one IP address, the router assumes that it is a source IP address and not a destination. If we don't want to specify a source IP address, we must use the any keyword.

For example, **access-list 101 deny udp any gt 50000 10.10.10.0 255.255.255.0 lt 1000** will deny any UDP traffic from any source IP address, with a source port that is greater than 50000 and has a destination on the network 10.10.10.0 to 10.10.10.255 and a destination port less than 1000.

We create the extended access list the same way as we did with the standard access list. We add the extended access list to the router interfaces the same way. The router applies the list the same way – it stops processing the list when it sees a match.

Here is a tip. If we create a complicated access control list, we might want to leave a comment so that later we can figure out what it does.

Using the remark command, we can write **access-list <access list number> remark <text>**, where <text> is the comment that we want to leave.

A Named ACL works exactly like a Numbered ACL, except that it has a name. The name makes it easier to remember what it does. Also, we configure a Named ACL kind of like we configure an interface – through subcommands.

To configure a Named ACL, I would type **ip access-list <type> <name>**, where type is either standard or extended, and the name is the name of the list. This would take me into the Named ACL configuration. I would then enter each rule one line at a time.

For example, if I want to create a standard list called "serverlist" and allow traffic from 1.2.3.4 but deny traffic from 5.6.7.8, I would type

```
ip access-list standard serverlist

      permit 1.2.3.4

      deny 5.6.7.8
```

If I had a numbered ACL, I would type

```
access-list 1 permit 1.2.3.4

access-list 1 permit 5.6.7.8
```

While configuring a named ACL, I can use the remark command inside the ACL configuration.

Across the standard and extended named and numbered ACLs, I can delete a command by typing "no" in front of the command.

For example, if I wanted to delete **access-list 1 permit 1.2.3.4**, I would type **no access-list 1 permit 1.2.3.4** in global configuration mode.

If I wanted to delete **permit 1.2.3.4** from the standard list I created, I would first enter the configuration mode for that list, then I would type **no permit 1.2.3.4**.

Going back to my earlier example

```
Router#show access-lists
Standard IP access list 1
    10 deny host 10.0.0.0 (2034 matches)
    20 permit host 9.9.9.9 (8 matches)
    30 permit host 4.4.4.4
```

Notice that the router added numbers (10, 20, and 30) to the start of my ACL rules. Why? It makes it easier to edit later. Remember that each rule is applied in order. If I create several rules, the router will save them, and then apply them in the order that they were created.

We can (and in some cases must) configure a numbered rule just like a named rule. To enter the numbered rule configuration, we type **ip access-list <type> <number>**.

If I want to add a new rule but insert it in between the existing rules, I can do so from here. I just give it a number that is in between the existing rules I want to insert it between.

For example, if I want to create a new rule between rules 10 and 20, I could type **15 deny host 5.4.3.6**. But first, I would type **ip access-list standard** 1 to enter the configuration for List 1.

Notice that my router prompt changed to "config-std-nacl," which stands for standard numbered access control list.

```
Router>enable
Router#conf t
Enter configuration commands, one per line.  End with CNTL/Z.
Router(config)#ip access-list standard 1
Router(config-std-nacl)#15 deny host 5.4.3.6
Router(config-std-nacl)#
Router#
%SYS-5-CONFIG_I: Configured from console by console
```

The configuration on my router now is

```
access-list 1 deny host 10.0.0.0
access-list 1 deny host 5.4.3.6
access-list 1 permit host 9.9.9.9
access-list 1 permit host 4.4.4.4
```

Even though we have configured the numbered rule like a named rule, the router will store the configuration like a numbered rule, as a list of global access-list commands.

If I type **show ip access-lists**, I can see the rules with their numbering

```
Router#show ip access-lists
Standard IP access list 1
    10 deny host 10.0.0.0
    15 deny host 5.4.3.6
    20 permit host 9.9.9.9
    30 permit host 4.4.4.4
```

If I want to delete a rule, I can type **no <rule number>**. For example, if I want to delete rule 30, I would type **no 30**.

```
Router#conf t
Enter configuration commands, one per line.  End with CNTL/Z.
Router(config)#ip access-list standard 1
Router(config-std-nacl)#no 30
Router(config-std-nacl)#
Router#
%SYS-5-CONFIG_I: Configured from console by console
show ip access-lists
Standard IP access list 1
    10 deny host 10.0.0.0
    15 deny host 5.4.3.6
    20 permit host 9.9.9.9
|
```

5.3 Configure device access control using local passwords

Remember that there are three ways to access a Cisco router: Telnet, SSH, and Console. And remember that when we create a local account, the password is stored on the router.

The old way to store passwords was in plain text. If we made a back up of the configuration, or if we chose to show the configuration on the router, the password would appear.

To avoid this, in the global configuration, we should type **service password-encryption**. This command encrypts the passwords that were created with the following commands

- The console password created with the **password <password>** command
- The console username/password combination created with the **username <name> password <password>** command
- The enable password created with the **enable password <password>** command

In my example, I chose a password called "blueberries".

```
Router#conf t
Enter configuration commands, one per line.  End with CNTL/Z.
Router(config)#enable password blueberries
Router(config)#show running-config
```

When I show my configuration, the password is stored in plain text

```
!
!
enable password blueberries
!
!
.
```

If I go back and enable the password encryption

```
Router#conf t
Enter configuration commands, one per line.  End with CNTL/Z.
Router(config)#service password-encryption
Router(config)#
Router#
%SYS-5-CONFIG_I: Configured from console by console
```

I see that my password has been changed to something encrypted. I also see the number "7" in front of the password. The "7" tells the router that the password has been encrypted, so that it knows that the random text that follows isn't actually the password.

```
.
!
enable password 7 0823405B0C1B000500020917
!
!
!
```

We can disable the encryption by typing **no service password-encryption**, but the router will not automatically decrypt the existing encrypted passwords – we would still need to change the password for it to be decrypted.

It is easy to reverse engineer the encrypted password that is created with this command via tools on the internet that use rainbow tables.

When setting the enable password, use the **enable secret <password>** command instead of the **enable password <password>** command. Why? The secret command encrypts the password. How does it work?

- When you create the password, the router hashes the password. It puts it through a one-way math equation that results in some random text. It is generally not possible to reverse this equation. The hash equation (or algorithm) is called MD5, but two other forms of hashes are available – SHA-256 and Scrypt. Both are more secure than MD5.

- The router stores the password hash.

- When you try to log in, the router puts the password that you entered through the same hash equation.

- The router compares the hashe it just calculated with the hash that it is storing and if they match, then the router knows you entered the correct password.

If you want to choose a different encryption method, type

- **enable algorithm-type sha256 secret <password>** for SHA-256

- **enable algorithm-type scrypt secret <password>** for Scrypt

On a router, I can configure both an enable password and an enable secret, but I can't configure multiple enable secrets using different algorithms. If both are configured, the enable password command must have a different password than the enable secret command. If both are configured, the user is expected to enter the enable secret password – the router won't accept the enable password password.

```
Enter configuration commands, one per line.  End with CNTL/Z.
Router(config)#enable password blueberries
Router(config)#enable secret blueberries
The enable secret you have chosen is the same as your enable password.
This is not recommended.  Re-enter the enable secret.
Router(config)#enable secret blueberries1
Router(config)#
Router#
```

In my configuration, the secret is stored as "enable secret" and has a "5" in front of it. Notice that the secret is more complicated – it contains special characters that the password doesn't have, even though we encrypted the password.

```
enable secret 5 $1$mERr$.jHJ3J6ga0OF3KscGJrAM/
enable password 7 0823405B0C1B000500020917
!
```

We can change any password by just typing the command again. For example, to change the enable secret, we would just type in **enable secret <password>** in the global configuration mode.

We can go one step further and restrict logins from specific IP addresses. If we know that logins to our router originate from a specific IP address or subnet, we can create a "permit" ACL. For example, if my logins originate from 192.168.5.0 to 192.168.5.255, I would create an ACL that says

access-list 10 permit 192.168.5.0 0.0.0.255

I could go back to my router configuration and add the access-class command. In particular, I would write

access-class 10 in

This command verifies that the user's Telnet or SSH connection originates through the network specified by the ACL list number 10. Remember that a user can also connect to my router and then use it to Telnet or SSH into another router. I could write

access-class 10 out

The "out" in this command restricts connections to the network specified by ACL list number 10. The out command checks the IP address of the device that you're trying to connect to against the ACL, not the IP address of the device that you're trying to connect from.

Remember that this happens in the "line vty" or "line aux" configuration. Below, I've configured an ACL, and then entered the "line vty 0 4" configuration to add that ACL to it.

```
Router(config)#access-list 10 permit 192.168.5.0 0.0.0.255
Router(config)#line vty 0 4
Router(config-line)#access-class 10 in
Router(config-line)#
Router#
%SYS-5-CONFIG_I: Configured from console by console
```

If we look at the configuration, it now shows an ACL present on the line vty 0 4 section.

```
!
line aux 0
!
line vty 0 4
 access-class 10 in
 login
!
!
!
```

5.4 Describe security password policies elements, such as management, complexity, and password alternatives (multifactor authentication, certificates, and biometrics)

How can keep unauthorized users out?

One strategy is to use strong passwords. This is known as password **complexity**.

- A password policy may require a user to have capital letters, numbers, special symbols and/or lowercase letters in their password
- A user cannot repeat a character
- A user cannot use a dictionary word or their name in the password
- The password must have a minimum length

Passwords that are easy to guess represent security risks because they can be broken by brute force.

We can manage user passwords centrally through an Active Directory or RADIUS server. A good password policy

- Requires users to choose complex passwords
- Requires users to change their passwords often (at least every three months)
- Locks a user account if the password is entered incorrectly several times in a short period

But even complex passwords can be guessed or seen by unauthorized users. As phishing and social engineering attacks grow more complex, it is more likely that a user will be tricked into giving up his credentials without realizing it. How can we keep our network safe if the hackers can trick our users into handing over their passwords? There are three ways

- Multifactor authentication
- Certificates
- Biometrics

Multifactor authentication means having to provide more than just your username and password. The principles of **multifactor authentication** (formally two-factor authentication) are important. The three main factors are Something You Are, Something You Have, and Something You Know. Basic authentication methods combine Something You Have (a username/access card) with either Something You Know (a password) or Something You Are (biometric).

- **Something You Are** – something you are refers to a biometric identity such as facial recognition, fingerprints, voice recognition, or a retinal scan. Select the best type of biometric for your environment. A construction site or hospital may have employees with gloves or

- **Something You Have** – something you have refers to a smartcard, identification card, or username; it could also refer to a randomly generated password (such as an RSA SecurID or authenticator app)
- **Something You Know** – something you know refers to a password or PIN
- **Somewhere You Are** – somewhere you are refers to your physical location. In the case of connecting to the internet, somewhere you are is your IP address. If a hacker compromises a username/password and logs in through a computer or network location that is not recognized, then the login may be denied. Websites have sophisticated ways of detecting users – IP address, web browser version, computer version, date/time of the login, other user behaviors. If the username/login is correct, but the other factors aren't it could be that the account was compromised, or it could be that the user is travelling/bought a new computer. The site can ask the user for additional verification (such as through an automated phone call)
- **Something You Do** – something you do is an observation of the user's action's or behaviors. In Windows a user can choose a picture password; in an Android phone the user can interact with a pattern.

Instead of entering a username and password, a user can present a certificate to the authentication server. A certificate is a digital file that confirms the identity of a user or device. A certificate must be signed by a certification authority. IEEE 802.1X is a standard for Network Access Control. It allows a device to authenticate when connecting to a LAN or WAN.

There are three devices in the protocol

- The **supplicant** is the device that chooses to connect to the LAN/WAN. It could be a laptop, desktop, smartphone, tablet, or other computing device
- The **authenticator** is a network device that allows/denies access. It could be a switch, a router, a firewall, or a proxy server.
- The **authentication** server is a server that decides whether a device should be granted access

The procedure works as follows

- The supplicant connects to the network
- The authenticator (switch) detects the new supplicant and automatically sets the port to an unauthenticated status. Only traffic related to 802.1X is permitted.
- The authenticator sends frames to the supplicant. These frames demand that the supplicant provide credentials such as a user ID. The frames are sent on the local network segment to a specific address (01:80:C2:00:00:03). The supplicant listens for messages on this address.
- The supplicant replies to the message with an EAP-Response Identity frame
- The authenticator sends the supplicant's response to an authentication server

- The authentication server and the supplicant negotiate an authentication method. The server and the supplicant may support different methods and must agree on one that both understand. The negotiation methods are transported through the authenticator.
- The authentication server attempts to authenticate the suppliant. If successful, the authenticator changes the port status to authorized. If unsuccessful, the authenticator keeps the port status as unauthorized.

When the supplicant logs off or is disconnected, the authenticator changes the port status back to unauthorized. When the supplicant logs off, it sends an EAPOL-Logoff message to the authenticator.

Biometrics are used in combination with other devices to provide an additional layer of authentication. These include

- Facial recognition
- Finger print reader
- Voice recognition
- Palm reader
- Retinal scan

A biometric reader takes a photograph of a human body part and then converts it into a mathematical model. For example, a fingerprint reader understands the bumps and ridges on a fingerprint and compares their relative sizes. There are many different algorithms and each one is different.

Not every scan is perfect. Most biometrics have a false positive because of the algorithm. The false positive rate for a fingerprint sensor is approximately 1 in 50,000.

A biometric reader does not (and cannot) create a pixel-by-pixel comparison of a person. Imagine taking a photograph of your face 100 times. Each photo will be slightly different. The lighting, the reflection, the angle of your head, and the position of your hair will be slightly different each time.

What are some pros and cons of the different biometric devices?

- **Fingerprints**
    - A fingerprint scanner maps a person's fingerprint and converts it into a mathematical signature. This signature is stored.
    - It later compares new scans to the original mathematical signature.
    - Advanced fingerprint scanners can verify that a real finger has been scanned (as opposed to a mold of a finger)
    - Fingerprint scanners are cheaper than other biometric sensors

- **Retinal Scan**
  - A retinal scan uses a laser to examine the blood vessels in the back of the eye
  - Retinal scans are unpopular because they require a user to have a laser shined into his eye; the user must also put his eye up against the sensor
- **Iris**
  - An iris scan photographs the front of the eye from a distance
  - Iris scanners are more popular than retinal scanners
- **Voice Recognition**
  - Voice recognition is hard to implement
  - Voice recognition sensors have a high rate of false positives and false negatives
- **Facial Recognition**
  - Facial recognition scans features that are present on the user's face
  - Facial recognition systems work well

5.5 Describe remote access and site-to-site VPNs

An employee might want to work from home or on the road but needs access to the corporate network. We can't build a WAN link to each user because that would be too expensive.

A VPN or Virtual Private Network allows us to connect to the corporate network and pretend that we are physically on the network. The user uses his own personal internet connection, and the VPN software transports the data back to the corporate network over a tunnel. The VPN also encrypts the traffic.

We can also use a VPN to connect a remote site to our main network when a WAN is not available or too expensive.

There are several types of internet connections available to end users and VPNs can be established over all of them.

A DSL or **Digital Subscriber Line** is delivered over a phone line. It may provide speeds of up to 150 Mbit/s. A subscriber will require a **DSL modem** to convert the signal from a phone line to an ethernet cable. The same phone line can be used to transmit voice simultaneously because internet traffic is transmitted at a different frequency from voice traffic. At the ISP's network, voice and data are filtered and sent to different types of equipment. Voice traffic is routed to a telephone switch, while data traffic travels to an internet router. The device that performs this filtering is called **a digital subscriber line access multiplexer** or **DSLAM**. When a DSL modem powers on, it must synchronize with the DLSAM so that they can agree to filter out noise and errors. After synchronization, a DSL modem is ready to transmit data. A DSL modem will typically have a "link" or "DSL" light that shows its synchronization status. Below is a photo of a common DSL modem.

Cable Broadband is a product competing with the DSL. While DSL is typically provided by a phone company Cable Broadband is provided by a cable television provider and is delivered over a coaxial cable. A subscriber requires a **cable modem** to connect to the network. At the provider's facility, a device known as a **cable modem termination system** is installed. This device synchronizes with the subscriber cable modems and transfers their data to the internet. It is necessary for the ISP to filter video and internet traffic at their data center.

Another option is to install a **Wireless** WAN like a 4G, LTE, or possibly 5G. A cellular modem connects to the ISPs cellular network via an antenna. Each cell tower contains a fiber optic connection back to the ISPs main network. The modem uses a SIM card to authenticate to the network. Many Cisco routers can connect directly to a cellular internet connection via an expansion card. Some Meraki routers can accept a SIM card and connect to a cellular network.

Fiber is quickly replacing copper, even in residential neighborhoods. Most fiber is being installed by the phone companies, which typically have the right to install underground cable. Cable companies and cellular providers own some fiber as well. Metro Ethernet is typically delivered over fiber, although it could be delivered over copper.

The VPN must be able to do the following

- Authenticate each user so that the network can confirm he is legitimate and that he only has access to the resources that he is entitled to.
- Authenticate each network so that the user can confirm that he is connecting to a legitimate corporate network.
- Provide data integrity to confirm that the data received by the network is the data that was sent.
- Provide anti-replay protection to prevent a man-in-the-middle attack – a situation where a hacker can intercept a legitimate packet and resend it in order to gain access to a protected resource
- Encrypt the data so that nobody on the internet can see it.

A **site-to-site VPN** allows two sites to create a connection, like a point-to-point tunnel. At the edge of each network is a router that connects to the internet. We configure the edge routers to create a tunnel between each other, which is always on. The routers use the tunnel to transport data between their locations.

Any internal device at one site can communicate with any internal device on another site without having to create a separate VPN tunnel because the edge routers handle the traffic.

We use a technology like **Generic Routing Encapsulation** to create the tunnel.

Consider this scenario. Computer A is connected to Router A, and Computer B is connected to Router B. Each computer is on a separate LAN, but we don't have a WAN connection between the two LANs.

Router A and Router B create a tunnel so that they can transport traffic between their respective networks. Computer A and Computer B continue to speak with their routers as normal. They do not know anything about the tunnel.

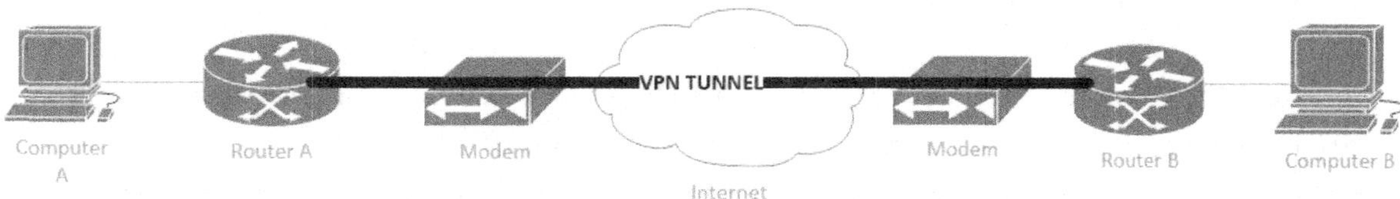

An **IPSec architecture** defines how the VPN will encrypt traffic, but the member devices are free to use any type of protocol to provide encryption or communication. When establishing a tunnel, the two devices must agree on an encryption key. How do two devices agree on an encryption key and share it over the internet without anybody seeing it?

Each device generates two encryption keys. The first encryption key is called the **private key** and can only decrypt data. The device uses the private key to generate a **public key**. The public key only encrypts the data. It is possible to generate a public key from a private key, but it's not possible to generate a private key from a public key.

The device shares its public key with the sender (the other party to the communication). The sender uses the public key to encrypt the data and send it to the recipient. The public key can be placed on the internet without any harm because it can't be used to decrypt the data.

Upon receipt of an encrypted message, the recipient uses its private key to decrypt the data. A device might generate a different set of keys for each party that it communicates with.

There are many algorithms that can be used to generate and exchange the keys. The keys might be known as a **shared secret**. One popular algorithm is called the Diffie-Helman Key Exchange.

There are two problems with using a public/private encryption key. First, it takes a lot of system resources to encrypt and decrypt each message. Second, there is a risk that the private key gets leaked. If a hacker intercepted and stored all our encrypted messages, he could wait until he obtained the key, and then used it to decrypt everything we said.

What we need to do is generate a second simpler key from the encryption key. This key is called a **session key** or an **ephemeral key**. It requires less system resources to encrypt and decrypt data with the session key.

In a communication, we generate a new session key for each message, thereby encrypting each message with a different session key. If a session key is compromised, a hacker will only be able to view the contents of a single message, instead of the entire conversation. The original private key cannot be used to decrypt any messages, so if it is leaked, no communications will be compromised. This is known as **perfect forward secrecy**.

For a user working from home, a better tunnel is a **VPN over TLS**. TLS, or **Transport Layer Security** is a replacement to SSL. TLS is also used to encrypt traffic between a user and a web server. Instead of using an unsecure HTTP protocol, a user's web browser and the web server agree to establish a TLS session and send the HTTP traffic inside it.

Cisco AnyConnect Secure Mobility Client is a software program that we can install on any end user's computer. The Client helps the user connect to the corporate network over a VPN tunnel. Unlike a site-to-site VPN that is always on, a user only activates a remote VPN when he needs to access internal resources.

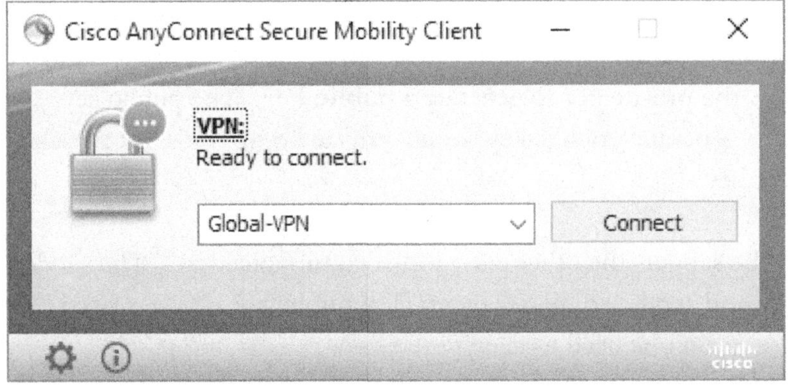

5.7 Configure Layer 2 security features (DHCP snooping, dynamic ARP inspection, and port security)

We've talked about DHCP. What if a hacker installs a rogue DHCP server on your network? He could intercept DHCP messages from clients on your network and give them the wrong IP address, DNS, or gateway information. He could set up a fake gateway or DNS. If a client is configured with the address of this fake DNS or gateway, the hacker could intercept its traffic.

To protect against that, Cisco switches have a feature called **DHCP snooping**. Imagine if we have a remote DHCP server and a hacker installed a rogue DHCP on our local network.

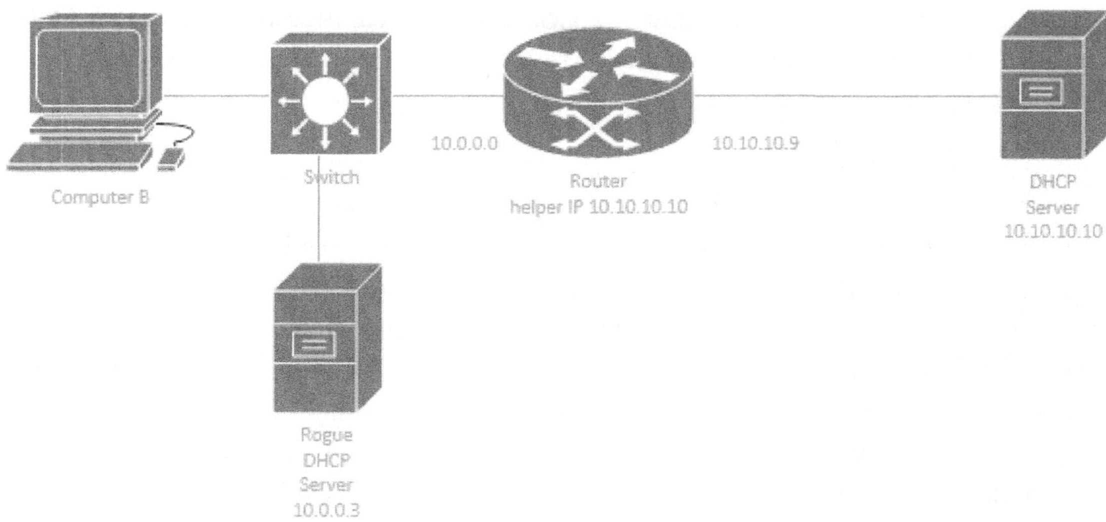

Remember that a DHCP Discover message is a broadcast message. That means that all hosts on our local network will see it. The rogue DHCP server would see our DHCP Discover messages before the remote server because it takes longer for a message to travel through the router.

The DHCP server can give our computer a default gateway that is incorrect and intercept the traffic. For example, it could give our computer a default gateway of 10.0.0.3, which is the IP address for the rogue DHCP server.

Our router will pass the message to the remote DHCP server, which will also respond with a DHCP Offer message. But by then, our computer already received a valid DHCP Offer from the rogue DHCP server. It will most likely not accept a second DHCP Offer.

The way that we fix this is by enabling DHCP snooping on our switch. When snooping is enabled, by default, all switch ports are untrusted. That means that the switch will assume that any DHCP Offer messages entering an untrusted port have originated from a rogue DHCP server, and it will not forward them.

On an untrusted port, the switch will accept DHCP messages from clients. These messages include the DHCP Discover message.

The switch creates a table called the **DHCP Snooping Binding Table**. Each time a client accepts a DHCP Offer, the switch creates an entry in that table. It records the MAC address of the client and the IP address that was assigned to it. It also records the VLAN and interface that the client is connected to.

Say your computer's IP address is 10.5.5.5, and I'm a hacker. I want to kick you off the network, so I send the DHCP server a release message saying, "release IP address 10.5.5.5". The DHCP server will release the IP address and try to assign it to somebody else, which will disrupt your network connection.

DHCP snooping can protect against this kind of attack as well. When the switch sees a new DHCP Release message, it checks that message's sender's MAC address against the table. It will see that the request to release 10.5.5.5 came from my MAC address instead of yours. It knows that the message isn't valid and doesn't let it through.

A hacker might try to lease many hundreds or thousands of DHCP addresses so that nobody else can get any. The switch can protect against this as well. If a client sends a Discover or Request DHCP message, the switch checks its MAC address (the MAC address inside the Ethernet header) against the MAC address inside the actual message. Remember that a DHCP message is something like "hey, my MAC address is aa:bb:cc:dd:ee:ff, can I please have an IP address". This message is encapsulated inside an IP packet which is encapsulated inside an Ethernet frame. If the MAC address sending the message is different from the MAC address inside the message, then the switch knows something is wrong, and doesn't let it through. A hacker might send many DHCP requests from the same MAC address.

When we know which switch ports are connected to legitimate DHCP servers, we tell the switch to trust them.

To configure DHCP snooping

- First, we enter the global configuration and enable DHCP snooping by typing **`ip dhcp snooping`**.
- Second, we enable DHCP snooping on each individual VLAN that requires it by typing **`ip dhcp snooping vlan <VLAN ID>`**.
- Third, we enter the configuration for any interface that is connected to a trusted DHCP server and enable the trust by typing **`ip dhcp snooping trust`**. By default, all other interfaces are untrusted.

On my switch, I enabled DHCP Snooping on VLAN 1 and made port three a trusted port.

```
Switch(config)#ip dhcp snooping
Switch(config)#ip dhcp snooping vlan 1
Switch(config)#interface FastEthernet0/3
Switch(config-if)#ip dhcp snooping trust
Switch(config-if)#
Switch#
%SYS-5-CONFIG_I: Configured from console by console
```

If we look at the new configuration, we can see that DHCP snooping is enabled.

```
ip dhcp snooping vlan 1
ip dhcp snooping
!
spanning-tree mode pvst
spanning-tree extend system-id
!
interface FastEthernet0/1
!
interface FastEthernet0/2
!
interface FastEthernet0/3
 ip dhcp snooping trust
```

I can verify the snooping by typing **`show ip dhcp snooping`**

```
Switch#show ip dhcp snooping
Switch DHCP snooping is enabled
DHCP snooping is configured on following VLANs:
1
Insertion of option 82 is enabled
Option 82 on untrusted port is not allowed
Verification of hwaddr field is enabled
Interface                  Trusted    Rate limit (pps)
-----------------------    -------    ----------------
FastEthernet0/3            yes        unlimited
```

The switch shows that snooping is enabled on VLAN 1 and that FastEthernet0/3 is trusted.

There is a message that says, "Insertion of option 82 is enabled". When a router is configured with a helper IP address to relay DHCP messages to an external DHCP server, it adds additional information into the DHCP request header. This information is known as "option 82". If our switch is a Layer 3 switch and acts as a DHCP relay agent, it will also add "option 82" information.

If our switch isn't acting like a DHCP relay agent, it will change the DHCP messages in a way that will prevent the DHCP server from accepting them. Thus, if our switch isn't a DHCP relay agent (for example if it is not a Layer 3 switch, or if a DHCP server isn't directly connected to it), we should turn this option off. We can do so by typing **no ip dhcp snooping information option**.

Notice also that there is a rate limit. Our interface's rate limit is unlimited. A hacker can attack DHCP Snooping by sending many DHCP messages to overload our switch. If we receive too many DHCP messages on the port and we have set a rate limit, the switch will change that port's status to err-disabled.

We can set the rate limit by typing **ip dhcp snooping limit rate <number>** on each interface. We can set the rate limit on both trusted and untrusted interfaces.

```
Switch(config-if)#ip dhcp snooping limit rate 100
Switch(config-if)#exit
Switch(config)#interface FastEthernet0/3
Switch(config-if)#ip dhcp snooping limit rate 20
Switch(config-if)#
Switch#
```

Now if we look at our snooping status we see FastEthernet0/2 is not trusted and has a rate limit of 100. FastEthernet0/3 has a rate limit of 20. An interface won't appear in our list unless it is either trusted or has a rate limit or both.

```
show ip dhcp snooping
Switch#Switch DHCP snooping is enabled
DHCP snooping is configured on following VLANs:
1
Insertion of option 82 is enabled
Option 82 on untrusted port is not allowed
Verification of hwaddr field is enabled
Interface                  Trusted    Rate limit (pps)
-----------------------    -------    ----------------
FastEthernet0/2            no         100
FastEthernet0/3            yes        20
Switch#
```

The second feature is called **Dynamic ARP Inspection** or **DAI**. Remember that a hacker can send us fake ARP information. If my computer wants to learn the MAC address of another computer (and knows its IP address) on the same network, it sends out an ARP Request. The request says "Hey, if this is your IP address, reply with your MAC address". The other device replies with a message called an ARP Reply.

Each ARP Request and ARP Reply message will list the sender's IP address and MAC address. That means that a device can learn the sender's MAC address from the ARP Request.

If a new device joins the network, it might send a broadcast ARP message to let everybody know about its MAC address. This message is called a **gratuitous ARP** message. It is sent in the format of an ARP Reply to the Ethernet broadcast address.

In my network, Computer B is legitimate. It has an IP address of 10.0.0.4 and a MAC address of AAAA. Computer H belongs to a hacker. It has an IP address of 10.0.0.5 and a MAC address of BBBB. Everybody knows that my computer's IP address is 10.0.0.4 and has a MAC address of AAAA.

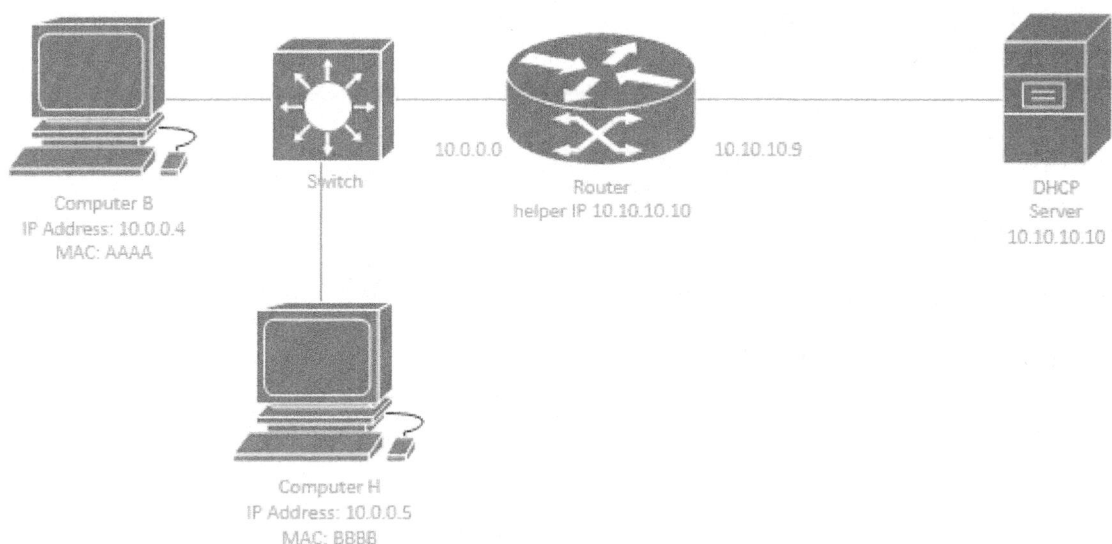

The hacker might send out a fake gratuitous ARP message and tell people that Computer B's MAC address is BBBB. The other devices on the network will update their ARP table to say that IP address 10.0.0.4 belongs to MAC address BBBB.

When a device decides to send Computer B some traffic, it addresses it to IP address 10.0.0.4, but encapsulates that in an Ethernet frame with the MAC address BBBB. The result is that the switch forwards the frame to Computer H, because Computer H has the MAC address BBBB.

If the hacker was really sneaky, Computer H would receive the frames and change their destination to MAC address AAAA, and then send them back over the network to Computer B. Computer B wouldn't notice that its messages were being intercepted.

When we turn on DAI, the switch checks each ARP message's sender's IP address and MAC address against the DHCP Snooping table. If the ARP message matches what's in the table, the message is allowed through. Otherwise, it is blocked.

The drawback of DAI is that a device might have a static IP address and still need to send ARP messages. In that case, it won't appear in the DHCP Snooping table. Thus, we may also need to manually configure some IP Address-MAC Address pairs in our switch. These are called ARP ACLs.

Just like ARP Snooping, we can make some ports trusted and some untrusted. We can also limit the number of ARP messages that a port receives before it is shut down.

To enable ARP Snooping, we type **ip arp inspection vlan <VLAN ID>** in the global configuration for each VLAN that we want to enable ARP snooping on.

Then we add **ip arp inspection trust** to any interface that should be trusted. By default, all ports are untrusted and subject to ARP Inspection.

In this case, I have configured inspection on VLAN 1, and trusted Port 2. ARP messages sent on Port 2 are not inspected.

```
Switch(config)#ip arp inspection vlan 1
Switch(config)#interface FastEthernet0/2
Switch(config-if)#ip arp inspection trust
Switch(config-if)#exit
```

We can verify the ARP by typing **show ip arp inspection**.

```
show ip arp inspection

Source Mac Validation      : Disabled
Destination Mac Validation : Disabled
IP Address Validation      : Disabled

 Vlan     Configuration    Operation   ACL Match          Static ACL
 ----     -------------    ---------   ---------          ----------
    1     Enabled          Inactive

 Vlan     ACL Logging      DHCP Logging      Probe Logging
 ----     -----------      ------------      -------------
    1     Deny             Deny              Off

 Vlan      Forwarded         Dropped     DHCP Drops      ACL Drops
 ----      ---------         -------     ----------      ---------
    1             20              11              0              0

 Vlan   DHCP Permits    ACL Permits  Probe Permits   Source MAC Failures
 ----   ------------    -----------  -------------   -------------------
    1              0              0              0                     0

 Vlan   Dest MAC Failures   IP Validation Failures   Invalid Protocol Data
 ----   -----------------   ----------------------   ---------------------
    1                   0                        0                       0
```

The switch provides me with many statistics for each VLAN, including the number of ARP messages that were forwarded and the number that were dropped.

We can also type **show ip dhcp snooping binding** to view the IP Address-MAC Address bindings that the switch has learned.

I can add a rate limit by typing **ip arp inspection limit rate <Rate>**. By default, the rate is the number of messages per second.

I can also type **ip arp inspection limit rate <Rate> burst interval <interval>**. For example, if I wanted to allow 100 messages every 60 seconds, I would type **ip arp inspection limit rate 100 burst interval 60.**

```
Switch(config)#interface F0/2
Switch(config-if)#ip arp inspection trust
Switch(config-if)#ip arp inspection limit rate 100 burst interval 60
Switch(config-if)#
Switch#
%SYS-5-CONFIG_I: Configured from console by console
```

We can check the status of our ARP inspection on each interface by typing **show ip arp inspection interfaces**. Note that the default rate is 15 messages per second.

```
show ip arp inspection interfaces
Interface         Trust State      Rate(pps)     Burst Interval
---------------   -----------      ---------     --------------
Fa0/1             Untrusted               15                  1
Fa0/2             Trusted                 100                 60
Fa0/3             Untrusted               15                  1
Fa0/4             Untrusted               15                  1
Fa0/5             Untrusted               15                  1
Fa0/6             Untrusted               15                  1
Fa0/7             Untrusted               15                  1
Fa0/8             Untrusted               15                  1
Fa0/9             Untrusted               15                  1
```

Remember that ARP Inspection validates the ARP message's sender's MAC address and IP address. We can also validate its source MAC address, destination MAC address, and/or IP address. We do so by **typing ip arp inspection validate <method>**, where the method is **dst-mac**, **ip**, or **src-mac**, for destination MAC address, IP address, or source MAC address, respectively.

On the below switch, I have configured all of three methods in the same command. I ran the show command after to verify that all three methods are enabled.

```
Switch(config)#ip arp inspection validate dst-mac ip src-mac

Switch(config)#exit
Switch#
%SYS-5-CONFIG_I: Configured from console by console

Switch#show ip arp inspection

Source Mac Validation       : Enabled
Destination Mac Validation  : Enabled
IP Address Validation       : Enabled
```

A key feature on a Cisco switch is **port security**. Remember from the earlier part of this book that each switch remembers the MAC addresses of devices connected to each port. It uses these MAC addresses to forward traffic.

We can use the MAC address table to detect unauthorized devices. If an unauthorized device connects to the switch (as determined by its MAC address), we stop its traffic.

The switch keeps track of the number of unique MAC addresses that it sees on each interface. It also keeps a counter. If the counter exceeds a certain number, it knows that a violation has occurred and turns the port off. For example, if the maximum number of unique MAC addresses is five, and the switch sees six unique devices on a port, it shuts it down.

Port security is activated on a port-by-port basis. Before we can activate port security, we must have manually configured the port to be either an access port or a trunk port.

Remember that we can configure a port mode by typing **switchport mode access** or **switchport mode trunk** from the interface configuration.

Once we have configured the mode, we can enable the port security interface configuration by typing **switchport port-security**.

- We type **switchport port-security maximum <number>** to set the maximum number of unique MAC addresses that a port can see before activating the security measures.

  The port learns MAC addresses of connected devices dynamically and stores them in the MAC address table. To clear the list of MAC addresses that the switch has learned, we must shutdown and no shutdown the port.

  If we want the switch to automatically clear MAC addresses of devices that haven't sent traffic for some time, we type **switchport port-security aging time <time in minutes>**. The timer is between 0 and 1440 minutes. If a MAC address hasn't sent traffic in the time specified by the command, it is removed from the list. This gives another new device the opportunity to use the port.

- We type **switchport port-security mac-address <MAC address>** to set specific MAC addresses that are allowed on the port. We can set multiple MAC addresses with this command by typing this command more than once, each time with a different MAC address.

  The MAC addresses configured by this command count towards the total number of MAC addresses that the switch will see before activating the security measures. For example, if the maximum number of MAC addresses is five, and we have configured three MAC addresses with this command, the switch will learn two more MAC addresses dynamically. This will happen even if the MAC addresses that we configured do not send any traffic.

- We type **switchport port-security mac-address sticky** so that the switch can remember the MAC addresses that it learned dynamically.
    - As soon as we turn this on, the switch will add a **switchport port-security mac-address** entry for each MAC address that it sees or that it had learned dynamically. This configuration will remain until the switch is rebooted.
    - If we set a limit to the number of MAC addresses the switch can learn on that port, then the switch will stop learning MAC addresses after it reaches the limit. If we don't set a limit, the default is one MAC address.
    - This is a useful feature when for example we install a new switch and connect some devices to it. We enable the sticky security and the switch remembers the MAC addresses of the devices connected to each port.

```
Switch#conf t
Enter configuration commands, one per line.  End with CNTL/Z.
Switch(config)#interface FastEthernet0/1
Switch(config-if)#switchport mode access
Switch(config-if)#switchport port-security
Switch(config-if)#switchport port-security mac-address 0001.2222.3333
Switch(config-if)#exit
Switch(config)#interface FastEthernet0/2
Switch(config-if)#switchport port-security
Command rejected: FastEthernet0/2 is a dynamic port.
Switch(config-if)#switchport mode access
Switch(config-if)#switchport port-security
Switch(config-if)#switchport port-security mac-address sticky
Switch(config-if)#exit
Switch(config)#interface FastEthernet0/3
Switch(config-if)#switchport mode access
Switch(config-if)#switchport port-security
Switch(config-if)#switchport port-security maximum 5
Switch(config-if)#
```

In the above, I set the switch to accept only the MAC address 0001.2222.3333 on Port 0/1. I tried to set port security on Port 0/2, but the switch rejected the command because I didn't choose whether the port was an access or trunk port. I then set Port 0/2 to have a sticky MAC address. I set Port 0/3 to allow a maximum of 5 MAC addresses.

When we enable security on a port, by default, the switch allows only one MAC address. Port 0/1 will only accept traffic from the one MAC address – the one that we configured.

We type **`switchport port-security violation <response>`** to set the action that the switch will take once a security violation is detected on that port. A violation occurs when the switch receives traffic from more MAC addresses than the limit specifies or when it receives traffic from a MAC address that is not permitted.

There are three possible responses

- **Protect**. Protect drops the traffic in violation and does nothing else. Traffic from permitted MAC addresses continues to flow through the port.

- **Restrict**. Restrict drops the traffic and keeps a log of the incident. Traffic from permitted MAC addresses continues to flow through the port.

- **Shutdown**. Shutdown drops the traffic, keeps a log of the incident, and shuts down the port. Now no traffic can get through. The port status changes to "err-disabled", and the security status changes to "secure-down". The port will not come back up until we manually shut it down with the **`shutdown`** command, and then turn it back on with the **`no shutdown`** command.

  Having to shutdown and no shutdown ports due to security violations could get annoying, so if we want to avoid it, we can configure the switch to turn the port back on automatically. We type

  - **`errdisable recovery cause psecure-violation`**. This is a global command that applies to all ports and allows the switch to restore the port to functional status after the security shuts it down.

  - **`errdisable recovery interval <time in seconds>`**. This command tells the switch how much time it should wait before restoring the port.

  - **`errdisable recovery cause dhcp-rate-limit`**. This command tells the switch to restore the port if the error was caused by the DHCP Snooping.

  - **`errordisable recovery cause arp-inspection`**. This command tells the switch to restore the port if the error was caused by ARP Inspection.

If we configure port security on a trunk port, we must be careful. A trunk port may see legitimate traffic from dozens or hundreds of MAC addresses. We must configure trunk port security on each individual VLAN within the trunk port. This is beyond the scope of the CCNA, but to enter the VLAN sub-sub configuration, first enter the interface configuration, and then type **`vlan-range <VLAN number or range>`**. Then configure the port security commands as before.

If we configure port security on an EtherChannel, we should do so on the EtherChannel interface, and not the physical interfaces inside the EtherChannel.

We can verify the port security by typing **show port-security interface <interface name>**. For example, if I want to see the port security on GE0/1, I would type **show port-security interface G0/1**.

```
Switch#show port-security interface G0/1
Port Security              : Enabled
Port Status                : Secure-up
Violation Mode             : Shutdown
Aging Time                 : 0 mins
Aging Type                 : Absolute
SecureStatic Address Aging : Disabled
Maximum MAC Addresses      : 1
Total MAC Addresses        : 1
Configured MAC Addresses   : 1
Sticky MAC Addresses       : 1
Last Source Address:Vlan   : AABB.CCDD.EEFF:1
Security Violation Count   : 0
Switch#
```

What does this tell us?

- Port Security tells us that the port security is enabled
- Port Status tells us whether the port is operational. If the status was "**secure-shutdown**", that would mean that the switch shut the port down due to a security violation.
- Violation mode tells us what the switch plans to do with the port when it detects a violation.
- Maximum MAC addresses tells us what the maximum number of different MAC addresses a switch is willing to see on the port before it determines that a security violation has occurred.
- Sticky Mac Addresses tells us the number of sticky MAC addresses that the switch saw.
- Last Source Address:Vlan tells us the last MAC address that the switch saw on that port and the VLAN that it was on.
- Security Violation Count tells us the number of times that the port has been shut down (if shutdown is the violation mode) or the number of invalid frames received by the port (if restrict is the violation mode). If our violation mode is protect, then the security violation count will remain at zero regardless of the number of violating frames received.

After we have enabled port security, MAC addresses for that port stop appearing in the switch's MAC address table, even if the switch learned them through the sticky command. To see them, we must type **`show mac address-table static`**, instead of **`show mac address-table dynamic`**.

5.8 Differentiate authentication, authorization, and accounting concepts

How does a secure system provide access to an individual? Through **IAAA** – also known as **AAA** (**Authentication, Authorization, and Accounting**)

- **Identification** is the process of identifying a person. The person has presented credentials to the system (such as a smart card, an access card, an identification card, or a username). It is possible that the credentials have been compromised, so the system has not verified the person's identity at this stage.
- **Authentication** is when the person has been positively identified. Circumstances where authentication takes place
    - User presented a smart card and entered their PIN correctly
    - Presented an identification card to a security guard who positively compares the photograph on the card with the face of the individual
    - Entered the correct username and password into a computer
    - Scanned an access card at a card reader (the access card is a weak form of authentication because a lost/stolen access card can be used by an unauthorized individual)
- **Authorization** is the process of providing the user with access to the resources that he requested. Just because a user requested access and entered the correct username/password does not mean that the user is entitled to access.
    - For example, a user comes to work on a weekend but is not permitted. The security guard recognizes the employee as a legitimate employee and verifies his identification but does not permit access.
    - A user logs in to an HR system with the correct username and password but is not authorized to access the system.
- **Accounting** is the process of keeping track of who accessed what. Accounting is important for audits, and to ensure that all access attempts are legitimate. For example, patients have the right to know who accesses their personal health data. A nurse at a hospital may have the ability (authorization) to access the electronic health records of any patient at the hospital but should only do so if she has a legitimate need (and not because she is curious). The system should be able to track every time a patient record was accessed.
- We should log the following
    - What credentials were used (username, password, etc.)?
    - What system did they log in to (computer, door, entrance, etc.)?
    - What resources did they access (shared folder, printer, etc.)?
    - When did the access take place?

5.9 Describe wireless security protocols (WPA, WPA2, and WPA3)

How do we keep our wireless network secure when we are sending bits of data out in the air that anybody with a packet sniffer can pick up. The goal of security is four-fold

- Ensure that only authorized users can access the network and ensure that each user has access to only the resources that he needs.
- Ensure that users connect to the legitimate network and not to a fake SSID that is pretending to be part of the real network (a rogue AP).
- Keep the data secure so that unauthorized users can't view it.
- Keep the data intact so that it is not tampered with on its way to the destination.

The most basic type of security requires the user to enter a passcode when connecting to an SSID. All users are given the same passcode and it is not possible to determine which users connected or when. An unauthorized user who knows the passcode can also connect.

The second type of security requires the user to enter a username and password when connecting to the network. The LAP or WLC verifies the username and password with a central database like Active Directory or RADIUS. It is less likely that an unauthorized user will guess the correct username and password combination. Also, we can determine which users have connected to the network, monitor their activities, and provide them with access to only the resources that they require.

What if I set up a fake LAP and used it to broadcast the same SSID as your real network? Your users would connect to it, thinking that it is the real thing. I could capture data from your users. I could also forward the data to a real LAP so that users don't notice that they have connected to a fake LAP. This is called a man in the middle attack.

If I just wanted to be annoying, I could send signals to clients connected to legitimate LAPs which tell them to disconnect from the LAPs. These signals are called management frames.

How do we keep the data secure between each host and the LAP? Each LAP and each host encrypts data right before it transmits it, and decrypts data upon receipt. A LAP (an entire wireless network actually) will only support one form of encryption, but each client chooses a unique encryption key to communicate with the LAP so that other users cannot read its communication.

There are several forms of encryption

- **Open Authentication**. We do not encrypt any data. Anybody who wants to connect to our network can.
- **WEP** or **Wired Equivalent Privacy**. The client must enter a password (known as a WEP key) to connect to the wireless network. The client and LAP use the WEP key to choose an

encryption key. The data between the client and the LAP is encrypted with the chosen key. All the clients must use the same WEP key, which must be shared ahead of time.

WEP has been broken and is not considered secure. We should not use WEP.

- **802.1x/EAP** or **Extensible Authentication Protocol**. When WEP was introduced, it was considered the standard for encryption, and network devices were built around it. When it became insecure, administrators were left panicking because their devices had to be replaced.

  Thus, EAP was invented. EAP lets a host authenticate with a network, but the host and the network can choose their own authentication method within EAP. That way, if some of the authentication methods become insecure, we can choose new ones and continue to use EAP, without having to replace the network devices.

  Using EAP, a client can associate with a WAP, but is not allowed to access deeper parts of the network until it is authenticated. This is different from WEP where a client can authenticate with the WAP.

  There are three devices
    - The **supplicant** is the client that chooses to connect to the LAN/WAN. It could be a laptop, desktop, smartphone, tablet, or other computing device
    - The **authenticator** is a network device that allows/denies access. It could be a switch, a router, a firewall, or a proxy server. In the Wi-Fi case, it is probably a WLC.
    - The **authentication server** is a server that decides whether a device or user should be granted access

  The procedure
    - The supplicant connects to the network
    - The authenticator (switch) detects the new supplicant and automatically sets the port to an unauthenticated state. Only traffic related to 802.1X is permitted.
    - The authenticator sends frames to the supplicant. These frames demand that the supplicant provide credentials such as a user ID. The frames are sent on the local network segment to a specific address (01:80:C2:00:00:03). The supplicant listens for messages on this address.
    - The supplicant replies to the message with an EAP-Response Identity frame
    - The authenticator sends the supplicant's response to an authentication server
    - The authentication server and the supplicant negotiate an authentication method. The server and the supplicant may support different methods and must agree on one. The negotiation methods are transported through the authenticator.
    - The authentication server attempts to authenticate the suppliant. If successful, the authenticator changes the port status to authorized. If unsuccessful, the authenticator keeps the port as unauthorized.

    - When the supplicant logs off or is disconnected, the authenticator changes the port status back to unauthorized. When the supplicant logs off, it sends an EAPOL-Logoff message to the authenticator.
- **Lightweight Extensible Authentication Protocol** or **LEAP**. LEAP was developed by Cisco to plug the hole created by WEP. The client must provide a username and password, which are checked by the authentication server. The server authenticates the client and the client authenticates the server. LEAP used WEP to encrypt the traffic but changed the keys every few minutes. Eventually, LEAP was found to be insecure, but it can still be configured on a Cisco WAP.
- After LEAP, Cisco developed **EAP-FAST**, or **Flexible Authentication via Secure Tunneling**. The supplicant sends the authentication server a credential called a **Protected Access Credential**, or **PAC**. The PAC is a shared secret that only the server and client know. This shared secret is generated via the Diffie-Hellman key exchange. The process
    - Phase 0: The PAC is generated by the client
    - Phase 1: The client and server authenticate each other and create a tunnel
    - Phase 2: Optionally, the server can authenticate the end user (not just the client hardware). We call this an inner and outer authentication.
- **PEAP** or **Protected Extensible Authentication** Protocol. Originally, EAP assumed that communications would be secure; therefore, it did not provide a mechanism to secure the data being transmitted. PEAP corrects this by providing a secure TLS tunnel.

  The authentication server has a digital certificate that it presents to the supplicant. This certificate is signed by a third party (a certificate authority or CA) that the supplicant and authentication server trust. Since the supplicant trusts the CA, it trusts the certificate signed by the CA, and therefore, it trusts the authentication server. We want to make sure that we have connected to a legitimate authentication server and not a fake, so that we don't provide the fake server with our username and password.

  How does the server know that the client is legitimate? Once the client and the server have established a TLS tunnel, they can use a second authentication method to verify the identity of the user. PEAP permits the use of **MSCHAPv2**, or **Microsoft Challenge Authentication Protocol version 2**, or **GTC** or **Generic Token Card**.
- **EAP-TLS** or **EAP-Transport Layer Security u**ses TLS (Transport Layer Security) as its protocol. All wireless manufacturers support EAP-TLS, and it is considered secure.

  The authentication server maintains a certificate and every client device maintains a certificate. To establish a connection, the authentication server and the supplicant must exchange certificates and then create a TLS tunnel. Again, these certificates are usually signed by a third party.

  Once we have a secure tunnel, we can authenticate a user through the tunnel.

The problem with EAP-TLS is that we must install a certificate on each client device. This is not easily done manually when there are many devices. We must also be aware that many devices (industrial devices, medical devices, etc.) do not support the use of certificates for authentication. Thus EAP-TLS is not always a practical option.

The recipient also needs to make sure that the message I sent hasn't been modified. Before a device sends a message, it creates a fingerprint of the message by performing a specific calculation on its contents. The fingerprint is sent with the message. The recipient calculates the same fingerprint upon receipt and compares it with the fingerprint inside the message. If the results match, then the recipient knows that the message was not modified during transmission. This is known as **integrity**. How can we verify the integrity of the message? There are several algorithms.

- **TKIP** or **Temporal Key Integrity Protocol** was used ensure integrity in transmissions over WEP. TKIP was invented when WEP was found to be insecure, but the industry needed a temporary solution to encrypt wireless transmissions over the existing hardware until a better system could be developed.

  Each time we send a frame, we perform a calculation known as **MIC**, or **Message Integrity Check**. What does the MIC contain?

  - A signature (hash value) of the message contents
  - A time stamp. We add a time stamp so that a hacker can't intercept the message and send it again. If he does, the message will appear to arrive late.
  - The sender's MAC address
  - The TKIP sequence counter. Each time the sender creates a new message, it increments the counter by one. If a hacker intercepts the message and sends it again, the recipient will receive two messages with the same sequence number and will know that the second message was fake. This prevents a replay attack.

  TKIP uses a key mixing algorithm to generate a new WEP key for each frame sent. It also uses a 48-bit initialization vector which prevents a hacker from brute forcing the frames. The initialization vector, or IV, is a random set of data that is included in the key generation process.

  TKIP is no longer considered secure.

- CCMP or Counter/CBC-MAC Protocol was developed after TKIP. It uses two algorithms

  - AES or Advanced Encryption Standard

- CBC-MAC or Cipher Block Chaining Message Authentication Code

  CCMP is used by WPA2

- GCMP or Galois/Counter Mode Protocol. It also uses two algorithms
  - AES or Advanced Encryption Standard
  - GMAC or Galois Message Authentication Code

  GCMP is used by WPA3

After the failure of WEP, the industry (the Wi-Fi Alliance) developed WPA or Wi-Fi Protected Access. There are three types of Wi-Fi Protected Access (WPA): WPA, WPA2, and WPA3.

While the IEEE was still working on a regulation for protecting Wi-Fi, WPA was created by the Wi-Fi Alliance using the 802.1x authentication and TKIP. WPA is no longer considered secure.

After the IEEE released 802.11i, the Wi-Fi Alliance used it to create the WAP2 standard, which uses the CCMP algorithm. WPA2 is the current standard, but WPA3 has been introduced to replace it. It uses a better encryption algorithm.

In summary

Feature	WPA	WPA2	WPA3
Pre-shared Key Authentication and 802.1x Authentication	Yes	Yes	Yes
TKIP Encryption	Yes	No	No
Encryption	AES and CCMP	AES and CCMP	AES and GCMP

Providing a user with a pre-shared key is also known as **personal mode**. In personal mode, we give each user a key string. The key string is used by the LAP and the client to exchange data and to generate encryption keys via a four-way handshake. The key is not transmitted, but if a hacker were to capture the data, he could perform a brute force attack and guess the key.

While personal mode under WPA and WPA2 can be broken, personal mode under WPA3 has forward secrecy and **Simultaneous Authentication of Equals**. That means that each message is transmitted with a different key. If the encryption key is broken, the hacker can only intercept message that was sent with that key and not new messages or previous messages.

802.1x authentication is called **enterprise authentication**. All three versions of WPA support enterprise authentication through the EAP scheme, but no specific EAP method is required.

Enterprise authentication means that a user authenticates through a third-party server such as a RADIUS or Active Directory server.

How can my users determine that they have connected to a legitimate LAP? We would create a certificate for the network, which is digitally signed by our organization or by a third party. We configure each end user device to trust this certificate and to only connect to networks that present a trusted certificate. When an end user device connects to our legitimate network, it verifies the presence of the trusted certificate.

A rogue network will not hold a certificate but might broadcast the same SSID. When an end user device attempts to connect to a rogue network, it will notice the lack of the signed certificate and refuse to connect.

5.10 Configure WLAN using WPA2 PSK using the GUI

The CCNA requires us to know how to configure a WLAN with WPA2 PSK security on a Cisco WLC via the web-based GUI. It does not require us to configure it via a console, but this is possible.

Go to Configuration > Wireless > WLAN > WLANs. Create a new WLAN as before.

Once the WLAN is created, go to the Security tab inside the WLAN configuration. Check the WPA2 Policy box. Check the WPA2 Encryption AES box. Enter a Pre-Shared Key under the PSK section.

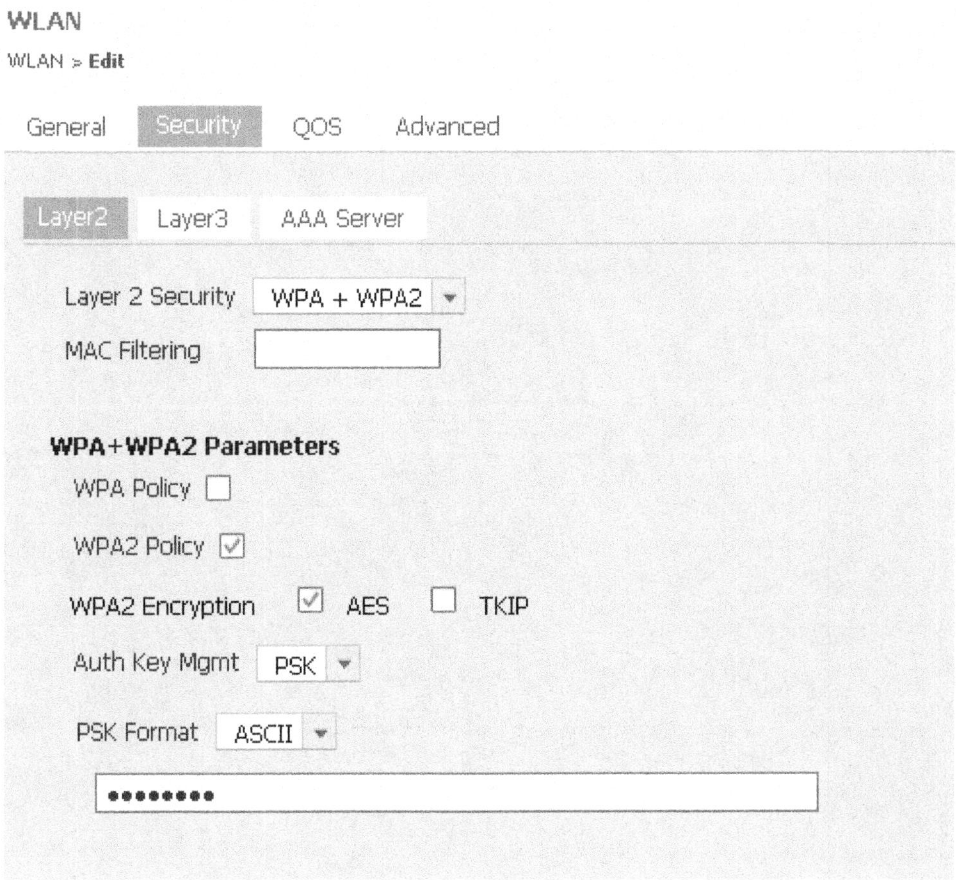

6.0 Automation and Programmability

6.1 Explain how automation impacts network management

Eventually, the first five chapters of this book will become obsolete and all networks will be automated.

Automation allows us to configure a network without thinking about the granular management of each physical device. Instead of configuring VLANs, duplex, speed, PoE, etc on each switch port, we create policies that tell us how the network will function. A controller interprets those policies and automatically configures the devices.

Network Management also allows us to automatically gather data from multiple devices and verify that they are functional. We can be alerted in the event of an issue.

I mentioned the "show" command many times in this book. Think about the output of the **`show ip interface brief`** command.

```
Router#show ip interface brief
Interface              IP-Address      OK? Method Status                Protocol
GigabitEthernet0/0/0   unassigned      YES unset  up                    down
GigabitEthernet0/0/1   unassigned      YES DHCP   administratively down down
GigabitEthernet0/0/2   unassigned      YES unset  administratively down down
Loopback0              100.100.100.100 YES manual up                    up
Vlan1                  unassigned      YES unset  administratively down down
```

It tells us the status of each router interface, including its IP address and whether it is up or down.

Now think about how we could obtain this information from each router automatically

- We would need a list of router IP addresses
- We would create a script that automatically logged in to each router
- The script would enter the enable mode and enter the enable password
- It would write the **`show ip interface brief`** command and record the output
- We would create another script and use it to process the results from the output, including the types of interfaces available and their status. It would have to understand the columns from each output.
- If we had different models of routers that required different commands, the script would need to figure out which command to enter for each router.

If each model of router provided the output in a different format, our script would need to interpret the different formats.

We can use this data to create a graphical user interface or store it in a database. With a script, we don't have to manually log in to each router and check its status. We can look at a dashboard and automatically see the status of dozens or hundreds of router interfaces at the same time.

It is much easier to automate a network when devices allow us to automatically collect data. That requires some effort on the part of the manufacturer.

Some of the benefits of automatic device configuration

- We can configure each device from a template, instead of manually. This reduces the risk of error.
- We can change device configuration based on the time of day or day of the week, which would not be possible if we had to do so manually.
- We can change device configuration based on user demand.
- We are better able to analyse data.

An example of an automation tool is the Cisco Meraki dashboard

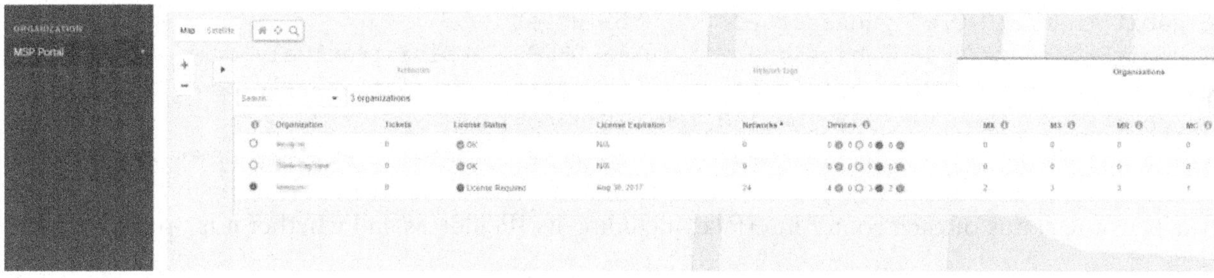

6.2 Compare traditional networks with controller-based networking & 6.3 Describe controller-based and software defined architectures (overlay, underlay, and fabric)

6.3.a Separation of control plane and data plane

6.3.b North-bound and south-bound APIs

A **Software Defined Network** or **SDN** is also known as **Software Defined Architecture** or **SDA**, **Programmable Networks**, or **Controller-Based Networks**.

With an SDN, we don't need to worry about manually configuring each device and each interface. We draw out a policy framework, and the controller configures the underlying devices. This is faster and reduces errors.

Earlier, I spoke about the data plane and the control plane. The data plane carries user traffic while the control plane carries configuration and monitoring for the network devices. The control plane operates the protocols that help the data plane function.

What does the data plane do?

- Adds and removes Ethernet headers and trunk headers
- Adds and removes IP headers
- Decides how to forward a frame based on its MAC address
- Decides how to forward a packet based on its IP address
- Operates Network Address Translation
- Encrypts and decrypts data
- Establishes a VPN connection
- Enforces the Access Control Lists, Port Security, DHCP Snooping

What does the control plane do?

- Manages ARP
- Manages Spanning Tree Protocol
- Manages Neighbor Discovery Protocol
- Allows a switch to learn MAC addresses

- Manages routing protocols such as OSPF, EIGRP, and BGP

The management plane allows us to configure and monitor the network devices. It includes

- Telnet
- SSH
- SNMP
- Syslog

Inside the switch is a circuit called the **Application-Specific Integrated Circuit** or **ASIC**. The ASIC is a custom-designed circuit that only knows how to forward ethernet frames by checking the switch's MAC address table. We use an ASIC because standard hardware won't perform as efficiently. This is important because the switch might be forwarding millions of frames per second.

The MAC address table is stored inside the **ternary content-addressable memory**, or **TCAM**. The TCAM is a special type of memory that lets us search the table instantly. If we give the TCAM a MAC address, it gives us the matching entries instantly.

The idea now is to use a Software Defined Network to centralize the control of our network. In a traditional network, the control plane is distributed across all the devices. That means that every router or switch makes its own decisions. For example, every router makes its own decisions about forwarding packets, and each switch makes its own decision about forwarding frames.

A centralized control plane can be more efficient. We use a SDN controller. The amount of centralized control varies from network to network. The controller can be anywhere in the physical network, but it must be able to reach every network device.

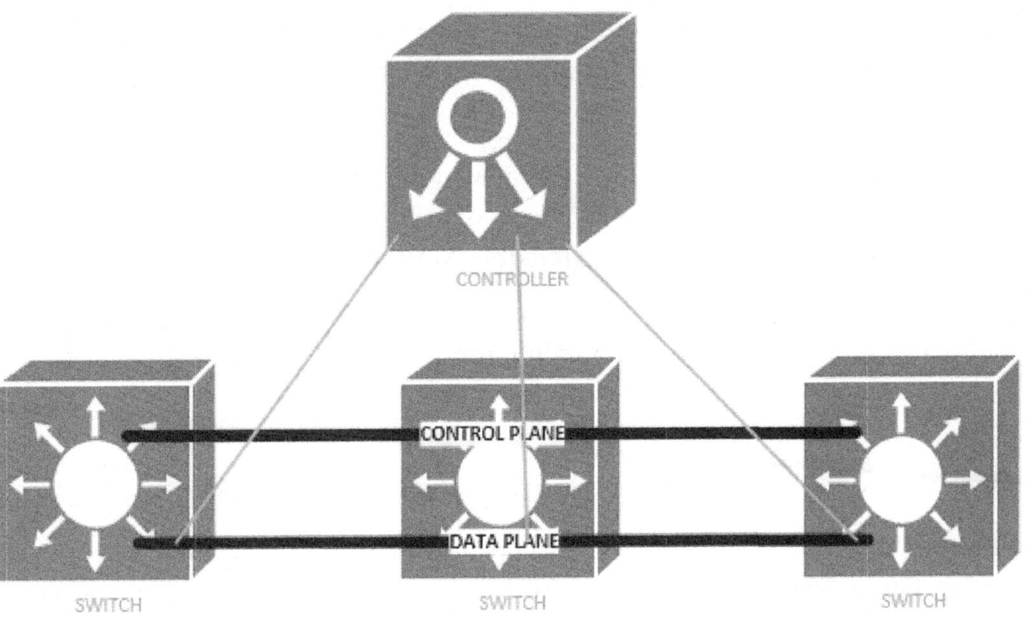

In a controller there are two interfaces

- The **Southbound Interface** or **SBI** is the interface between the controller and its devices that it controls. Its name comes from the fact that in network diagrams, the controller sits above the devices that it controls.

  The Southbound Interface is not just a physical interface, but also a set of protocols that allow the controller to control network devices. It might also include an **API** or **Application Programming Interface**. An API lets two different programs talk to each other. The developer of each program creates a common set of instructions or words that one program can use to talk to another program.

  There are many different models of SBIs. The official Cisco SBI is called **OpFlex**. Other programs include OpenFlow, Telnet, and SNMP.

- The **Northbound Interface** or **NBI** allows us to read the data inside the controller. We can send commands to the controller, and the controller can send commands to the network devices that it manages.

  Technically, the controller can be a software program that is on a server. Another application can connect to the controller via an API. We can create programs or workflows that interact with the controller for monitoring, filtering, or controlling traffic.

A **REST API** or **Representational State Transfer API** is one that allows different APIs to exist on different physical devices. The APIs communicate via HTTP or HTTPs messages. We communicate with a Rest API by visiting a specific URL. We will see some examples further in this section.

An API is designed to return structured data. If we understand the format of the data that we will receive, we can write a program to interpret it. The two main API languages are **JSON** or **JavaScript Object Notation** and **XML**, or **eXtensible Markup Language**.

Our Application sends the Controller a request over its API by sending a message called an **HTTP GET URI**. The Controller replies with an **HTTP GET Response**, which includes the data.

There are three main controllers: OpenFlow, OpenDaylight, and Open SDN.

The **Open Networking Foundation** produces an open-source Software Defined Networking framework called **OpenFlow**. The Foundation works with many network engineers and vendors of network equipment so that they can help create an SDN framework that works on all devices. That means any brand of network equipment can work with any other brand of network equipment.

OpenFlow defines network devices as abstract ideas with standard capabilities. For example, the idea of a switch is a device that forwards traffic based on its destination MAC address. Most of the control plane is centralized by OpenFlow. The controller and applications that talk to the controller control the network.

The **OpenDaylight Controller** is an open-source controller based on the ONF Framework. Any SDN controller vendor can use the OpenDaylight Controller as the basis for their own commercial controller. The controller supports several SBIs including BGP and OpenFlow. Any vendor can take this controller and customize it for their own use.

Cisco's version of the OpenDaylight Controller is called the **Open SDN Controller**, or **OSC**, but it is no longer available. The current version is called the **Software-Defined Access** or **SDA** and the **Software-Defined WAN** or **SD-WAN** (SD-WAN is supported by many other vendors).

When designing an SDN, instead of thinking about the physical layer (Layer 1) of the OSI model, we should focus on the application layer (Layer 7). What resources do applications on Layer 7 need to function? Once we understand that, we can build a network to support them. We call this **Application Centric Infrastructure** or **ACI**.

One feature of the new software defined network is not worrying about manually configuring each physical interface. Remember from our earlier part of the book that on a single switch interface, we can give it a speed, duplex, description, ACL, VLAN, make it trusted or untrusted, etc. Across an entire network, we may have thousands or hundreds of thousands of switch ports.

Going back to the beginning of the book, I talked about a Spine Leaf topology. We also call it a Clos network. Each leaf switch is connected to each spine switch, but no leaf switches connect to each other, and no spine switches connect to each other. An end user device connects to a leaf switch. Most of the end user devices will be routers and servers. An end user device can connect to multiple leaf switches.

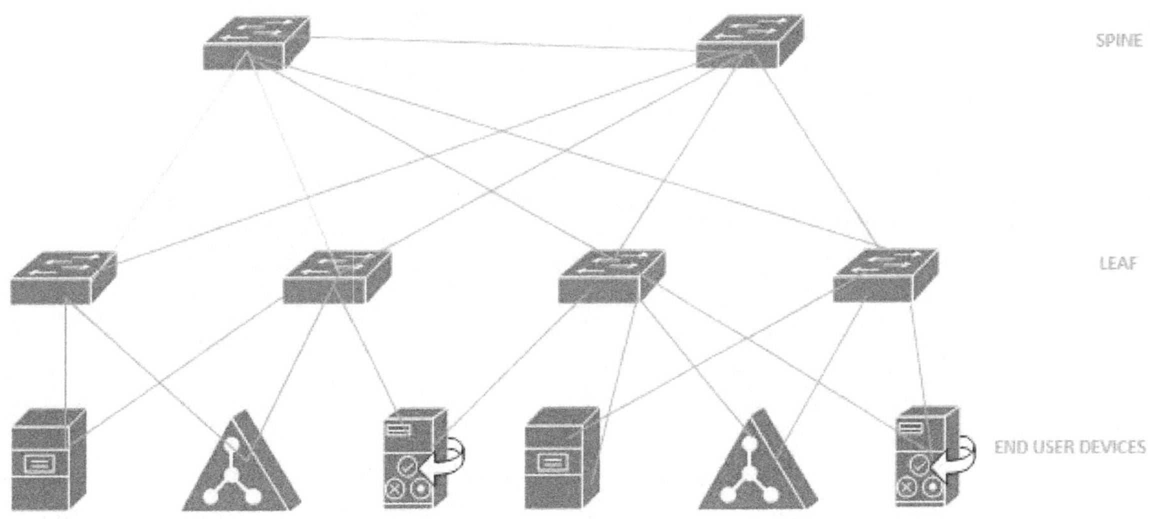

An **Application Policy Infrastructure Controller** or **APIC** controls the ACI. ACI uses an **Intent-Based Networking model**, or **IBN**. Instead of manually configuring each switch interface, we create some policies that tell the network what type of devices can communicate. The controller analyses these policies and configures the physical network hardware to match the intent of the policies. If we move equipment to other physical locations within the network, the ACI reconfigures the hardware so that it continues to match the intent of the policies.

Think about a large website like Amazon.com

- It has a front-end website that serves the product catalog, pages, reviews, etc.
- It has a content delivery network that provides product photographs, videos, etc.
- It has a database that holds product information, reviews, etc.
- It has a payment application that processes credit cards.

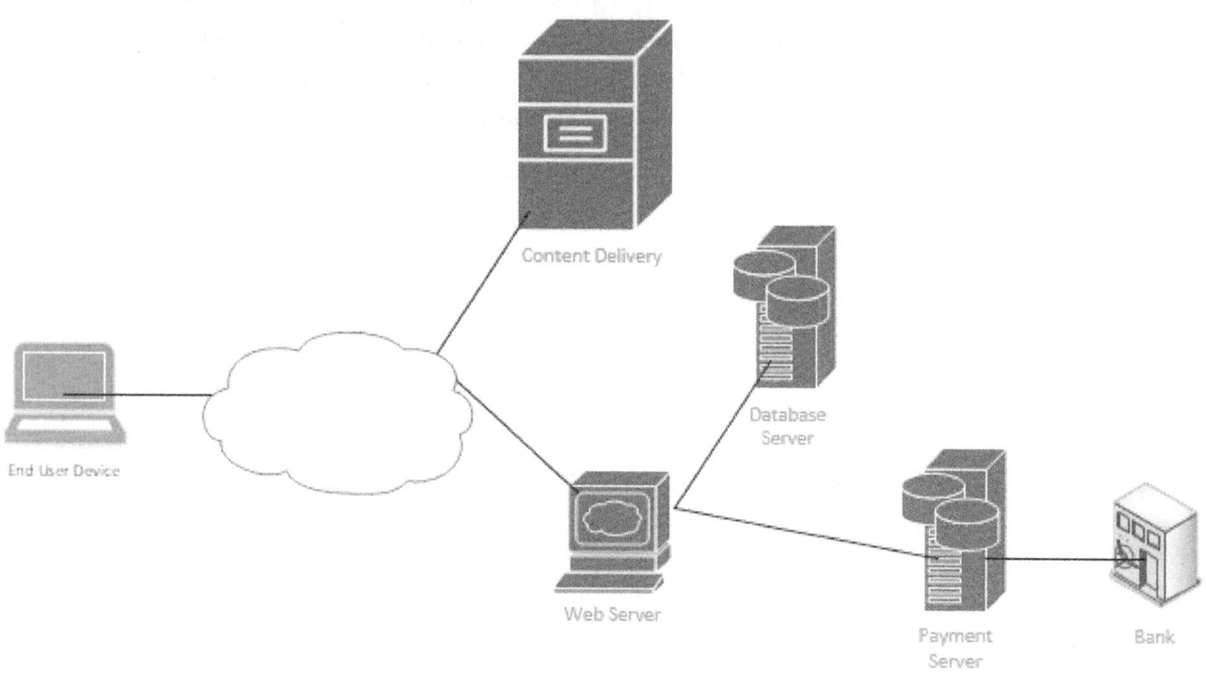

When you visit the website, your computer requests a specific page from the Web Server. Every Amazon product page is just a template. Amazon's server figures out the product number of the page that you visited and calls up a database that contains the product's price, properties, and reviews. It fills out the product page template and sends it to your web browser. The page also includes links to photographs. Your web browser manually downloads the photographs from Amazon's content delivery network and inserts them into the page.

At no time should you be able to directly connect to Amazon's database – only to its web server and content delivery network. If Amazon uses a controller, it can create these kinds of policies on its network. For example, it would create a policy that allows only web servers and database administrators to connect to its database server.

It's not that our switch doesn't have VLANs, access ports, trunk ports, speeds, duplex, or security settings. But we don't have to worry about it anymore. We just create policies and the APIC creates all the configurations.

In an Enterprise network, we can use the **APIC Enterprise Module** or **APIC-EM**. One problem is that many networks have legacy devices that don't support SDN. Cisco knew that a customer would not purchase an SDN if they had to replace all the underlying network hardware such as switches and routers, thus they introduced the APIC-EM. It allows us to keep the same equipment but configure it via an SDN controller instead of via Telnet, SSN, or a console cable.

What can the APIC-EM do?

- It allows us to automatically map out the topology of our network
- It can show us how data flows through our network (if we provide it with a source and destination, it can create a diagram demonstrating the pathway)
- It can show us how the network makes forwarding decisions at each router or switch interface
- It allows us to automatically configure new devices as soon as they are connected to the network
- It allows us to manage Quality of Service

APIC-EM can't automatically configure any devices that do not support automatic configuration, but it can automatically configure them via Telnet, SSH, or SNMP. It can also verify the configuration on any device. On legacy devices it can't make deep configuration changes such as changes to a switch's MAC address table.

APIC-EM is no longer being sold by Cisco, but it is still in use. As customers continue to upgrade their networks, some will replace their hardware with cloud managed equipment and some won't.

At the top of our network is our controller. We can connect to it via an App, a GUI, or a Script. The controller connects to the physical network through its Southbound Interface. We call the physical switch structure below the fabric. The fabric contains two components

- The overlay creates VLAN tunnels (called **VXLAN** tunnels) between different switches. The overlay allows us to move traffic from one end user device to another.
- The underlay connects each end user device with an IP address. The underlay helps us discover the different connected devices on the network.

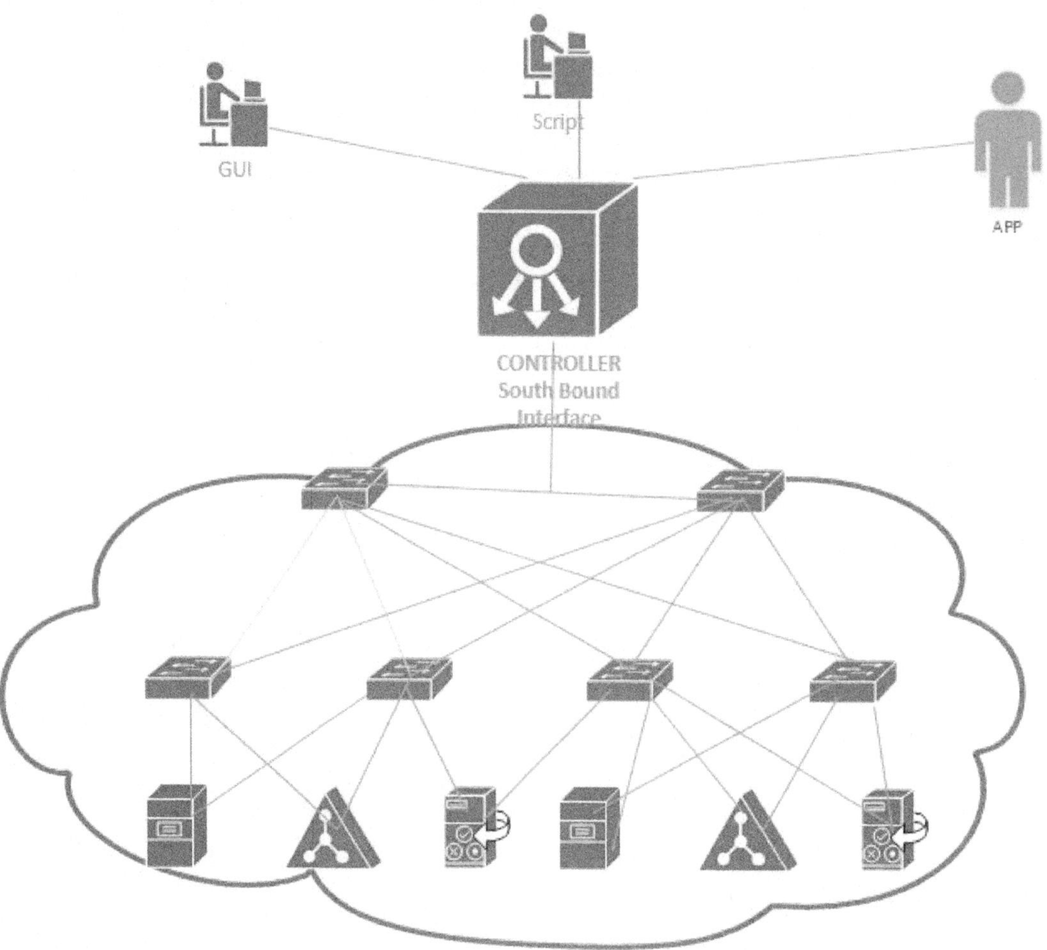

We create a VXLAN tunnel between each switch. The VXLAN tunnel allows end-user traffic to flow through the network. This is supported by the **Cisco Virtual Extensible LAN** protocol.

A VXLAN is a tunnel that allows end-user traffic to flow through the network. A computer on the left wants to talk to a computer on the right. The switches in the pathway create a VXLAN tunnel between the two devices and transport their traffic.

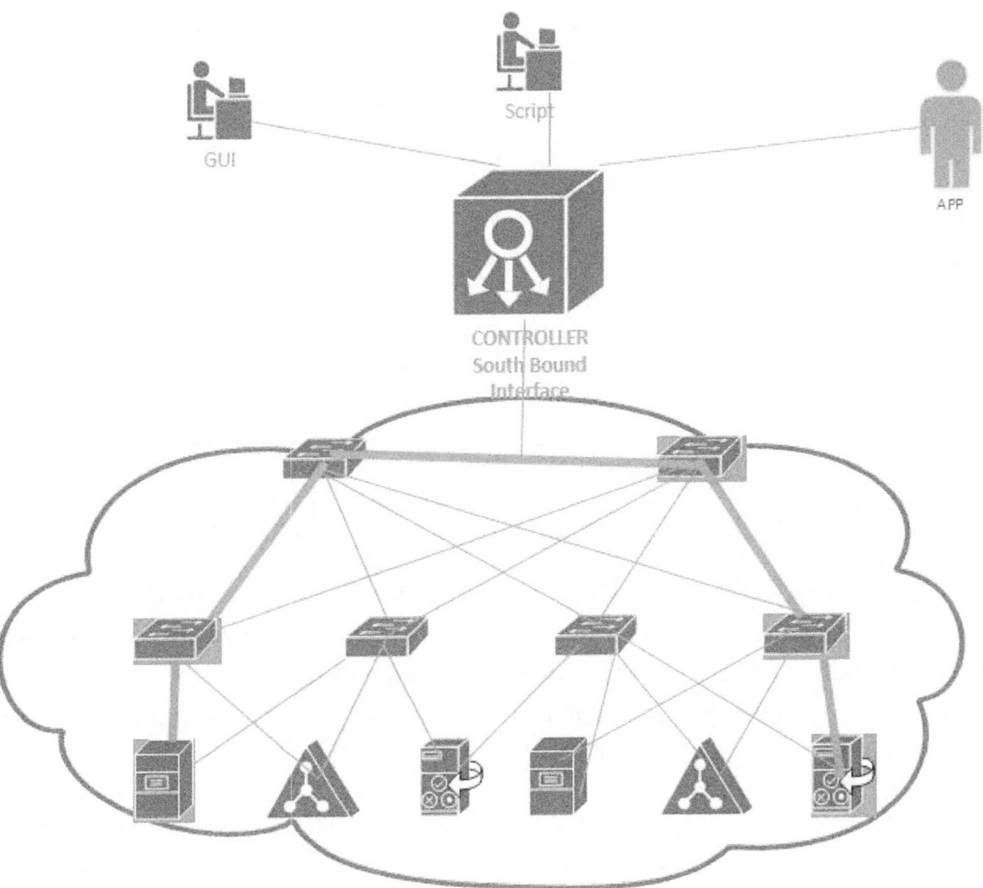

This tunnel is created by the overlay but supported by the physical underlay. We can use an existing network to build an underlay, and add configuration to each device to allow it to support an SDA. This is a cheaper option than purchasing all new devices.

We should make sure that our legacy hardware is compatible with SDA. We should verify that the network devices have compatible operating systems and hardware features for their roles. These roles include

- A **Fabric Edge Node**. This is a switch that connects to an end user device. It's like an access switch.
- A **Fabric Border Node**. This is a switch that that connects to devices that don't use the SDA. That could include devices like WAN routers.
- A **Fabric Control Node**. This is a switch or router that helps the control plane operate.

The question is – does your network have the hardware to support the new SDA network? You will need to check the specifications for each device.

If we can't use the legacy equipment, we can build a new SDA network in parallel to the existing legacy network, and slowly migrate end user devices to the new network. This option is more expensive. More accurately, this option has a higher up-front cost. Eventually, all network hardware is replaced due to failure or age.

We should verify the following hardware features

- How many physical ports do we need and where?
- How fast does each interface need to be – Gigabit, 10 Gigabit, etc.?
- Do we need PoE?
- How much power do we need overall?
- What kind of cabling is installed – cat5e, cat6, multi-mode fiber, single-mode fiber?
- How much overall traffic will the network need to support?

When we connect physical switches in an SDA network, we don't need to worry about EtherChannels or HSRP. We can use something called a **routed access layer design**. By default, all LAN switches in an SDA are Layer 3 switches. Cisco DNA will configure the devices to support the routed access layer by default. Any link between two switches is a Layer 3 link. The switches use the **IS-IS** routing protocol instead of STP or RSTP.

Access switches are located on the edges of the network. Each access switch becomes the default gateway for any end user device that is connected to it.

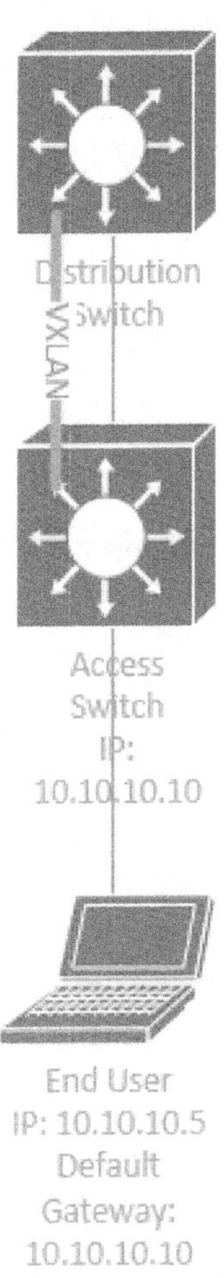

How does a device on an SDA communicate?

- It encapsulates the data in in a frame
- It sends the frame over the fabric (network) and sends it to the Access Switch.
- The Access Switch encapsulates the data inside a VXLAN header and sends it to the destination switch. The other switches in the network forward this frame based on the contents of its header.
- The exit switch (also an access switch) removes the VXLAN header and sends the frame to the end user device (known as an **endpoint**).
- The switch uses its ASIC to process the VXLAN header; therefore, an SDA doesn't slow down any switches.

Why do we need an VXLAN? It allows us to encapsulate any type data inside a tunnel and deliver it to its destination. The VXLAN is flexible enough to support a range of header fields so that changes to the protocol can be implemented in the future, without having to make changes to the underlying hardware or software. At the same time, the VXLAN header can be supported by existing equipment.

A VXLAN encapsulates the entire frame, not just the IP packet because it must support Layer 2, not just Layer 3.

The first switch (known as the **ingress switch**) to receive a frame encapsulates it inside a VXLAN header and sends it through a tunnel to the egress switch.

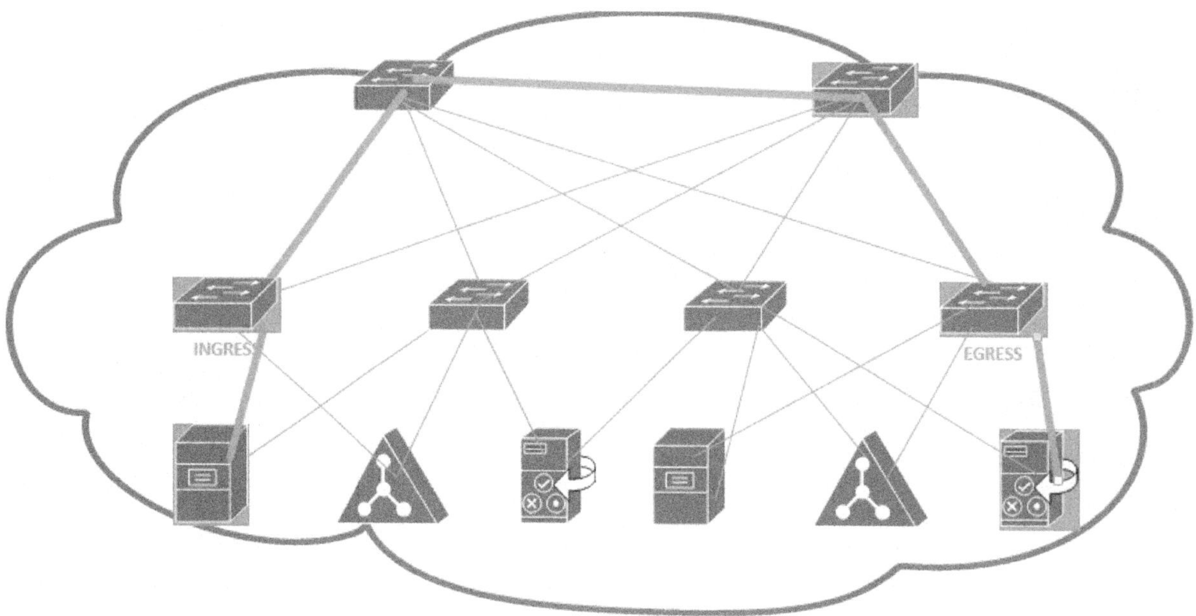

Each switch has two IP addresses – an overlay IP address that uses the same subnet as the end user devices, and an underlay that uses a different subnet. Why? We need to build an underlay subnet that allows the controller to communicate with the switches. We also need an overlay subnet to transport end user data.

In the diagram below, each switch has two IP addresses. One IP address is an overlay IP address in the 10.10.1.0/24 subnet, which transports end user data. The second IP address is an underlay IP address in the 172.172.172.0/24 subnet.

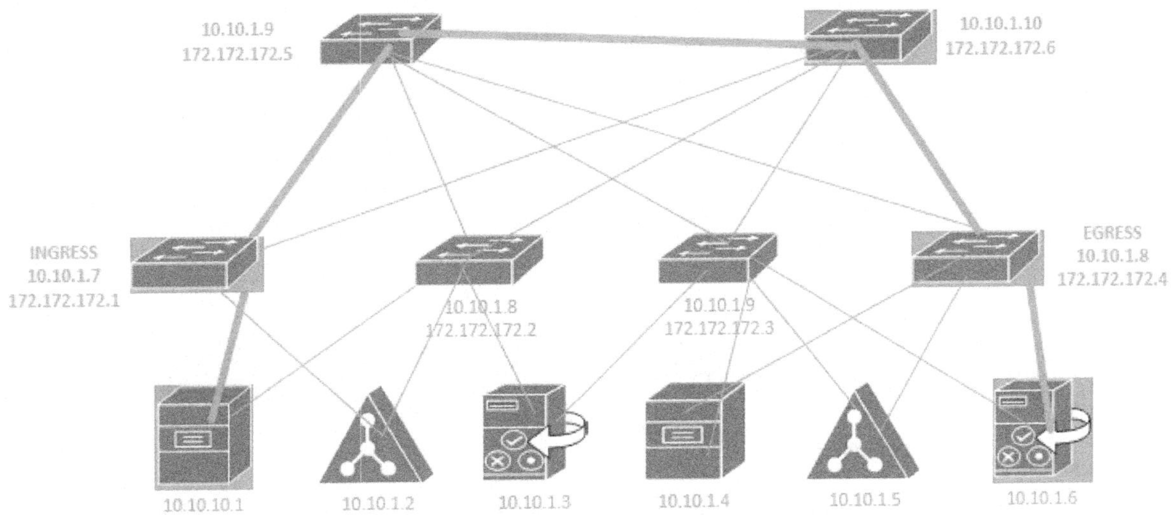

The overlay establishes a pathway in the fabric between two edge nodes. It uses the same IP address space as the endpoints. For example, the Ingress switch sends the end user data to 10.10.1.8.

Remember that a switch uses layer two to learn device MAC addresses from their frames, and that a router uses layer three to learn about neighboring routers through a discovery protocol. We call this the control plane.

Well, access switches (also known as **edge nodes**) can do the same thing as routers and switches. They can learn about connected endpoints through their MAC addresses, IP addresses, and subnets. Each connected endpoint is given unique ID called the **endpoint identifier**, or **EID**.

In our setup we also have a **LISP**, or **Location ID Separation Protocol** map server. Each fabric edge node tells the LISP map server about the endpoints that it has identified, and thus its ability to reach them. The server stores this information into a database. Now the server can create a **routing locator** or **RLOC** for each device.

That means that the server can identify a pathway to each endpoint. When the fabric needs to send a message to a specific device, it asks the LISP server for the appropriate destination. The LISP server checks its database.

The LISP server holds a database that shows each RLOC and corresponding EID. This database contains the underlay IP address of the edge node and the overlay IP address of the edge node.

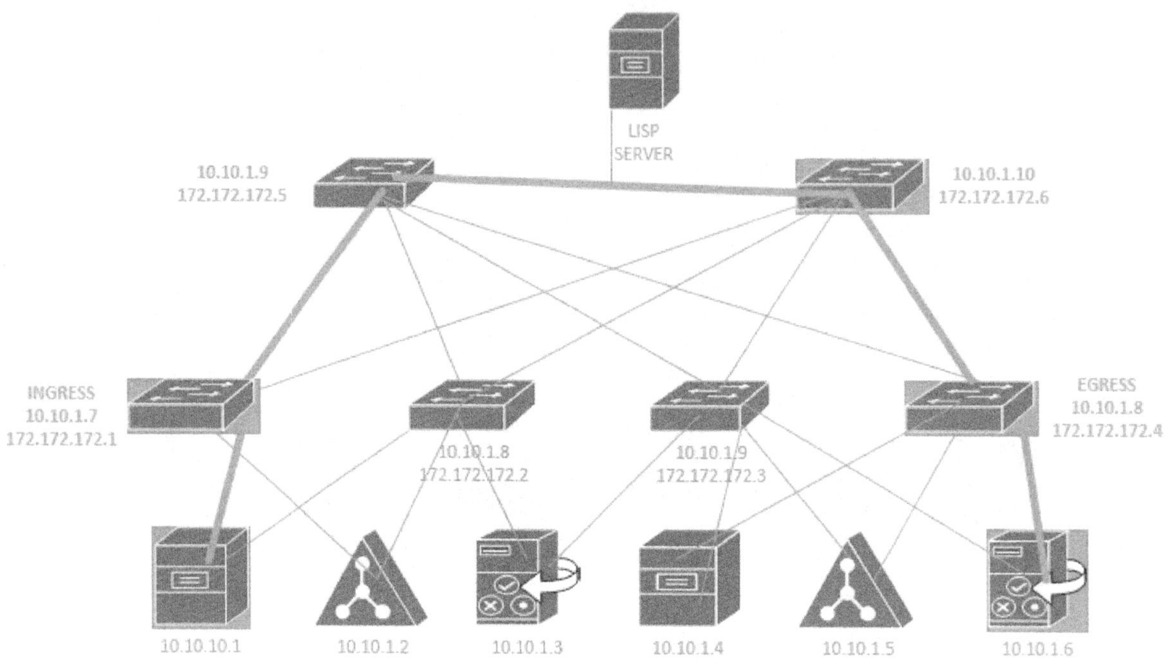

The **Ingress Tunnel Router** (**ITR**) receives frames from outside the fabric. It must decide on a tunnel to send the frame to. When it doesn't know where to forward the frame, the ingress node contacts the LISP server and asks it how to reach the destination. If the LISP server has a destination in its database, it checks the IP address. It calls the egress router in the database and asks it if is still the correct router for that endpoint. The egress router verifies that it is still correct. Now the original ingress can encapsulate the frame with the destination.

In the above example, the LISP server knows that 172.172.172.1 can reach 10.10.10.1 and it knows that 172.172.172.4 knows how to reach 10.10.1.6. If 10.10.10.1 wants to send a message to 10.10.1.6, first the ingress router 172.172.172.1 asks the LISP server if it knows how to reach 10.10.1.6. The LISP server verifies that it does know how to reach 10.10.1.6. It contacts the egress router 172.172.172.4 and asks it if it is still a valid router for 10.10.1.6. If the egress router says yes, then the LISP server tells the ingress router to send its message to 172.172.172.4. The ingress and egress routers establish a VXLAN tunnel to forward their traffic.

The destination in the VXLAN header contains the IP address of the RLOC (172.172.172.4), but the destination of the IP packet contains the IP address of the actual end user device (10.10.1.6).

6.4 Compare traditional campus device management with Cisco DNA Center enabled device management

Cisco DNA or **Cisco Digital Network Architecture** is Cisco's software-defined architecture controller. Cisco DNA is managed from the Cisco DNA Center.

We should be careful not to use **Cisco DNA Center** with an operational legacy network because it might reconfigure existing equipment, which would cause disruptions.

We use Cisco DNA as a controller in a network that uses SDA or as a controller to manage a traditional network. We can install Cisco DNA and then gradually migrate our network. A Cisco DNA Center Appliance comes preinstalled with the Cisco DNA Center application.

We can connect to the Cisco DNA Controller via

- The Controller's GUI
- A script that accesses the controller's REST API
- A third-party app that accesses the controller via a REST API
- A script that accesses a third-party app via a REST API (which in turn accesses the controller via a REST API)

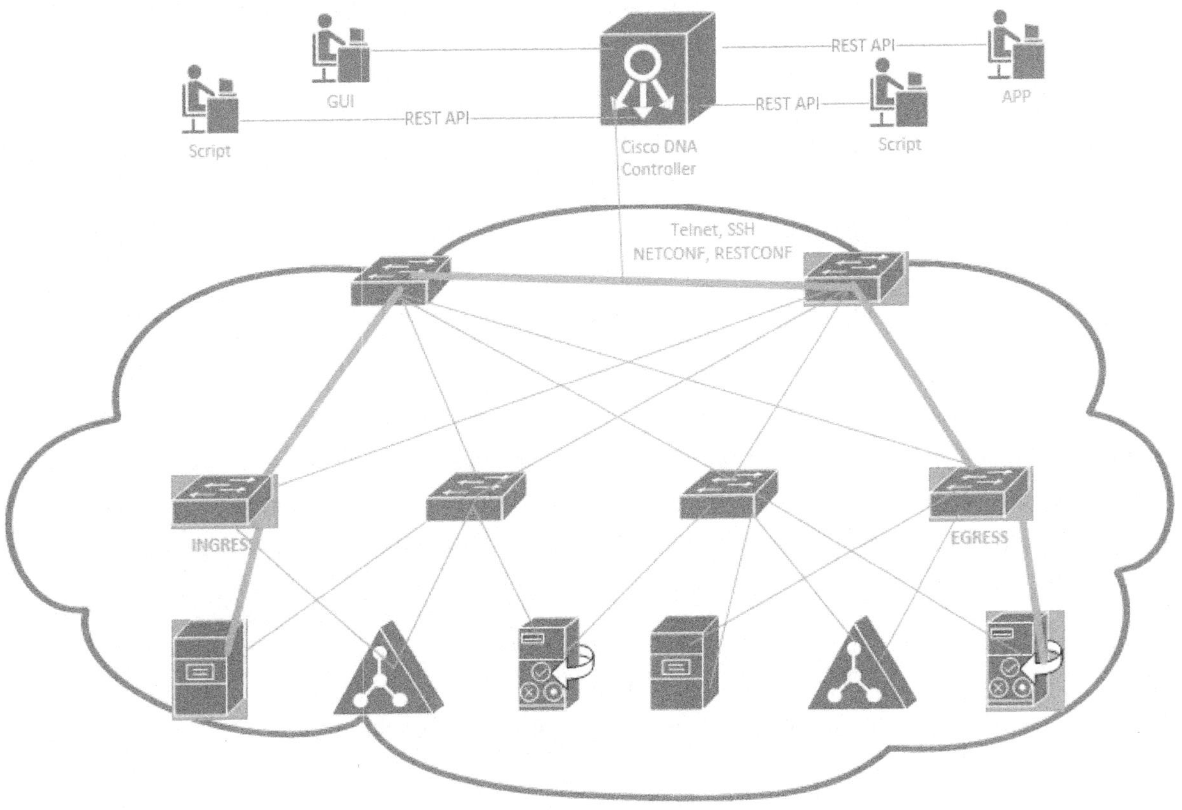

Th Cisco DNA Controller has a Northbound REST API and many Southbound APIs. We use the northbound API and the GUI access the Controller and make changes to the network.

The southbound API can configure traditional devices over Telnet, SSH, or SNMP. It can configure newer devices via **NETCONF** and **RESTCONF**. More and more Cisco devices support NETCONF and RESTCONF.

On a traditional network, we can create ACLs to filter traffic. An ACL contains several rules, and the router applies each rule in order. As our network grows, we might add more and more rules. When there are dozens or hundreds of rules, it becomes difficult to edit or remove a single rule.

With Cisco DNA, we just create security policies. We define what types of devices can communicate, and what they're allowed to communicate with. We don't have to worry about their IP addresses. We don't have to analyse the logic behind each ACL. Cisco DNA modifies the SDA fabric to reflect the policies we create. We can manage each policy separately without having to worry about how it affects other policies.

We can do this by creating users and groups. A user is a single individual. We can add a user to one or more groups. Each group is assigned specific policies. For example, the administrator group might have full access to the entire network. Users in the HR group have access to personnel records. Users in the engineering group have access to engineering documents.

Cisco calls these groups **scalable groups** and each group is assigned a **scalable group tag**, or **SGT**. We create a grid that specifies which groups can send traffic.

			Destination	
Source	**Engineer**	**HR**	**Administrator**	**Support Staff**
Engineer	N/A	Permit	Permit	Permit
HR	Permit	N/A	Deny	Permit
Administrator	Permit	Permit	N/A	Permit
Support Staff	Permit	Deny	Deny	N/A

Now, when a device tries to send traffic, the ingress node first contacts the Cisco DNA Center. The Cisco DNA Center figures out which user is sending the traffic and what group he belongs to. Then it pulls up the appropriate policy. If the traffic is permitted, then the DNA Center tells the edge node that it can create a tunnel between itself and the destination edge node. If the traffic is not permitted, the DNA Center does not permit the tunnel to be created.

For example, if a member of the Support Staff group wants to send a message to a device in the Engineering group, it would be permitted. If a member of the Support Staff group wants to send a message to a device in the HR or Administrator group, it would be denied.

The benefit of using a group is that we are now basing security on the role of a user instead of the physical device connection. When devices can be shared by multiple users, providing security based on the physical device does not make sense.

The predecessor to Cisco DNA was **Cisco Prime Infrastructure**, or **PI**.

- PI allows us to manage all the network from a "single pane of glass". That means we can manage the network from a single control panel instead of having to log in to each device separately.
- PI also manages the entire enterprise's LAN, WAN, and device inventory.
- PI can determine a network's entire topology. Cisco DNA can work with PI to obtain the data that PI discovered so that DNA does not have to rescan the network.
- Uses Telnet, SSH, CDP and LLDP to configure and manage traditional devices
- Allows us to install, configure and monitor devices
- Allows us to configure QoS
- Allows us to manage Wi-Fi and wired networks
- Maintains images of network operating systems through the **Software Image Management** or **SWIM**
- Allows plug and play configuration of new network devices. If we connect a new device, PI automatically configures it

PI is a software application that can be purchased and installed on your server or can be purchased as part of a separate physical appliance.

Cisco DNA supports SDA, whereas PI does not. But Cisco DNA is missing some of PI's management features. Cisco DNA is still under development and will eventually contain all of the features included in PI. Some of Cisco DNA's features

- **EasyQoS** allows us to manage Quality of Service through a graphical user interface
- **Encrypted traffic analysis** can detect malware inside encrypted traffic by looking for patterns and signatures
- **Client health check** allows us to view the health of any connected client. It provides a quality score from zero to ten. This feature might be known as **Device360** or **Client360**.
- **Network Time Travel** allows us to go back in time and see how a client was performing. If we're troubleshooting an issue, Network Time Travel allows us to return to the conditions that created the issue.

- **Path Trace** shows us the path a packet travels from the source to the destination. We can use this to detect latency and inefficient network layouts. It also shows us any ACLs that would interrupt the transmission.

6.5 Describe characteristics of REST-based APIs (CRUD, HTTP verbs, and data encoding)

I mentioned APIs earlier. We use the APIs to communicate with software applications. In the Cisco CCNA, we use a **RESTful API** or **Representational State Transfer API**. What makes an API a RESTful API?

- **Client/Server Architecture**. An original application is known as a server. A software developer creates an API as part of his application, which operates on a physical device.

  A REST Client executes code called the **REST API call**. It makes requests to the server, and the server provides information in response.

  For example, the government maintains an accurate clock API server. If I want to know what time it is, my client sends the government API a call and the government's server responds with the time.

- **Stateless Operation**. Each API request is independent of any other API request. The API does not use any previous request history in deciding how to respond to a new request. That makes it stateless. If an API was stateful, it would maintain variables that are affected by the previous requests.

- **Statement of whether it is Cacheable or Uncacheable**. If an API is **cacheable**, we can reuse the data from its response. We can cache the data and use it again in the future instead of having to make another request.

  If an API is **uncacheable**, then we can't reuse the data. We must make a new request each time we want to reuse the data.

  For example, if we were obtaining historical data, such as the price of a stock last month, we would cache it because that data doesn't change. If we are obtaining current data such as the price of an airline flight, we would not cache it.

  When an API provides a response, it must tell us whether we can cache it or not. If we can cache it, the API must also provide an expiry date.

- **Uniform Interface**. That means that the all requests to the API should follow the same format, and that all responses from the API should follow the same format. The format of the actual resource is separated from its representation.

- **Layered**. The system is layered. When we connect to an API, we don't know what part of the physical infrastructure we are connected to.
- **Code-on-Demand**. A server can provide the client with additional functionality by sending it executable code.

A v**ariable** is a piece of information that could change. For example, if I was building an application to trade stocks, the current stock price would be stored inside a variable. I might have two variables, one that lists the current stock price, and another that lists the number of shares I want to purchase. I could multiply these variables to get the total transaction cost, and store that in a third variable.

If we're monitoring a router, the interface's current status could be stored in a variable. When the interface is up, the variable's value is "up". When the interface is down, the variable's value is "down".

When we create an application, we must give each variable a name (this is known as declaring a variable). Depending on the type of programming language we are using, we might also need to tell the computer the type of data that it will store – text, integer number, decimal number, Boolean (true/false), etc..

A group of related variables is called an **array**. For example, I could create an array for the status of the ports on my switch. If I called the variable SwitchPortStatus, then SwitchPortStatus[1] could hold the status of Switch Port #1, SwitchPortStatus[2] could hold the status of Switch Port #2, etc..

We might call an array a **list** or a **dictionary**. I might create an array that contains the status of a switch port. Let's say I want to track the following data:

- Speed: 100
- Duplex: auto
- VLAN: 20

I might give the variables the names speed, duplex, and VLAN. In a dictionary, the name of the variable is known as the **key**, and the value is known as the **value**. We can report these variables as **key:value** pairs. For example, if I ask the API to report the status of a switch port, it may reply with

[Speed:100, Duplex: auto, VLAN:20]

I can parse this data to understand the value of each variable.

Most REST APIs use HTTP, but they don't need to. The benefit of an HTTP API is that the HTTP protocol is understood by many devices and operating systems. It is easy to access an HTTP API via a URL.

The HTTP API needs to allow us to do the following. We call it **CRUD.**

- **Create** a new variable
- **Read** the contents of an existing variable
- **Update** the value of an existing variable
- **Delete** a variable

There are several types of HTTP messages. Each one contains a variable which tells the server what it wants to do. The HTTP message is contained inside a TCP/IP header.

- **HTTP POST** – create a new variable
- **HTTP GET** – read the contents of an existing variable
- **HTTP PUT** – update a variable
- **HTTP DELETE** – delete a variable

Each HTTP request also contains the name of the resource that we want to access. For example, if we want to delete a variable, we must specify the name of the variable.

How do we know what variables are available? How do we know what to ask the API? The creator of the API must create a document that tells us not only the variables but also the syntax so that we can contact the API.

Our App must send an HTTP request that is directed to a specific URL. For example

https://www.cisco.com/api/switchinterfacevalue?duplex=fullduplex might be a URL where we are informing the API that the duplex is a full duplex. What are the different parts of the URL?

- This URL uses the HTTPS protocol to contact the API.
- The hostname of the server is www.cisco.com (https://www.cisco.com)
- The resource we're trying to access is api/switchinterfacevalue. This value is unique for each resource.
- The question mark after the resource tells us that variables will follow.
- The variable name and value. In this case the variable name is 'duplex, and the value we're trying to set it to is 'fullduplex'. If we have multiple variables, we can separate them with an & sign. For example ?duplex=fullduplex&speed=100&name=port1

The HTTP header can also contain authentication information.

sandboxdnac2.cisco.com is a website that we can use to experiment with Cisco DNA. A reply from Cisco DNA will be returned in JSON format.

The software on the client needs to be able to separate the variable names and values automatically. This is known as **parsing**.

A **resource** is a set of variables. For example, the settings on a switch port can include the variables such as speed, duplex, VLAN, etc., and can be combined into a resource. If we request a resource from the server, namely, the status of a switch port, the server takes the values of the variables and encodes them into a JSON format. Our client reads the response, extracts the variables and stores them.

JSON works well as an API response because many different programs and languages can understand JSON automatically and parse the data from its response without any additional programming. Each language stores its variables in its own way, but many languages can convert their variables into a JSON format so that programs written in different languages can understand each other. We can call JSON a **data serialization language** or a **data modeling language**. We will look at some JSON examples in the last section.

The other type of language is called XML. An XML variable is nested between tags that look like <variablename> and </variablename>. For example, if my variable name is "duplex" and my value is "full", I would encode the data like this

```
<duplex>full</duplex>
```

XML also lets me nest my data so that it is meaningful. For example, I could write

```
<switch>
    <ports>
        <port1>
            <duplex>full</duplex>
            <speed>100</speed>
        </port1>
        <port2>
            <duplex>full</duplex>
            <speed>100</speed>
        </port2>
    </ports>
```

```
        <hostname>MainSwitch</hostname>
        <default-gateway>10.10.10.1</default-gateway>
</switch>
```

The outer nest is called <switch> and tells us that we have a switch configuration. There are three nests on the second layer - <ports>, <hostname>, and <default-gateway>. The <ports> nest lists variables for each port such as <port1> and <port2>. Inside each of the <port1> and <port2> nests are additional variables for the speed and duplex.

We can give the variables any name we want, but it is better to give them meaningful names. In the previous example, you can understand the XML just by looking at it.

We can indent the variables to make them easier to read, but a computer will ignore the indents. It wouldn't make a difference if I wrote the whole thing like this.

```
<switch><ports><port1><duplex>full</duplex><speed>100</speed></port1><
port2><duplex>full</duplex><speed>100</speed></port2></ports><hostname
>MainSwitch</hostname><default-gateway>10.10.10.1</default-
gateway></switch>
```

6.6 Recognize the capabilities of configuration management mechanisms Puppet, Chef, and Ansible

Why do we need configuration management? When we first set up our network, we have something called a **baseline**. The baseline is the standard configuration for our network. Every device configuration should follow the baseline.

Later, if an administrator makes a change to a network device, it must be documented. We don't want to introduce undocumented changes because it will become difficult to troubleshoot the network, we will introduce potential security risks, and make the network inefficient.

The problem is that when manually change the configuration of a device, we have no way to automatically track the change. If I console into a router and change the speed or interface on a port or modify an ACL, there is no documentation of this change.

Nobody knows what was changed, who changed it, when it was changed, or why. The solution is to centralize the configuration of each device. A simple solution is to store the configuration in plain text on a server or shared folder. But can we trust the configuration files in the shared folder? What happens if we manually update the configuration on a device but forget to update the configuration in the server?

For example, say I install a new router and configure the interfaces. We save this configuration on our server as a baseline. A few months later, our internet connection changes and I update the static IP address on one of the interfaces. A few months after that, the router malfunctions and needs to be replaced. The administrator who replaces the router downloads the original configuration and configures the router, but it doesn't work. Why not? The original configuration doesn't contain the correct interface settings. The administrator spends several hours troubleshooting the connection with the ISP.

A better approach is to use a **configuration management tool**. The tool keeps track of each configuration file, the changes made, when the changes were made, who made them, and why. The configuration management tool keeps copies of the older versions of each configuration, so that we can go back in time and compare different versions of the file.

We should make the changes to the file in the configuration management tool, and let the tool use the file to update the configuration on the device.

We also use the configuration management tool to regularly check the configuration on each device to ensure that it hasn't changed. This is known as **configuration monitoring**. Even with a configuration management tool, it is still possible for an administrator to manually change a device's configuration or for the configuration to become corrupted.

Configuration provisioning is the concept of making the changes after the configuration file has been edited. We should be able to

- Choose the number and type of devices whose configurations will be updated. We could update all devices, or a subset of devices such as switches, or switches of a certain model, or switches in a specific location.
- We should be able to revert to an older configuration if the new one causes undesired operations.
- We should be able to validate the change to ensure that it will work as expected before we implement it. This might involve a simulation, or at least a verification of the logic or syntax in the configuration.
- We should be able to verify that the change was made correctly.
- We should be able to choose whether the change is made to the running-config or both the running-config and startup-config.
- We should be able to create templates for different device configurations, such as a standard switch configuration or a standard router configuration.
- We should be able to schedule a configuration change. For example, we might schedule a configuration change for after hours.

The template helps us configure devices quickly. It also reduces errors associated with manual configuration. If we have a standard configuration, we can replace the names and other parameters with variables. We can use an application to generate a configuration for a new device by entering some values.

Ansible is a tool that allows us to create configuration templates. Here is part of my router configuration

```
hostname Router
!
interface Loopback0
 ip address 100.100.100.100 255.255.255.0
!
interface GigabitEthernet0/0/0
 ip address 100.100.100.101 255.255.255.0
 duplex auto
 speed auto
!
interface GigabitEthernet0/0/1
 ip address 100.100.100.102 255.255.255.0
 duplex auto
 speed auto
!
```

I could create a template out of this configuration and then use it to configure many other routers. I have replaced the variable portions of my configuration with actual variables, which are surrounded by curly braces.

```
hostname {{hostname}}
!
interface Loopback0
 ip address {{IP address IF1}} {{subnet mask IF1}}
!
interface GigabitEthernet0/0/0
 ip address {{IP address IF2}} {{subnet mask IF2}}
 duplex {{duplex 2}}
 speed {{speed 2}}
!
interface GigabitEthernet0/0/1
 ip address {{IP address IF3}} {{subnet mask IF3}}
 duplex {{duplex 3}}
 speed {{speed 3}}
!
```

If I plug the following variables into my Ansible script, it automatically uses them and the template to generate a configuration file.

```
hostname
IP address IF1
subnet mask IF1
IP address IF2
subnet mask IF2
duplex 2
```

```
speed 2
IP address IF3
subnet mask IF3
duplex 3
speed 3
```

The template helps me focus on configuring the device by specifying the necessary parameters. It makes sure that I don't miss any fields. If I forget something, I won't be able to save the configuration.

If many devices use a common template, and I make changes to the template, I can use the software to automatically update all the devices that use the same template. For example, I could use the template to change the enable password on all my switches at the same time.

Ansible is open source and available for free. It requires us to create several files

- A **Playbook** is a file that lists actions Ansible should perform
- The **Inventory** lists the hostnames of all the devices we have, as well as the role that each one performs
- **Templates** are templates of the configuration without the details
- **Variables** list the data that Ansible will substitute into the template

After we create a configuration, Ansible uses SSH or NETCONF to update the device configuration. Ansible "pushes" the device configuration to each network appliance. When Ansible configures a device over SSH, it is doing so exactly like a human user. Ansible uses SSH when a device can't be configured via NETCONF.

Ansible can also monitor each device to ensure that its configuration has been successfully updated. Ansible uses the playbook to determine how to respond when it detects a device with the wrong configuration. It can either notify the administrator or update the configuration automatically.

The second tool we will learn about is called **Puppet**. Puppet is also open source and available for free. Once we install Puppet, we create several files

- **Manifest**. The manifest tells Puppet how we would like a device to be configured. Inside the Manifest is a Resource, a Class, and a Module, which are distributed as a hierarchy of configurations. Each module contains several classes, and each class contains several resources.
- **Templates**. Puppet uses a template and variables to generate a Manifest.

Unlike Ansible, we use the Manifest to tell Puppet what the device configuration must look like in the end. Puppet figures out what steps it must take to configure the device.

Puppet must install an "agent", or software application on each device that requires configuration. Puppet communicates with the agent, and the agent configures the device. Some versions of Cisco IOS do not support Puppet.

If a Cisco device doesn't support Puppet, Puppet can configure the device over SSH. It must install an **External Agent** on another device and let the other device connect to the Cisco device over SSH.

Puppet makes changes through a Pull mechanism. We create the Manifest and Template files on the Puppet server. We also install the Puppet agent on each device. The agent regularly checks the server for updates to the configuration, and "pulls" the manifest and other data from the server so that it can understand how to configure the device. The agent (and not the server) updates the device configuration.

In other words, every device with a Puppet agent is asking the Puppet server "is my configuration correct or do I need to make some changes?".

The third tool is called Chef Automate (better known as **Chef**), which operates like Puppet. We create several files

- **Resource**. The resource is a set of objects that Chef must manage. It is like a list of ingredients in a recipe book – ingredients that can be used in multiple recipes.
- **Recipe**. A recipe is a set of instructions that can be applied to a resource. It tells us how to modify a resource.
- **Cookbooks**. A cookbook is a group of recipes that are related. We group recipes so that we can manage them better.
- **Runlist**. A runlist is a set of recipes that can be run against a device. Chef runs the recipes in the order that they appear on the list.

Chef installs an agent on each device and pulls configuration data from the server as required. It also pulls the necessary recipes and resources so that it can keep the device updated. Chef is not supported on many devices.

Puppet and Chef use HTTP and a REST API to communicate between the server and the agent.

6.7 Interpret JSON encoded data

Like XML, it's easy to interpret JSON data. If you look at a set of JSON data, you can probably guess what it means.

The JSON data is written in the format of Key:Value. The key is the data before the colon, and the value is the data after the colon. Each Key:Value pair is separated by a comma. If a key has multiple values, they are enclosed in square brackets.

For example, the following data specifies the configuration of a switch port

```
{
        "speed": "100",
        "duplex": "full",
        "VLAN": "20"
}
```

We can write the JSON data like this instead

```
{"speed": "100", "duplex": "full", "VLAN": "20"}
```

The spaces don't matter. The curly brackets enclose the set of JSON data delivered from the server. This is also known as an object.

We can write a script to interpret JSON data received from a server, but most programming languages include functions to automatically parse the data.

We can also create a JSON **object**. An object is like a set of variables. For example, a port configuration might be an object. We enclose an object with {}. For example, the configuration of Port 1 might be an object with the following data

```
{"speed": "100", "duplex": "full", "VLAN": "20"}
```

An array is enclosed in []. For example, the API might return the list of switch ports like

```
["FastEthernet0/1", "FastEthernet0/2", "FastEthernet0/3"]
```

It could also return an object that includes an array, for example.

```
{
        "ListofACLs": ["1", "2", "3", "4"],
}
```

What if I have two variables – **ListofACLs** (List of ACLs), and **ACLIPAddresses** (ACL IP Addresses). Each variable has an array with four variables.

When interpreting the JSON data, we need to understand that an object is surrounded by curly braces {}. Inside the object is one or more variables. The variable name is to the left of the colon and the variable value is to the right.

The value of a variable can be a single value, an array, or another object. For example, we have returned an object showing the configuration of three ports, and the configuration of each port is an object with three variables

```
{
        "FastEthernet0/1" : {"speed": "100", "duplex": "full", "VLAN":
        "20"},
        "FastEthernet0/2" : {"speed": "1000", "duplex": "full", "VLAN":
        "20"},
        "FastEthernet0/3" : {"speed": "10", "duplex": "half", "VLAN":
        "20"}
}
```

I could also write it like this, so that it's easier to read

```
{
        "FastEthernet0/1" : {
                "speed": "100",
                "duplex": "full",
                "VLAN": "20"
        },
        "FastEthernet0/2" : {
                "speed": "1000",
                "duplex": "full",
                "VLAN": "20"
        },
        "FastEthernet0/3" : {
                "speed": "10",
                "duplex": "half",
```

```
        "VLAN": "20"
    }
}
```

The entire JSON is an object (the switch is an object), and each variable is an object (each interface is an object). We might have an API that returns the configuration of all the ports, and an API that returns the configuration of a single port.

I can write the JSON in any number of ways, adding spaces or tabs where necessary to make it easier to read, but when we send a JSON over the internet, the computers cut out all the white space.

Made in the USA
Coppell, TX
05 February 2024